KIMONO

STYLE

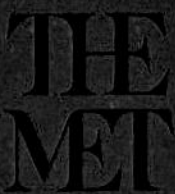

THE METROPOLITAN MUSEUM OF ART, NEW YORK
DISTRIBUTED BY YALE UNIVERSITY PRESS, NEW HAVEN AND LONDON

KIMONO

EDO TRADITIONS TO MODERN DESIGN

MONIKA BINCSIK

with contributions by

KAREN VAN GODTSENHOVEN

ARAI MASANAO

THE JOHN C. WEBER COLLECTION

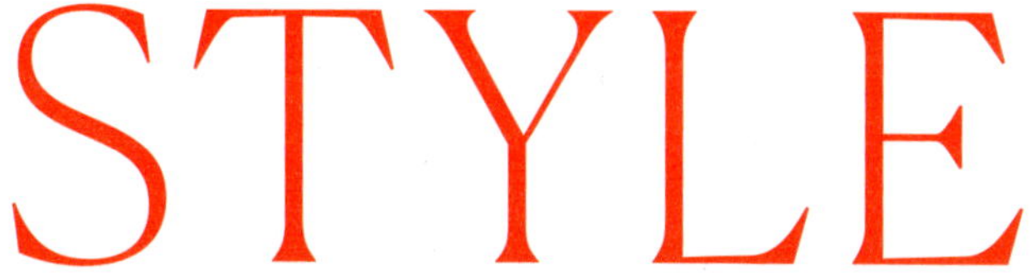

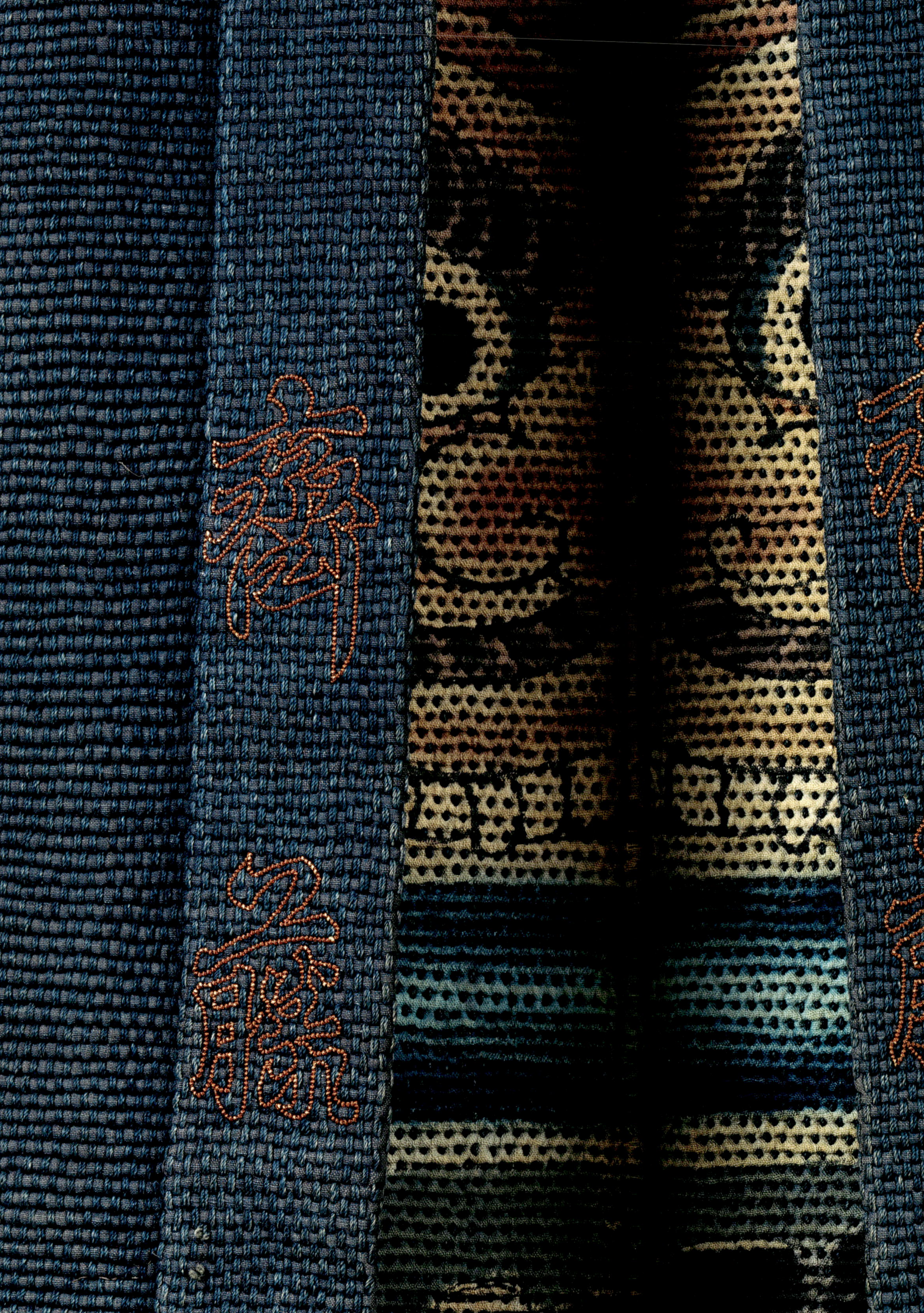

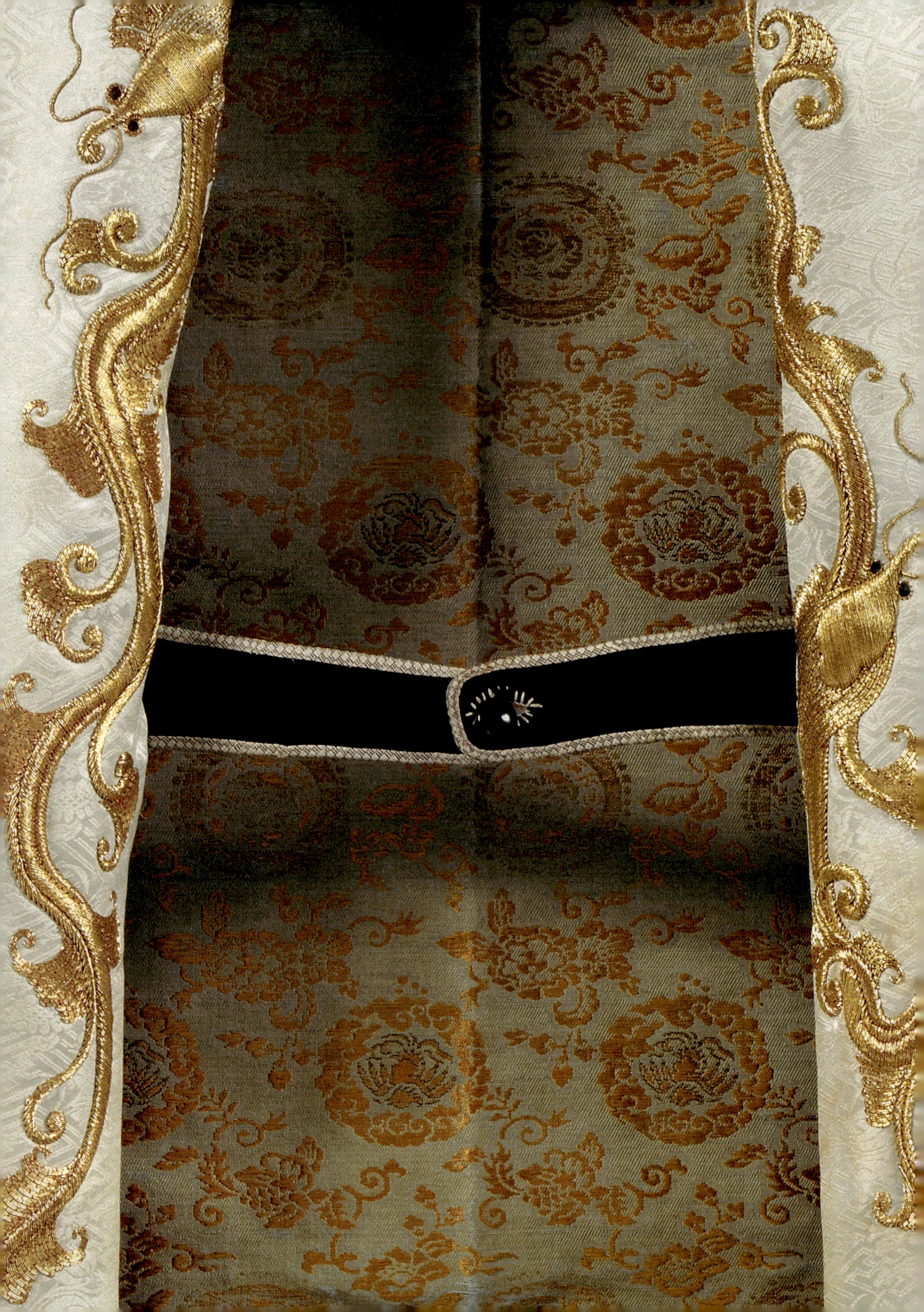

DIRECTOR'S FOREWORD

The kimono is one of Japan's most visible art forms. Resonant with unique cultural significance, the T-shaped garment is also an emblem of Japanese fashion's continuous evolution and enduring influence on clothing in the West.

From the seventeenth century on, Japan developed a sophisticated system of production, distribution, and consumption of fashion that was further transformed by its encounter with the West in the second half of the nineteenth century. The introduction of Western apparel, manufacturing techniques, popular culture, and democratic ideals stimulated modernization and social change. More women than ever before gained access to silk kimonos, many patterned with fashionable new designs informed by Western art. Affordable ready-to-wear kimonos (*meisen*) became popular by the 1920s, reflecting a more Westernized lifestyle. They were sold in department stores modeled on Western retailers, following Western-style marketing strategies.

At the same time, the kimono's comparatively loose, enveloping silhouette and rectilinear cut had a profound and lasting influence on Western fashion, as we can see in the haute couture creations of Paul Poiret, Madeleine Vionnet, and Callot Soeurs. The garment's continued impact on designers around the world is represented in these pages by the designs of Hanae Mori, Yohji Yamamoto, Issey Miyake, Rei Kawakubo, and John Galliano, which collectively redefined "fashion."

This publication and its accompanying exhibition present outstanding kimonos from the eighteenth century through the 1930s, highlighting the artistic conversations between Japan and the West. Featuring approximately seventy superb garments from the renowned John C. Weber Collection as well as a selection of haute couture from The Met's Costume Institute, this project presents the art of the kimono from a transnational perspective. It also celebrates the promised gift of forty modern kimonos from John C. Weber to The Met.

We are grateful to Dr. Weber, a well-known collector of Japanese art who started acquiring kimonos in 1997, for that promised gift, his loans to this exhibition, his generous support of this publication, and his long-term support of Asian art. Over the years he has built a significant collection of Japanese textiles: theatrical costumes, battle flags and surcoats, firemen's jackets, garments for high-ranking samurai women and wealthy merchant-class ladies, elegant wedding robes, and a variety of clothes made by farmers and other commoners. One of the unique features of his collection is a comprehensive selection of *meisen* kimonos, bright, modern garments that were not yet collected in the West when he developed a taste for them. Textiles have a distinguished role in his encyclopedic collection of Japanese paintings, sculptures, and decorative arts, demonstrating the interconnectedness of these art forms.

For their excellent work on this project, I wish to thank Monika Bincsik, Diane and Arthur Abbey Associate Curator for Japanese Decorative Arts at The Met, and guest cocurator Karen Van Godtsenhoven, previously an associate curator in The Met's Costume Institute and currently a fashion curator and PhD candidate at Ghent University, Belgium. We are pleased to present not only their contributions to this volume, but also an essay by Arai Masanao, a well-known specialist on *meisen* kimonos based in Kiryū, Japan, and a glossary compiled by Kristine M. Kamiya, a conservator in The Met's Department of Textile Conservation. Their work was thoroughly supported by the Departments of Asian Art, Textile Conservation, and Scientific Research, The Costume Institute, and the entire Met team. This is truly a cross-departmental, as well as a cross-cultural, project.

We recognize the Mary Livingston Griggs and Mary Griggs Burke Foundation Fund, 2015, for supporting this presentation. We are grateful to the Florence and Herbert Irving Fund for Asian Art Publications for making this catalogue possible. Additional support is provided by the Richard and Geneva Hofheimer Memorial Fund.

MAX HOLLEIN
Marina Kellen French Director
The Metropolitan Museum of Art, New York

ACKNOWLEDGMENTS

Realizing the exhibition *Kimono Style: The John C. Weber Collection* and this accompanying catalogue has been a complex undertaking. The exhibition was conceived in 2017 after a series of discussions I conducted with John T. Carpenter, Mary Griggs Burke Curator of Japanese Art; Maxwell K. Hearn, Douglas Dillon Chair of the Department of Asian Art; Dr. John C. Weber, a well-known collector of Japanese art for whose unstinting generosity toward every facet of this project I am deeply grateful; and Julia Meech, former curator of Japanese art at The Metropolitan Museum of Art, current curator of the Weber Collection, and editor of *Impressions: The Journal of the Japanese Art Society of America*. My interest in exploring the cross-cultural artistic influences between the kimono and Western fashion coincided with Dr. Weber's desire to further investigate his extensive Japanese textile collection; Julia, who has studied Japanese textiles for decades, facilitated our shared vision. The concept was immediately supported by Andrew Bolton, Wendy Yu Curator in Charge of The Costume Institute, who has been a wonderful collaborator throughout the project.

First and foremost, I thank Karen Van Godtsenhoven, who cocurated the exhibition, made a terrific selection of Western haute couture from The Costume Institute collection, and provided an insightful essay for this volume. Kristine M. Kamiya, a conservator in The Met's Department of Textile Conservation, was indispensable, lending her expertise in Japanese textiles and overseeing the photography and display of more than seventy kimonos. She also compiled the glossary of Japanese textile terms and took the micrographs that illustrate them. Arai Masanao, a specialist on *meisen* kimonos, generously contributed an essay, highlighting the little-known technical history of these ready-to-wear garments from the first half of the twentieth century.

Thought-provoking discussions with many colleagues, viewings, advice on literature, and guidance in the field helped me to prepare for this exhibition. Numerous curators beyond The Met kindly gave their advice, but special thanks go to Nagasaki Iwao, Professor of Textile and Clothing at Kyoritsu Women's University, Tokyo, who visited the Weber Collection and conducted a detailed study of several garments; Oyama Yuzuruha, Chief Curator of Asian Textile and Clothing at Tokyo National Museum; Anna Jackson, Keeper of the Asian Department at the Victoria and Albert Museum, London; and, at Kyoto National Museum, Yamakawa Aki, Senior Curator of Costume and Textile, and Melissa Rinne, Specialist, Department of Research and Curatorial Collaboration, Curatorial Division. Sawada Kazuto, National Museum of Japanese History, lent support in many ways.

At The Costume Institute, whose collaboration was crucial to this work, I am especially grateful to Jessica Regan, Associate Curator, and Amanda B. Garfinkel and Mellissa J. Huber, Assistant Curators. Glenn O. Petersen, Conservator, made sure the garments were in top condition. Marci K. Morimoto, Associate Collections Manager, and Elizabeth D. Randolph, Collections Manager, helped set up viewings and compile checklists, and Joyce Fung, Senior Research Associate, created a beautiful installation with great sensitivity to cultural context. Michael Downer, Principal Departmental Technician, helped with all aspects of the installation.

It is impossible to list all the other colleagues at The Met who worked with us on or helped facilitate this endeavor, but on behalf of the curatorial team I extend thanks to Janina Poskrobko, Conservator in Charge of Textile Conservation, for her steadfast support. At the Antonio Ratti Textile Center, thanks go to Eva L. Labson, General Manager of Collections, and her team, as well as to Amelia Peck, Marica F. Vilcek Curator of American Decorative Arts and Supervising Curator, Antonio Ratti Textile Center.

In the Publications and Editorial Department, Mark Polizzotti, Michael Sittenfeld, Peter Antony, and Lauren Knighton guided the publication of the catalogue. I am especially grateful to my editor, Nancy E. Cohen, for her insightful comments, attention to details, and partnership throughout the preparation of the manuscript. Our bibliographer, Alicia Badea, carefully double-checked the sources and citations. The book design was elegantly conceived by Lucinda Hitchcock and Cara Buzzell. Elizabeth De Mase, Image Acquisition Manager, and Josephine Rodriguez, Image Acquisition Specialist, made sure that all illustrations were at hand. For the brilliant photographs, special gratitude is due to Paul H. Lachenauer, Senior Photographer. William Scott Geffert, Christopher Heins, and others in the Imaging Department ensured through careful postproduction work that all the images were of the highest quality. The exhibition labels were edited by Elizabeth Benjamin.

A collaborative project on dye analysis with The Met's Department of Scientific Research, an ongoing investigation, will shed light on the mid-nineteenth-century transition from natural plant dyes to Western aniline dyes. The dye-chronology study is led by Marco Leona, David H. Koch Scientist in Charge, with Nobuko Shibayama, Research Scientist, and Maria Goretti Mieites Alonso, Associate Manager of Laboratory.

To realize any exhibition at The Met, curators rely on teams of professionals at every turn. Daniel H. Weiss, President and Chief Executive Officer, and Max Hollein, Marina Kellen French Director, embraced this project early on. Andrea Bayer, Deputy Director for Collections and Administration, and Quincy Houghton, Deputy Director for Exhibitions, provided advice and support. Amy Bogansky, Hannah Korn, and, later, Aileen Marcantonio, Exhibition Project Managers, helped oversee logistical details, and Elsie Alonso, Assistant Registrar, made sure the loans were safely transported. Jennifer Isakowitz, Senior Publicist, helped promote the exhibition. The Education Department created programming related to the show.

Daniel Kershaw, Exhibition Design Manager, oversaw the beautiful gallery layout and designed a discerning installation, while Alexandre Viault, Design Manager, and Abby Chen, Graphic Designer, created the splendid graphics, all under the creative direction of Alicia Cheng, Head of Design. Taylor Miller, Buildings Manager for Exhibitions, together with Matthew Lytle and Maria Nicolino, created new cases and installation furniture, which were expertly lit by Clint Ross Coller, Richard Lichte, Amy Nelson, and Grace Mennell in Exhibition Design.

In the Department of Asian Art, Maxwell K. Hearn and Stephanie Kwai, Senior Manager, Administration and Operations, coordinated the administrative and financial details, assisted by Mary Hurt and Inae Rurup. Our Collections Management team, led by Hwai-ling Yeh-Lewis, provided crucial help, particularly Jessica Kuhn, who coordinated the installation, Alison Clark, and Jacqueline Taeschler. Our team of art handlers and technicians—Beatrice Pinto, Imtikar Ally, Lori Carrier, and Djamel Haoues—installed the galleries. Jennifer Perry, Mary and James Wallach Family Conservator of Japanese Art, and Masanobu Yamazaki, Conservator, oversaw the works on paper in the exhibition. In the Department of Objects Conservation, Conservators Christina Hagelskamp, Vicki Parry, and Daniel Hausdorf worked on the lacquerware, ceramics, and sculpture, respectively.

The Museum's volunteers and interns provided invaluable assistance with the preliminary research and various preparatory tasks. My volunteer, Makiko Kawada, helped compile the bibliography; Maria Puzyreva, intern in the Asian Art Department, collected relevant articles and illustrations; and Ayaka Sano, an intern in The Costume Institute, supported Karen's research and contributed to the translation of Arai Masanao's essay.

The Mary Livingston Griggs and Mary Griggs Burke Foundation Fund, 2015, deserves special recognition for making this exhibition possible. Thanks also go to the Florence and Herbert Irving Fund for Asian Art Publications and the Richard and Geneva Hofheimer Memorial Fund for their support of this book.

Finally, I would like to acknowledge my mother for her unwavering support from afar.

MONIKA BINCSIK
Diane and Arthur Abbey Associate Curator for Japanese Decorative Arts
The Metropolitan Museum of Art, New York

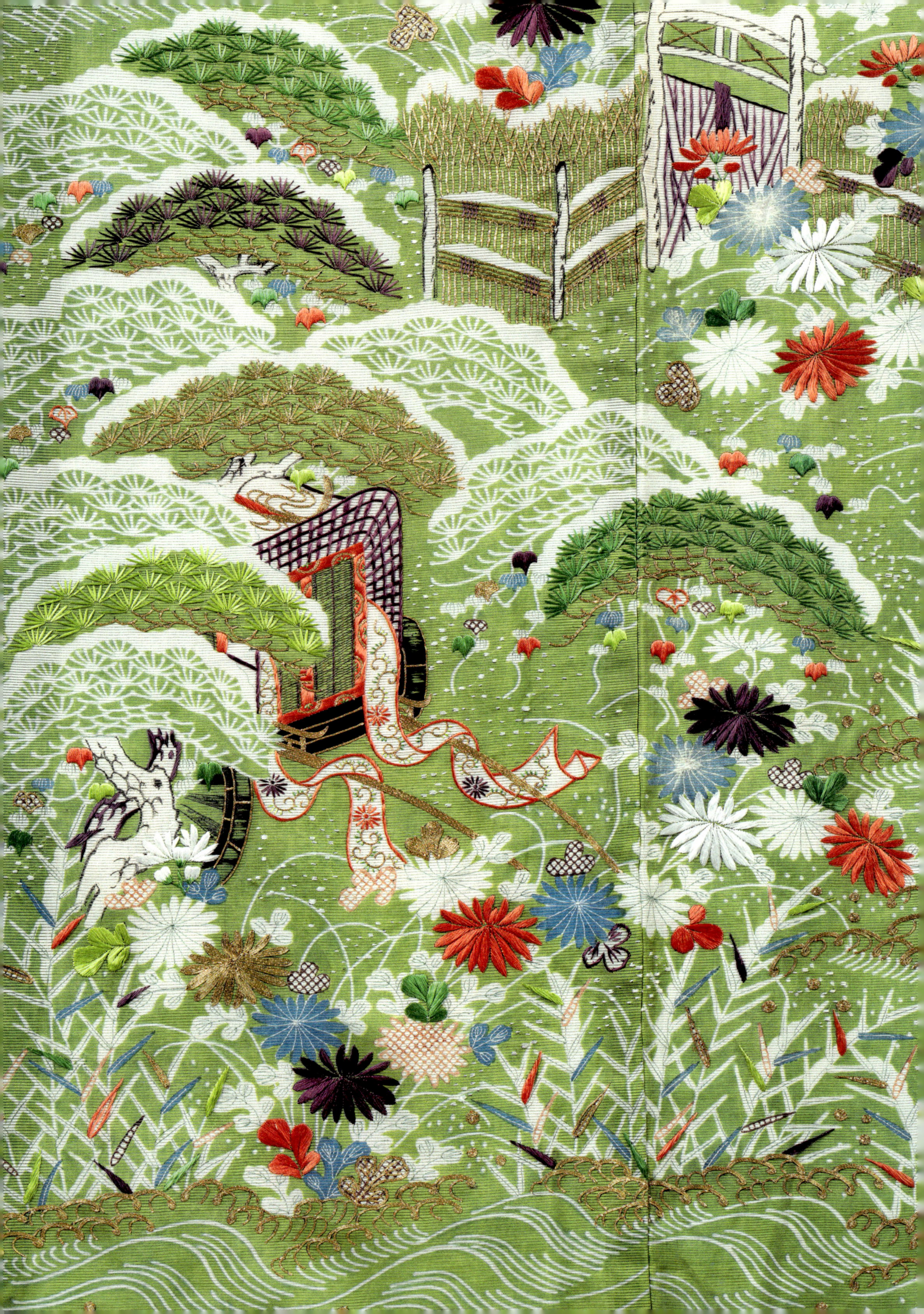

JAPANESE

FROM EDO TO

MONIKA BINCSIK

THE MODERN ERA

FASHION

IN THE ELEVENTH MONTH OF 1681, INOUE TSŪJO, A TWENTY-TWO-YEAR-OLD LITERARY PRODIGY FROM A SAMURAI FAMILY,

began a journey with her father and attendants from their home on Shikoku to Edo, the center of the Tokugawa shogunate. At a border checkpoint, the officials who inspected her travel documents did not allow Tsūjo to pass: the documents described her as a woman, but her *furisode* robe, a long-sleeved garment worn by maidens, indicated that she was a girl. "[W]hatever one does there are so many obstacles if one inhabits the body of a woman," Tsūjo wrote unhappily in her diary.[1] She was defined by the style of her robe, which was as important to border inspectors as her official travel papers.

Like the *furisode*, most clothing of the Edo period (1615–1868) signaled the wearer's age, marital status, and social position. Red was deemed appropriate for young women. *Tomesode* robes, with shortened sleeves, were typically worn by adult, married women. Robes made of silk indicated status or wealth, while certain colors, patterns, and decorative techniques were exclusively reserved for the robes worn by elite women (cat. 18). Many formal garments, especially for samurai men and women, were embellished with family crests that revealed the wearer's name at a glance. At the beginning of the Edo period, only the elite were privileged to wear elegant, stylish, luxurious clothing, a visual expression of high social rank.

In a society strictly controlled by a military government, dress was not an entirely free, personal choice. Many aspects were regulated by the shogunate; others, by social convention. That is not to say that fashion was absent from Edo-period Japan. The simplicity and the unchanged cut of the kimono are deceptive. Indeed, the T-shaped garment's seeming changelessness gave rise to a long-standing misapprehension that Japan, along with other Asian countries, lacks fashion—that is, quickly changing styles of dress adopted by a group of people at a given time and place. The main reason is that most Western historians considered only changes in silhouette and tailoring, the fundamental aspects of European styles, overlooking trends in patterns, decorative techniques, and fabrics, which are the key elements of kimono fashion. As kimonos are traditionally made of a single bolt of fabric with minimal cutting and are unfitted, easily made at home, and can without alteration be handed over to another wearer, they were seen as timeless.[2] However, the richness of its variations throughout its long history attests to the kimono's endless

fig. 1 Robe (*nuihaku kosode*) with shells and sea grasses. Late Momoyama (1573–1615)–early Edo (1615–1868) period, late 16th–early 17th century. Plain-weave damask silk patterned with warp floats (*saya*), with tie-dyeing, silk embroidery, and gold-leaf application; 60½ × 49 in. (153.7 × 124.5 cm). The Metropolitan Museum of Art, New York, Gift of Mr. and Mrs. Paul T. Nomura, in memory of Mr. and Mrs. S. Morris Nomura, 1992 (1992.253)

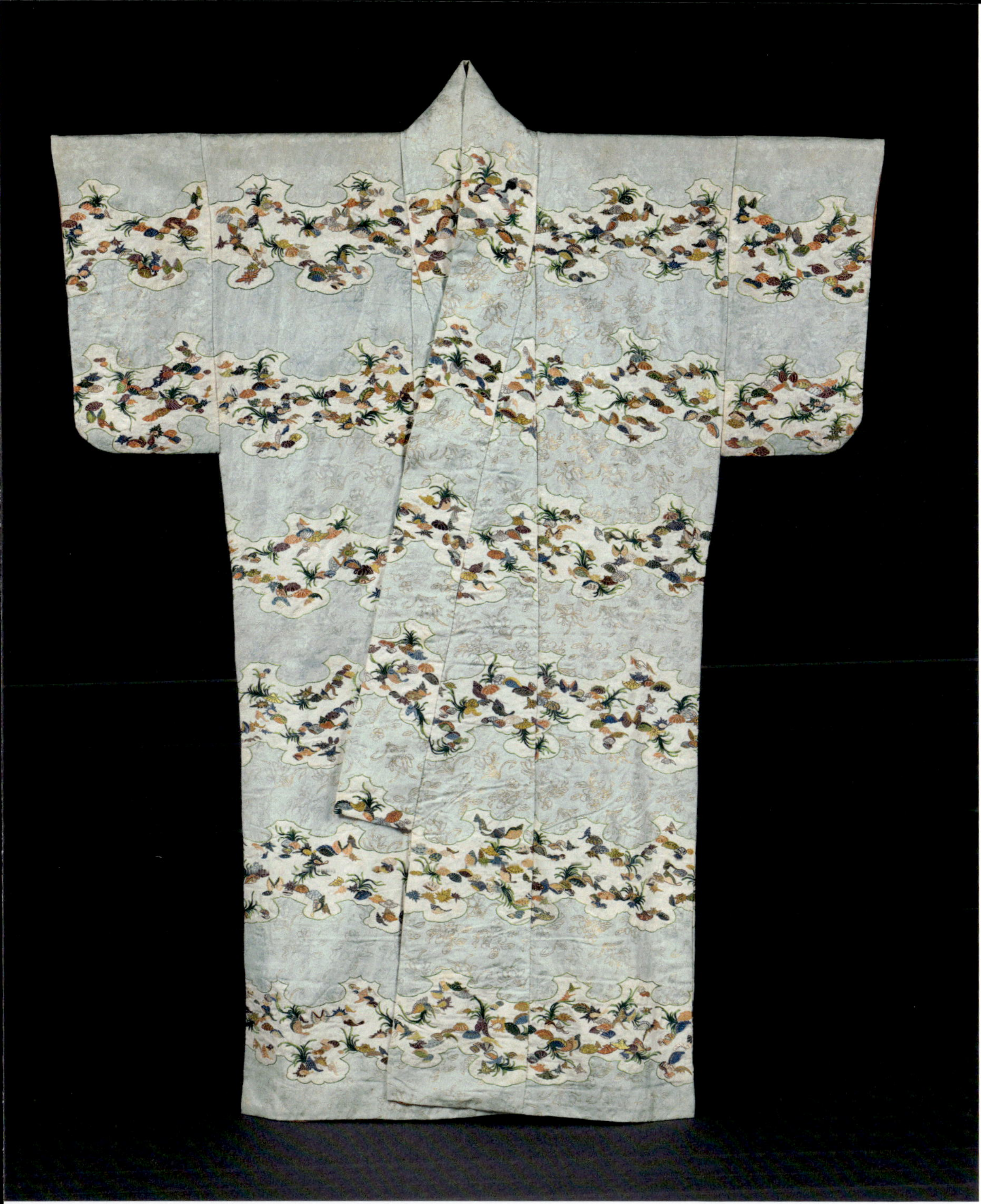

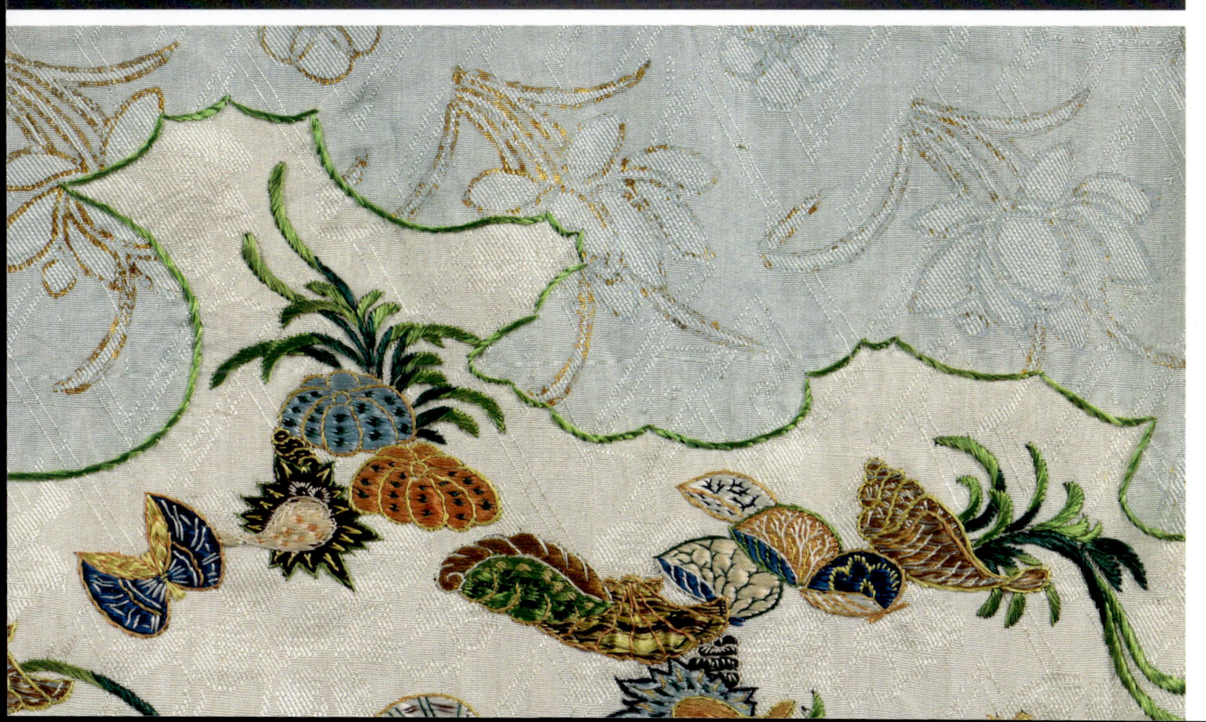

reinvention. Furthermore, the kimono is always worn as an ensemble with an obi and other accessories and is sometimes combined with a *haori* jacket and *hakama* pants, allowing for updated looks and the expression of personal style.

Only in the last decades of the twentieth century did scholars begin to consider fashion as a global cultural phenomenon, not one isolated to the West.[3] One of the first authors to address the field's Eurocentrism was Eric Wolf, in his seminal work *Europe and the People without History* (1982). His global anthropological approach, which considered the interconnectedness of economy, culture, and identity, provoked other anthropologists and fashion historians gradually to recognize that courtly garments in non-Western cultures exhibit the same fundamental elements of fashion, including rapidly changing styles and the signaling of social status, as in Europe,[4] and that non-Western dress has its own fashion system.[5] Indeed, many aspects of Japan's fashion system during the Edo period were comparable to contemporary European examples, and from the late nineteenth century they developed in tandem with Western concepts such as department stores and modern marketing strategies. Not only did Japan have fashion trends; it had an apparatus for the design, production, promotion, and sale of fashion every bit as complex as in the West.

Fashion is often said to have originated as a way for the elite to distinguish themselves from those lower on the social scale. Sixteenth- and seventeenth-century Italian sources, such as Baldassare Castiglione's *The Book of the Courtier* (1528), which provides insight into the customs and manners of Urbino's court life, suggest that fashion is a social institution of modernity and that clothing can be interpreted at both a personal and a political level.[6] The history of Edo-period dress unfolded within a similar framework, defined by political currents and the rise of the market economy in Japan. Fashion also shaped the identities of Kyoto and Edo, the two major cities. Innovations in textile production and a flourishing publishing industry that disseminated the latest styles in pattern books and woodblock prints are evidence of a pursuit of novelty dating to the seventeenth century.

Shifting fashions and even choices of patterns also reflect the mutable expectations of women's conduct and appearance, which can be gleaned from the influential instructional texts (written by men) that were published for women throughout the Edo period. These provided women moral guidance, social direction, education on subjects from child rearing to literature to the arts, and useful information on how to run a household, including sewing and cooking. The changes in such texts over time mirror men's evolving image of the ideal woman, which was continuously reshaped by economic and social conditions, such as changes in the traditional family structure and expanding literacy.[7] The Kyoto fashion trends and conventions summarized in an instructional text from 1692 (republished in 1847) suggest how circumscribed were women's options and how harshly they might be judged for failing to keep up with the new styles, which changed every five or eight years: "If a samurai wife went out dressed in [a *kosode* with] old-fashioned patterns with a lot of gold- or silver-thread embroidery on red or white backgrounds . . . she'd look like a country bumpkin and people in the capital would laugh at her." The text further advises that young women might wear fashionable patterns but that, by thirty, following trends "looks immature. Only subdued patterns stitched in dark colors are appropriate."[8]

SOCIAL AND FASHION SYSTEMS

The word "kimono" first appears in written sources in the Kamakura period (1185–1333) — not as the name of a specific type of garment but as a general word for clothing. When the Portuguese, the first Europeans to reach Japan, arrived in 1543, they noted that "qimono or qirumono"

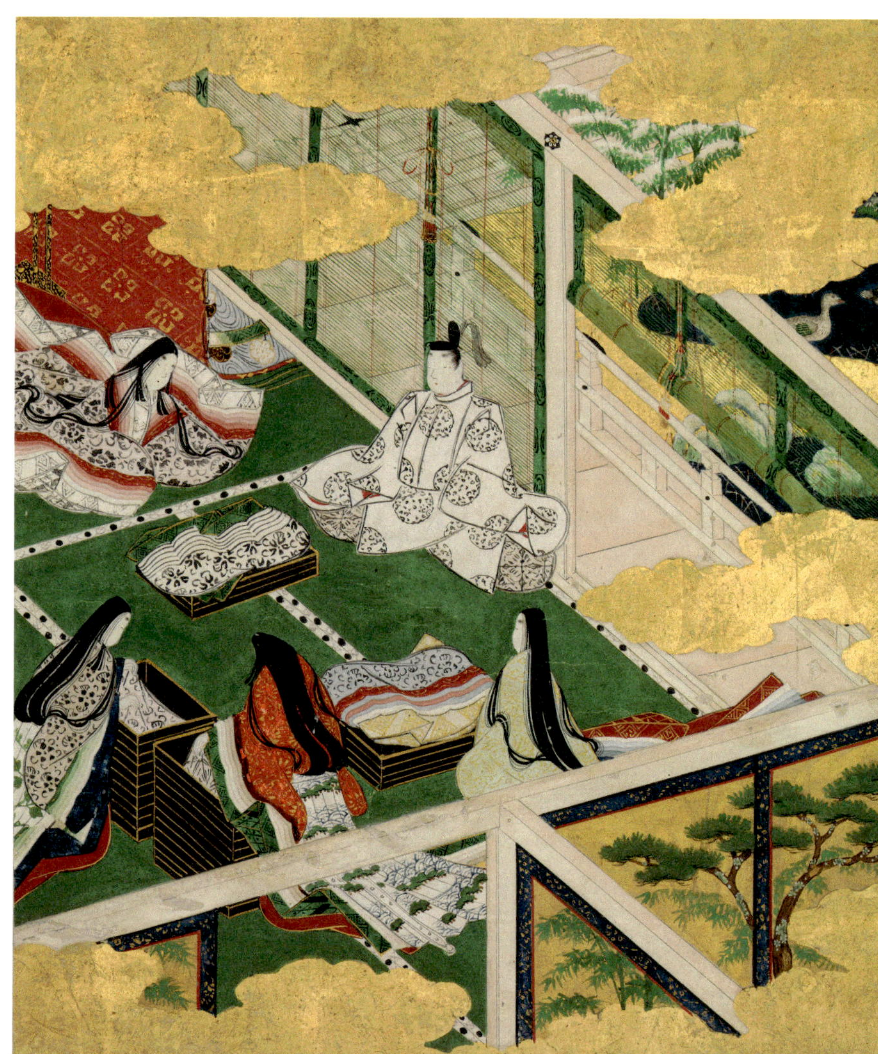

means "clothes" and that there are versions for summer (*katabira*), autumn (*awase*), and winter, and that the latter, with added lining, is generally called "kimono."[9] Various types of garments had individual names; the closest predecessor of what we now call a kimono is the *kosode*, the most common garment throughout the Edo period (fig. 1). *Kosode* means "small sleeve," which refers to the narrow opening around the wrist. By contrast, *ōsode* were robes with large sleeve openings. Aristocratic ladies wore silk *kosode* as an undergarment beneath several layers of *ōsode*, combining colors and patterns in a sophisticated manner (fig. 2). Commoners also wore *kosode*, typically made of hemp, as both undergarment and outer clothing. As merchants gained financial power, eventually they too were able to afford silk.[10]

Both men and women wore similar *kosode* as outer robes. They were loose fitting, held together by thin sashes, relatively wide, and shorter than present-day kimonos, with long collars. From the early seventeenth century, after the establishment of the Tokugawa shogunate, the garments reflected a strictly hierarchical social system. In 1688 the poet and novelist Ihara Saikaku expressed the contemporary view of clothing as a marker of class distinctions: "A merchant wearing fine silks is an ugly sight. Not only is homespun [pongee] better suited to his station, but he also looks smarter in it. With samurai, of course, for whom an imposing appearance is essential in the course of duty, even those without any servants should not dress like ordinary persons."[11]

At the top of the Edo-period social hierarchy, based on Confucian principles, were the samurai, members of the warrior class, which itself had an elite tier consisting of the daimyos, or feudal lords, and the shogun, or military commander, the de facto ruler of the country. The samurai were followed by three tiers of commoners: farmers, artisans, and merchants, last in class as they produced nothing, only profited from trade. The latter two were collectively called townspeople, or *chōnin*. Within this structure, women were deemed secondary to men, and commoners inferior to samurai, who were the retainers of the daimyos. Above these four tiers existed a prestigious but politically weak aristocracy, with an imperial court led by the emperor.

The establishment of a centralized military government by the shogun Tokugawa Ieyasu (1543–1616) in Edo in 1603 had marked the beginning of a peaceful, prosperous, politically stable period after centuries of warfare. With tight regulations, the shogunate cultivated a harmonious society and orderly behavior. Although the emperor's role was largely ceremonial, Kyoto, site of the Imperial Palace, remained both the capital and the hub of artists and craftsmen, with a vibrant and sophisticated cultural life (fig. 3). An extensive trade system developed within the country, with Edo, Kyoto, and Osaka being the major centers of the economy and the arts. More than two hundred regional daimyos under the rule of the shogun were required to spend every second year in Edo. This policy of "alternate attendance," known as *sankin-kōtai*, secured the shogunate's political power and regulated the wealth of the daimyos. When in Edo, the daimyos were in service to the shogun, attending audiences in the castle and assigning their samurai to guard the castle gates and fight fires. Their wives and children were required always to live in Edo. Women related to the shogun were relegated to the "great interior" (Ōoku) of Edo Castle, and there were similar living spaces for women in the daimyos' residences. The women were effectively held hostage so that the daimyos would not rebel. The daimyos' elaborate processions between their estates and Edo necessitated the construction of an extensive road system, with inns, restaurants, and teahouses built along the routes, boosting the economy. Edo gradually evolved from being a small military city to being the center of the shogunate, and by the eighteenth century had become one of the world's largest cities, with a population of one million, approximately half of which were women.[12]

Although women are prominently featured in histories of Japan's medieval and later modern eras, they were marginalized in official Edo-period historiographies and records; their experience is revealed mainly through letters, diaries, and wills. One explanation for women's relegation to the sidelines in written sources was the dominant influence of *Onna daigaku* (*Greater Learning for Women*), a set of moral codes based on neo-Confucian ethics supported by the shogunate; first published in 1729, it served as a guide to the daily life of women.[13] The main text consists of a nineteen-point lesson that emphasizes filial piety—not only toward the woman's own parents but, more important, toward her husband's—and wifely obedience: "A woman should look on her husband as if he were Heaven itself and

fig. 2 "A Lovely Garland" (*Tamakazura*), from *The Tale of Genji*. Circle of Tosa Mitsuyoshi (1539–1613). Momoyama period (1573–1615), early 17th century. One of a pair of album leaves mounted as a hanging scroll; ink, gold, silver, and color on paper; each leaf: 9⅝ × 8⅜ in. (24.4 × 21.3 cm). The Metropolitan Museum of Art, New York, Mary Griggs Burke Collection, Gift of the Mary and Jackson Burke Foundation, 2015 (2015.300.33a, b)

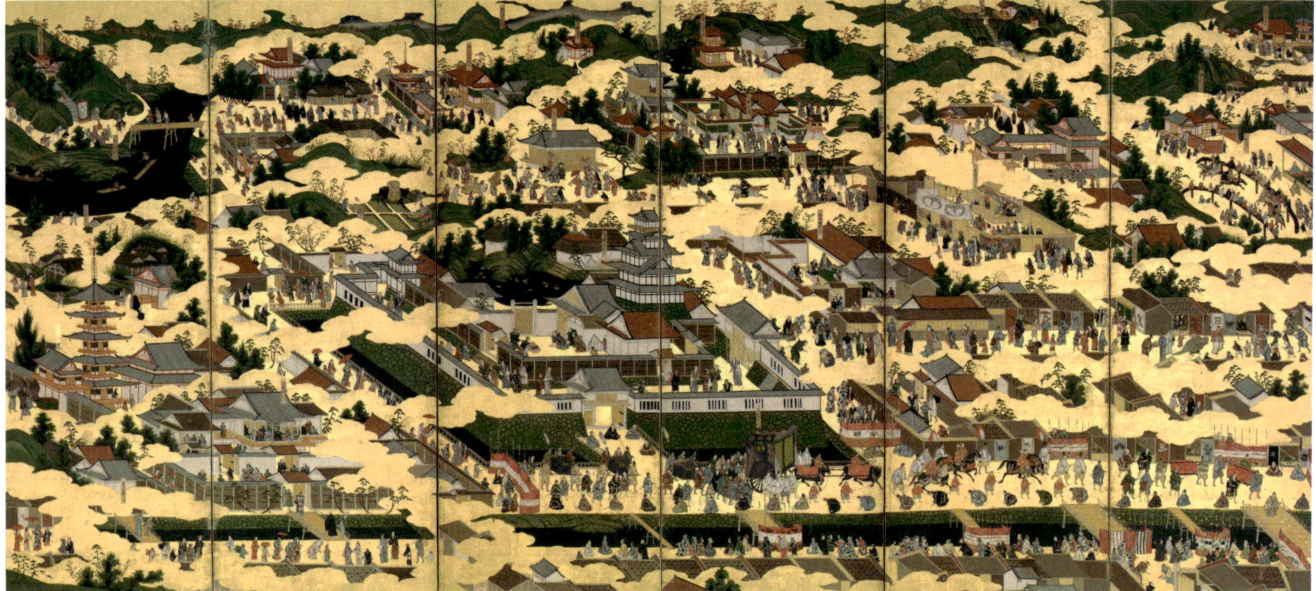

never weary of thinking how she may yield to her husband and thus escape celestial castigation."[14] It also underscored women's inferiority to men, stating that the majority of women were afflicted by "indocility, discontent, slander, jealousy, and silliness."[15] While such views may not have reflected women's actual, everyday experience, they became the norm for Edo-period texts.

Gentleness, humility, and restraint defined the ideal woman. The Edo-era attitude toward females is captured by instructions for teaching girls (*Joshi wo oshiyuru hō*, 1710) by the renowned scholar Kaibara Ekiken, the author of *Onna daigaku*: "Do not let them go outside after the age of ten; make them stay in the inner quarter and make them learn weaving, sewing, and spinning wheels. . . . *Kouta* (popular songs), *jōruri* (puppet shows), and shamisen (a three-stringed instrument) are fond of inappropriate tones so [if a girl hears them] her heart will be ruined."[16]

In an effort to regulate public decorum and align consumption with status, the Tokugawa shogunate repeatedly issued sumptuary laws; by controlling the materials and decorative techniques each class could use for apparel, it aimed to create and make visible rigid class distinctions, as well as to constrain spending. In the late seventeenth century, a series of edicts permitted merchants to wear only ordinary silk, pongee, cotton, and ramie. Thin crepe silk (*chijimi*), embroidery, and tie-dye (*shibori*) were prohibited, and the price of one length (*tan*) of material for a padded robe was strictly limited. In 1713 a warning was issued against such luxuries as unusual and intricate patterns, new dyes, expensive brocaded silks (*nishiki*), and labor-intensive techniques. The Kansei reforms in 1789–1801 and the Tenpō reforms in the early 1840s imposed a policy of frugality and restricted numerous aspects of production.[17] The sumptuary laws were often issued in years of devastating fire or poor rice harvests so the shogunate could reinforce its position in the economy. These regulations were not always strictly enforced, however, and the townspeople were able to find ways around them, including by using luxurious materials on the lining of a garment, where they were concealed. Sumptuary laws perhaps inadvertently had a strong influence on fashion, driving the popularity of the materials that were not regulated and of the methods used to mimic the forbidden techniques or dyes.

In its efforts to codify dress, the shogunate unwittingly was articulating a system of fashion much like the one that existed in Europe. Italy appears to have been one of the first places in Europe that attempted to classify dress by gender, status, and geography, including by the issuance of sumptuary laws. The emergence of a wealthy and influential bourgeoisie in the sixteenth and seventeenth centuries prompted Italy to regulate appearances so as to define social standing — and to prevent the newly rich from presenting themselves as upper class. Sumptuary laws also limited the amount spent on jewelry and luxury fabrics.

fig. 3 *Scenes in and around the Capital*. Edo period (1615–1868), 17th century. Pair of six-panel folding screens; ink, color, gold, and gold leaf on paper; each overall: 67 in. × 12 ft. ¼ in. (170 × 366.2 cm). The Metropolitan Museum of Art, New York, Mary Griggs Burke Collection, Gift of the Mary and Jackson Burke Foundation, 2015 (2015.300.106.1, .2)

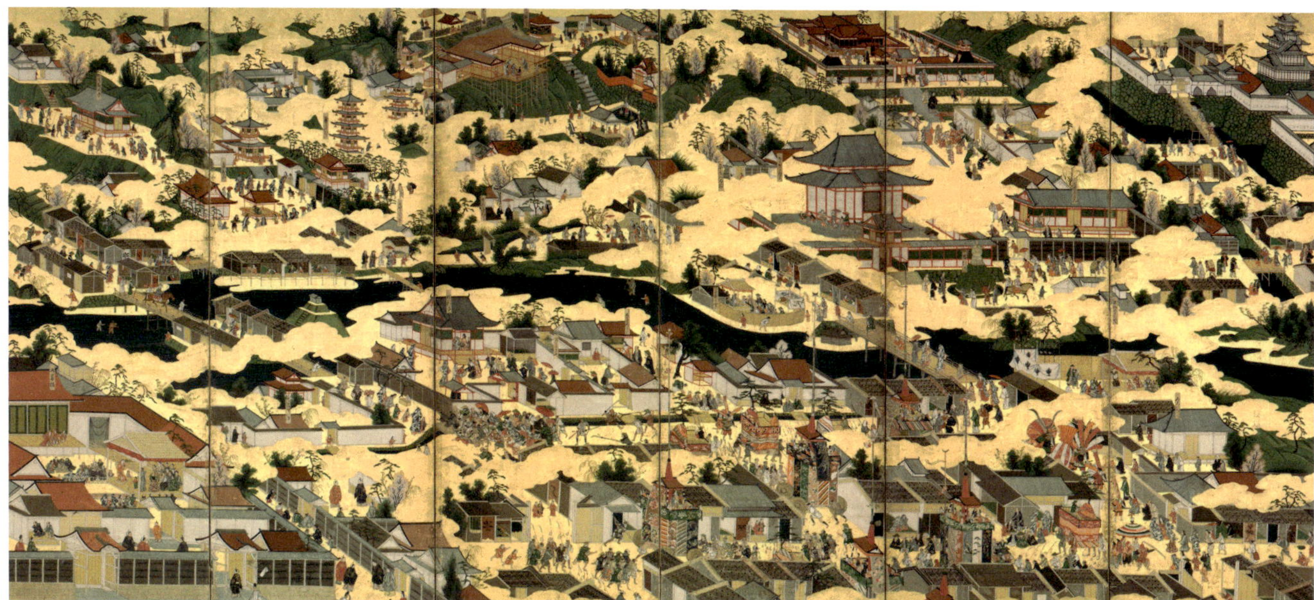

Complex structures of codes such as those underpin fashion systems across the globe, as does the development of a manufacturing industry, all of which were well established in Japan during the Edo period.

The Nishijin district of Kyoto had been the center of silk weaving since the late fifteenth century, but the roots of silk production in the city go back hundreds of years earlier. By the mid-sixteenth century the silk weavers' guild received protection from both the shogunate and the imperial court, as high-quality silk was required by both high-ranking samurai and the nobility. From about the beginning of the Edo period, wealthy merchants could afford silk clothing too, and the silk-weaving industry started to expand in response to increased demand. In particular, Nishijin became known for complex, brocaded fabrics woven on a raised loom (*takahata*) (fig. 4). By 1706 more than two thousand households were included in the silk weavers' guild. The guild protected its members as a kind of monopoly with advantageous trade conditions, including access to the Chinese silk yarns that came into Japan in limited quantities. The abolishment of the yarn-importing guild a few decades later led to fierce competition for silk yarn in Kyoto and to surging prices.[18]

In response, the shogunate promoted the production of silk yarn in northern Japan and in the Edo area, and Japanese silk gradually replaced the Chinese import. The industry further expanded

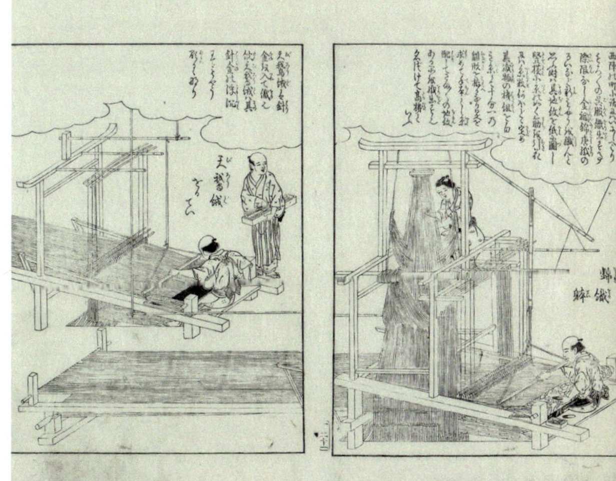

in 1730, when the Great Fire of Nishijin destroyed almost half the operating looms in Kyoto, devastating the city's silk industry. Not only did the silk-spinning and weaving centers north and west of Edo — in Tangō, Kiryū, Isesaki, and Hachioji — increase output to take advantage of Kyoto's setback; Kyoto weavers who had to relocate introduced advanced weaving techniques and looms to the provincial workshops. Competition among the various silk centers intensified as the quality of their silk improved significantly.[19]

While Kyoto has always been the center of silk production, in the Edo period Osaka was the center of the cotton trade, expanding cotton cultivation and production in the sixteenth century

fig. 4 *Nishijin*, from *Illustrations of Famous Places in Kyoto* (*Miyako meisho-zue*). Edo period (1615–1868), 1786. Woodblock-printed book; ink on paper. International Research Center for Japanese Studies (Nichibunken) Collection

and cotton processing by the seventeenth century. By the mid-eighteenth century, however, rural cotton production began to flourish in the Kinai region. Osaka-based wholesalers purchased cotton cloth and sold it to dealers for storage and distribution, including merchants who shipped to Edo.[20]

EDO-PERIOD MERCHANDISING

Dry-goods stores or fabric merchants (*gofukuten* or *gofukuya*) sold high-quality, made-to-order *kosode* of silk or fine hemp called *gofuku*.[21] The *gofuku* shops' clients were principally men and women of the samurai and wealthy merchant classes.[22] From about the mid-eighteenth century, when aristocratic women's everyday dress became standardized, they too ordered robes from a *gofukuya*. Farmers and commoners with low incomes mainly made their own clothing, either from cotton or bast fiber they cultivated or perhaps purchased, or from pongee, a slub-weave silk. The best-known *gofukuya* were Echigoya, Shirokiya, Matsuzakaya, and Daimaruya, all of which had branches in multiple cities, including Kyoto; they all ordered fabrics from Kyoto through their offices there and worked with Kyoto craftsmen to custom-make their clients' robes. The exteriors of the large one-story shops were draped with curtains emblazoned with crests identifying the business, concealing the interiors from passersby (fig. 5). Shoppers could not freely enter to browse.

Kosode orders were placed differently by each social class, as Professor Nagasaki Iwao illustrated in a 2017 study. For high-ranking samurai households, the *onando-yaku*, a steward in charge of the wardrobe, arranged orders with the *gofukuya*, principally for the head of the family. The orders were carefully recorded in ledgers, including the ground fabric, the patterns, the decorative techniques, the calculation for the price of each robe, and the grand total. For lower-ranking samurai families, a representative of the shop may have visited the home to take the orders directly.[23]

While the *onando-yaku* may occasionally have ordered clothing for the wife or other female relatives of the daimyo or high-ranking samurai, more often a senior lady-in-waiting in charge of the women's wardrobe placed the orders and handled the payment. After the lady-in-waiting briefly described what was needed, the fabric shop created a detailed plan, including a rough sketch of the robe depicting the patterns. The senior lady-in-waiting might also order the clothing that the daimyo and high-ranking samurai men wore privately in the women's quarter, but the *onando-yaku* always ordered the clothing men wore in their public life.

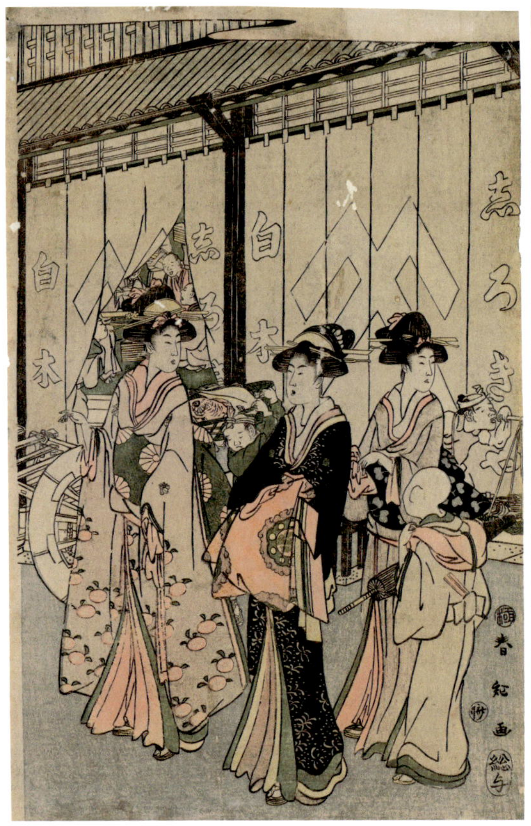

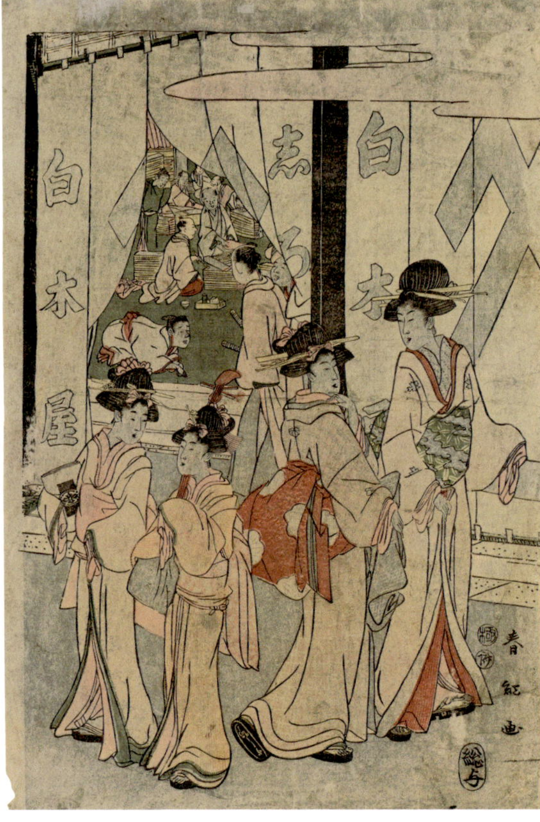

fig. 5 Women walking by the Shirokiya shop. Katsukawa Shunkō (active 1789–1818). Edo period (1615–1868), late 18th century. Woodblock print (*nishiki-e*); ink and color on paper; overall: 14⅞ × 19¾ in. (37.8 × 50 cm). Museum of Fine Arts, Boston, William Sturgis Bigelow Collection

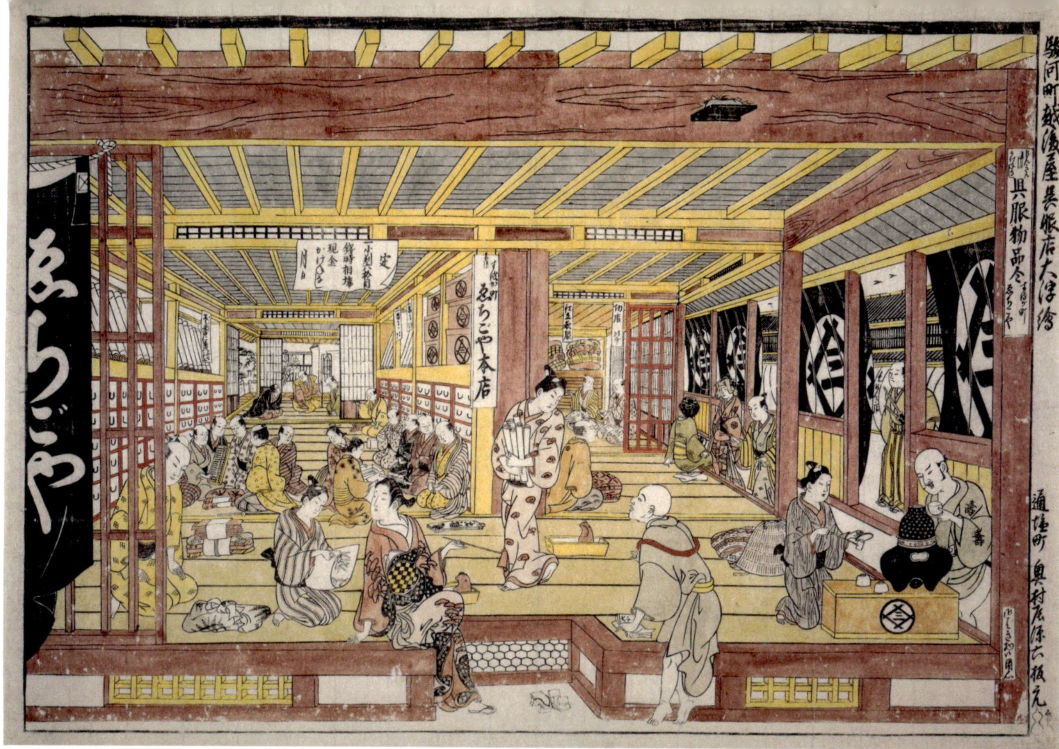

Elite men existed in the socially visible "front" world, while women of the samurai class were confined to the interior of the residence, strictly secluded from male visitors and with very limited social roles. Yet their duties within the household — controlling its members' religious and ritual life and managing the affairs of the women's quarters, including marriages, childbirth, and child rearing — were considered vital to maintaining the political and social order. They complemented men's work in the public sphere.[24]

On the rare official occasions when elite samurai women were seen in public, they wore garments rooted in traditions codified by samurai etiquette dating to the Muromachi period (1392–1573). The silk and the decorative techniques were of the finest quality, but the patterns were typically conservative, based on traditional, auspicious motifs and literature. While adhering to those high standards and the requirements of the shogunate, each garment was individually designed and unique. For a high-ranking samurai lady, approximately thirty garments were ordered at a time, twice a year, for the opposite season. A daimyo lady would wear a robe perhaps ten times, but never again after the end of the year.

Clothing orders for high-ranking samurai women indicated the season, occasion (such as the New Year celebration), and decorative techniques but included few detailed instructions regarding the patterns. Pattern books of hand-painted sketches created by the fabric shop were used only to help guide the selection. After the order was copied into a ledger dedicated to the client, the designer created several versions of the garment, unique compositions derived from standard patterns and designs, to present to the client. The final selection was recorded in the order book, and written instructions and sketches were created for all the craftsmen who would work on the robe, sometimes accompanied by lifesize drawings. The selected bolt of undyed fabric was cut and temporarily stitched together in the shape of the garment, and the underdrawing, or outline of the patterns, was applied to the fabric with light blue dye. Then the piece was taken apart and sent to specialized craftsmen for dyeing, embroidery, the application of gold foil, and so forth. Sewn together in its final form and completed with a lining, the garment was carefully examined and compared with the order. The date of completion and the cost of the execution (including all the charges by the individual craftsmen) were registered in the order book. The final price, including the *gofukuya*'s profit, was recorded in a separate ledger. Finally, the garment was sent out, accompanied by a statement of delivery and invoice.[25]

By contrast to samurai men, *chōnin* men had little choice in fashion, in compliance with regulations pertaining to social status. Their wives made

fig. 6 Large perspective view of the interior of Echigoya in Suruga-chō, Edo. Okumura Masanobu (1686–1764). Edo period (1615–1868), ca. 1745. Woodblock print (*urushi-e*); ink on paper with hand-applied color and *nikawa* (animal glue); 18¾ × 26⅜ in. (47.7 × 66.8 cm). Museum of Fine Arts, Boston, William Sturgis Bigelow Collection

or ordered their garments, typically patterned with stripes in subdued colors, such as indigo blue, brown, or gray. For formal attire, *chōnin* men wore a *haori* jacket with *hakama* pants; for special occasions and ceremonies, a two-piece *kamishimo* — a vest (*kataginu*) and a *hakama* in matching fabric — worn over a *kosode*. For everyday wear and privately, they wore *kosode* of cotton, bast fiber, pongee, or occasionally silk.

Chōnin women had more freedom to decide what to wear. Although their outfits were supposed to reflect their social position and conform to the sumptuary laws, they often disregarded such rules to be fashionable, to show off wealth, and to compete with other women, including courtesans; unlike their social superiors, *chōnin* women could go out freely and parade on the streets of Edo and Kyoto. They could attend poetry circles and learn calligraphy and music, expected to be at once educated, attractive, and unthreatening. Summing up the challenge for women in the Edo period, the historian Marcia Yonemoto observed: "A learned woman was the essential foundation of a reputable household, yet an overly clever one was inclined to haughtiness and unseemly ambition; a cultivated and presentable woman was an asset to the family and society, while a flamboyantly attractive one was bound to stir up chaotic desires."[26]

Chōnin women placed orders themselves, either in the comfort of their homes or at the *gofukuya*, for bolts of fabric that in most cases were sewn into garments at home. A woodblock print of the Echigoya store conveys the eighteenth-century retail experience (fig. 6). The store's floor was covered in tatami, and clients removed their footwear before entering. A few bolts of fabric were displayed on shelves, but most were not readily visible; sales clerks would bring out bolts that were stored in drawers and, kneeling with their customers, discuss the choice of fabrics and patterns.

Women's education and role in society, as well as their age and marital status, were all captured on the surface of their robes. Both the designers of the patterns and the clients reacted sensitively to shifts in culture, the economy, and the law. Women's knowledge of literary classics was reflected in their choices of patterns or in what was deemed to be appropriate for them; auspicious and didactic themes were often integrated into the designs (fig. 7). *Kosode* and *uchikake* (over robe) patterns with references to stories about filial piety

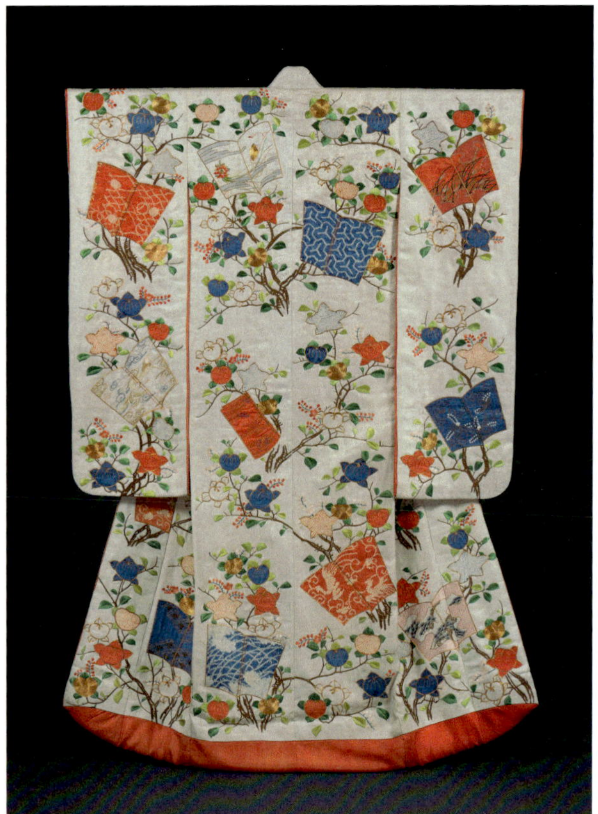

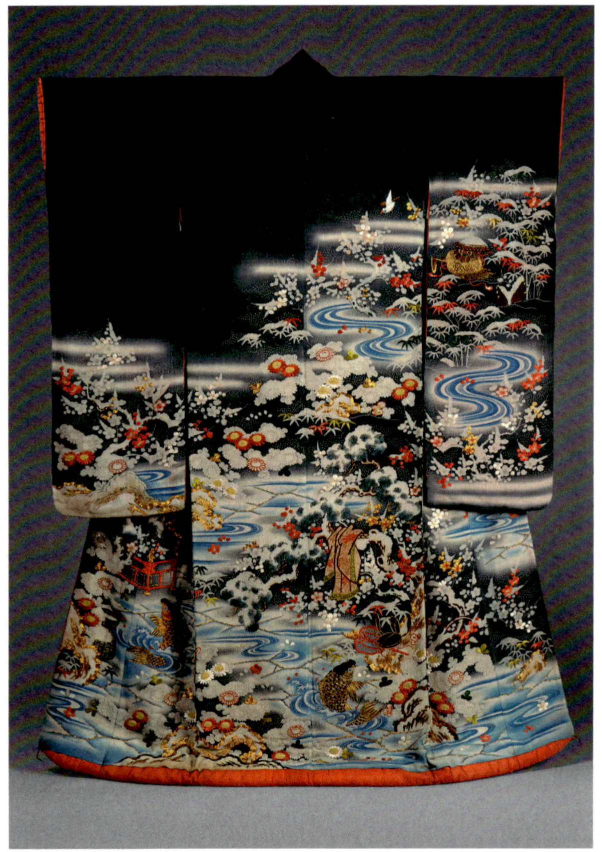

fig. 7 Over robe (*uchikake*) with books and mandarin-orange branches. Edo period (1615–1868), late 18th–early 19th century. Figured satin-weave silk (*rinzu*) with paste-resist dyeing, tie-dyeing, silk embroidery, and couched gold thread; 68 × 49 in. (172.7 × 124.5 cm). The Metropolitan Museum of Art, New York, Gift of Mr. and Mrs. Earl Morse, 1972 (1972.18)

fig. 8 Over robe (*uchikake*) with scenes of filial piety. Edo period (1615–1868), first half of 19th century. Crepe silk with paste-resist dyeing, silk embroidery, and couched gold thread; 68¾ × 49 in. (174.6 × 124.5 cm). The Metropolitan Museum of Art, New York, Anonymous Gift, 1949 (49.32.109)

were common in the late Edo period, especially for samurai women (fig. 8). In a similar way, Chinese characters (kanji) were often incorporated into patterns beginning in the early eighteenth century, when women, who had typically used kana characters (syllabaries), were encouraged to learn the Chinese characters previously reserved for men (cat. 23); they were also urged to read Chinese books based on neo-Confucian ideals.

Unlike samurai women, merchant-class women could readily follow the latest trends and freely choose patterns and decorative techniques. In consultation with shop representatives, they referred to woodblock-printed pattern books, or *hinagata-bon*. *Hinagata-bon*, which were available in bookshops, were similar to today's fashion magazines. *Chōnin* women enjoyed perusing them at home but also used them as a tool for ordering the most up-to-date *kosode* fashions. An illustration from 1718 shows three women looking at pattern books while contemplating the bolts of fabrics nearby (fig. 9). Their conversation sounds familiar: "What an unusual, new pattern!" "Let's see if we can find something we like." "I will pick this one."

From 1666 to 1820, approximately 180 *hinagata-bon* were published in Japan. They serve as essential resources to date popular patterns and the changes in the distribution of the motifs on the surface of the *kosode*. They also document the development of dyeing and decorative techniques; for example, *Genji hinakata* (Genji patterns) of 1687 details twenty-seven types of dyeing.[27] Most of these books contain schematic drawings of the *kosode*, spread out flat, that clearly depict the motifs and are accompanied by comments about the patterns, recommended colors, and decorative techniques (fig. 10). However, some of the books illustrate the robes in use to indicate the appropriate styling and the types of women they fit best, much as today's fashion magazines show garments on models. Most patterns were created by unknown designers, but well-known ukiyo-e artists such as Hishikawa Moronobu (1618–1694) and Nishikawa Sukenobu (1671–1750) also produced *hinagata-bon*. The surviving examples of garments that can be matched with published patterns testify that the customer's taste dictated the colors and modifications to the design. She sought both to follow the latest trends and to express a distinct individual style.

The production of pattern books declined in the late Edo period, one of the last being *Banzai hiinakata* (Patterns for ten thousand years), in 1820. The waning need for *hinagata-bon* can be explained by the slowing development of new fashions and decorative techniques, the weakening economy, the standardization of designs, and a simplification of the distribution of patterns across the garment and thus of the design process: motifs were increasingly concentrated below the waist from the late eighteenth century, as the width of the obi increased; upper sections of

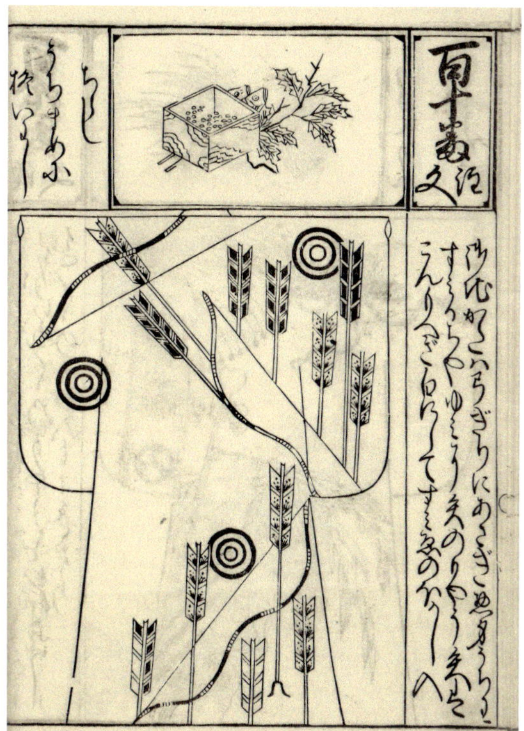

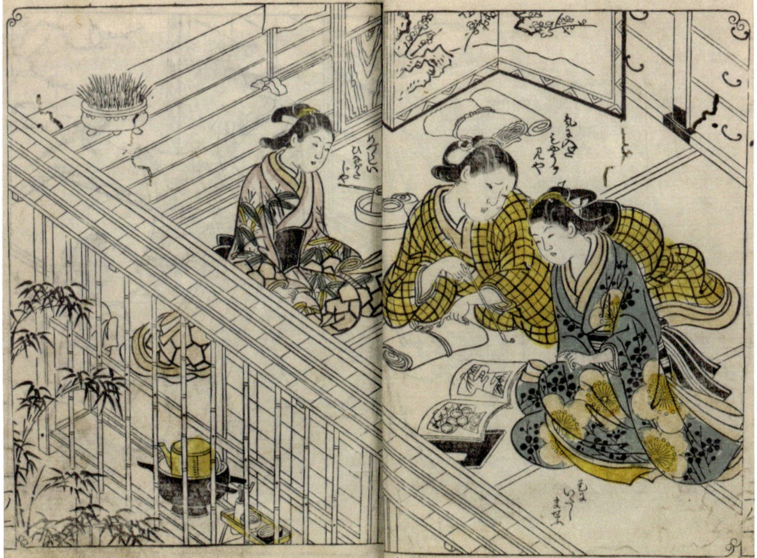

fig. 9 *Nishikawa's Book of Patterns (Nishikawa hinagata).* Nishikawa Sukenobu (1671–1750). Edo period (1615–1868), 1718. Woodblock-printed book; ink on paper. The New York Public Library, Spencer Collection

fig. 10 *Order Book of Kosode Patterns (Chūmon no hiinagata).* Imura Katsukichi (active early 18th century). Edo period (1615–1868), 1716. Woodblock-printed book; ink on paper; 9 ¾ x 7 ⅛ in. (24.8 x 18 cm). The Metropolitan Museum of Art, New York, Gift of Betty and Paul Nomura, in memory of Nomura Shōjirō, 2018 (2018.954.8a)

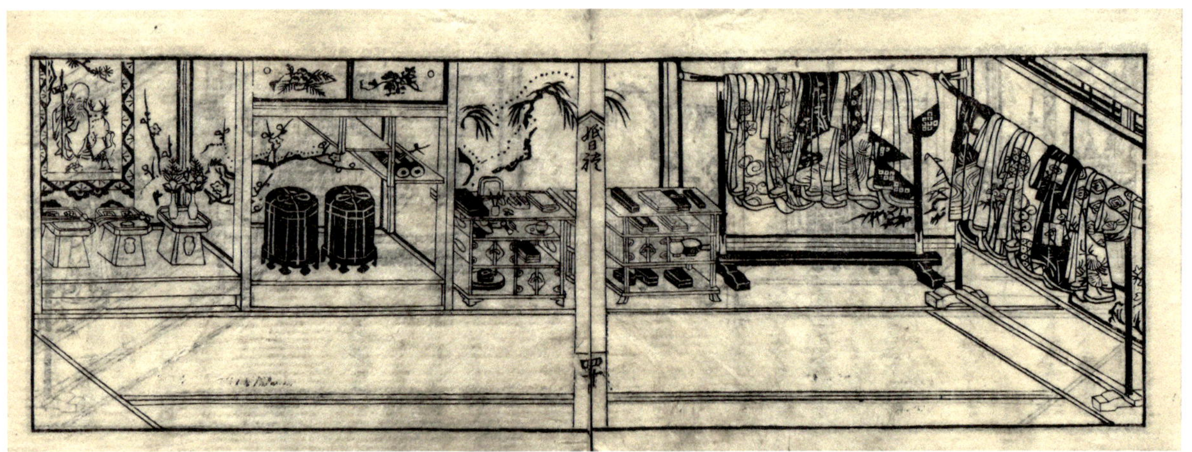

the garment were left largely undecorated. Three new locations for patterns emerged as trends: on the front flaps and the front lower hem (*tsuma moyō*); around the hem (*suso moyō*); and on the inner lining (*ura moyō*). In addition, small, refined, uniform patterns (*komon*) on monochrome surfaces became fashionable, a response to the sumptuary laws and changing tastes. By contrast to earlier, colorful designs enriched with gold and other luxurious materials and labor-intensive techniques such as embroidery or tie-dyeing, the new patterns were produced in great variety with relatively inexpensive stencil-dyeing (*katazome*). They represented a subdued sensibility, or *iki* (chic simplicity). The beauty of usually hidden details — such as patterns on the inner lining — characterizes the aesthetic of *iki*.[28] As the emphasis shifted to colorful obis made of luxurious materials, *kosode* took on understated shades of gray, brown, and blue. Accordingly, albums of dye color and *komon* pattern samples, with both swatches and woodblock-printed stencil samples, replaced the printed pattern books.

WEDDINGS

A successful marriage was seen as a fulfillment of filial duties and a woman's most important accomplishment in the Edo era. And, at a time when parents typically left all their property to their firstborn or adopted son, marriage was among the few ways a woman could ensure that she was provided for. Far from a romantic union, it was a government-regulated means of preserving the patrilineal system, maintaining strict class distinctions, and, especially for high-ranking samurai, preventing upward mobility and the increase of wealth and status, ultimately sustaining the shogun's privileged position. Samurai marriages in particular were strictly controlled, and marriage across class lines was generally forbidden.

Women's education was one means for their families' economic or social advancement within a given class, conforming to the Confucian idea that self-improvement leads to the stabilization of society.[29] Skills such as reading and writing, keeping accounts, managing the household budget, and weaving and sewing were viewed as assets toward securing a good marriage. Once a bride was sent to the groom's home, she became the daughter of her husband's parents, more bound to them by the ties of filial piety than to her own family.

A woman from an elite family had little to no say in the choice of her spouse; for example, Princess Chiyo-hime (1637–1699), the eldest daughter of Tokugawa Iemitsu, the third shogun, was married at the age of three in an effort to stabilize the power of the shogunate. A family's financial, social, and political considerations took precedence over a bride's personal preference, and the shogunate's consent was required for a daimyo wedding. Educated women from low-ranking samurai families and the wealthy merchant class had more influence over the selection of husband, and women in farming communities, where marriage was relatively informal, held even greater sway.

Upon announcement of an engagement, wealthy and powerful daimyos began preparations for magnificent wedding trousseaux for their daughters, significant investments and symbols of the political alliance. The trousseau was an important part of the dowry taken to the groom's estate in an elegant wedding procession. Such bridal processions were depicted on folding

fig. 11 Pages from a wedding manual (*Konrei shiyōkeshi-bukuro*). Edo period (1615–1868), 1706. Woodblock-printed book; ink on paper; each: 4⅞ × 7¼ in. (12.3 × 18.2 cm). Center for Open Data in the Humanities, Collection of Ajinomoto Foundation for Dietary Culture

screens and handscrolls, visual records of the marriage that documented even the names of the participants.[30]

From the mid-Edo period onward, all the dowry furnishings were formally displayed at the groom's home, with the garments carefully arranged in the dressing room on lacquer kimono racks (fig. 11). The wedding ceremony followed Muromachi-period traditions codified in a wedding handbook compiled by Ise Sadamichi (1463–1521), a high-ranking samurai in charge of warrior etiquette. The bride was dressed in a white ensemble, while the groom wore a formal navy-blue *kamishimo*. The ceremony included the presentation to the groom of a pair of lacquer shell-matching-game boxes, the ritual drinking of sake, and a celebratory meal of auspicious ingredients and dishes. Next, the bride changed into richly embroidered white, red, and black *uchikake*, layered on one another or worn in sequence, and was officially introduced to the groom's family (fig. 12).

Chōnin had a similar but simpler tradition, imitating the customs of the samurai, and well-to-do merchants ordered expensive and refined household utensils, furniture, and clothing for their daughters. However, their trousseaux, strictly regulated by sumptuary laws, could be transferred to the groom's home in a few chests.[31]

The preparations for one commoner's marriage in 1833, as recounted by the scholar Amy Stanley, provide rare insight into the contents of garment dowries and exemplify how both a woman's worth and her family's social standing were measured by her wardrobe.[32] Tsuneno was preparing to marry a wealthy farmer in Echigo province (today's Niigata prefecture). Her older brother, Giyū, catalogued her clothing, which included fifty-seven items: five lined silk kimonos; fifteen cotton-padded robes in pongee, crepe silk, and striped and patterned cotton; six obi sashes, some of satin and damask; five unlined cotton robes; crepe silk underwear; and outerwear such as a rain jacket, a sleeveless jacket, and two wrappers. Though her wardrobe was extensive, Tsuneno's family decided to buy fifty-three additional pieces: bolts of white cotton, raw cotton, glossy silk, and ramie; prefabricated cuffs, collars, and hems; accessories such as hairpins and hand towels; a set of white clothing, possibly for the wedding ceremony; and a formal kimono in black silk with an obi. When the bill for those items exceeded Giyū's estimate for the wardrobe, the groom's family

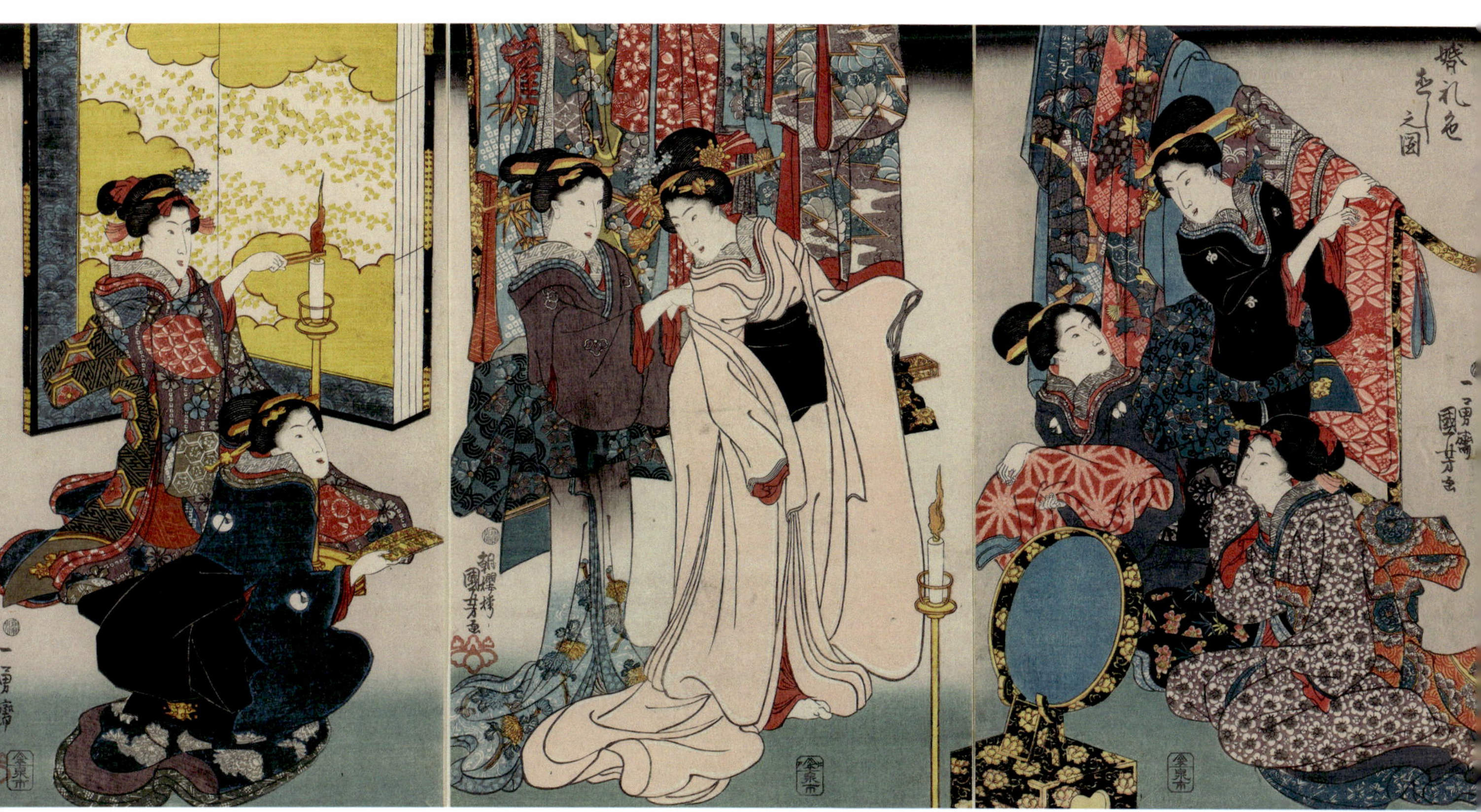

fig. 12 *The Bride Changing Clothes after the Wedding Ceremony* (*Konrei ironaoshi no zu*). Utagawa Kuniyoshi (1797–1861). Edo period (1615–1868), ca. 1843–47. Woodblock print (*nishiki-e*); ink and color on paper; 14⅛ × 28¾ in. (35.8 × 72.9 cm). Museum of Fine Arts, Boston, William Sturgis Bigelow Collection

agreed to contribute funds toward Tsuneno's garments, an unusual gift at that time.

Despite the importance placed on marriage, the rate of divorce among samurai and commoners alike was relatively high. Tsuneno's marriage — her second — lasted only four years. She was obliged to return to her brother's home but was fortunate to be able to retain her full set of clothes. Her former in-laws could not have sold the kimonos to recover their investment without the embarrassment of revealing that they had contributed to the wardrobe. Tsuneno went on to marry and divorce twice more. Later, when she set out to start a new life in Edo, she owned only her clothing and had to pawn almost all of it to survive. Ultimately she became a maid, which other than marriage was among the few options available to women at the time.

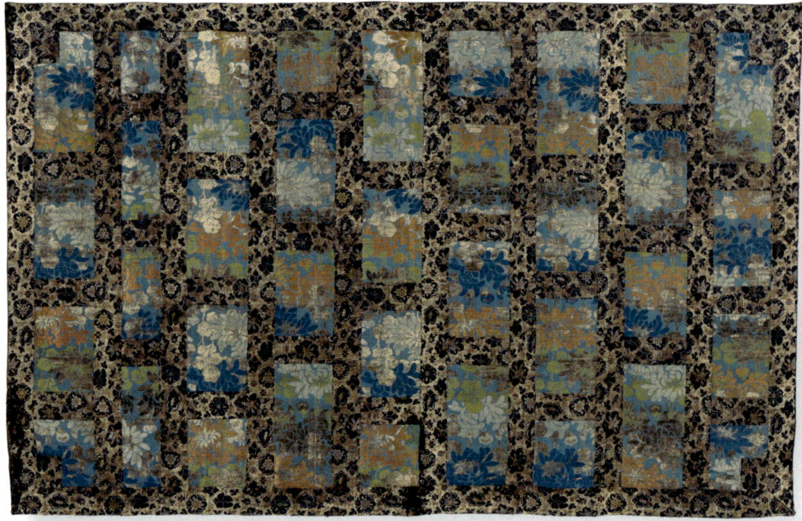

CLOTHES FOR THE COMMON PEOPLE

While fine silk was a defining characteristic of clothing worn by Japan's affluent and elite, it was far beyond the reach of the masses. Cotton was available in the warmer regions, such as Ise and Kinai, where cotton cultivation had been introduced in about the fifteenth century, but pricey cotton clothing was not typical for farmers elsewhere until the mid-Edo period. In colder areas, the only locally available fabrics were made of hemp, ramie, mulberry, wisteria, and other bast fibers. These traditional fibers were strong but not warm, and they were laborious to produce. During the long winters, when there was no work in the fields, women would painstakingly make yarns from plant fibers and weave cloth for the family.

Farmers with the means bought cotton cloth to make new garments, but access to the precious fiber increased in the middle of the Edo period with the establishment of the *kitamaesen*, a commercial shipping route between northern and central Japan, which enabled the secondhand clothing trade to flourish. Used silk kimonos were transported from Kyoto to Edo, and cast-off cotton clothing was brought from Edo to Osaka to be dispersed to other parts of Japan, especially the north. Nothing was wasted. Peasants recycled used clothes from the cities into homespun. A respect for and ingenious use of scarce materials led to the emergence of regional folk textile traditions such as *sakiori*: torn strips of castaway cotton cloth woven with bast-fiber warp yarns into a thick material and made into sturdy and warm jackets and vests (cat. 30). Another folk textile tradition is *sashiko*, which derives from stitching or quilting cotton yarns onto bast-fiber cloth or layers of cotton fabric, converting them into durable, relatively warm textiles for work clothes and coverlets (cat. 29). These humble garments were typically dyed with indigo.[33]

Japan's long tradition of reusing and preserving fragments of textiles has roots in Buddhism. *Kesa*, the outer garments or vestments worn by Buddhist monks, originally were pieced together as a patchwork from scraps of fabric salvaged from worn-out clothing, often donated by members of the community. The practice reflects the historical Buddha's renunciation of wealth and waste. Later, wealthy people would donate the *kosode* of deceased women and Noh costumes to Buddhist temples in exchange for ceremonies and prayers, and these luxurious secular garments were transformed into banners, altar cloths, or *kesa* (fig. 13).

A NEW ERA

Decisive change came to Japan near the end of the Edo period. The country's exposure to the West's military and technological might, after the United States' warships arrived in 1853, and the opening of its ports to international trade the following year ushered in an era of industrialization and modernization that was motivated in part by the threat of being overpowered by foreign countries and their goods.

Other historical and social developments had been longer in the making. By the mid-Edo period, the stratification of Japanese society

fig. 13 Seven-panel *kesa* (Buddhist monk's vestment) with chrysanthemums and stylized flowers. Edo period (1615–1868), 18th century. Twill-weave silk with silk- and gold-thread supplementary weft patterning (*kinran*); 49 x 68¾ in. (114.3 x 183 cm). Lent by John C. Weber Collection

had begun to loosen, as the *chōnin* accumulated wealth but remained without political power, while the samurai retained power but were unable to increase their wealth. Their fixed income was calculated in rice that was converted to cash at a price defined by the shogunate and not by the market. The difference between the "posted price" of the rice and its market value, combined with high taxes and the cost of maintaining men at arms, horses, and equipment, contributed to the bankruptcy of the samurai and the prosperity of the merchants. Even daimyos had to borrow funds from Kyoto merchants and moneylenders. This imbalance factored into the eventual collapse of the Tokugawa shogunate, the dismantling of the hierarchical system, and the return of imperial rule.

In 1868 the Tokugawa shogunate was overthrown by supporters of Emperor Meiji (1852–1912). The restoration of the emperor's political power brought sweeping changes to the bureaucratic and economic systems and led to the establishment of a modernized form of government. Edo was renamed Tokyo and became the capital, and the young Meiji emperor moved from Kyoto to the castle formerly occupied by the shoguns. Meiji-period (1868–1912) reforms introduced a constitutional system in which the hereditary rights and powers of daimyos and high-ranking samurai were abolished and the four-tier social system was dissolved; a host of other measures was directed toward the industrialization and urbanization of the country. Public museums, universities, and parks were opened. The export of silk and tea helped defray the investment in infrastructure and naval ships. The samurai class had a leading role in the creation of a militarily powerful nation-state, represented by the emperor in a European-style uniform, and many upper-class samurai became politicians and civil servants.

Clothing played an important role in how Japan tried to present itself on the world stage as it balanced pride in its traditions with an embrace of the modern, as defined by the West. Male government officials and military personnel followed the Meiji emperor's lead and adopted Western-style uniforms and suits to project an up-to-date image of Japan. From the 1880s Empress Shōken (1849–1914) and her court promoted the adoption of Western-style fashion — made of Japanese materials — along with advancements in domestic textile manufacturing. The Singer sewing machine, which was introduced to Japan in the 1870s, symbolized the modern method of making clothing at home even as it clashed with a long tradition of homemade, needle-stitched kimonos (fig. 14). High-ranking Japanese ladies for the first time sported imported bustles, corsets, and boots, although they sometimes required modifications of Western styles. As the couturier

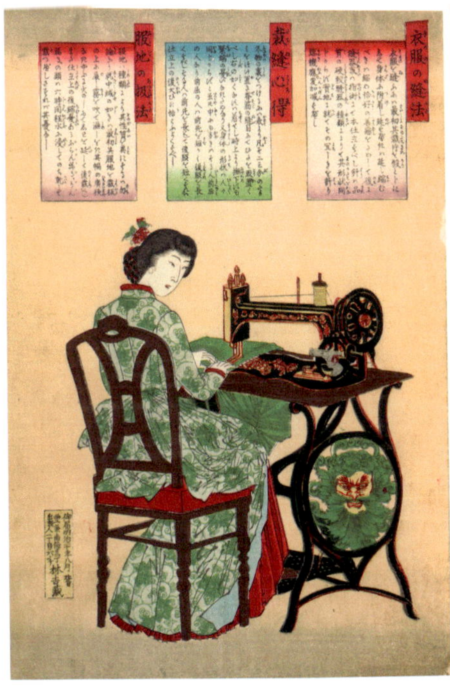
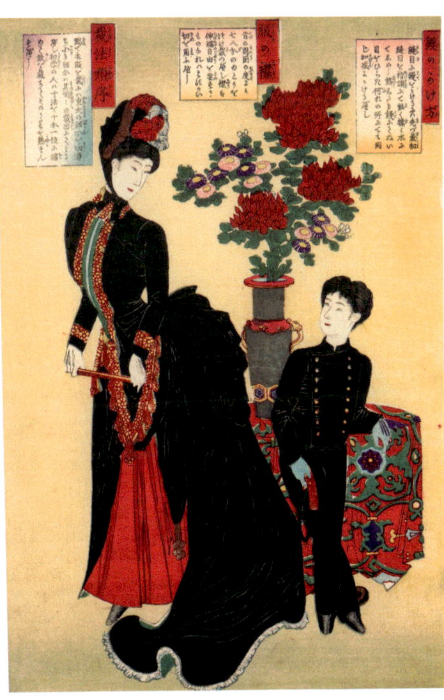
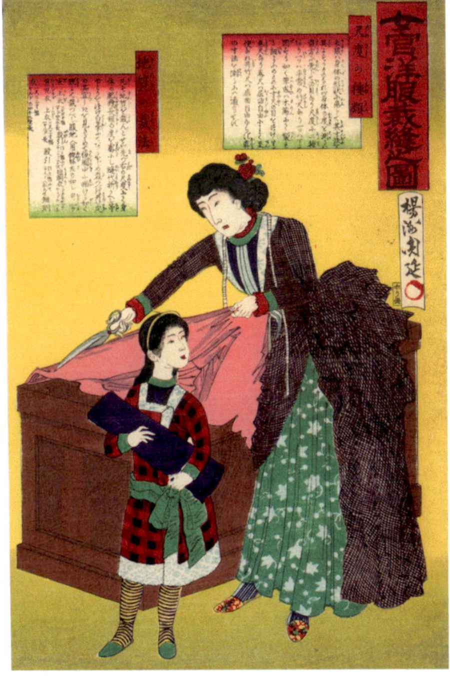

fig. 14 Court ladies sewing Western clothing. Yōshū (Hashimoto) Chikanobu (1838–1912). Meiji period (1868–1912), 1887. Triptych of woodblock prints (*nishiki-e*); ink and color on paper; 14⅜ × 29¾ in. (36.4 × 75.4 cm). The Metropolitan Museum of Art, New York, Gift of Lincoln Kirstein, 1959 (JP3340)

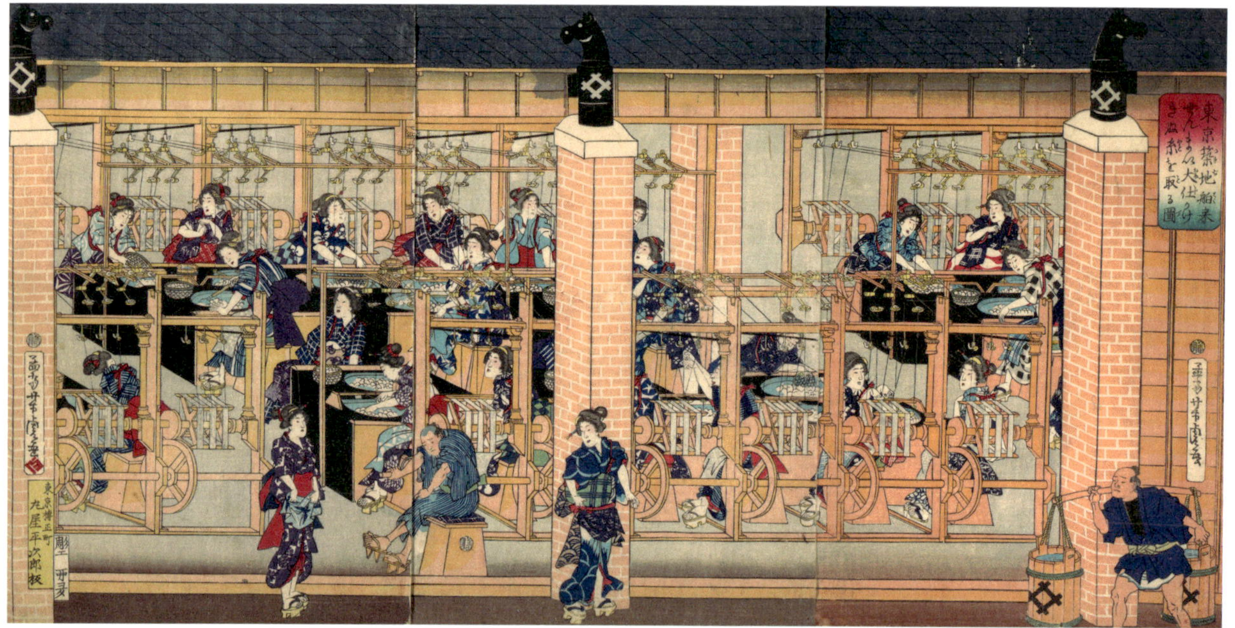

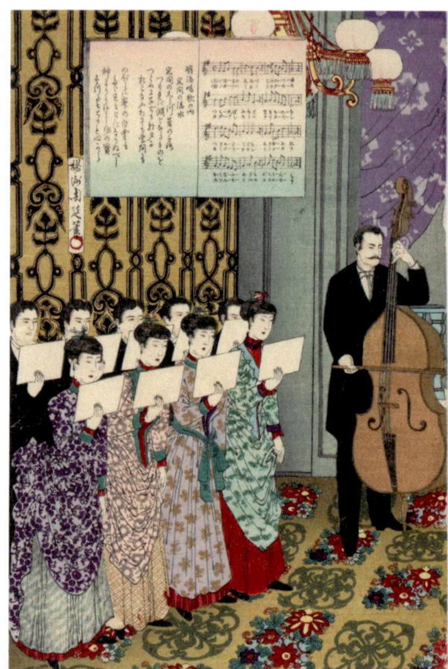

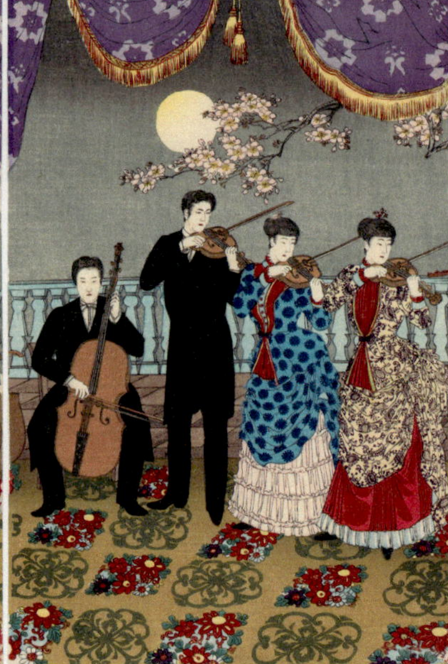

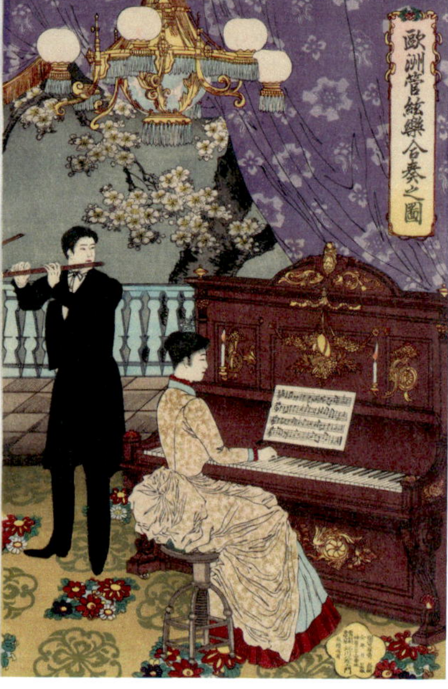

Jean Philippe Worth noted in his 1928 history of the House of Worth: "One of the most difficult sovereigns to dress was the Empress of Japan. The Nipponese Protocol . . . was very strict in the eighties. Certain parts of the body had to be covered, and no bodice could be décolleté. Price, however, never bothered them."[34]

Nevertheless, the adoption of Western dress was gradual. Men took to it sooner, while most women continued wearing kimonos. (At the beginning of the Meiji period, the price of Western dresses was exceedingly high.) In a sign of change, however, women, especially students, began to wear *hakama* pants and *haori* jackets, which were previously worn only by men. While some Japanese sought to preserve their heritage to the greatest possible degree, many took a middle road, modernizing their traditional aesthetics by, for example, wearing kimono patterns inspired by Western oil painting. The influx of styles from abroad was reflected in new terminology that distinguished Japanese clothing (*wafuku*) from Western clothing (*yōfuku*). Also for the first time, the word "kimono" became widely used

fig. 15 Imported silk-reeling machine at Tsukiji in Tokyo. Utagawa Yoshitora (active ca. 1850–80). Meiji period (1868–1912), 1872. Triptych of woodblock prints (*nishiki-e*); ink and color on paper; 14½ × 28¾ in. (36.8 × 73 cm). The Metropolitan Museum of Art, New York, Gift of Lincoln Kirstein, 1959 (JP3346)

fig. 16 Concert of European music. Yōshū (Hashimoto) Chikanobu (1838–1912). Meiji period (1868–1912), 1889. Triptych of woodblock prints (*nishiki-e*); ink and color on paper; 14½ × 29 in. (36.8 × 73.7 cm). The Metropolitan Museum of Art, New York, Gift of Lincoln Kirstein, 1959 (JP3276)

to designate Japanese garments, as opposed to Western-style apparel and instead of the varied terms used in the Edo period for specific types of clothes. Indeed, the kimono became a cultural signifier for Westerners, who identified it as the national costume of Japan.

As part of a broader policy to increase production and encourage industry (*shokusan kōgyo*) to protect the domestic market, the Japanese government emphasized the advancement of the textile industry. Perhaps the most significant change was the importation of Western machinery, techniques, and materials that modernized textile manufacturing (fig. 15). The Japanese did not merely adopt Western weaving technology and chemical dyes but used them in innovative ways—for example, mixing traditional rice paste (*utsushi nori*) with synthetic (aniline) dye and applying the paste through paper stencils (a new stencil-printing method called *kata-yūzen*).[35] The introduction of the jacquard loom from the West revived silk production in Kyoto's Nishijin district, which had lost its most significant patron after the imperial court relocated to Tokyo. This new automated weaving technology made possible the production of complex brocaded silk fabrics with traditional patterns at relatively affordable prices. Similarly, the aniline dyes from Europe allowed vivid colors to be produced at a lower cost than the previously used plant-based dyes.[36]

One of the earliest aniline dyes to gain popularity in Japan was mauveine, a deep purple created by William Henry Perkin in 1856.[37] In the Edo period, purple had been reserved for aristocratic women, as its production from the root of the gromwell plant (*murasaki*) was laborious. The use of mauveine is first documented in Takasaki, a silk-production area north of Edo, in about 1863. Later this purple became widely available to both textile dyers and woodblock-print workshops; it can be seen in a print from 1889 (fig. 16). The intense color of an elegant robe for a court lady from the early Meiji period also came from this aniline dye (fig. 17). The availability of aniline dyes in the Meiji period fostered new kimono fashions, such as bright flower designs on colorful grounds. Many of these robes were decorated with *yūzen* paste-resist dyeing, primarily with the innovative *kata-yūzen* technique.[38] Combined with improvements in transportation and trade networks and a recuperating economy, these late nineteenth-century advancements in the textile industry supported the dissemination of widely available, quick-changing fashion in the early twentieth century and the modernization of the kimono itself.

MODERN MERCHANDISING

One of the first shops to sell Western clothing for women was Shirokiya in Tokyo, purveyors to the Imperial Household. The business, which began as a *gofukuya* in 1662 in Edo, quickly adjusted to the times and in 1886 announced that it had hired its first female tailor from England and had started to take orders for women's apparel. Mitsukoshi, which was founded in 1673 under the name Echigoya by Mitsui Takatoshi, started to sell Western clothing in 1888. It was among the first Japanese department stores to adopt Western business and marketing methods, drawing upon its executives' studies of the John Wanamaker Department Store in Philadelphia and Harrods of London. Mitsukoshi introduced a showcase display system in 1900 and departmentalized sales floors with a greatly expanded range of merchandise in 1904. The following year the retailer increased its inventory of foreign products and promoted the sale of Western dresses,

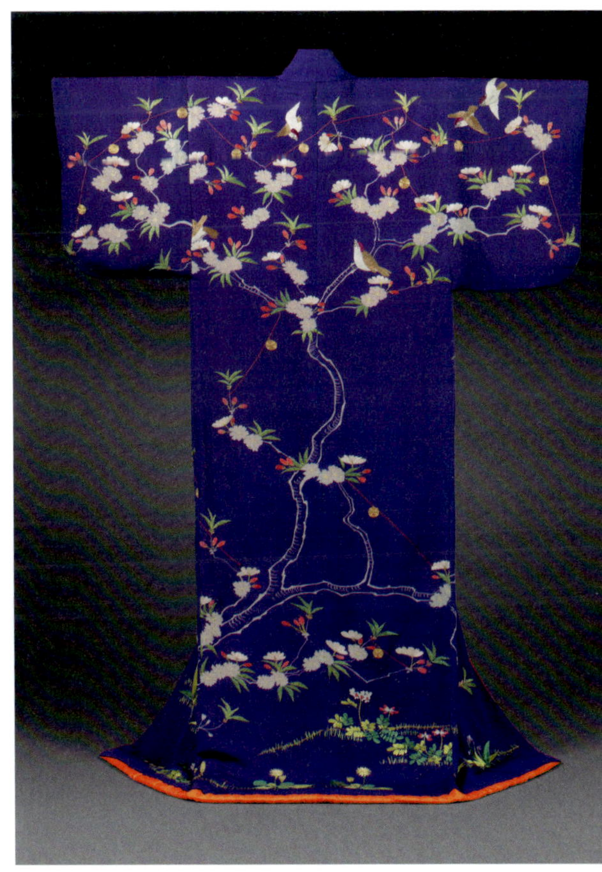

fig. 17 Court lady's robe (*kosode*) with swallows and bells on blossoming cherry tree. Meiji period (1868–1912), mid-19th century. Crepe silk with silk embroidery and couched gold thread; 69¼ × 46¼ in. (175.9 × 117.5 cm). The Metropolitan Museum of Art, New York, Purchase, Tomoko Trust, The Robert and Joyce Menschel Family Foundation and Josephine L. Berger-Nadler Gifts, 2018 (2018.559).

while continuing staunchly to advertise kimonos. In-house designers created kimonos exclusively for Mitsukoshi's own brand.

Takashimaya, which was founded in Kyoto in 1831 as a small *gofukuten* by Iida Shinshichi, was also early to adopt Western retail practices. Its Kyoto branch was Japan's first store to install plate-glass windows, in 1896, and shortly thereafter added kimono-clad mannequins to the window displays. The company had by then already become a pioneer of the export trade, bringing Japanese textiles to the world market as early as 1876. In the following decades, Takashimaya representatives traveled throughout Europe and the United States, visiting international expositions and textile factories, exploring business opportunities, and establishing trading partners. They recommended that Takashimaya design export products specifically for the Western customer (see fig. 23). The company established foreign offices in Lyon in 1899 and in London in 1906.[39]

With Japan's industrialization and urbanization in the early twentieth century, a burgeoning upper middle class emerged, including civil servants, military officers, university professors, doctors, and other white-collar workers who settled their families in the cities. This was the prime market the department stores sought to capture, and to do so the retailers positioned themselves as repositories of the most advanced knowledge about modern life and all the goods attendant to it: not only kimonos and their necessary accessories but also cosmetics and Western-style clothes, hats, bags, shoes, umbrellas, stationery, tableware, and furniture (fig. 18), which had been sparingly imported before the 1890s.[40]

Japanese retailers by the 1920s served not only as purveyors of goods but also as centers of leisure and entertainment, incorporating restaurants, cafes, barbershops, and musical performances, shaping the idea of modern daily life in the Taishō (1912–26) and Shōwa (1926–89) periods. Many department stores hired young women as clerks, which turned out to be a smart strategy, as they could persuasively make recommendations based on their own experience.

The department-store companies also invested in comprehensive market and product research to support the creation of contemporary fashions, and in advertising, in-house magazines, and in-store events to promote them.[41] To stay in tune with quickly evolving urban life, develop products appealing to the modern, educated consumer, and build the store's brand, Mitsukoshi engaged prominent artists, scholars, and journalists to offer ideas and advice on kimono fashion and launched the Society for Fashion (Ryūkōkai), which also served as a research committee. (Takashimaya had a similar organization, Hyakusen-kai.) Between 1905 and the 1920s, the department store's team included the author and critic Fukuchi Gen'ichirō, educator and economist Nitobe Inazō, and folklorist and scholar Yanagita Kunio. The group met regularly, hosted design contests, held exhibitions, and arranged public lectures.[42] At the same time, Mitsukoshi developed splashy, themed, in-store exhibitions to promote new styles, creating trends based, for example, on the modern urban lifestyle, Western fashions, and Edo-period culture; its Genroku style triggered a craze for dress and hairstyles that were last in vogue in the late seventeenth century.[43] Mitsukoshi promoted its fashions through lavishly illustrated, self-published magazines in the mold of the Harrods catalogue and *Harper's Bazaar*.[44] These publications played an important role in conveying the latest trends, much as the Edo-period

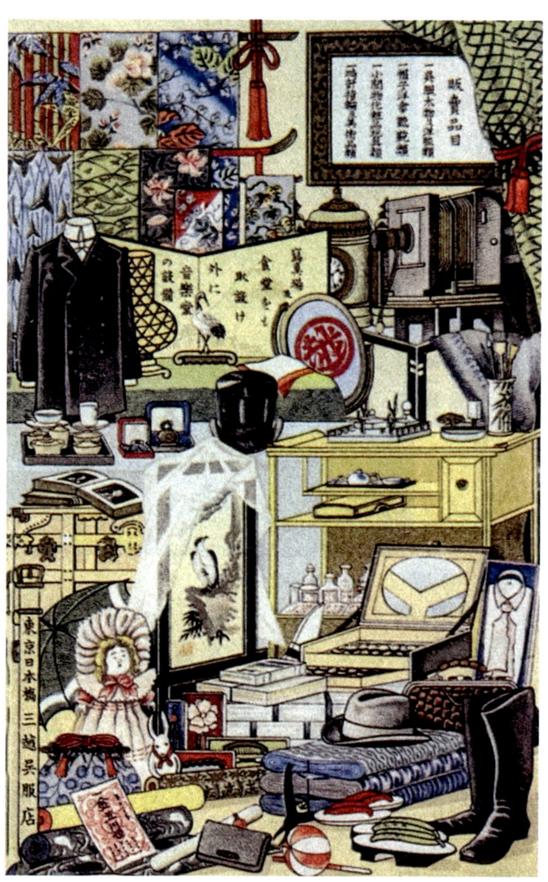

fig. 18 Advertisement for the Tokyo Nihonbashi Mitsukoshi Department Store's new products, including kimono fabrics, obis, a Western-style jacket, a hat, and a camera. Meiji period (1868–1912), 1907. Japan Archives Association (jaa2100.org)

hinagata-bon had done. All this retail showmanship was aimed not only at selling merchandise but also at establishing Mitsukoshi as a trendsetter, merging elements of the Eastern and Western fashion systems.

Japan's emporiums more dramatically patterned themselves after their Western counterparts following the devastating Great Kanto Earthquake of 1923. Most had to rebuild, and they replaced their eclectic, often Renaissance-style stores with modern multistory buildings of concrete and steel, with escalators and elevators. Customers no longer had to remove their footwear upon entering. The leading department stores, such as Mitsukoshi, had originally positioned themselves as high-status retailers but gradually catered to a broader customer base. As competition among department stores intensified, they turned to less affluent urban customers, adding discount sales and intensely marketing inexpensive kimonos and other low-priced goods. New department stores were built around big railway stations in Tokyo, Osaka, and Nagoya to take advantage of the large number of suburban commuters. Further developing a consumer culture among the lower middle class, department stores began to appear in the provinces, where the metropolitan retailers also organized temporary sales events and exhibitions.[45]

The retailers also worked closely with the textile workshops north and west of Tokyo, in Isesaki, Ashikaga, Chichibu, Kiryū, and Hachioji, to develop inexpensive, mass-produced *meisen* kimonos (see "*Meisen* and *Omeshi*: Kimonos for the Masses" in this volume).[46] *Meisen* were designed to be visually striking, with a great variety of bold patterns and bright colors; the department stores aggressively promoted them to turn over inventory quickly and to create fast-changing trends that would continually bring customers back.

MODERN WOMEN, MODERN STYLES

Fashion — and Japan itself — was caught between a past reexamined and an enthusiasm for modernism during the transformative years of the Taishō and early Shōwa periods. Venerable traditions coexisted with invigorating international trends as Japan sought, sometimes uneasily, to define its national character.

Fashion reflected the search for a vocabulary that integrated creativity with cultural pride. Contemporary garments reflected a hybrid nature described as *wayō-secchū*, "a compromise between Japanese and Western." The Art Nouveau style, which had been inspired in part by Japanese art, circled back in about 1903–15 to influence Japanese fashion with its sinuous lines and stylized floral and organic forms. The Art Nouveau trend led to a revival of similarly stylized textile designs developed by the painter Ogata Kōrin in the early eighteenth century (cat. 35). Mitsukoshi's promotional material extolled as "cutting-edge" the blend of influences, such as Western flowers rendered as Kōrin-style motifs or modernized versions of well-known elements from *hinagata-bon* (cat. 43).[47] Painters, graphic designers, and printmakers, including Sugiura Hisui, Hashiguchi Goyō, and Itō Shinsui, lent their talents to textile design and promotional material for department stores, elevating contemporary kimonos as art (fig. 19).

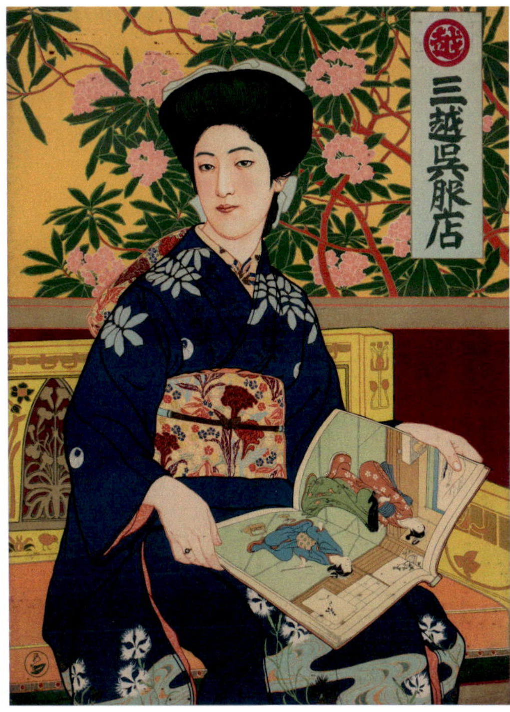

fig. 19 "Beauty," poster for the Mitsukoshi Department Store. Hashiguchi Goyō (1880–1921). Meiji period (1868–1912), 1911. Color lithograph; 41⅜ × 29½ in. (105 × 75 cm). Printing Museum, Tokyo

Another wave of modernization and Westernization followed the conclusion of World War I. As the country's economy flourished, film, radio, jazz recordings, and magazines transmitted the latest Western ideas and artistic trends. The interwar period can be characterized by an air of excitement, an active lifestyle, more leisure activities, and a blossoming consumer culture. Women were especially affected, as they gradually joined the workforce, earned their own income, and consequently gained some financial independence from

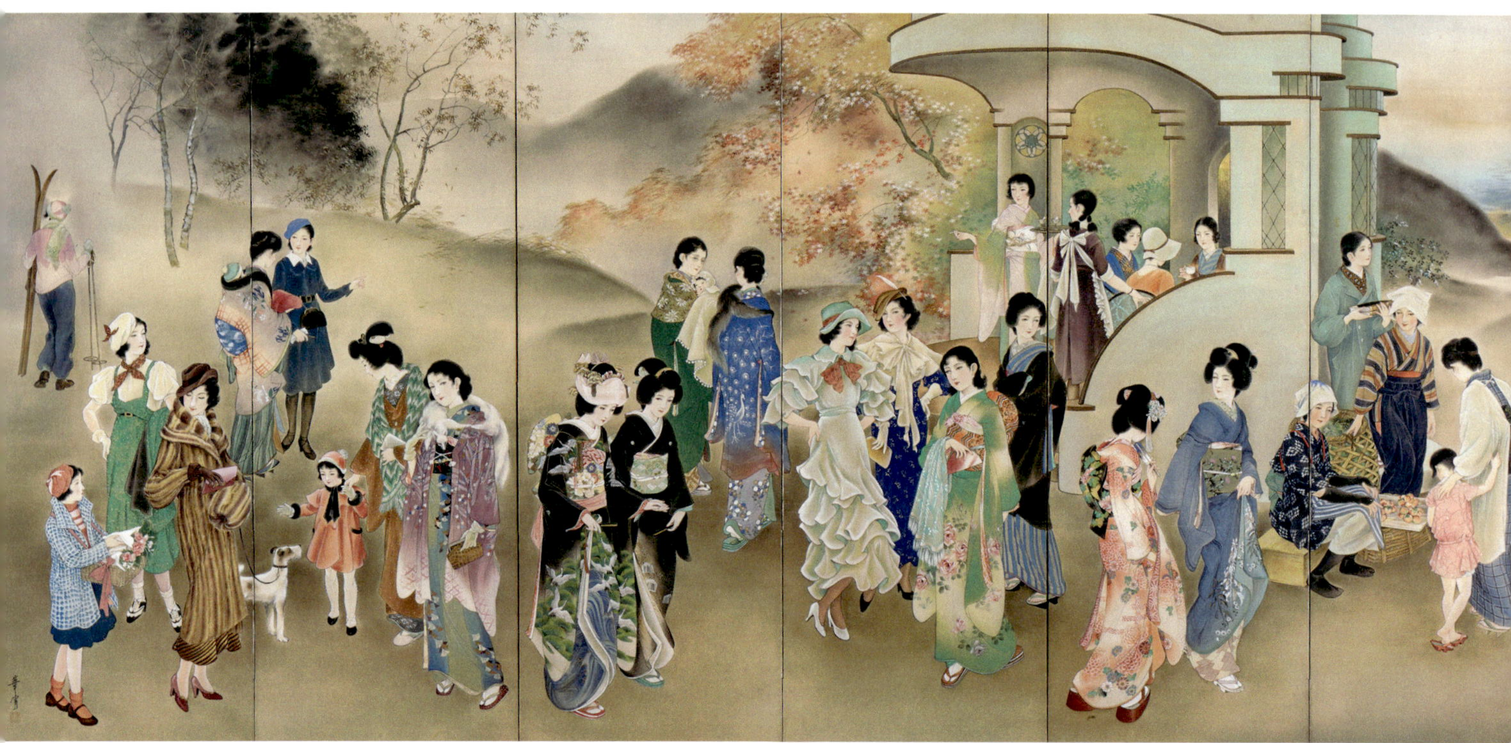

their fathers or husbands.[48] The rise of the "new woman" and the "modern girl," or *moga*, in the Taishō period spurred debates about women's cultural identity and role in society that mirrored the larger national discourse about Western-style modernization. With their newly public presence as shop assistants, telephone operators, and waitresses, young women spent their free time enjoying the recently established cinemas, dance halls, and department stores, which increasingly targeted a female clientele. Young ladies projected a newfound liberation by bobbing their hair, wearing makeup, smoking cigarettes, and frequenting bars. While many more, and more conventional, women — primarily homemakers raising children — dressed in kimonos, the *moga* opted for stylish Western dresses and high heels (fig. 20). The simple, columnar, draped silhouettes then in fashion were comfortable and easy to wear, and they fitted the Japanese body type well.[49] But however liberated the *moga* may have felt, women still had limited rights in matters of divorce and property under the Meiji Civil Code. Only in 1922 could women freely participate in political meetings and organizations, and universal suffrage was not established in Japan until 1947.[50]

Despite Western-style liberalism and entertainment in mass culture, the 1920s were a time of political unrest, with rice riots, violence against radical leaders, and the formation of labor unions and political parties. At the core were struggles with establishing Japan's identity and position on the world stage, which contributed to the rise of nationalism and military aggression, from annexing Korea in 1910 to invading Manchuria in 1931, entering war with China in 1937, and, finally, attacking the United States in 1941.

The shifting notions of "Japanese" and "Western," as well as the reshaping of the national identity, were manifested in department-store displays, where garments from both traditions were shown together; Matsuzakaya even featured its apparel with an automobile, the ultimate symbol of the modern age (fig. 21). Kimono patterns also captured the confluence of styles. For example, the rendering of Japanese motifs in Western style characterizes the Taishō Roman (Taishō Romantic) kimono aesthetic. Western patterns, such as tulips and dahlias, Art Nouveau motifs, and images representing a contemporary lifestyle, such as trains and cameras, were also popular. Silk ikat kimonos followed Edo traditions with stripes or geometric designs, but

fig. 20 *Passersby*. Takabatake Kashō (1888–1966). Shōwa period (1926–89), 1935. Pair of six-panel folding screens; ink and color on silk; each overall: 47½ × 106¾ in. (120.6 × 271.2 cm). Private collection, Japan

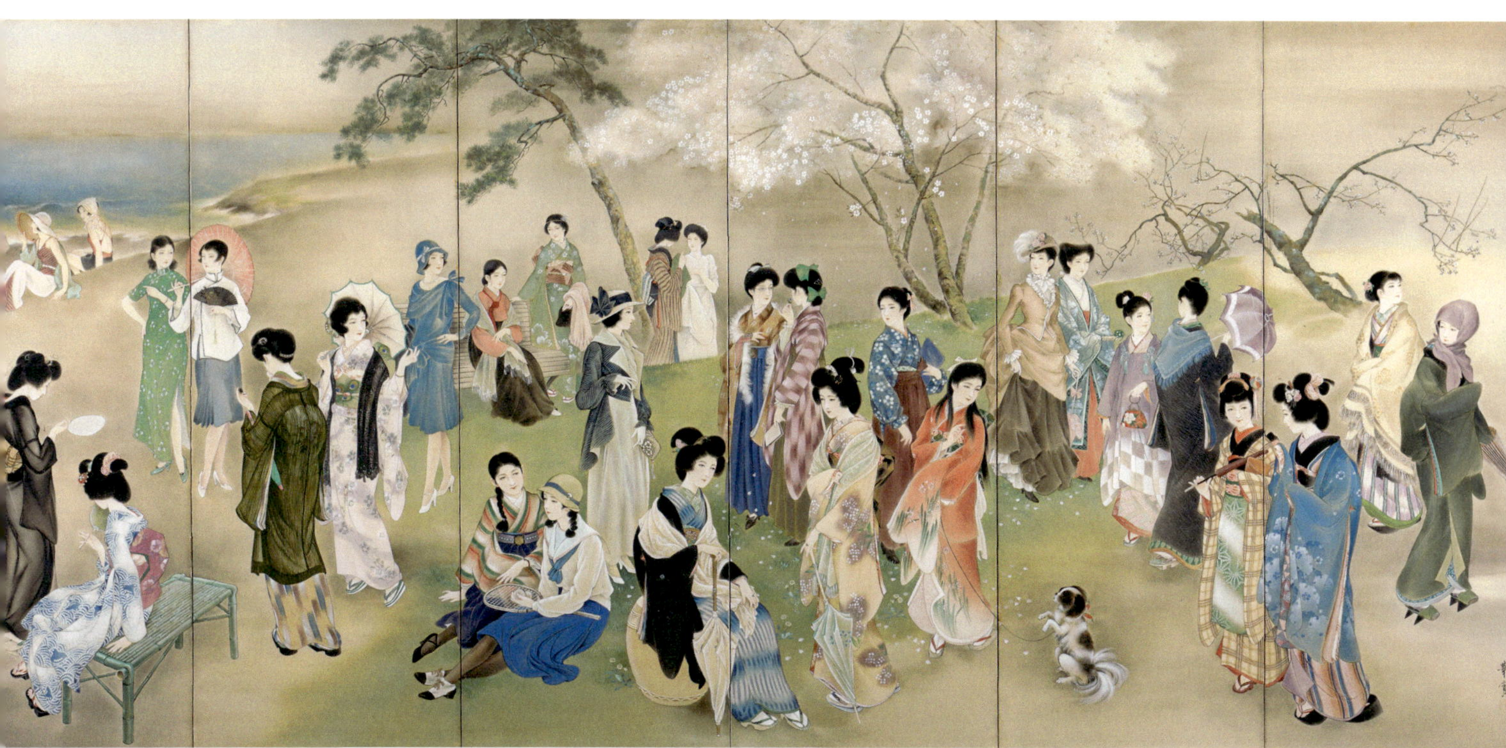

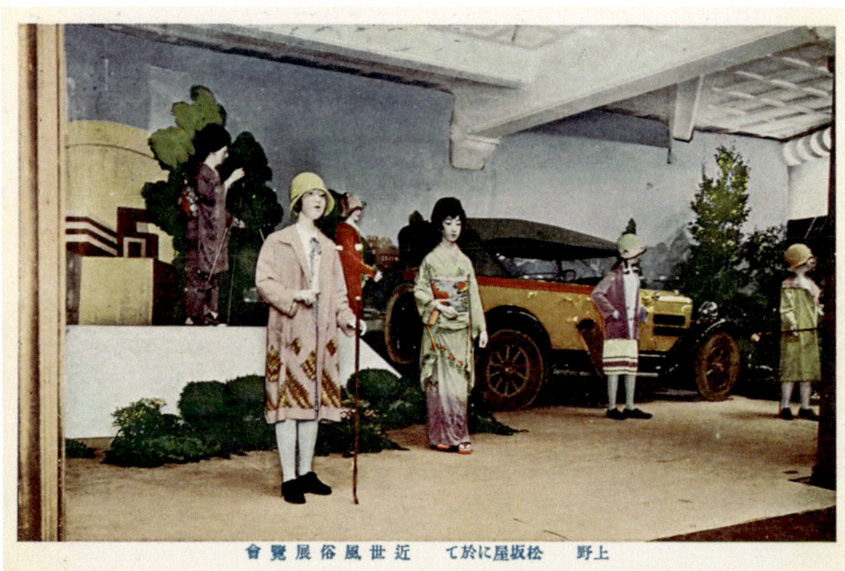

the patterns were revitalized by bold colors: vivid blues, pinks, purples, reds, and greens.[51]

Kimono fashions in the early Shōwa period were similar to the Taishō mode. Stylized, graphic, flat Art Deco–inspired motifs prevailed, along with the naturalistic depiction of flowers and plants. Western-style clothes and accessories were combined with kimonos or *haori* jackets. Contemporary art movements from abroad — notably Cubism, Constructivism, the Russian avant-garde, Italian Futurism, De Stijl, and Piet Mondrian's abstraction — strongly influenced *meisen* kimono patterns of the day, infusing them with a sense of novelty and freedom. *Meisen* kimono production peaked during that period. The brightly colored, brashly patterned kimonos became ubiquitous, serving as the everyday wear of working- and middle-class women and the uniform of female students at high schools and colleges.[52] Young women garbed in flamboyant colors and graphic patterns invigorated the cityscape. Their kimonos reflected Japan's embrace of the modern and its innovative application of influences from the West, which together yielded fashions that were uniquely Japanese.

fig. 21 Kimonos and Western clothing on display at the Ueno Matsuzakaya Department Store. Taishō (1912–26)–Shōwa (1926–89) period, 1920s. Postcard. Private collection

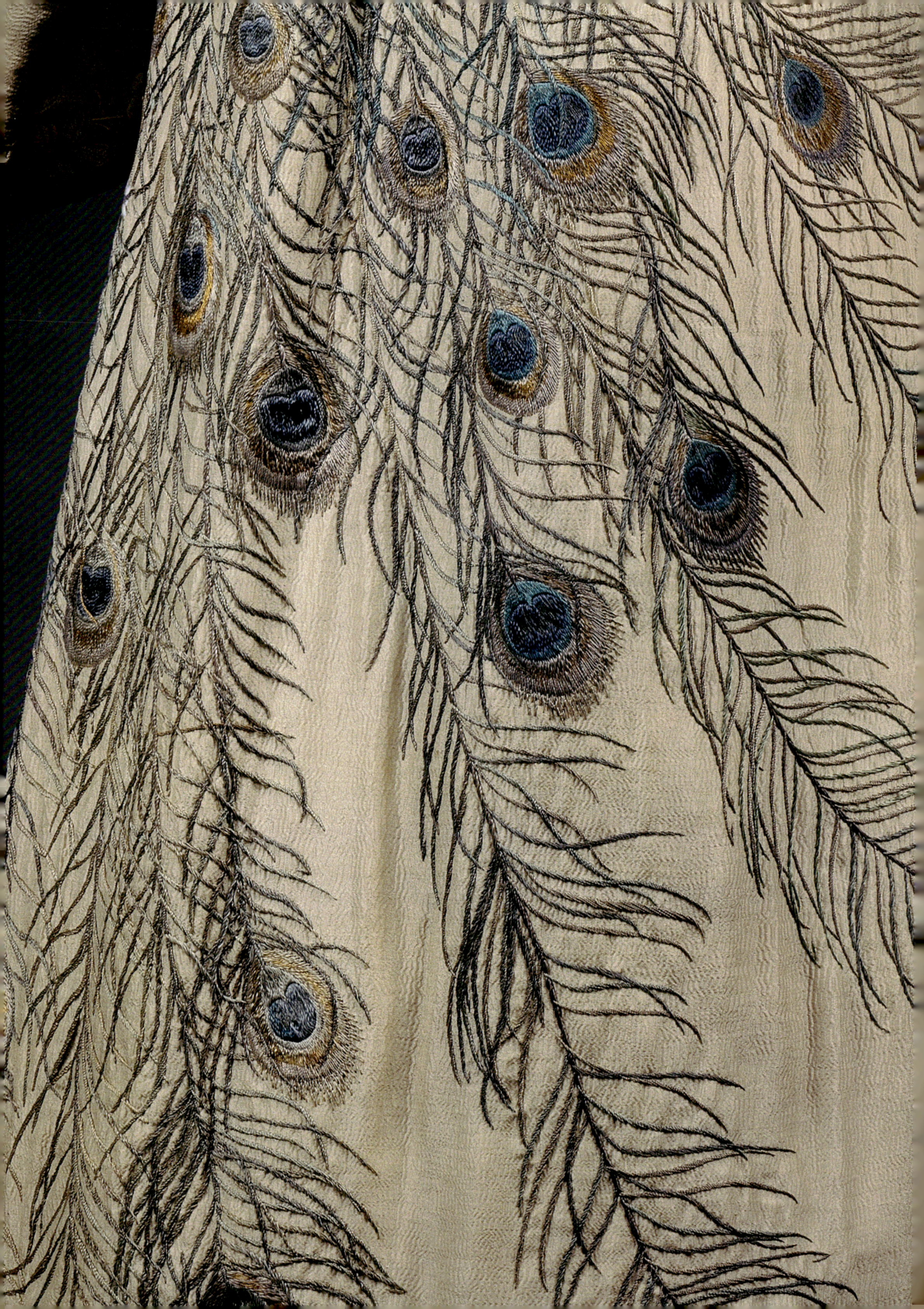

THE TIGER'S

KIMONOS AND

KAREN VAN GODTSENHOVEN

COUTURE

LEAP

A STRIKING GREEN TUNIC DRESS WITH A BROCADED GOLD FLETCHING MOTIF, CREATED IN 1925 BY COUTURIER PAUL POIRET, TESTIFIES TO THE SARTORIAL DIALECTIC

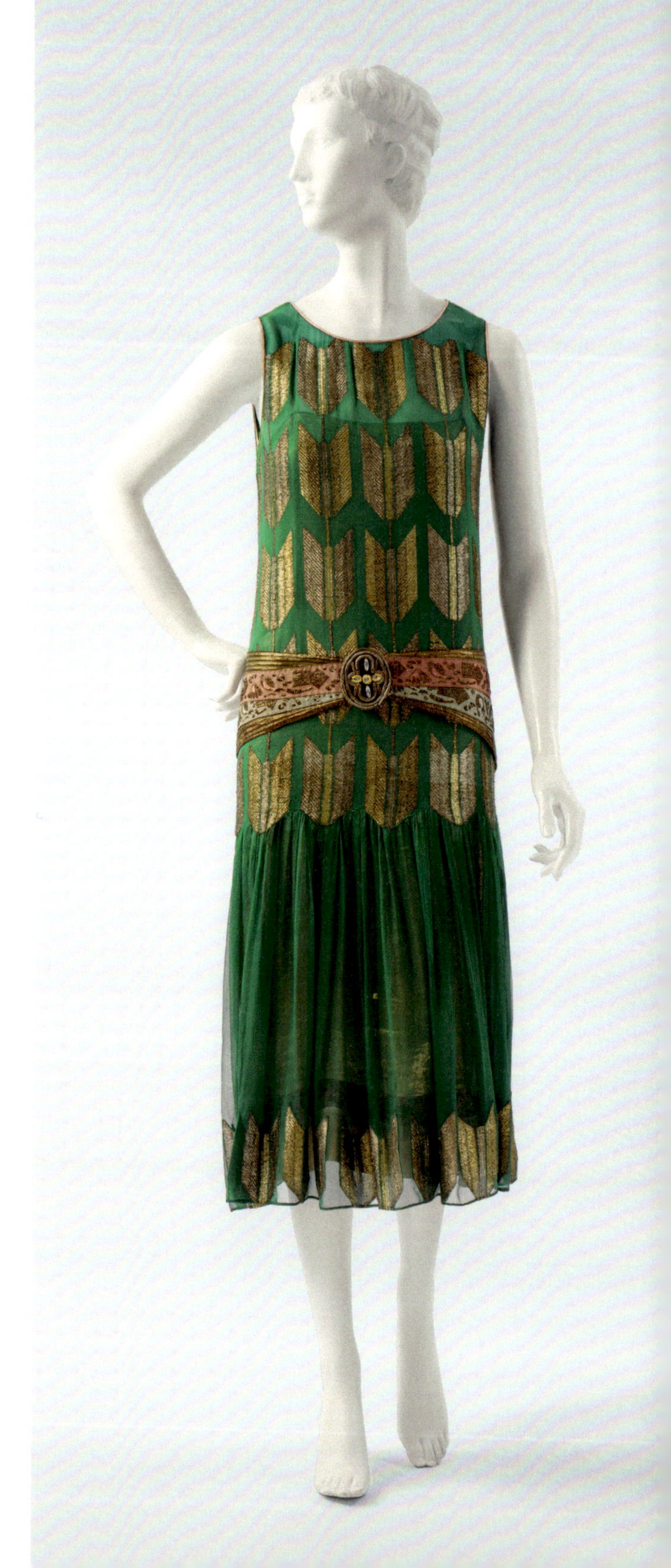

between Japan and the West (fig. 22). Most notable is the consonance between the Art Deco pattern of this dress and that of a summer kimono of roughly the same vintage from the Weber Collection (cat. 39). The fletching motif, popular in Japan before the 1920s, was at the time less visible in the West. It is possible that Poiret had come across this motif on a kimono or an image thereof, given his keen interest in Eastern modes of dress.

The kimono brought about two revolutions in Western dress, first in the 1920s and again in the 1980s, with profound liberatory consequences for women as they and their garments were freed from constraint. Perhaps its most influential attribute is that, unlike Western fashion, the kimono does not amplify gendered differences. Although kimonos for men and women differed slightly, notably in the cut of the armpit opening and of the closure and in the patterns — stripes and geometric figures for men, organic motifs of flowers, animals, and water for women — the essential structure is unisex. That underlying concept would emerge more emphatically in Japanese fashion of the 1970s, which, as the textile and fashion curator Fukai Akiko wrote, did "not exist to adorn women as sex objects but as logical attire."[1]

Through the silhouettes of garments in The Met's Costume Institute, it is possible to trace the waves of Japanism that reached the West and the stages of physical and psychic liberation they offered women, who were more significantly affected by the sartorial exchanges than were men. Before embarking on this journey, however, it is important to elucidate some crucial notions with regard to Japanism as a form of Orientalism. While acknowledging Edward Said's thesis about Orientalism as a Western style used to assert authority over the East[2] — and the kimono's gradual eclipse by Western clothes — it is also important to note that Europe never colonized Japan and thus did not regard it as a colonial "Other" or the static "East." The Japanism of the 1860s–80s was different from the Orientalisms that had come before. In contrast to those superficial appropriations, it was a two-way exchange of cultural artifacts: Japan and the West influenced and mirrored each other in a game of reciprocal adaptation and emulation.

The kimono filtered through European fashion as early as the seventeenth century, when Dutch traders exchanged *Japonsche rocken* (Japanese robes) with the shogunate. These long, loose garments resembled ornate gowns padded with silk wadding. In response to high demand, the Dutch East India Company began producing versions of these garments in the Coromandel region of India, "where the techniques of hand-drawn and woodblock-printed resist dyeing were well established."[3] Further evidence of the early global exchange in fashion is an eighteenth-century British version of the Indian banyan (1981.208.2), a T-shaped garment for men that was named after a caste of Indian merchants. (Like the other garments referenced but not illustrated here, this one is in The Met collection and is featured in the *Kimono Style* exhibition.) The banyan's non-Western influences range from kimonos to *Indiennes* (men's dressing gowns of Indian chintz) and later Turkish robes. The banyan was popular with intellectuals; because of its ease of cut, they wore it as a type of postprandial dressing gown, over a shirt and breeches. An early hybrid of Eastern modes of dress transformed by global trade, the banyan foreshadowed the kimono and its significance over the next two centuries. The kimono's influence on Western fashions exemplifies what the academic Ulrich Lehmann refers to as fashion's "tiger's leap," borrowing a term coined in 1942 by the philosopher Walter Benjamin, to describe how fashion leaps from the contemporary to the ancient and back again, without coming to rest exclusively in one temporal or aesthetic configuration.[4] In the kimono's case, this dialectical leap is between different places as well as between points in time.

THE FIRST LEAP

The arrival of United States' warships in Tokyo Bay in 1853 opened Japan to trade with the West in 1858 after more than two hundred years of isolation, ushering a Japanism wave in the West and dramatically increasing the long-standing European fascination with kimonos. The Meiji period (1868–1912) coincided with the advent of international exhibitions, which became important tools in the exchange of Japanese and Western goods. A Japanese government delegation visited the Great London Exposition in 1862, and in 1867, one year before the end of the Tokugawa shogunate, Japan officially participated at the Paris Exposition Universelle, displaying arts and crafts like lacquerware, ukiyo-e prints, and textiles in a teahouse pavilion. Concurrently, Japanese-style clothing began to appear in fashion magazines, like the *Journal des Demoiselles* of October 1867.

fig. 22 Paul Poiret (French, 1879–1944). "Arrow of Gold" dress, 1925. Silk, metallic thread. The Metropolitan Museum of Art, New York, Gift of Mrs. Robert A. Lovett, 1951 (C.I.51.70.19a–c)

Kimono-style garments were depicted as intimate, relaxed, and luxurious attire for affluent women to wear indoors. A pivotal exhibition was the 1873 Vienna World's Fair, where the Meiji government promoted Japan as a modern nation-state with rich Oriental traditions, including a sophisticated textile culture. On display was a wealth of Japanese products meant for export, including silks, hangings, screens, tablecloths, tapestries, fans, and kimonos.

At the time, many European painters, newly introduced to Japanese woodblock prints, were looking to Japan for inspiration. Initially, however, they used the kimono as an eroticizing prop, as seen in works by Claude Monet, Edgar Degas, James Tissot, Alfred Stevens, Henri Fantin-Latour, James McNeill Whistler, and George Hendrik Breitner. They portrayed seductive young women affecting varying degrees of indolence, surrounded by Japanese textiles and prints and wearing sumptuous kimonos, mostly open in the front. Breitner's thirteen-painting Girl with Kimono series exemplifies the subject. Compositionally, Edouard Manet was inspired by Japanese screens and prints; in *Boating* (1874; 29.100.115), in The Met collection, he explored broad planes of color and employed strong diagonals; in *L'automne* (1882; Musée des Beaux-Arts, Nancy) he placed his model in front of an embroidered kimono fabric, flattening the perspective, as in ukiyo-e depictions of beautiful women. As the art historian Shuji Takashina noted, the new compositional perspectives and vibrant colors offered by Japanism culminated in Monet's Water Lilies series (1914–26), inspired by Utagawa Hiroshige's and Katsushika Hokusai's ukiyo-e prints.[5] A similar trajectory from the superficial to the substantive took place in fashion, where the kimono first influenced the surface, its patterns figuring into the silks from Lyon used by designers like Charles Frederick Worth and Jacques Doucet in the 1880s. Only later, in the 1910s and 1920s, did the kimono more deeply inform Western fashion, its structure transforming it from the inside out.

Japan, spurred by the Japanism movement in the West, produced dressing gowns expressly for the foreign market. The Yokohama silk merchant Shiino Shobey had been dispatched to the 1873 Vienna World's Fair, and his research resulted in Yokohama robes, named for the port from which they were shipped between 1880 and 1890. They were made of quilted habutai (a glossy, plain-weave silk) and decorated with traditional

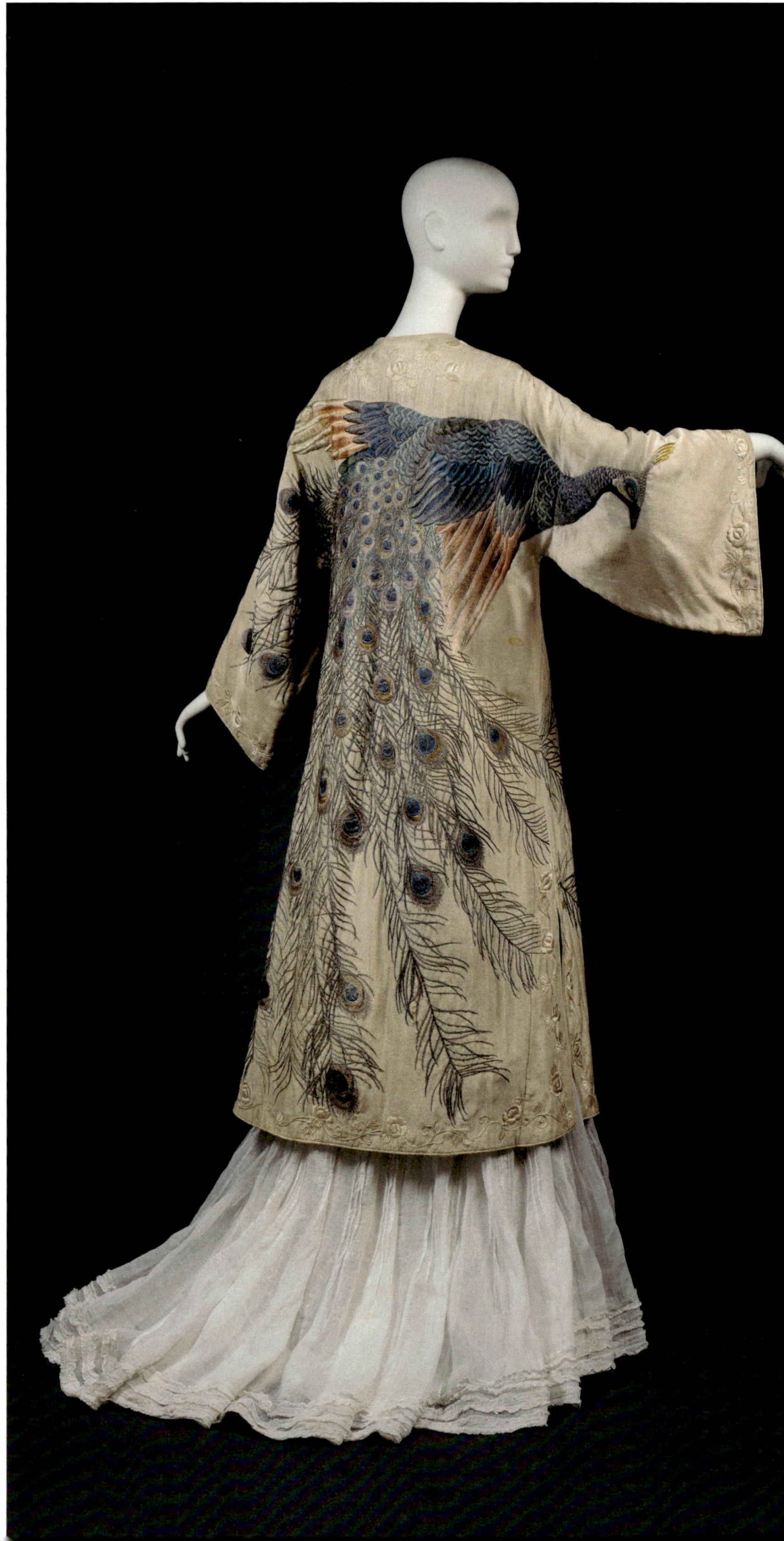

Japanese motifs like spring flowers (C.I.46.52.1). However, the gowns would never have been worn in Japan; the cut and construction were Japanese interpretations of Western style, unrelated to traditional Japanese dress. The garments are symbols of cross-cultural appropriation and the eagerness of Meiji Japan both to trade with Europe and to assert its own national identity. Japanese-style dressing gowns for the foreign market were followed by informal tea gowns for hostesses to wear at home. In one padded tea gown from 1898 (2009.300.558), the exchange between Japan and Europe is expressed in the asymmetrical Art Nouveau motif of embroidered lilies adorning an eighteenth-century robe à la française. The smocking at the top shows the influence of fashions of the period by the leading London retailer Liberty and Company. Art Nouveau's sinuous, floral patterns, inspired by Japanism, were all the rage at the end of the nineteenth century. The term "Japanese kimono" appeared in an 1898 Liberty catalogue and a 1902 Sears, Roebuck catalogue, attesting to the widespread interest in the garment among European and American shoppers.

Western fashion adopted Japanese elements more holistically than the other way around; in Meiji Japan, *yōfuku* (Western dress) and *wafuku* (Japanese dress) coexisted rather than blended.[6] A crucial development, on the Continent as well as in Japan, was the arrival of department stores, which had evolved from Parisian shopping arcades. They provided the bourgeois woman with an indoor shopping experience consolidating textiles, garments, housewares, and accessories. In this safe environment, women could spend a leisurely day away from home without chaperones and without risk of being perceived as "loose." In Japan, Edo-period *gofukuten* (stores specializing in fabrics for high-quality kimonos and obis) evolved into department stores with mass-produced, Westernized garments and kimonos targeting a new and burgeoning middle class.[7] The head of Takashimaya, a Kyoto shop that would become a leading department-store chain, visited his store's European counterparts for the first time in 1889; he returned to adapt the Kyoto store to the Western department-store layout, with display cases and oversize windows dressed with merchandise. From 1893 Takashimaya created goods specifically for the foreign market.

One such product is a lavish ivory robe embroidered with a peacock motif (fig. 23). The peacock was not commonly depicted on Japanese kimonos but often appeared in paintings and on folding screens, so the motif signified "Japan" to the Western eye.[8] Like the earlier Japanese dressing gowns, the robe combines Orientalist motifs with Western construction, such as shoulder seams, set-in sleeves, and inserted gores.[9] Though a ready-to-wear garment, it was fashioned as an example of fine art.[10] This robe exemplifies the self-Orientalizing, dialectical dream image of Japan as a highly cultured and sophisticated country producing artworks of exquisite beauty at the very time it was rapidly modernizing and expanding its export in an imperial way. As the art historian Mei Mei Rado stated, "Japan's political quest for national identity dovetailed with the Western cultural undercurrent searching for renewed exoticism."[11]

THE "BODY NATURAL"

European designers in the early twentieth century looked to other civilizations and epochs for alternatives to the constrictive S-shaped Edwardian silhouette. Most were familiar with the kimono through ukiyo-e prints, which usually depicted courtesans in a sumptuous Edo toilette — far more elaborate kimonos than those Japan produced for the foreign market.[12] At first Westerners wore the latter tightly wrapped, with corsets underneath to achieve the requisite S-shape.[13] As designers started exploring the technique underlying the kimono's shape, winding fabric around the body rather than covering it in complex, patterned pieces, the shoulder rather than the waist structured a new kimono-inspired silhouette, "a concept of clothing different from anything that had preceded it" in Western fashion.[14]

In 1903 Poiret made his first loose dress with hints of the kimono shape, and in 1906 he presented his first collection to be worn without a corset, based on the loose-fitting kimono. Poiret once wryly admitted that, being bad at sewing, he was not fully in control of his art.[15] However, this very deficiency might have pushed him to experiment with drape, creating directly on the body rather than relying on classical tailoring techniques.

Several designers emulated Poiret's new fluidity, including the House of Beer, Callot Soeurs, and Jeanne Paquin, whose loosely draped opera coat from 1912 appeared in *La Gazette*

fig. 23 Iida & Co./Takashimaya (Japanese, founded 1831). Tea gown, ca. 1900. Silk. The Metropolitan Museum of Art, New York, Gift of Joseph L. Brotherton, 1985 (1985.362.2)

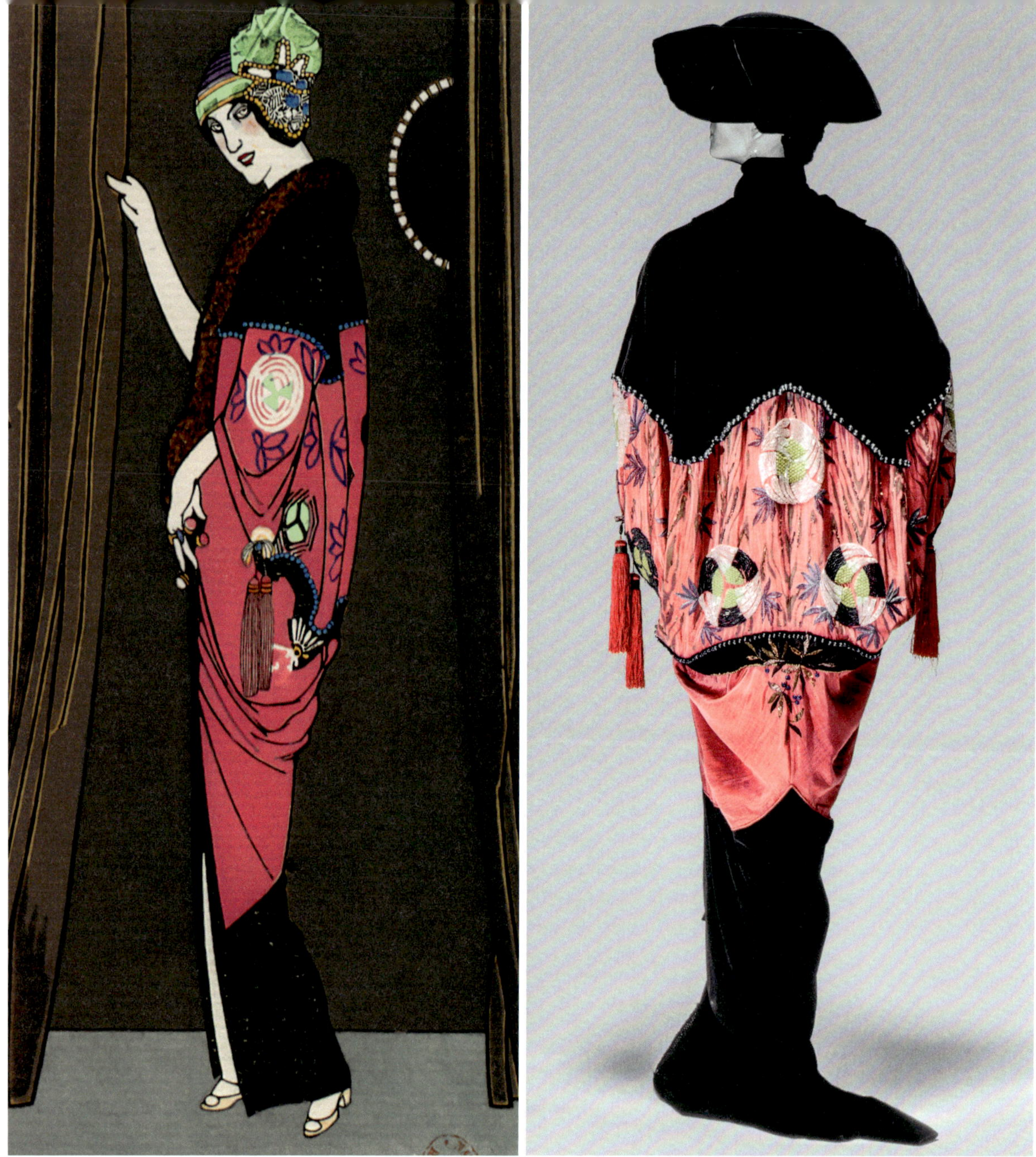

du Bon Ton (figs. 24, 25). Following the success of operatic productions with Japanese themes, like *The Mikado* (1885) and *Madama Butterfly* (1904), the kimono's popularity was linked to the stage costume, which represented a sexualized, "other" type of beauty to the Western gaze. This projection of exoticism was then transferred to the theatergoers who wore similar gowns. From 1907 the word "kimono," photographs of kimono silhouettes, and the concomitant vocabulary of "à la japonaise" became widespread in fashion magazines.[16] These fluid gowns transformed the kimono's status from a comfortable tea gown worn at home into a public fashion statement that showed the world its wearer's progressive, bohemian mind-set.

Poiret's "Paris" opera coat from 1919 (fig. 26) demonstrates his skillful, sculptural expression of two-dimensional fabric. A length of silk velvet with just one seam is draped without any cutting to create the sleeves and open front. Devoid of decoration except for the fastening, it

fig. 24 Illustration of the Paquin opera coat from *La Gazette du Bon Ton* 1 (1912–13), pl. VII

fig. 25 Mme. Jeanne Paquin (French, 1869–1936), House of Paquin (French, 1891–1956). Opera coat, 1912. Silk. The Metropolitan Museum of Art, New York, Gift of Mrs. Edwin Stewart Wheeler, 1956 (C.I.X.56.2.1)

is a masterwork of structural ingenuity. Western fashion here frees itself of the heavy decoration and complex patterning that had characterized it since the Renaissance.

The sartorial revolution the kimono had instigated advanced in the 1920s to achieve an "exceptional flatness of fashions"[17] and shapes that allowed greater freedom of movement. The short, loose-fitting flapper dress of the "new woman" and the *garçonne* look (featuring oversize jackets, blouses, and trousers) exemplify the liberating styles of the time. The flapper look also took hold in Japan, reflecting the feminist developments taking place there in the first decades of the twentieth century, as young women gained access to education and the workforce. (See "Japanese Fashion, from Edo to the Modern Era" in this volume. Although Western fashions pervaded Japanese fashion magazines and were sold alongside kimonos in Japanese department stores at the time, their influence on the kimono, including its colors and patterns, remains an avenue for further investigation.) In the West, bias-cut crepe de chine dresses by Madeleine Vionnet and rectangular suits by Gabrielle "Coco" Chanel, lacking curves and darts, were symbols of the "body natural." As Fukai put it, these designs were "attempts to actualize the new relationship between the body rediscovered and clothes," whereby "form extended along the vertical axis."[18]

Vionnet, who appropriated the structural composition of the kimono, perfected the new ideal of the body natural.[19] The flat, planar construction of her dresses created a fluid silhouette that allowed for the body's unencumbered movement and the emergence of a tactile and affective relationship between body and dress. Her early works, created between 1918 and 1920, feature flat construction and echoes of the kimono sleeve, an innovation of her mentor and employer Marie Callot Gerber (the eldest Callot sister), who had incorporated the sleeve into Art Nouveau dresses in the early part of the century.[20] (Madame Gerber, who was connected to Edmond de Goncourt, an art critic and expert on Japanism, had also introduced Vionnet to ukiyo-e prints, leading the younger designer to amass a collection of prints that she displayed on her atelier walls.[21]) From there, Vionnet developed the bias cut, which created a stretch that gave a body-skimming, rippling effect to the sensually draped fabric. According to the fashion historian Betty Kirke, Vionnet's revolutionary cut was based in part on the rectangular

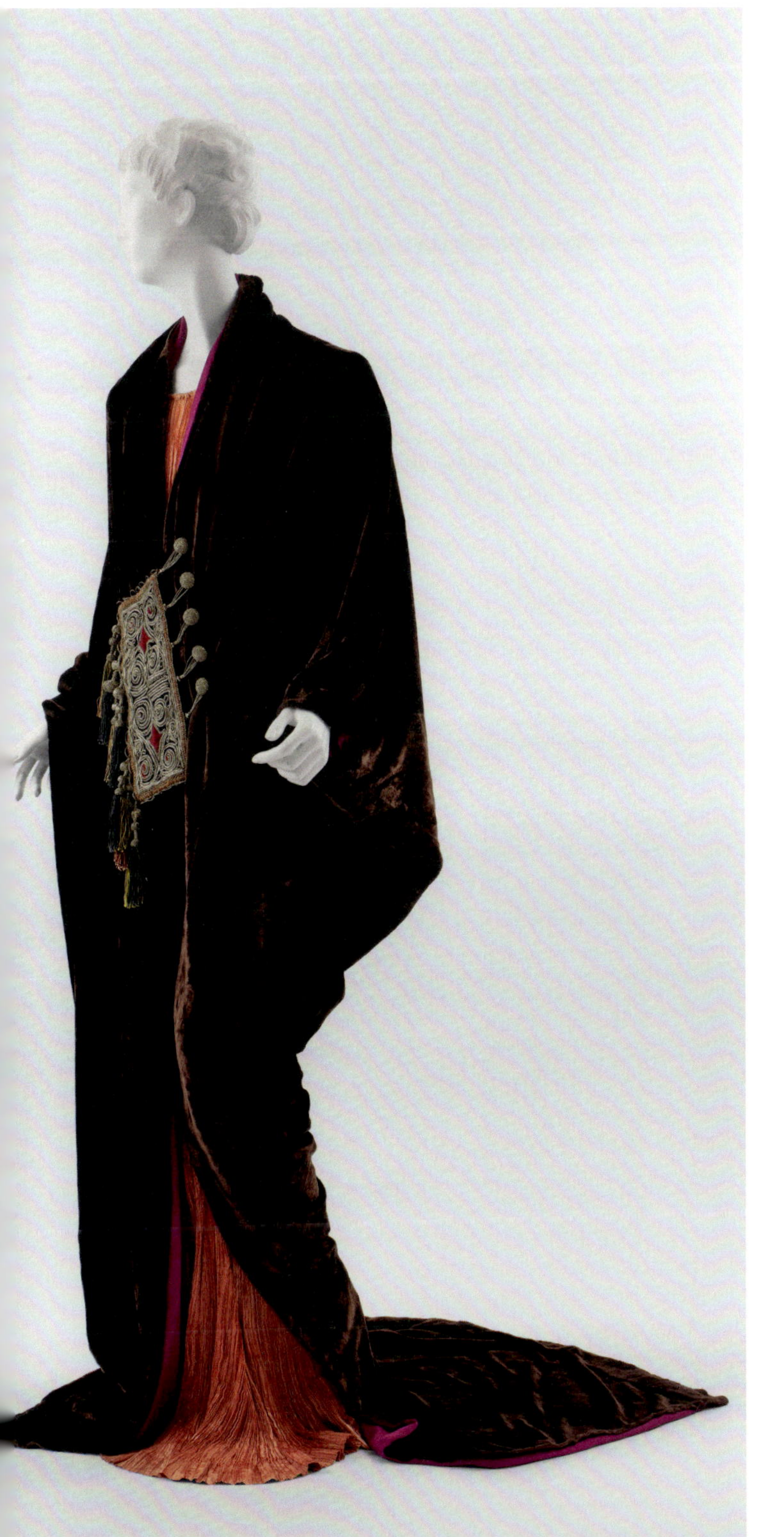

fig. 26 Paul Poiret (French, 1879–1944). "Paris" opera coat, 1919. Silk, wool, metallic thread. The Metropolitan Museum of Art, New York, Purchase, Friends of The Costume Institute Gifts, 2005 (2005.207)

cut of the kimono.[22] A 1923–24 dress of black satin-back crepe silk infuses Vionnet's kimono-type flat construction with a Cubist aesthetic (fig. 27).

A notable example of the tiger's leap is a sculptural dress from 1928–29 by Callot Soeurs in crepe chiffon with a dramatic lamé motif (fig. 28). Both historicist and avant-garde, it exemplifies the kimono's "one piece of cloth" philosophy, comparable to the Renaissance ex uno lapide method of making sculpture from a single block of marble. The dress is hung from a central point at the bust, then wound around the body on the bias in a continuous ribbon, culminating in a dramatic train that would impede the wearer's movement. Orientalist and utterly modern in its minimal drape, it announces the curvaceous silhouette of the 1930s, signaling the return to more traditionally gendered garments after the sartorial liberation of the 1920s.

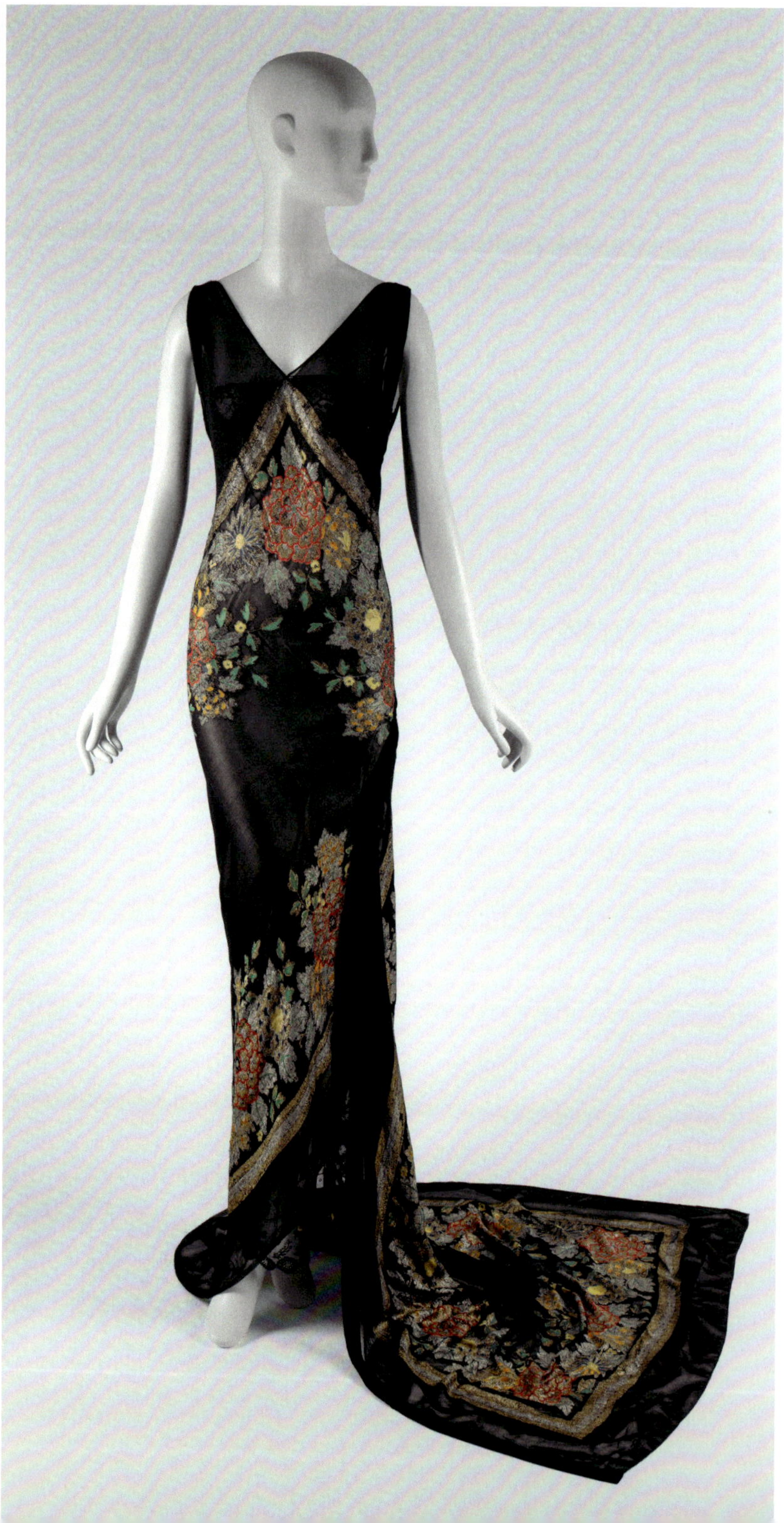

Revisiting the looser, volumetric silhouettes that Japanism had inspired at the turn of the century, Cristobal Balenciaga introduced his innovative cocoon or barrel lines in 1942 and 1947.[23] These created ample room around the midsection of the body in the backside, alluding to the way an outer kimono creates an elegant arc above the obi, abstracting the body underneath. He built upon this silhouette in the 1950s by developing a fluid, yet still structured, chemise line with an

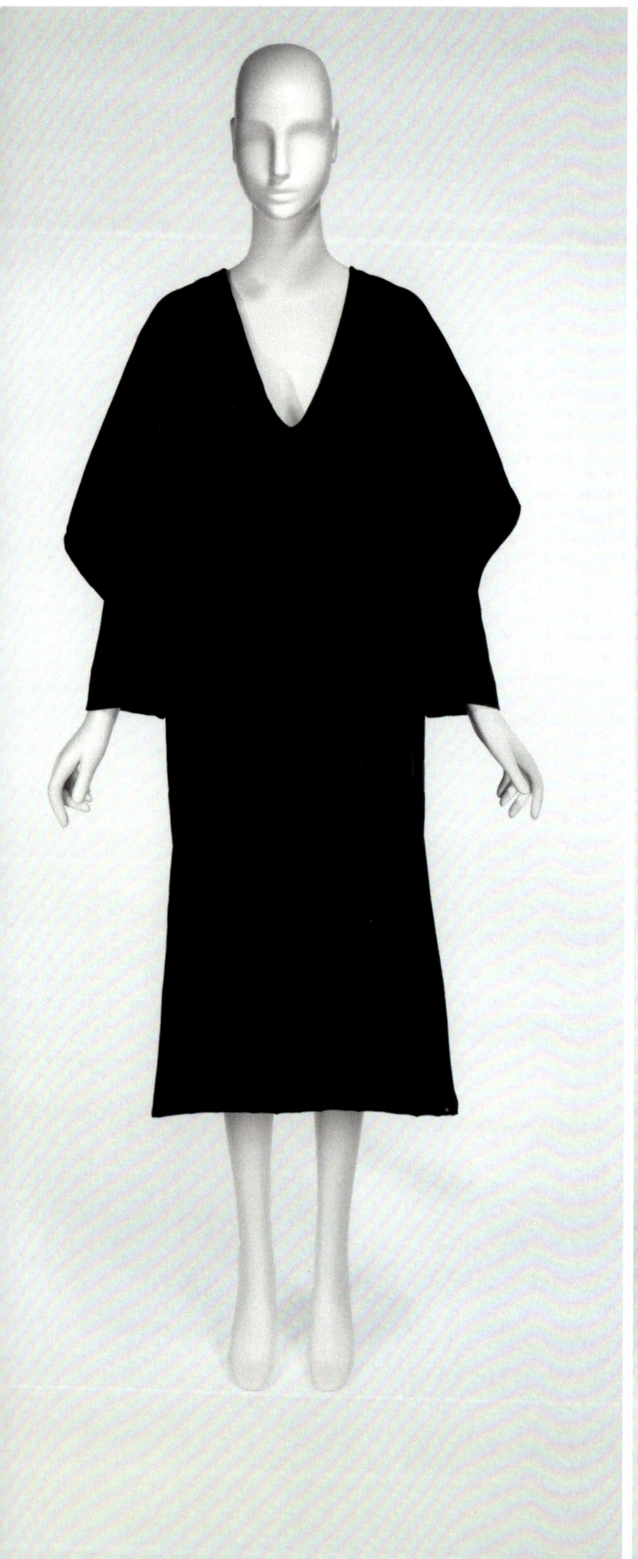

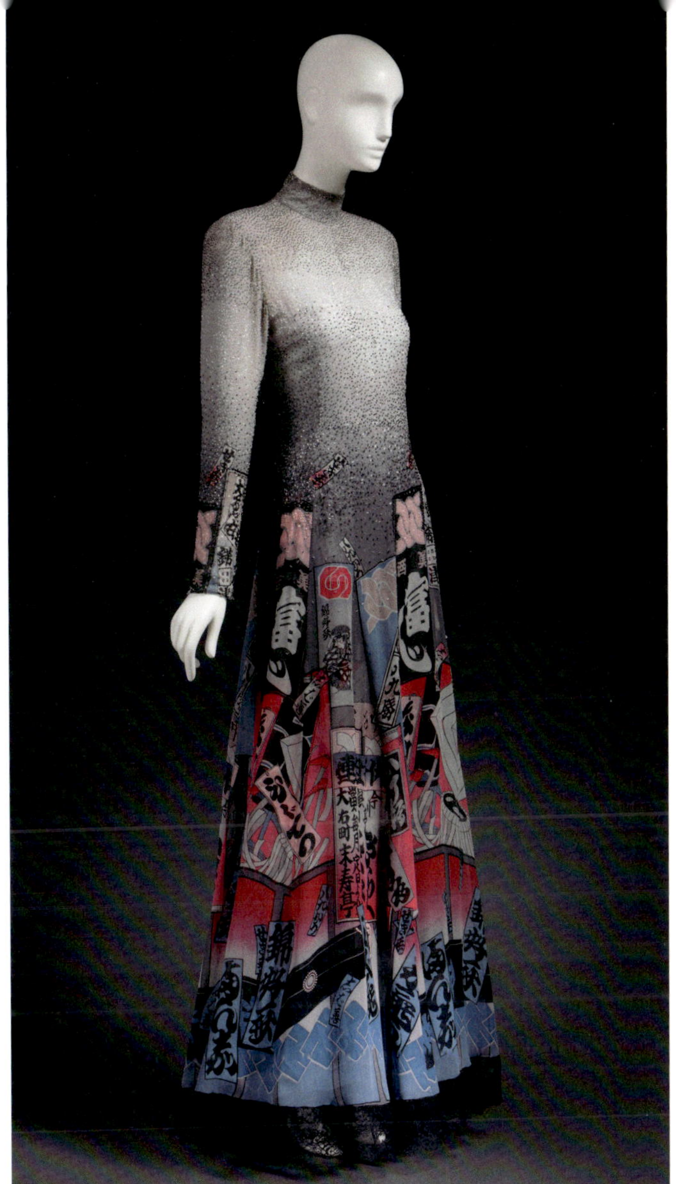

arched backside (C.I.64.4.3), to which he added a bias-rolled, stand-away collar, inspired by kimono collars. The kimono was a paradigm for Balenciaga's experiments with volume and shape, partially inspired by his admiration for Madeleine Vionnet and her bias-cut technique.[24]

His abstraction of the body culminated in the 1957 sack dress, which obliterated the waist's outline with fullness through the midsection, back and front, and a tapered hemline (1973.196.1). At a time when other designers were creating structured hourglass silhouettes with wasp waists, Balenciaga's sack obliterated the New Look. This iconoclastic midcentury silhouette anticipated Balenciaga's architectural volumes of the 1960s, which in turn prefigured the groundbreaking work of Issey Miyake a decade later.

THE SECOND LEAP: NEO-JAPANISM

After World War II, Western styles increasingly replaced kimonos as everyday wear in Japan. The Japanese designers who had grown up at that time — including Issey Miyake, Rei Kawakubo, and Yohji Yamamoto — sought to reinterpret their identity in a cycle of re-Orientalization and renewal Fukai called "neo-Japanism."[25] The movement started in the 1970s, when the Japanese designers took Paris by storm. By the 1980s it had fundamentally changed Western fashion, a new iteration of the tiger's leap. "The feeling is widespread that the Japanese fashion tide is coming and that, if nothing else, it will stimulate thinking about the kind of clothes we wear," *The New York Times* declared.[26] Revolutionizing the international fashion scene "is not just an indication of Japan's originality," Fukai predicted. "It may be a proposal for a clothing of the future that will transcend ethnic and gender differences and even the confines of an establishment called fashion."[27]

Before this dramatic turning point, a few Japanese designers had paved the way from Tokyo to New York and Paris. Hanae Mori was well established in Japan, where she was known for making Western-style clothes. A transitional figure, she presented evening garments inspired by the opulent materials of traditional kimonos at New York Fashion Week in 1965. *Women's Wear Daily* praised Mori's subdued approach, calling her "the first Japanese designer to break the Oriental mold and move into the fashions the West can wear without feeling like Madame Butterfly or a character in a Noh play."[28] Her signature style was sophisticated and feminine, inspired by courtly Edo fashions. The oscillation between Japanese and Western styles sometimes puzzled Western critics, to whom Mori responded: "Women always like women in other countries. I make a Japanese collection to bring here [New York], but I make an American collection for Japan."[29] Her "Ukiyoe" evening dress in chiffon silk from 1983–84 exemplifies Mori's incorporation of classical Japanese art in Western-style evening wear, with patterns inspired by woodblock prints enhanced by exquisite beading and embroidery (fig. 29). The primary motif on the dress is the votive slips of paper (*senjafuda*) traditionally posted on the gates or walls of Japanese shrines and temples.

fig. 27 Madeleine Vionnet (French, 1876–1975). Dress, 1923–24. Silk. The Metropolitan Museum of Art, New York, Purchase, Irene Lewisohn Trust Gift, 2020 (2020.159)

fig. 28 Callot Soeurs (French, active 1895–1937). Evening dress, 1928–29. Silk, metal. The Metropolitan Museum of Art, New York, Purchase, Friends of The Costume Institute Gifts, 2019 (2019.52)

fig. 29 Hanae Mori (Japanese, b. 1926). "Ukiyoe" dress, 1983–84. Silk, glass. The Metropolitan Museum of Art, New York, Gift of Hanae Mori, 2004 (2004.467.4)

In Mori's footsteps followed Kenzo Takada, who presented a relaxed, working-class aesthetic, and Kansai Yamamoto, whose theatrical, postmodern designs were popular with youth around the world. But Japanese designers truly arrived in Paris with Issey Miyake's 1974 collection, based on the "one piece of cloth" concept. Like the kimono, these garments were made of uninterrupted, flat cloth hung from the shoulder, creating a new relationship of garment to body through the intimate space left between them (*ma*). That space allows for free movement and, according to Fukai, "forms the significant difference between Western and Japanese clothes."[30] Miyake further developed the kimono-based structural innovations Vionnet and Balenciaga had introduced to the West, creating a gender-neutral architecture to house the body rather than allude to its shape. Miyake attempted to do away with size, fabric waste, gendered norms, and seasons in fashion, merging an avant-garde ethos with a traditional aesthetic, material taking precedence over shape.

By 1985 Miyake's work had become more sculptural, though still based on the single piece of cloth, and took its cue from organic forms. One example is his iconic "Seashell" cocoon coat (fig. 30), which was knitted with two kinds of thread to create a ribbed, undulating, shell-like form. Like Balenciaga's arched shapes, Miyake's cocoon floats around the body, creating ample *ma*.

Miyake's revolutionary APOC line, which had realized his aim to make garments of "a piece of cloth," evolved in the 1990s to combine the principles of the kimono's basic structure with high-tech design (fig. 31). By programming seams into tubes knitted from a single thread, he allowed wearers to cut out whatever garment they wished along the dotted seams, without the risk of the fabric unraveling. A mechanism for self-tailoring mass-produced, genderless, and universally sized garments, APOC drew the customer into the act of creation, instigating the designer's vanishing act: "My design is no design," he said.[31]

The initial reaction to the avant-garde work by Rei Kawakubo and Yohji Yamamoto, who arrived on the Paris fashion scene in 1981, can be compared to the shock that greeted the first production of Igor Stravinsky's *Rite of Spring* in 1913. Critics related their deconstructed look and pitch-black aesthetic to the devastation wreaked by the atomic bomb. Just one year later, however, critics and consumers alike began to understand the impact the two designers could have on the Western fashion

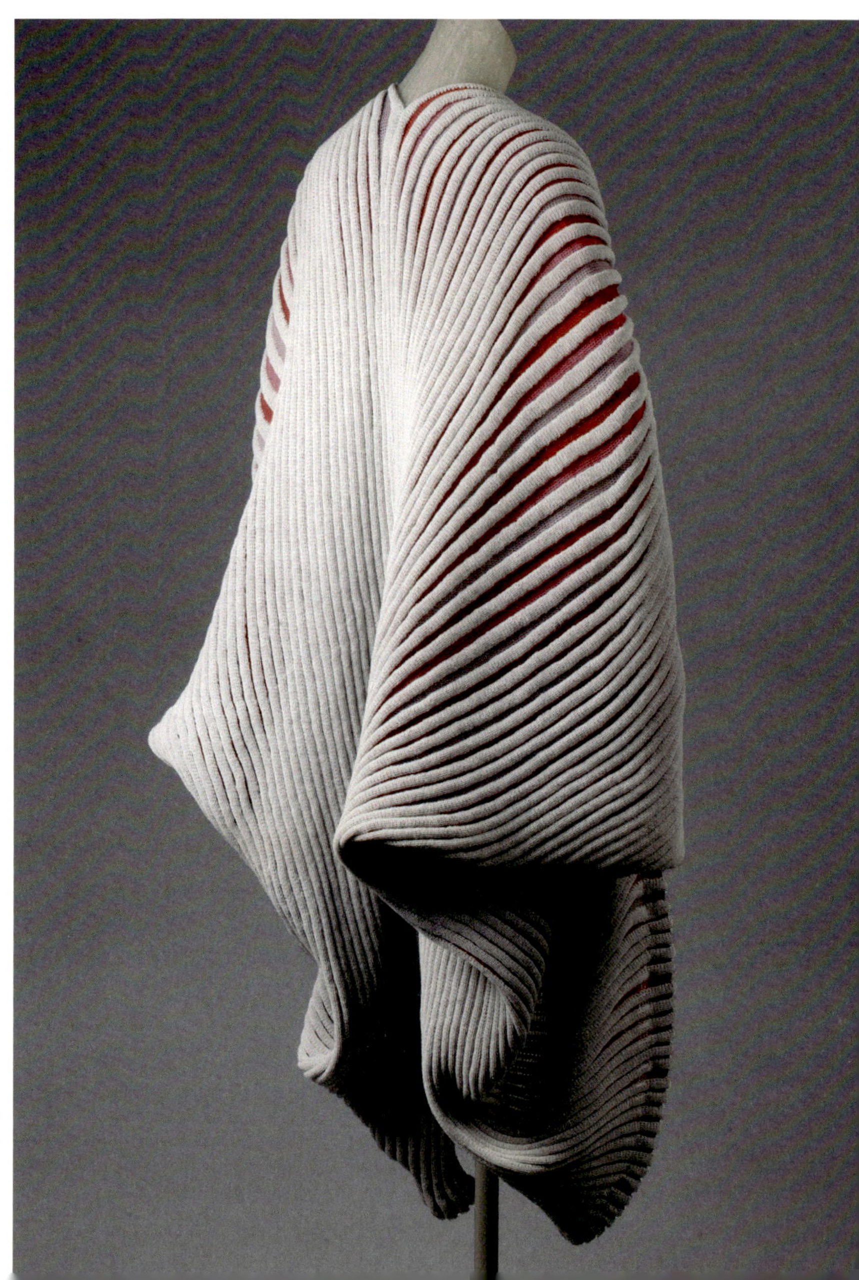

world: "Fads happen every five minutes in fashion, but a change of real strength and real importance is rare," said Geraldine Stutz, herself a pioneering retailer. "The Japanese are offering us this kind of change. They are certainly opening our eyes to a new way of looking at clothes."[32] Their unshaped garments embodied a different Japanese beauty than that expressed by earlier Japanese designers. Kawakubo and Yamamoto's designs integrated principles about negative space from Zen Buddhism and the *wabi-sabi* philosophy, which celebrates simplicity (*wabi*) and impermanence and imperfection (*sabi*). Deliberate imperfections, such as holes, knots, and unraveling seams, and minimal ornamentation characterized their garments.

Emancipatory principles accompanied the dramatic silhouettes. "We must break away from conventional forms of dress for the new woman of today," Kawakubo said in 1983. "We need a new strong image, not a revisit to the past."[33] The press recognized how her garments and Yamamoto's fit into the active lifestyle of the empowered woman of the 1980s: "Showing off the figure is not the point of their designs. . . . The big advantage of Japanese styles lies in their total comfort and absence of restrictions on body movement. . . . [As Kawakubo said,] 'They are for the woman who is independent, who is not swayed by what her husband thinks.'"[34]

Kawakubo's knitted, folded sweater from 1983 is made of one straight panel, shrouding the body in multiple layers in a puzzlelike, planar, kimono construction (fig. 32). Yamamoto often uses the kimono as a starting point too. His oeuvre features generous proportion and size, though he is sensitive to the precarious balance of experiment and exaggeration: "If you go too far with a kimono, the final conclusion is just fabric," he said. "That is not fashion."[35] The patterned floral cutouts of his humble T-shaped coat transform the fabric into a type of lacework, but they equally suggest the tatters worn by the destitute (fig. 33). In Yamamoto's words, "If one has only one piece of clothing in life, it becomes patched together, exposed to sun and rain, frayed from the course of daily life. I wanted to create clothing with the same kind of unconscious beauty and natural appeal."[36]

The success of the postwar Japanese designers precipitated a new way of thinking about fashion in the West, much as the kimono did at the beginning of the century. Subsequent designers such as Martin Margiela, Ann

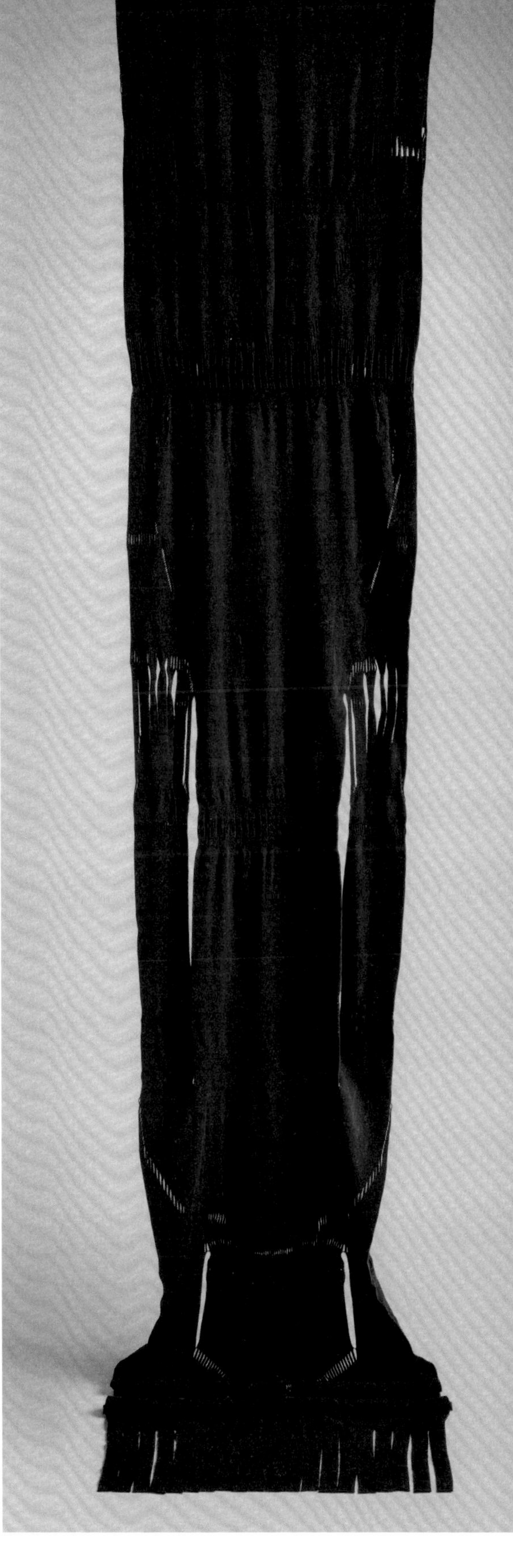

fig. 30 Issey Miyake (Japanese, b. 1938). "Seashell" coat, 1985. Cotton, nylon, linen. The Metropolitan Museum of Art, New York, Gift of Muriel Kallis Newman, 2003 (2003.79.16)

fig. 31 Issey Miyake (Japanese, b. 1938). "A Piece of Cloth" kit, 1999. Cotton, nylon, polyurethane. The Metropolitan Museum of Art, New York, Purchase, Funds from various donors, by exchange, 2015 (2015.417)

Demeulemeester, John Galliano, Alexander McQueen, and Iris van Herpen took their philosophy of creating an intimate space around the body, rather than enclosing it, a step further to revolutionize fashion. In a boundary-breaking collection for 1997, Kawakubo incorporated prosthetics and stuffing, creating lumps and bumps that concealed or deformed the shape of the body. She thereby announced new possibilities for fashion and for women in the twenty-first century, offering new ways to think about the affective relationship between body and garment.

THE KIMONO MIND

Almost a hundred and seventy years after the black ships arrived in Tokyo Bay, the "kimono mind"—a term coined in 1965 by the architect-historian Bernard Rudofsky[37]—has become an abiding metaphor for Japan in Western fashion design, a spur to liberate women's bodies from previous constraints. As Richard Martin, then curator in charge of The Costume Institute, wrote in 1995: "The 'kimono mind' is our contemporary perspective on fashion worldwide."[38] Rather than being regarded as an atavistic, static garment, the kimono was recognized as a futurist, utopian catalyst of innovation. Some of its enduring features, which endlessly emerge in fashion silhouettes, are the T-shape, the cocoon shape, the dropped, stand-away collar, the sleeves, and the obi.

Such influences can be seen in Alexander McQueen's tailoring innovations, for example, in an ensemble for 1998–99 (2010.208.2a, b). It is cut close to the body, in Western style, but the trailing sleeves, connected at the back, evoke the long sleeves of the *furisode*, the formal kimono style for young women.

The kimono continues to resonate through twenty-first-century couture, including John Galliano's 2015–16 collection for Maison Margiela. Galliano created a monastic, floor-sweeping dress with a draped collar at the nape of the neck and a large cobalt-blue bow reminiscent of an obi (fig. 34). The look recalls not only the Japanese kimono but also the innovations it inspired, from Balenciaga's architectural volumes to Miyake's use of *ma*, in another instance of the tiger's leap.

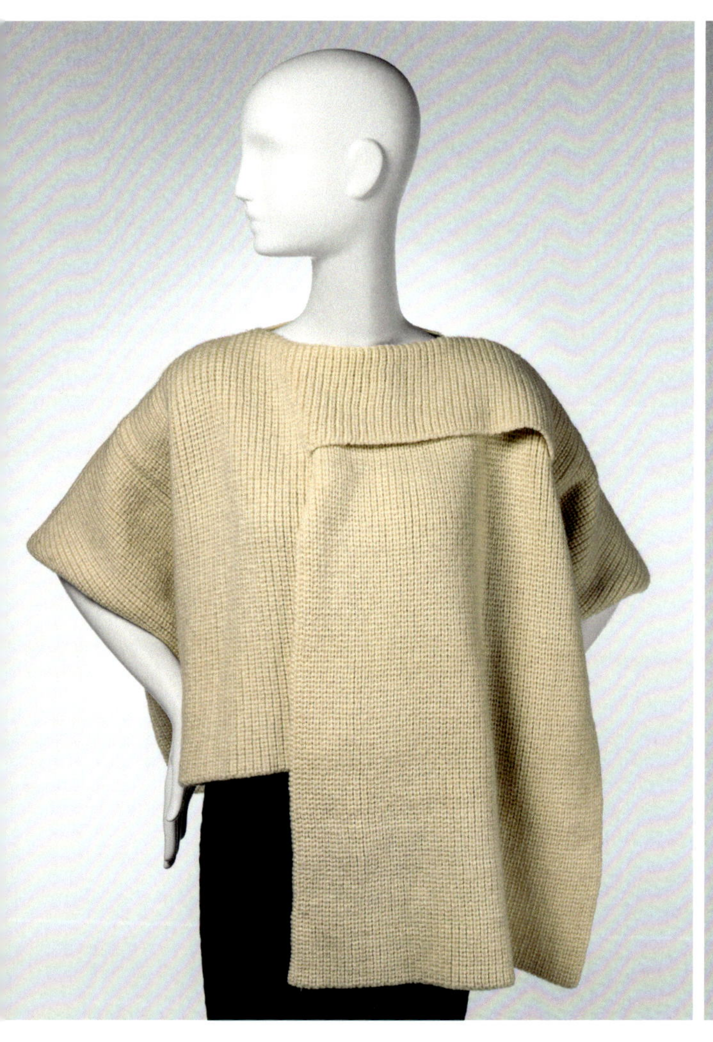

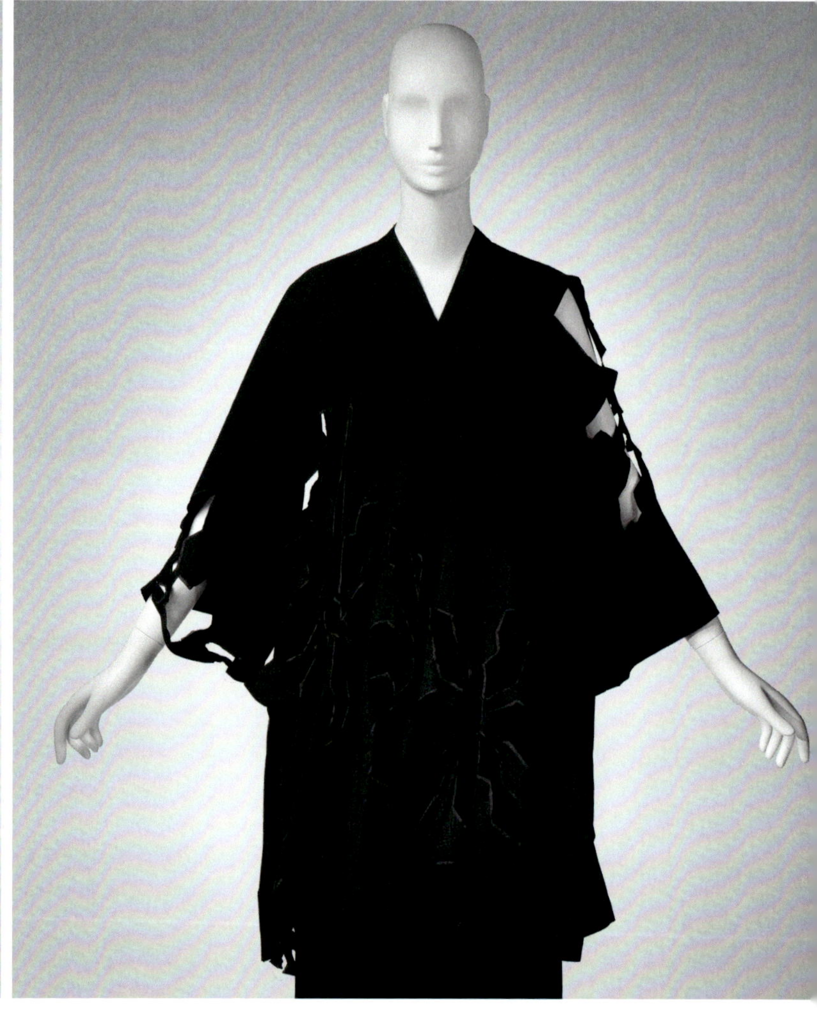

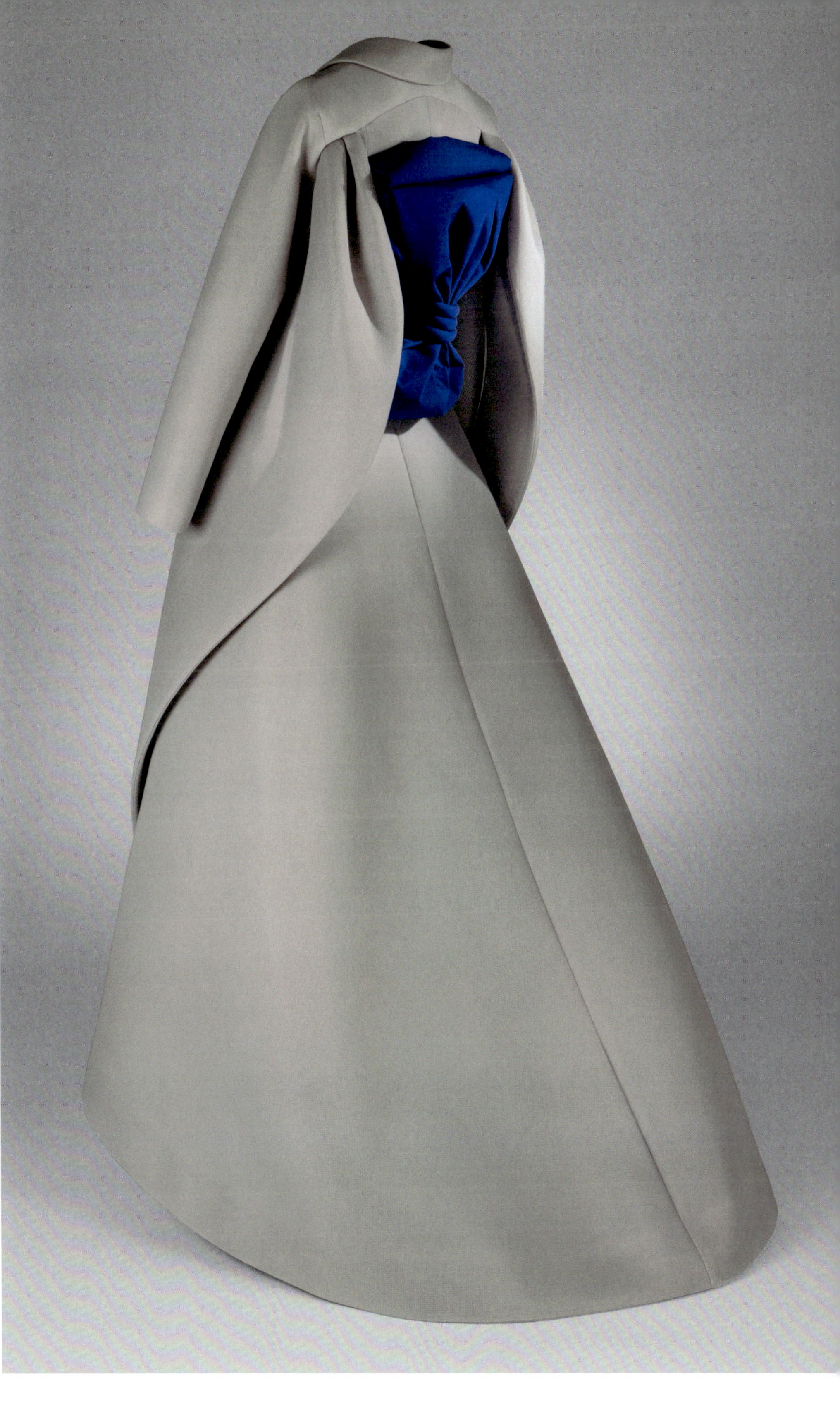

fig. 32 Rei Kawakubo (Japanese, b. 1942), Comme des Garçons (Japanese, founded 1969). Sweater, 1983. Wool. The Metropolitan Museum of Art, New York, Purchase, Gould Family Foundation Gift, in memory of Jo Copeland, 2019 (2019.153)

fig. 33 Yohji Yamamoto (Japanese, b. 1943). Coat, 1983. Cotton. The Metropolitan Museum of Art, New York, Purchase, Gould Family Foundation Gift, in memory of Jo Copeland, 2011 (2011.288)

fig. 34 John Galliano (British, b. 1960), Maison Margiela (French, founded 1988). Ensemble, 2015–16. Synthetic, silk, metal, leather. The Metropolitan Museum of Art, New York, Gift of Maison Margiela, in honor of Harold Koda, 2016 (2016.401a–c)

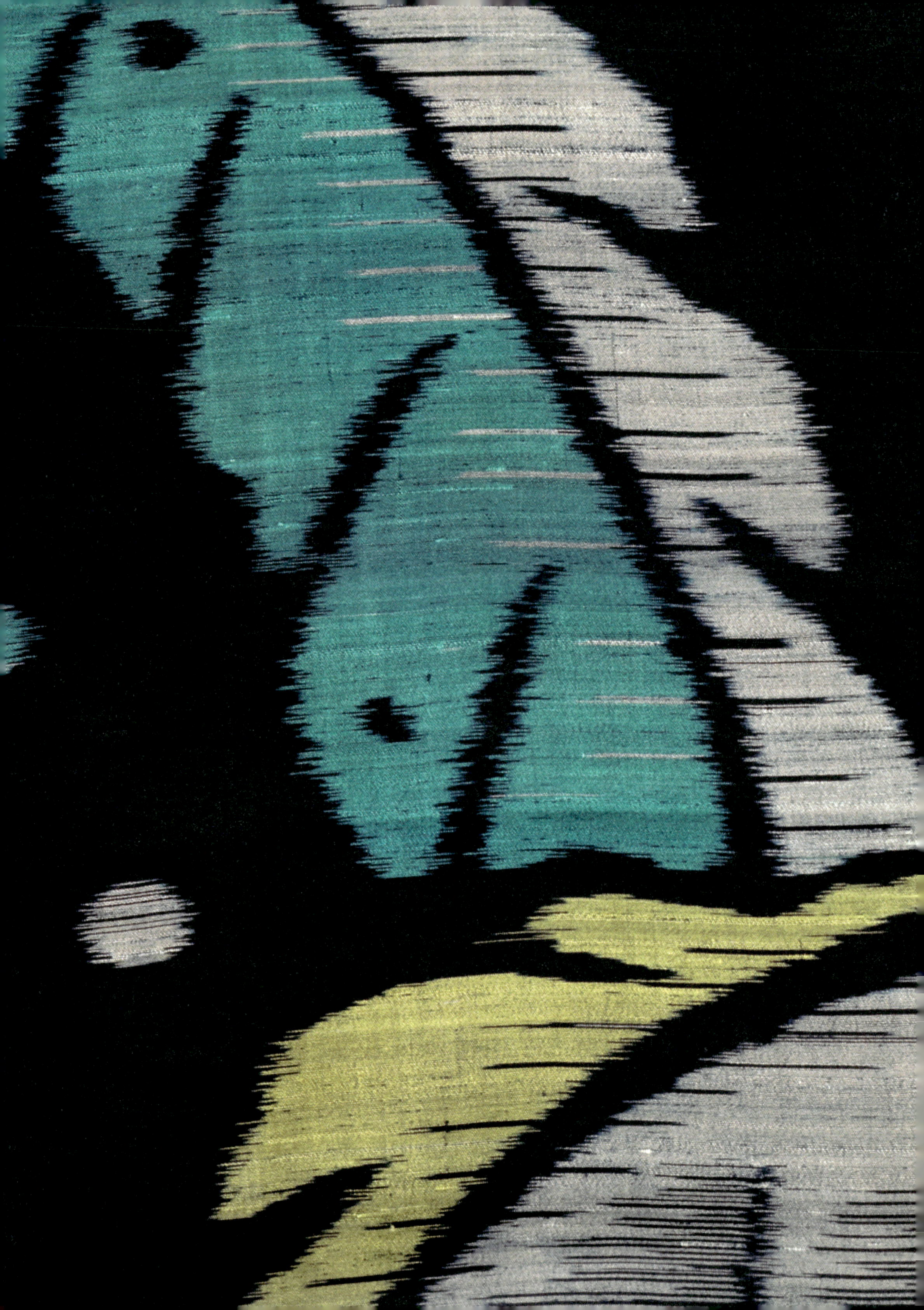

MEISEN AND

KIMONOS FOR

ARAI MASANAO

THE MASSES

OMESHI

FOR CENTURIES HIGH-QUALITY SILK IN JAPAN WAS GENERALLY AVAILABLE ONLY TO THE ELITE, THOUGH COMMONERS COULD USE INEXPENSIVE, DURABLE, HAND-SPUN pongee (*tsumugi* silk). This began to change in the late nineteenth century, when technology and materials imported from the West enabled manufacturers to increase production and drive down prices. Machine-spun silk, power looms, and aniline dyes all contributed to the creation of affordable, stylish kimonos made from *meisen*, an inexpensive silk woven with predyed yarns. By the 1920s–30s, working- and middle-class women, from high-school students to shop assistants, could clothe themselves in casual, bright-colored, modern kimonos with bold, graphic patterns that were released frequently to spark trends and inspire purchases (fig. 35).

Despite their importance to the democratization of Japanese dress — and their explosive sales in the 1920s and 1930s and again in 1951–55 — these popular textiles have scarcely been studied until now. Little was known about their techniques, the origins of their motifs, or even their precise dating. Recent research into the chronology of production techniques has helped contextualize *meisen* in Japanese textile history and facilitated more accurate dating and description of these kimonos, which are significantly represented in the Weber Collection.[1]

Meisen owe their invention and success to the silk yarn made from waste cocoons. Silkworm cocoons in Japan are typically categorized as good-quality cocoons, which can be reeled into thin, uniform filaments of raw silk, or waste cocoons. These lower-quality cocoons include double cocoons, formed by two or more silkworms, and cocoons that are stained or are pierced from the inside by the moths. They cannot be used to reel good-quality silk; instead, they traditionally were boiled together in a pot of water, from which filament fibers were pulled and wound on a reel by hand (fig. 36). Any pupae that were inside the cocoons and attached to the thread were carefully removed from the filaments by hand, but the small bits that were left behind created an uneven thread, known as dupioni silk (*tama-ito* or *fushi-ito*).[2] Noil silk (*noshi-ito*), another low-cost silk, is made of short filaments that yield an uneven, coarse yarn.

During the late Edo period (1615–1868), a warp (the lengthwise set of yarns) of dupioni silk and a slightly coarser weft (the yarns woven perpendicularly to the warp) of noil silk would be woven to produce *futo-ori* (thick weave), a durable, dense fabric with an uneven texture. Records dating to 1789 mention *mesen* (“a thousand

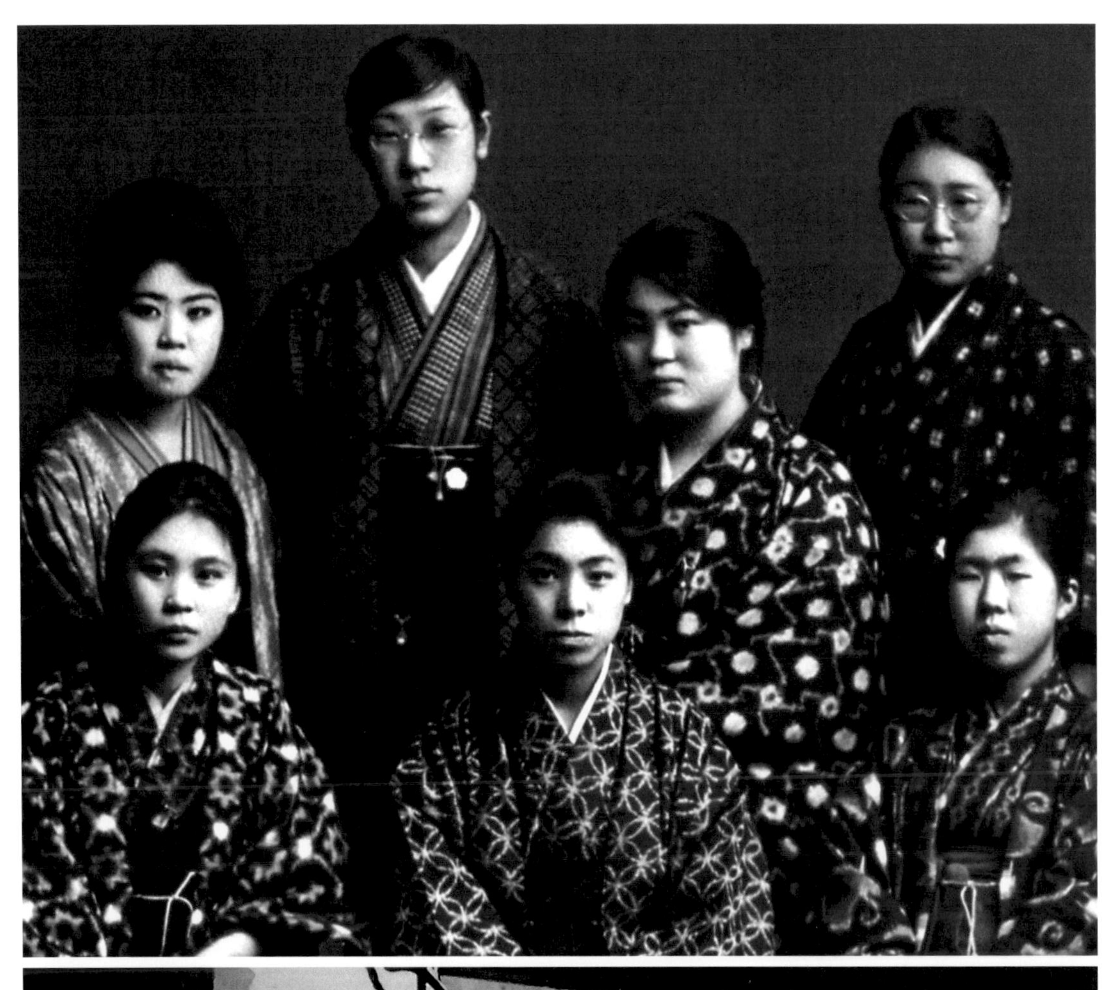

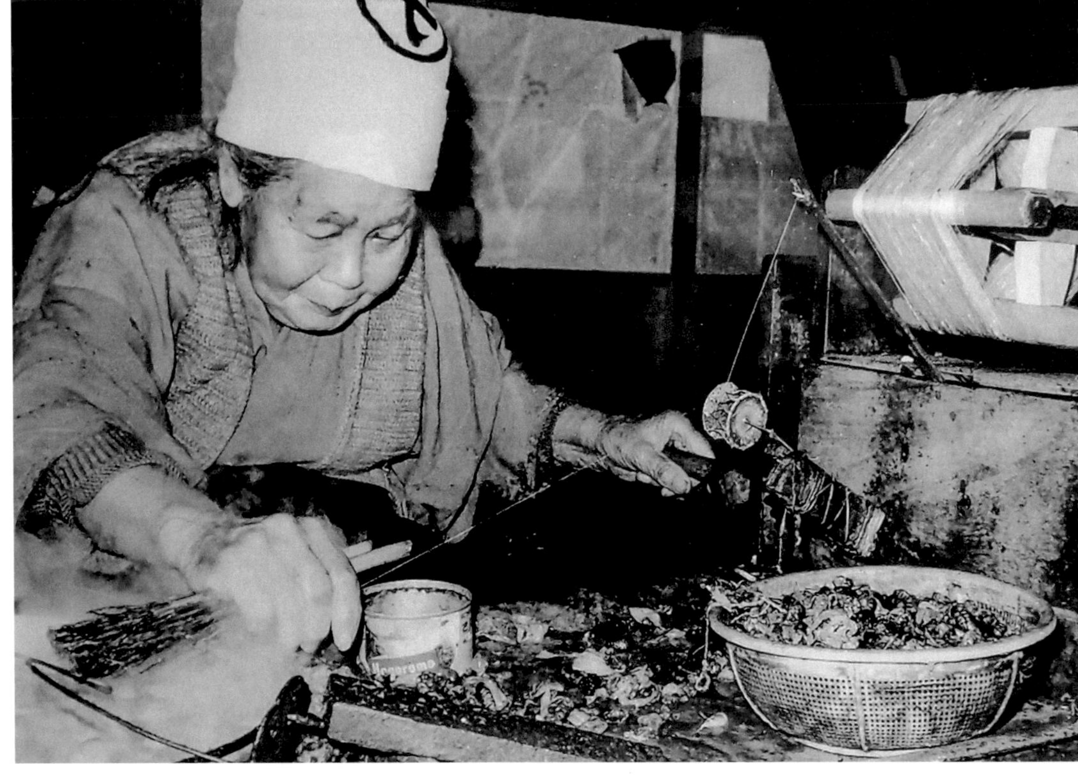

fig. 35 Students of the Tokyo Women's Higher Normal School (later Ochanomizu University), 1925

fig. 36 Reeling dupioni silk thread (*tama-ito*) by hand using *zaguri*, a traditional tool, 1954

weaves") *futo-ori*, suggesting that the fabric was woven with as many as a thousand warp yarns.[3] By the mid-nineteenth century *mesen* or *meisen futo-ori* robes were commoners' typical, understated, everyday clothing, usually featuring stripes of navy blue and brown.[4]

However, silk waste could be put to more profitable use, as was proven by the advanced silk-spinning industry in Europe — especially France, Italy, Germany, and Switzerland — to which China (and later Japan) exported silk waste. To compete in the global market and to protect its own manufacturers from an influx of foreign goods, the Japanese government in the early 1870s recognized the need to promote industrialization; the effort included the modernization of sericulture, silk reeling (for high-quality silk filaments), and silk spinning (for silk waste from damaged cocoons). As Japan had no such technology, it had to import all the necessary machines and know-how from Europe.

The first state-owned model silk-spinning mill was established in 1877 in Shinmachi, in Gunma prefecture, which boasted an advantageous location: near rivers to generate hydropower, proximate both to Tokyo's large market and business network and to the northern Kanto region's textile industry, and surrounded by traditional sericulture communities that could readily provide waste cocoons.[5] Following the lead of the Western textile trade, the new factory hired young women. Later, in 1897, the Shinmachi mill was privatized by the Mitsui clan, which had established one of the most prominent industrial and financial business conglomerates in Japan, including the Mitsukoshi department store.

The machine-spun silk (*kenshibōseki shi* or *kenbōshi*) produced in Shinmachi was sold to fabric manufacturers in neighboring Isesaki, Chichibu, Kiryū, Ashikaga, and later Hachioji, all of which had a long history of sericulture and became principal centers of *meisen* production (fig. 37). *Meisen* manufacturing rapidly increased in the Taishō period (1912–26) and reached its peak in 1930, when the production centers manufactured 6.52 million rolls of the flat, plain-weave fabric (each roll equal to two bolts and enough to make two kimonos); Isesaki alone produced 2.28 million rolls (fig. 38).[6] Total production from 1912 to 1937 was 98.05 million rolls. This vast output reflected both the dynamism of the trade network between the regional

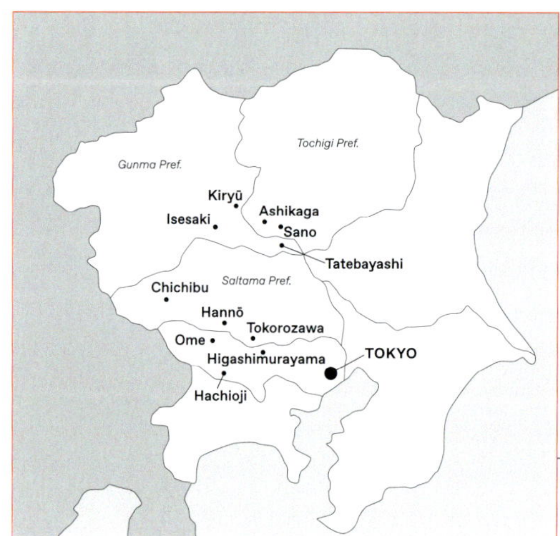

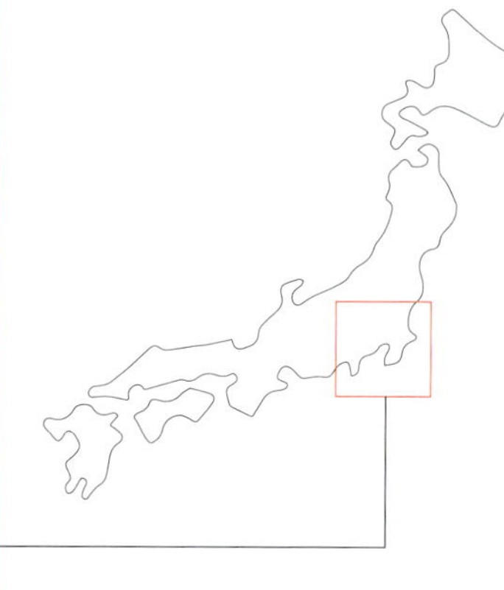

textile industry and its urban clients and the development of a consumer society in Japan.[7]

The growing demand for *meisen* may be attributed to the adoption of the chic, economical garments for girls' school uniforms and to the increasing number of women entering the labor force. Telephone operators, waitresses, shop assistants, and textile workers gravitated to it as workday wear or even for dress-up occasions. Middle-class women tended to wear it at home. The fabric was less lustrous than high-quality silk but strong and durable, ideal for everyday use, and it appealed to consumers as more precious than cotton.

EARLY *MEISEN* PATTERNS AND PRODUCTION TECHNIQUES

Ikat fabric in its ancient form was introduced from Southeast Asia to Japan (where it is known as *kasuri*) as early as the eighth century. However, it was only in about 1800 that *kasuri* became widely established in Japan, after the introduction of the hemp ikat technique from the Ryukyu Islands. By this method, yarns are resist-dyed to create a pattern before weaving, whereas other resist-dyeing techniques apply the resist to woven cloth. The difficulty in perfectly aligning the patterned yarns on the loom results in ikat's characteristic blurred outlines. The technique of weaving resist-dyed warp and weft yarns to create small white geometric patterns of the undyed sections of yarn was typically used for commoners' indigo-dyed fabrics of dupioni silk (*mesen futo-ori*). One hundred years later, *kasuri* would come to be one of the primary decorative techniques used for *meisen.*

fig. 37 *Meisen* production centers in the Kanto region

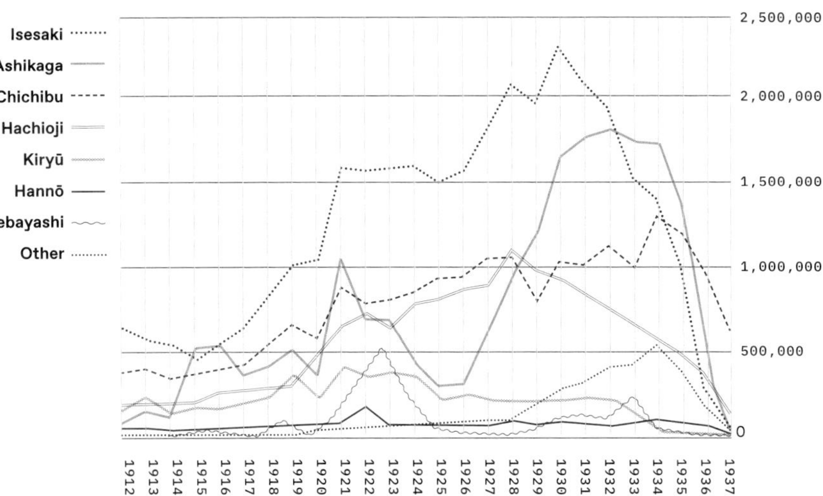

By the 1830s workshops in Nakano, near Isesaki, commenced weaving *kasuri* yarns that were resist-dyed to create *meisen* patterned with stripes, checks, and small geometric designs. The traditional method of making tied-resist (*shibari*) *kasuri* by hand is to stretch a bundle of twenty to thirty yarns between two upright iron rods, tightly wrap the parts that should remain undyed with cotton threads or hemp fibers, and immerse the bundle in a dye bath. After the yarns are washed and dried, the wrapped areas are released, revealing the patterns in white. The method creates straight-edged, geometric patterns but cannot produce curves or large pictorial compositions. Even after the use of imported chemical dyes became common, the fabrics were in subdued colors such as indigo, brown, and beige. Primary colors were featured only after 1926. The machine-spun silk that was available from about the 1880s facilitated *kasuri* production, as its uniform thickness and minimal irregularities allowed the patterns of the predyed yarns to be more precisely aligned on the loom.

In the *ōgasuri* (large ikat) version of the *shibari-gasuri* technique, which was developed in Isesaki in the 1920s and flourished in 1930–40, both the warp and weft threads were tied-resist dyed. A lined *meisen* kimono with a staggered checkered pattern in black, red, and yellow is an example of this *ōgasuri* technique (cat. 53). Another *ōgasuri* robe, which was inspired by Piet Mondrian's abstract paintings, features large patterns in raspberry red, turquoise, yellow, and white and is embellished with gold thread (cat. 52). The tied-resist techniques for *meisen* were used in Isesaki, Chichibu, Ashikaga, Kiryū, and Hachioji from the late Edo period through 1960.

As binding yarns with cotton threads by hand required tremendous time and dexterity, a simpler alternative, the board-clamped (*itajime-gasuri*) method, was developed in about 1890. Sections of yarns are clamped between wooden boards that keep those sections from being dyed. The technique transformed *meisen* production, as it could be used to print large quantities of fabric with rectilinear patterns. *Itajime-gasuri* was used in Isesaki and Ashikaga, and later in Chichibu and Murayama, until 1955.

THE PATTERNED *MEISEN* BOOM

Intense competition among the textile production centers led to continuous development of processes and dyeing techniques that would reduce costs, increase output, and create new, increasingly complex compositions, including curvilinear patterns with multiple colors. Some of those were inspired by the elegant designs made by the intricate, artisanal *kata-yūzen* method developed in Kyoto in the late nineteenth century, which used traditional Japanese paper stencils in the application of colored paste to fabric. This idea was simplified for industrial production in 1906, with a patented method of stencil-printing pictorial patterns on warp threads (fig. 39). Before dyeing the warp yarns, temporary wefts were sparsely interwoven to keep the warps in place. The fabric was stretched on a textile-dyeing table and printed with stencils. After steaming to fix the colors, the temporary wefts were removed

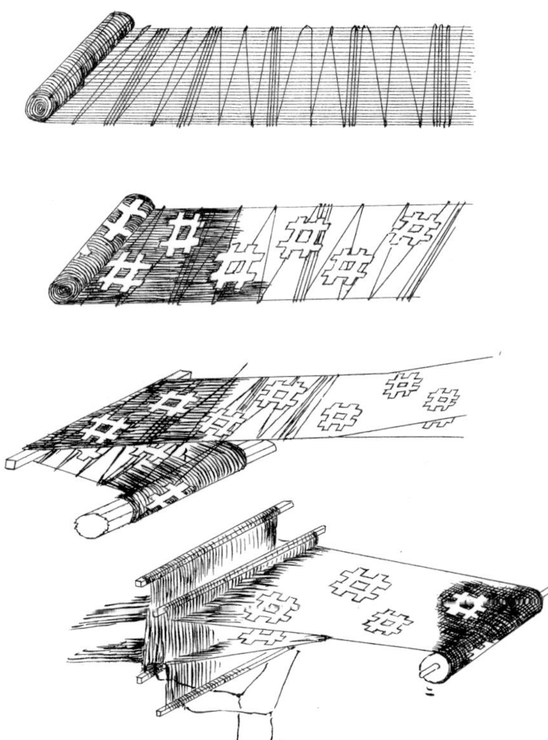

fig. 38 Volume of *meisen* (measured in *hiki*, a roll from which two kimonos can be made) generated by the leading production centers, 1912–37

fig. 39 Drawing for the patent application for the *senshō-gasuri seizōhō* method, which became known as *hogushi-gasuri* (unraveled ikat), 1906

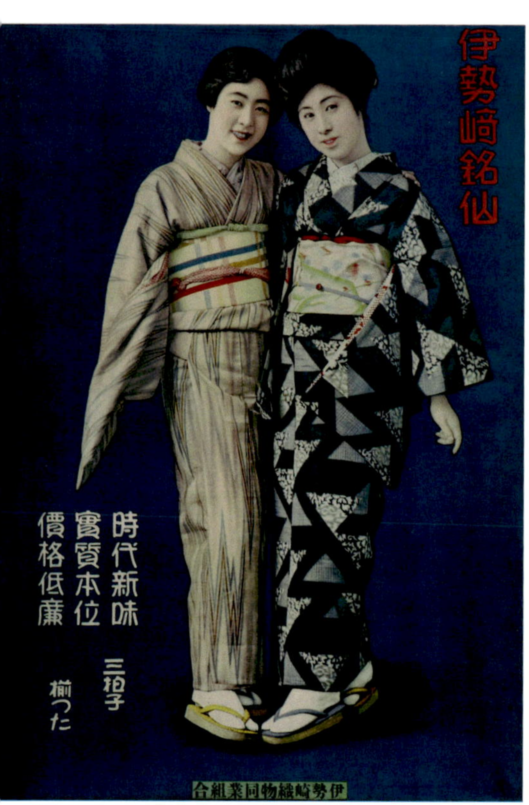

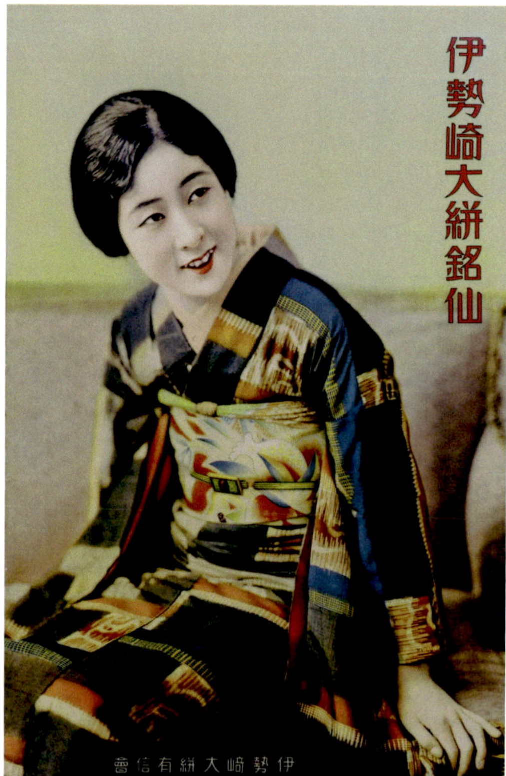

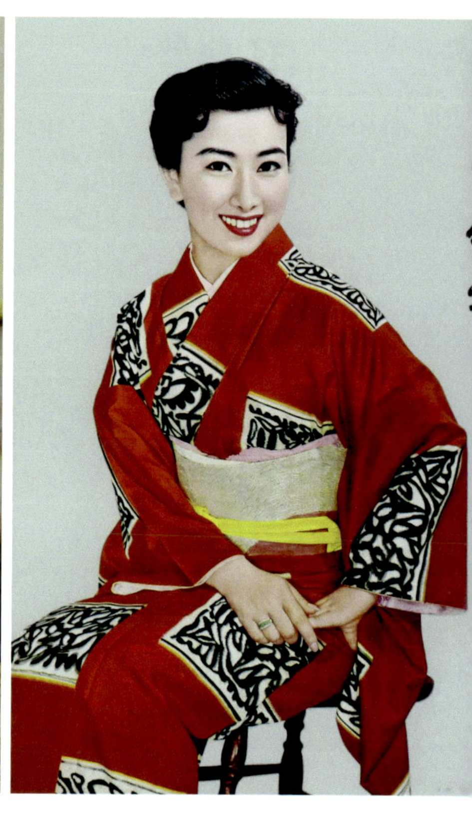

one section at a time while on the loom, leaving only the warps patterned, and the fabric was rewoven with unpatterned and monochrome permanent weft yarns. The unraveling of the temporary wefts gave the technique its name, *hogushi* (unraveled) *kasuri*. A starchy paste made of powdered konjac (*konnyaku*, elephant yam or devil's tongue), water, and pigment was key to the dyeing process. Suspending the dye in the paste allowed it to be precisely placed without bleeding, and the konjac paste did not harden, even after the steaming that follows dyeing; it could be easily removed from the fabric by washing after the yarns were woven. Konjac was cultivated in the mountains near the production centers and was easily accessible in pulverized form.

All the major production centers — Ashikaga, Isesaki, Chichibu, and Hachioji — used this process between 1905 and 1955. A host of new motifs emerged, as the stencil-dyeing technique provided the flexibility to create flower patterns, curvilinear forms, and realistic, painterly effects inspired by Western art. Kimonos with these attractive designs came to be known as "patterned *meisen*" (*moyō-meisen*) and evoked the luxurious *kata-yūzen* fabrics that were out of reach for working-class women. The *hogushi-gasuri* technique was used in 1935–40 to make a kimono with a motif of white rabbits and scouring rushes (cat. 54). The straight selvedges suggest that it was woven on a power loom (*riki-shokki*) or with a foot-operated loom (*ashibumi-shokki*). For this lively pattern, five stencils were prepared to apply the colors to the warp: gray, yellow, deep green, black, and dark pink. The weft is black.

With the development of more complexly patterned *meisen*, producers endeavored to present fresh artistic ideas and new fashion trends. From the early twentieth century they professionalized the textile design process by engaging designers and artists, including painters who worked in the Western style (*yōga*) and painters who followed the Japanese traditions (*nihonga*). Previously there were no designers per se; the weavers had created their own compositions by copying or modifying sample swatches. The establishment of research groups and associations for textile designers in Kyoto and Tokyo led to more sophisticated design processes and quickly changing styles. Expert designers approved by the Kyoto Design Association provided guidance and design drawings (*zuan*) to Tokyo-based

fig. 40 Poster for Taishō-style *meisen* produced by the Isesaki Textile Manufacturers' Association, 1927

fig. 41 Poster for *ōgasuri meisen* produced by Isesaki Ōgasuri Yūshinkai, a group of *meisen* manufacturers, 1932

fig. 42 Poster for Isesaki textiles, featuring the movie star Yamamoto Fujiko in a *heiyō-gasuri meisen* kimono, produced by the Isesaki Textile Manufacturers' Association, 1955

designers, and the information was simultaneously transmitted to the *meisen* production centers so they could keep up with the trends originating in Kyoto. Design research centers were also established in the Taishō period in Ashikaga, Kiryū, and Isesaki; their staffs consulted a wide range of design albums for inspiration for *meisen* patterns, including such titles as *Secession zuanshū* (Secession designs, 1921) and *Ōbei mohan kōkoku zuanshū* (Western advertisement designs, 1928). Woodblock-printed books like *Sōtatsu Kōrin byōgashū* (Folding screens by Sōtatsu and Kōrin, 1911) were used as references for Japanese-style patterns.[8]

As a result of such efforts, traditional motifs like plum flowers and hemp leaves were modernized, a range of new flower patterns emerged, and birds and butterflies were depicted in bright colors. The Art Nouveau and Art Deco styles had a major impact on *meisen* motifs, but modern compositions inspired by Fauvism, Cubism, De Stijl, Abstract Expressionism, Italian Futurism, and other modernist movements particularly characterize this genre. One of the significant changes in *meisen* kimono styles was the increased size of the patterns, which gradually became larger from the Taishō period on. A comparison of a 1925 photograph of students (see fig. 35) with promotional posters from 1927 to 1955 showing women (one a famous actress) wearing Isesaki *meisen* kimonos (figs. 40–42) reveals the aesthetic evolution.

Following the success of the *hogushi-gasuri* technique, manufacturers sought to create sharper images with more depth, shading, and hues by patterning the wefts in addition to the warps. Textile makers in Isesaki developed the *hogushi heiyō-ōgasuri* (double-ikat) method in the late 1910s, interweaving the wefts (dyed with the tied-resist *kasuri* technique) and the warps (dyed with the *hogushi-gasuri* method).[9] The dyed warps and wefts had to be carefully aligned on the loom to create these complex, painterly patterns. In 1930 the Isesaki Hiratō Company enhanced the technique by stretching the wefts around a board and printing the patterns on them with stencils on both sides, using different stencils for each color (fig. 43).[10] This double-ikat technique (with the simplified name *heiyō-gasuri*) became identified with Isesaki, which used it from 1930 to 1955 (fig. 44). While the technique produced dramatic, vividly colored motifs, the weaving process was painstaking, requiring a great deal of expertise and time, as it had to be done by hand on a floor loom, making this type of fabric very expensive.

Although the warps and the wefts would typically be printed with the same stencils in the *heiyō-gasuri* method, a lined kimono with a water droplet pattern made in Isesaki in 1930–40 is a rare exception (cat. 57). Three different stencils were used for the warps and four for the wefts. The overlapping of the variously sized roundels added depth to the pattern. As the warps were dyed with small black dots, the background appears gray, but a close look reveals a pixelated ground pattern. Another example of the technique is a lined kimono with a pattern of bobbins and books made about 1935–40 in Isesaki (cat. 58). Six stencils were used to print the pattern on both the warps and wefts, and silver threads were added to the bobbin patterns.

A summer garment with an overscale design of commas (*tomoe*) was also produced by the *heiyō-gasuri* technique in Isesaki at about the same time as the previous example (cat. 56). The blue, white, and black design was made with two stencils for the warps and three for the wefts. The warps were dyed with light blue and navy, and gray was added to the wefts, visible in the smaller commas. In this *omeshi meisen*, the silk *kasuri* wefts alternate with twisted dark blue rayon wefts to create lateral stripes and texture.

Producers in Ashikaga, which used modern foot-operated or automatic wooden looms, simplified the *heiyō-gasuri* technique so that they could create a similar effect in larger quantities. In this new technique, known as *hanheiyō-gasuri* (half *heiyō-gasuri* or partial double ikat), stencil-dyed warps were woven with tied-resist-dyed wefts with simple, large motifs in white or bright colors to create highlights in the design. The wefts gave the patterns depth and luminosity. This technique was less complex and time-consuming than the *heiyō-gasuri*, and the weaving could be done on automated looms. Chichibu producers also adopted the technique and used it from the 1930s to 1955. It generated many modern, dynamic compositions, including a colorful, lined jacket (*haori*) with fans and white flowers (cat. 59) that was made in Chichibu or Ashikaga in 1935–45. Four stencils were used for the warp, while the weft is tied-resist dyed. Tightly twisted three-ply wefts were woven in to create the slightly wrinkled, matte texture of a very fine crepe silk. Dyed warp threads form the fans and flowers, with wefts dyed white and black woven into the flower adding depth.

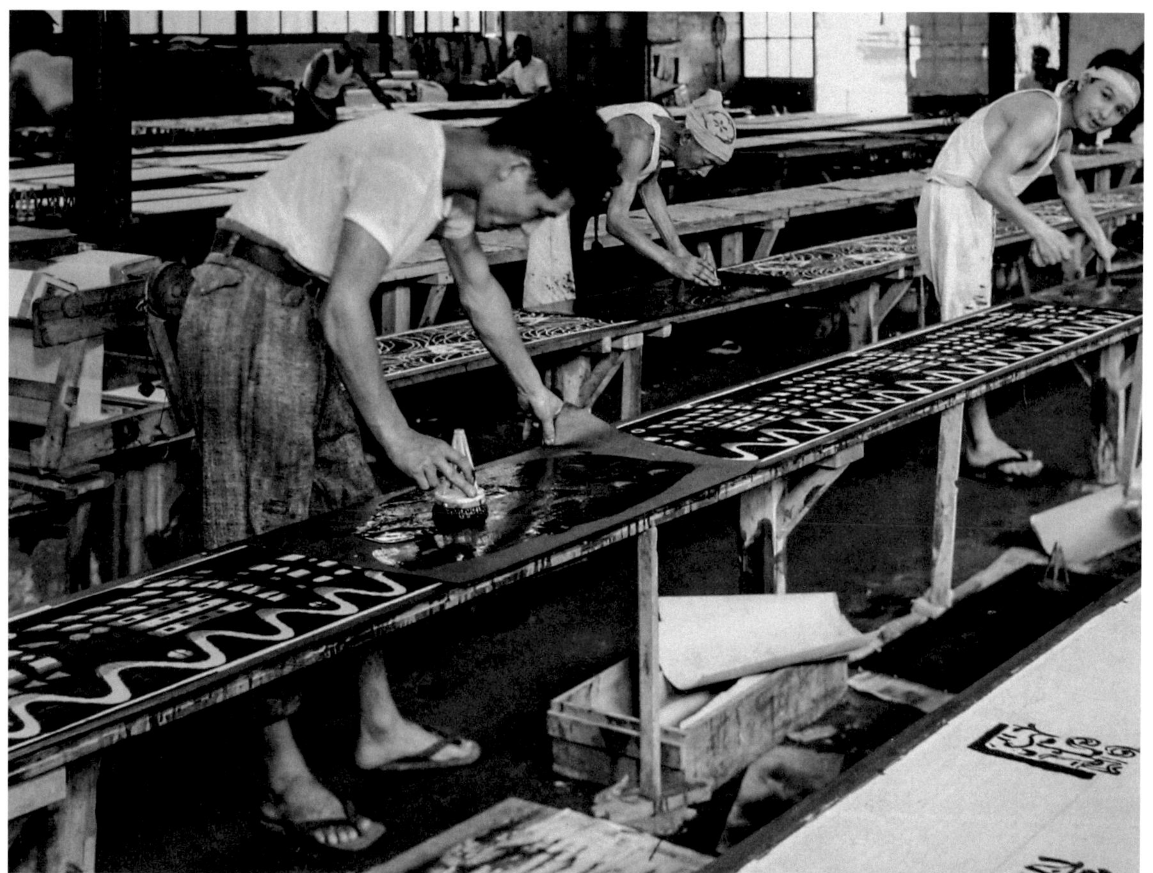

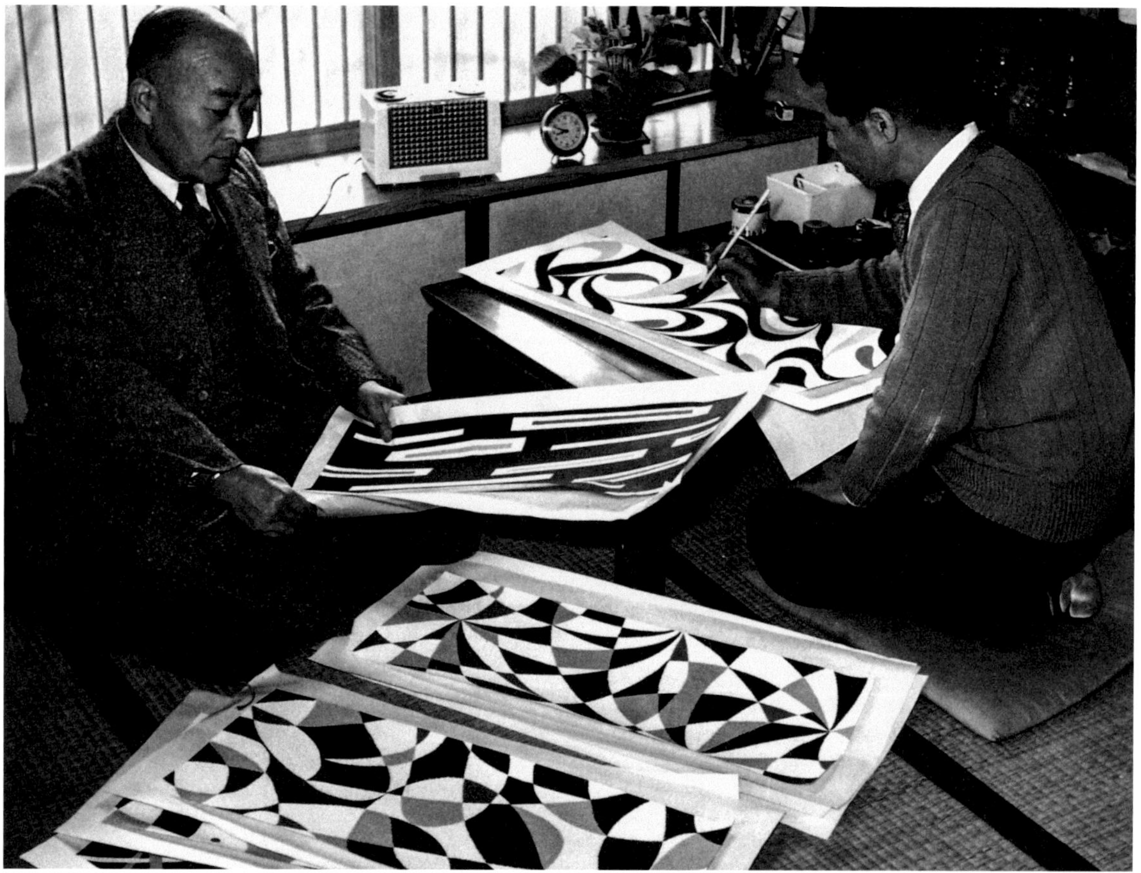

fig. 43 Printing *heiyō-gasuri* (double-ikat) patterns with stencils on white warp yarns stretched on a printing table in Isesaki, early 1950s

fig. 44 Abstract, Italian Futurist designs for *heiyō-gasuri* (double-ikat) patterns being selected by the director of a weaving workshop in a designer's studio, Isesaki, 1953

Large-scale patterns became increasingly prevalent, with motifs extending as much as twenty-four inches — almost half the length of the typical kimono — popular by 1941. The pattern of banana leaves with stylized snowflakes on a summer kimono made in 1940–45 has a vertical repeat exceeding thirty inches (cat. 60). It was made with an all-weft *kasuri* technique (*yokosō-gasuri*), which allowed for the creation of large, free-form, multicolored, continuous patterns. The warps are dark blue, while the wefts are tied-resist dyed with dark green, yellow, and white. A *haori* jacket from the 1950s was also made with the *yokosō-gasuri* technique (cat. 62). The wefts were dyed with four stencils to create a dynamic, graphic pattern of looping lines in brown, white, and gray on a red ground.

OMESHI MEISEN AND THE MEISEN REVIVAL

At the peak of *meisen*'s popularity, in 1930, manufacturers turned out enough fabric to make more than 26 million kimonos; at the time, Japan's population included about 32 million women.[11] Profit margins were thin, however, as department stores sought to keep prices for *meisen* kimonos within reach of the greatest number of customers. In search of larger profits, producers gradually shifted away from *meisen* and developed new techniques and superior fabrics, including luxurious *omeshi* (heavy crepe silk woven of predyed yarns).

Omeshi was made with a warp of machine-spun silk yarn (dupioni silk) and a weft of inexpensive rayon with a strong twist (about 2,300 twists per meter). A paste or glue was applied to the fabric, then the surface was finely patterned by sending the cloth through a heated roller press, which created a bumpy, crimped texture. This technique, called *semi-katō*, was invented in 1930 in Ashikaga.[12] The resulting fabric initially was called *omeshi meisen*, as only the weft yarns differed from those of *meisen*, and the yarns were similarly dyed with stencils. With the wartime suspension of imports in 1937, Japan dramatically increased the manufacturing of its own rayon, soon becoming the world's leading producer.[13] At the same time, the lack of an export market during wartime increased the domestic supply and depressed prices. From 1933 to 1944 the average cost of machine-spun silk was 14.67 yen per kilogram, while rayon cost about one-sixth of that, or 2.42 yen.[14] Rayon had already been used for items such as obis made in Kiryū and light crepe fabric (*kinsha chirimen*) produced in Ashikaga, paving the way for its adaption to *omeshi meisen*. In 1935, some 90 percent of *meisen* production consisted of *omeshi meisen*, which illustrates the sudden shift.[15]

World War II–era restrictions on the manufacture of certain goods interrupted the vogue for *meisen* kimonos, but production resumed in about 1951. The need to replace large quantities of clothing destroyed during the war and the special procurement demands of the Korean War (1950–53) led to a brief revival of the *meisen* industry. In 1953 *meisen* production in only five centers (Sano, Ashikaga, Tatebayashi, Kiryū, and Isesaki) reached 4.19 million rolls.[16] Bold, large-scale, abstract motifs emerged again, seeming to reflect the relief that followed the turmoil of war and to celebrate the beginning of a new era.

Several kimonos made with the *heiyō-gasuri* technique, all produced in Isesaki in the 1950s, exemplify postwar *meisen.* One is a striking red kimono with thunderbolt motifs (cat. 64). The dyer used a four-sided block instead of a flat board to dye the wefts, creating a sophisticated, gradated *kasuri* effect. Another, an unlined summer kimono (*hito-e*), features a modernized, abstract cracked-ice pattern, which has long been used in Japan to decorate ceramics and other works of art (cat. 63). The warps were dyed with two stencils and the wefts with three, and the patterns were carefully aligned on the loom.

The increasing popularity of synthetic fibers, the waning use of kimonos for daily wear, and a flourishing market for Western-style clothing caused the market for *meisen* to decline after 1955, and production soon ceased altogether. However, with the perspective of time and recent scholarship, these exuberant garments have assumed their place in kimono history as affordable silk styles for the masses.

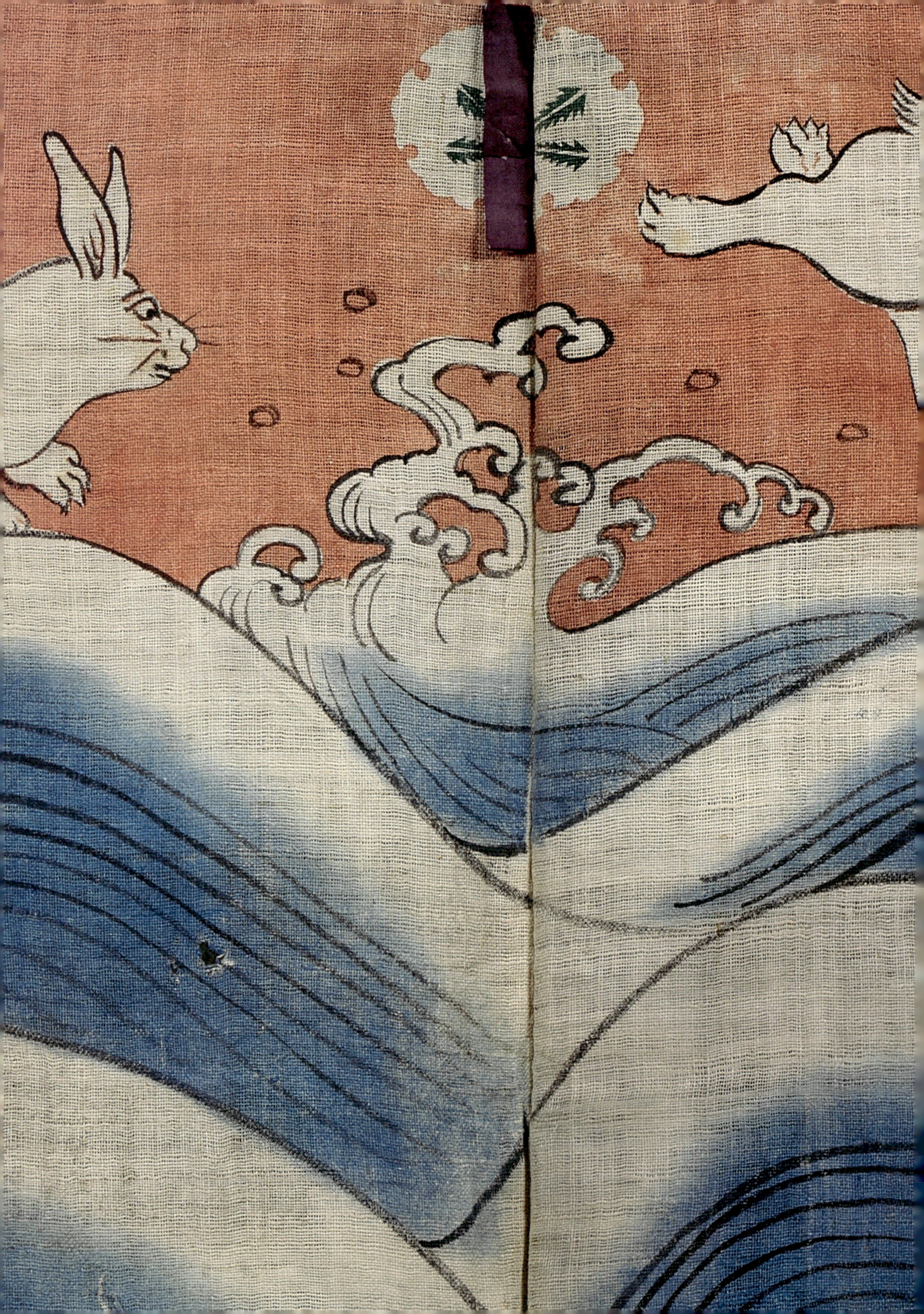

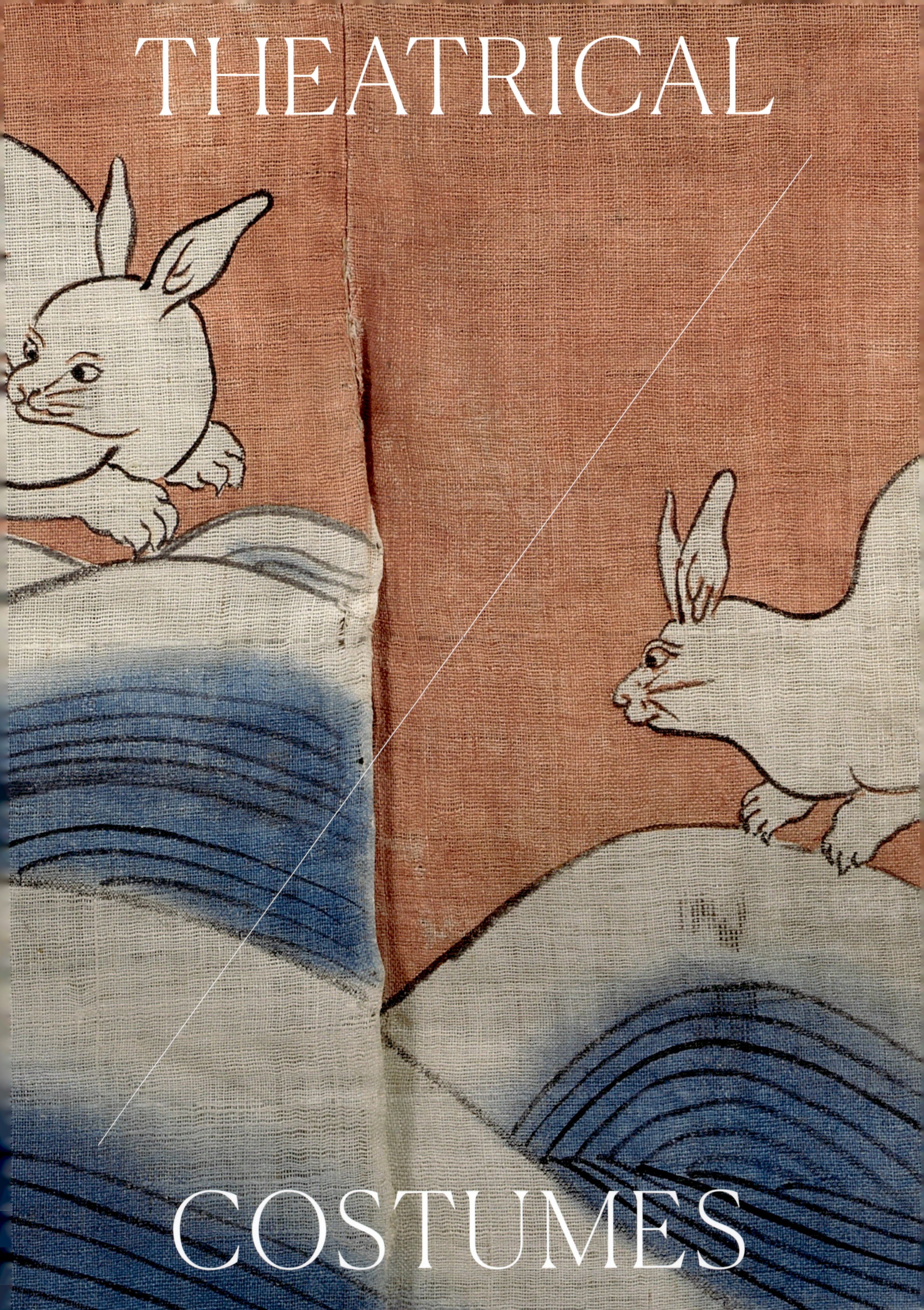
THEATRICAL
COSTUMES

JAPAN'S TRADITIONAL FORMS OF THEATER, NOH and Kyōgen, have the same roots but different stage conventions: Noh is solemn drama, with actors joined onstage by four musicians, a chorus, and attendants who assist with props and other tasks; Kyōgen is comic and emphasizes dialogue. They developed together in the fourteenth century, the one complementing the other, with Kyōgen pieces performed during interludes, or between acts, of the main Noh play. Their costumes—ornately decorated silk weaves, often made in Nishijin, for Noh; simpler dyed fabrics for Kyōgen—were integral to expressing the age, social status, and gender of the formalized characters, all played by male actors.[1]

Noh dramas, which are usually drawn from legends, history, and literature, were standardized by the actor and playwright Zeami Motokiyo (1363–1443). Tending to focus on forceful emotions overpowering the protagonist, they often recount a ghost's return to the site of a significant event that took place before his or her death. This reflects Buddhist teachings, according to which a person could not find spiritual release after death if possessed by strong emotion or desire. The music, dance, recitation, and codified acting are all directed toward the expression of that emotion, climaxing at the end of the play. Celebration is another fundamental aspect of Noh, and prosperity, peace, and benevolent rule are themes reflected in the text and in the costumes' auspicious patterns. In the Edo period (1615–1868) Noh theater was supported by the shogunate, and the troupes were often sponsored by Buddhist temples and Shinto shrines.

Three types of Noh robe in the *kosode* style (with small sleeve openings) are represented in the Weber Collection: the *karaori*, the *atsuita*, and the *nuihaku*. The first of these derives from the lavishly brocaded silk fabrics imported from China (*karaori* means "Chinese weave") as early as the Heian period (794–1185) and used for aristocrats' garments (*karaorimono*) in the Kamakura period (1185–1333).[2] Later, in the Muromachi period (1392–1573), members of the audience customarily gave items of their own clothing to the Noh actors in appreciation; these precious gifts were transformed into costumes, a tradition that likely led to the creation of exquisite garments for the stage (known as *karaori* from the sixteenth century).[3] *Karaori* were used as overgarments for women's and young noblemen's roles (cat. 1). The ones with red details were designed for roles of young women; costumes without red were for playing women who were elderly or of divine nature.

During the Edo period, costumes and ordinary clothing became increasingly distinct. Everyday robes were rarely made of stiff, woven fabrics like *karaori*; instead, they were made of supple silk embellished with dyeing and embroidery. By preserving aspects of the rich woven garments worn by aristocrats and high-ranking samurai prior to the Edo period, opulent Noh costumes uniquely shed light on Japanese textile history.

Atsuita are heavy silk robes designed for male roles, such as monks, old men, warlords, gods, or demons (cat. 2). The term means "thick board," referring to thick (*atsuji*) fabrics that were wrapped around wooden boards for transportation. Brightly colored, they were often embellished with brocaded geometric patterns, stripes, motifs from Chinese legends, or Buddhist implements. Generally worn as an inner layer, the *atsuita* was revealed when one of the large sleeves of the *ōsode*-style outer garment (for example, a *happi*, *kariginu*, or *chōken*) was pulled back from the shoulder.

Nuihaku refers to a lavish decorative technique combining silk embroidery and metal-leaf application, which became popular for high-ranking women's *kosode* during the Momoyama period (1573–1615). As *nuihaku* garments were donated to outstanding Noh actors, the term became synonymous with the Noh robes made by this method.[4] They were used primarily for female roles and sometimes for young men (cat. 3).

In contrast to the Noh theater's ornate and luxurious costumes of brocaded silks and other woven fabrics, early Kyōgen actors dressed in everyday clothes; Kyōgen costumes developed only in the early Edo period. Many Kyōgen plays are about the master-servant relationship, featuring an "everyman" servant, Tarō Kaja, who gets into humorous scrapes and with whom the audience can easily identify (cat. 7). Other stock characters include the daimyo, the master, and the mountain monk.

As the art form evolved in the seventeenth century, the previously improvised acting became formalized, and more attention was paid to appearance. Kyōgen costumes, which were specific to each character, were typically made of dyed bast fibers. They included *suō* ensembles (an *ōsode*-style jacket with double-width sleeves and matching *hakama* pants) for samurai roles and boldly patterned, often comic, *kataginu* vests, typically worn by actors playing servants.[5]

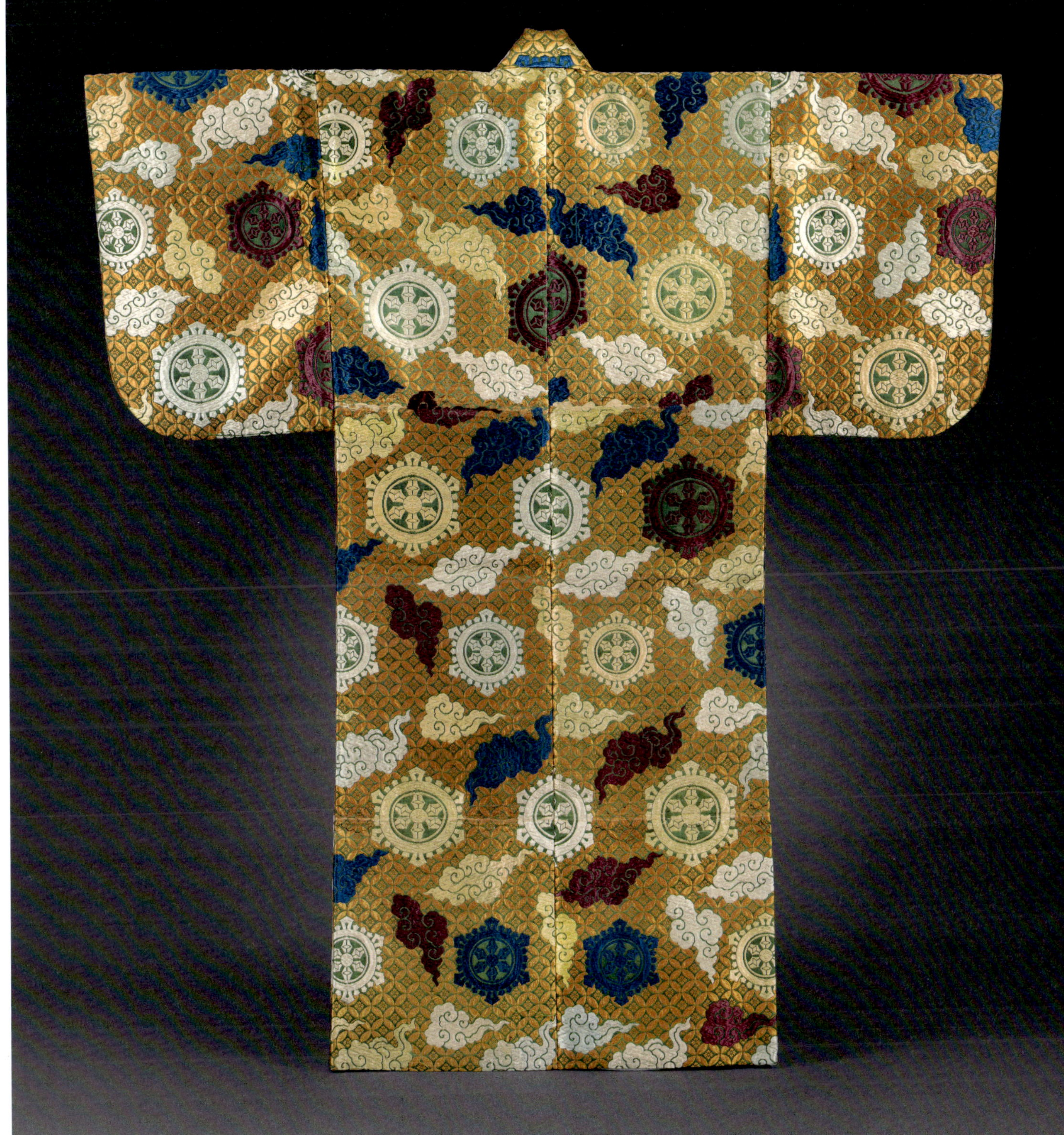

1 青竹色地輪宝瑞雲模様唐織
Noh costume (*karaori*) with dharma wheels and clouds.
Edo period (1615–1868), mid-18th century. Twill-weave silk with silk supplementary weft patterning, 56⅛ × 52⅜ in. (142.5 × 133 cm).
Lent by John C. Weber Collection

This Noh robe, or *karaori*, was inspired by sophisticated, layered patterns seen on early seventeenth-century examples. Weaving large raised patterns against a background of smaller motifs in semirelief was a novel technique borrowed in the early Edo period from China. Here, auspicious clouds and dharma wheels—the latter referring to the act of teaching by Buddha Shakyamuni—in white, beige, purple, and blue are represented on a ground of interlinked circles (*shippō*) with stylized flowers in the center, a felicitous pattern. Both the raised patterns and the golden-brown silk-floss ground motifs are woven with floating supplementary wefts on a dark green twill-weave ground, a technique also known as *karaori*. The word *karaori* (literally "Chinese weave") originally referred to luxurious brocaded silks with supplementary weft patterning imported from China but later became associated with this particular weave and then came to signify the Noh robe for which the woven fabric was used. Though *karaori* were worn for women's and young noblemen's roles, this costume likely served as an inner garment for the latter, as Buddhist implements such as dharma wheels are typically considered masculine.

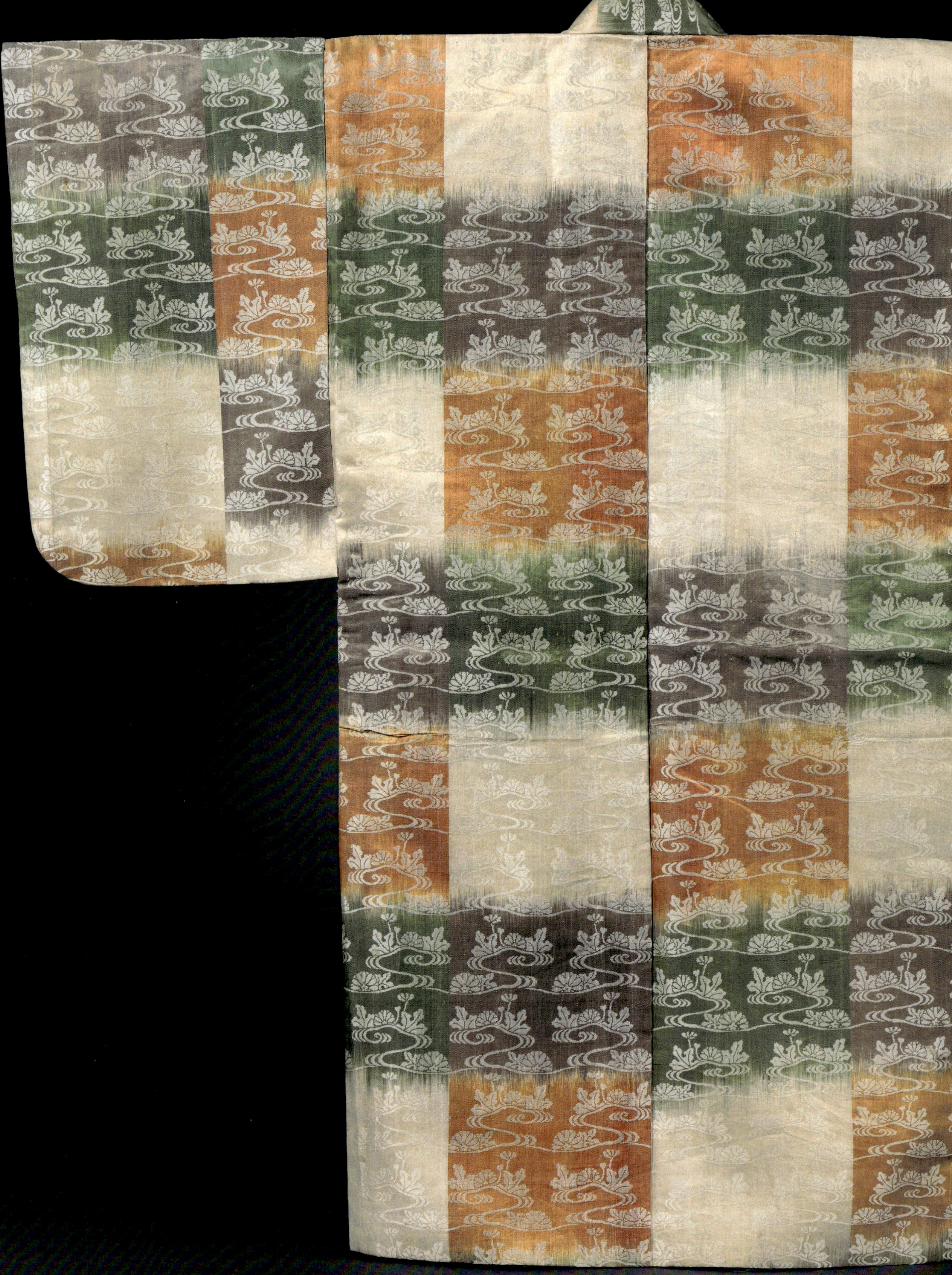

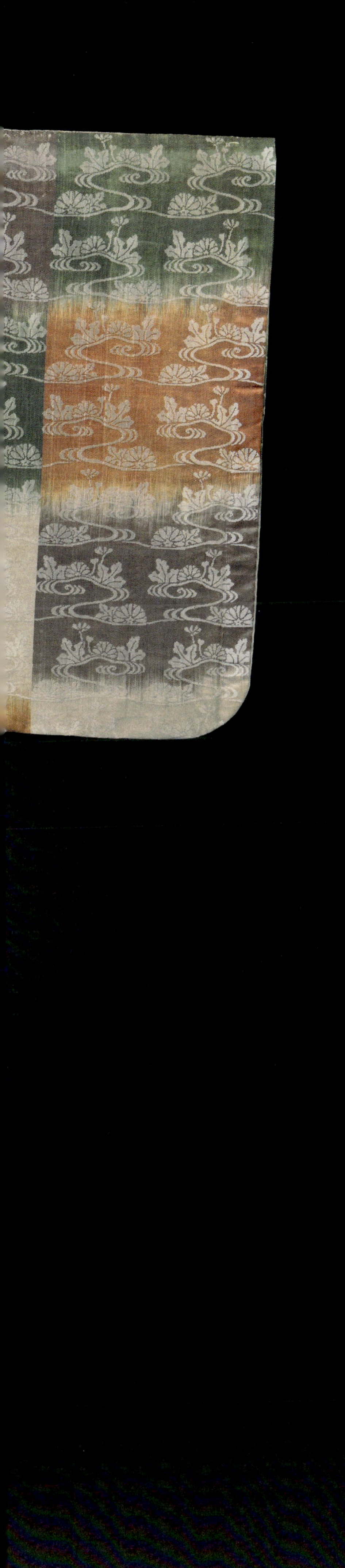

2 白地紅緑濃茶段替菊流水模様厚板
Noh costume (*atsuita*) with checkered ground and chrysanthemums in stream. Edo period (1615–1868), 18th century. Twill-weave silk with silk supplementary weft patterning, 54 × 53 in. (137 × 134.6 cm). Lent by John C. Weber Collection

Green, orange-red, white, and brownish-purple blocks form a colorful, contrasting background for white chrysanthemums drifting on flowing water. The pattern refers to the ancient Chinese legend of the Chrysanthemum Boy (Kikujidō) or the Noh play based on that story. It tells of a youth who is banished from court and spends centuries diligently copying a couplet from the Lotus Sutra, one of Buddhism's most important scriptures, on chrysanthemum leaves. Having drunk miraculous water from the stream where dewdrops had fallen from the chrysanthemums, he was freed from aging and illness and was unaware of the lapsed time.

This robe's warp yarns were tie-dyed before they were woven, resulting in the characteristically blurry ikat pattern. Supplementary glossed silk wefts were used to express the flowers and waves. *Atsuita* robes with checks, geometric patterns, and Chinese motifs were worn mainly by male leads as undergarments, but this example was shortened and refashioned for a child's role, probably after being damaged at the hem.

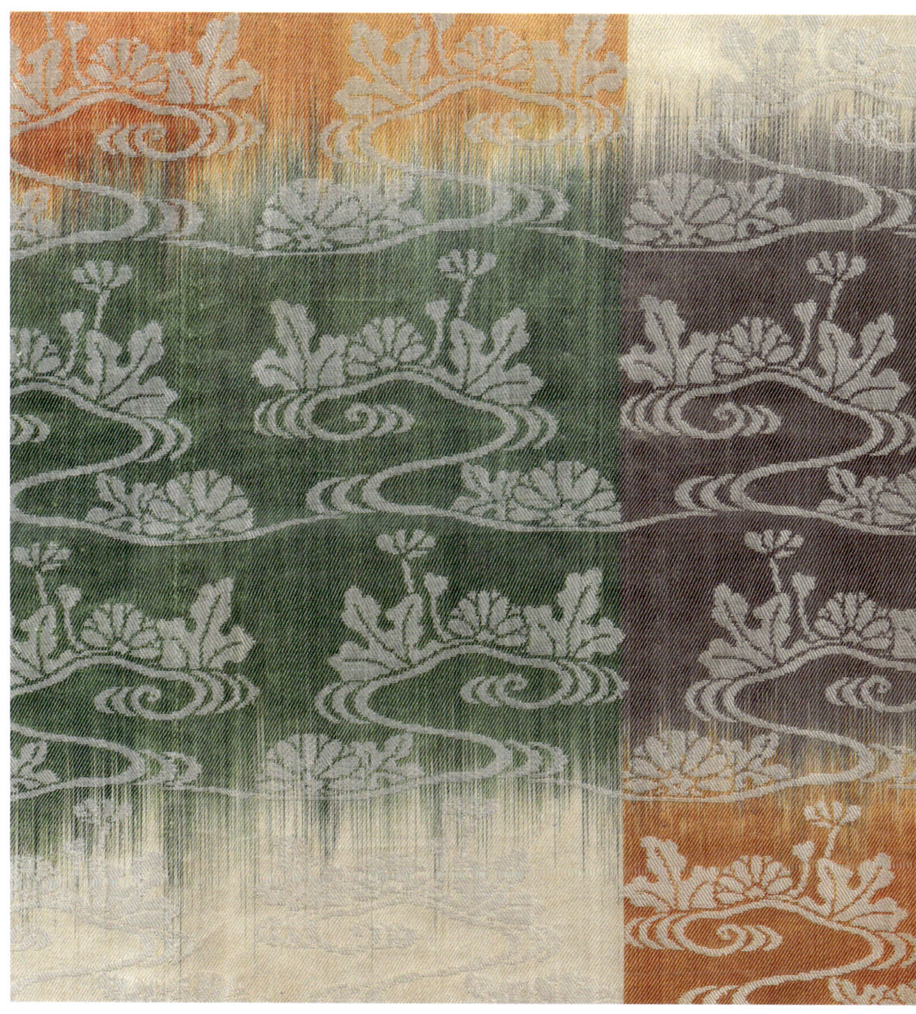

3 茶緑段蘭七宝模様縫箔

Noh costume (*nuihaku*) with orchids and interlinked circles. Edo period (1615–1868), 18th century. Plain-weave silk with gold- and silver-leaf application and silk embroidery, 59⅞ × 53⅛ in. (152 × 135 cm). Lent by John C. Weber Collection

The alternating bands of green and brown on this Noh robe are embellished with two distinctive patterns, recalling an earlier style of *nuihaku*. The green bands feature interlinked circles (*shippō*) with stylized flowers in their centers, all done in satin-stitch embroidery in yellow, white, purple, blue, gray, and brown silk floss. *Shippō* is an auspicious pattern associated with the Seven Treasures of Buddhism, as well as with the prosperity of descendants, good relationships, and harmony. The swaying orchids that fill the brown bands are a type (wind orchid, or *Vanda falcata*) popular among samurai as a symbol of bravery. They were executed in silk embroidery and stenciled gold and silver leaf; the reflective metallic decoration was particularly well suited for the stage. Most of the silver patterns are lost to oxidation, but the gold ones remain visible. *Nuihaku* are worn for roles of women and young men.

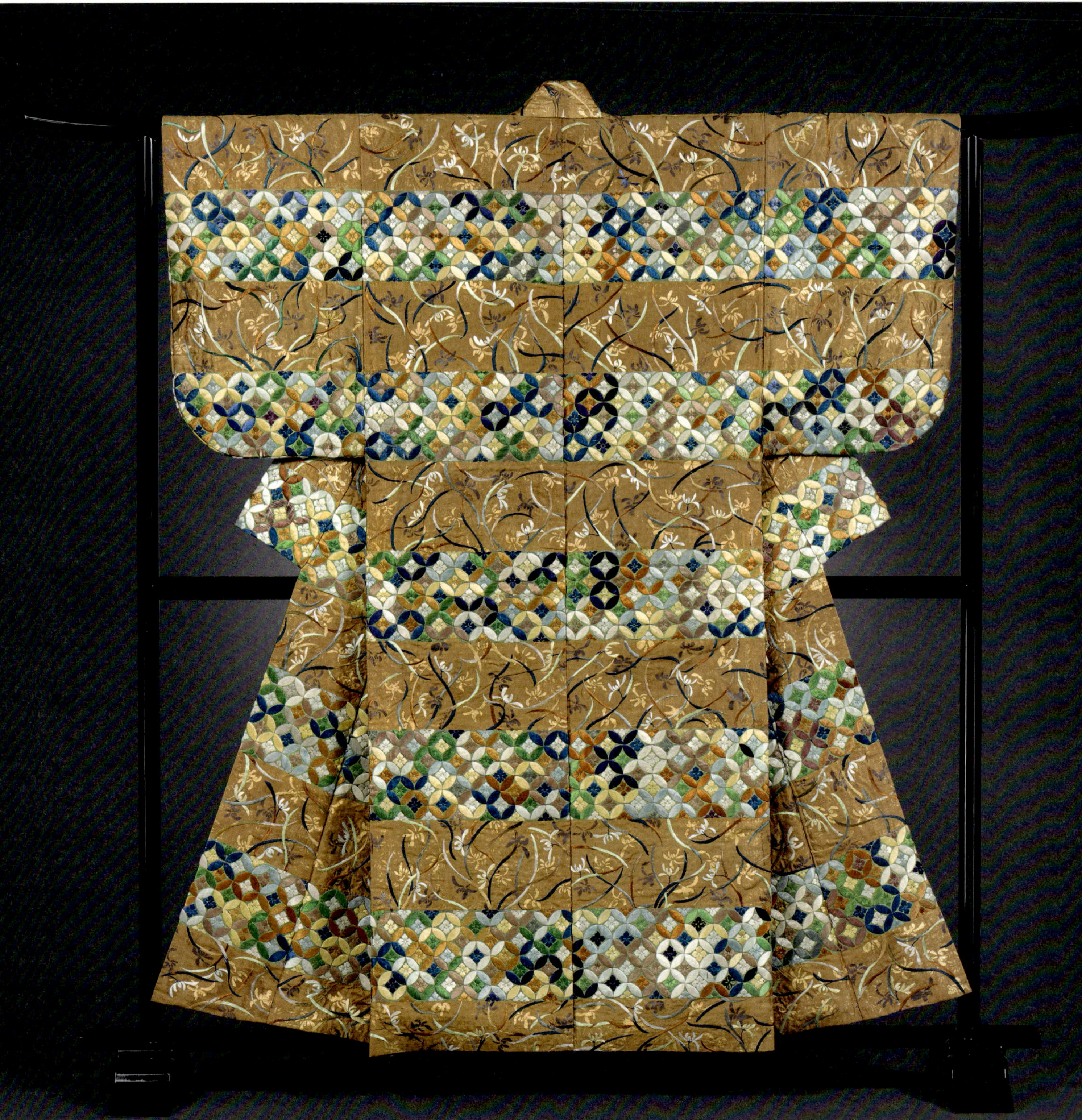

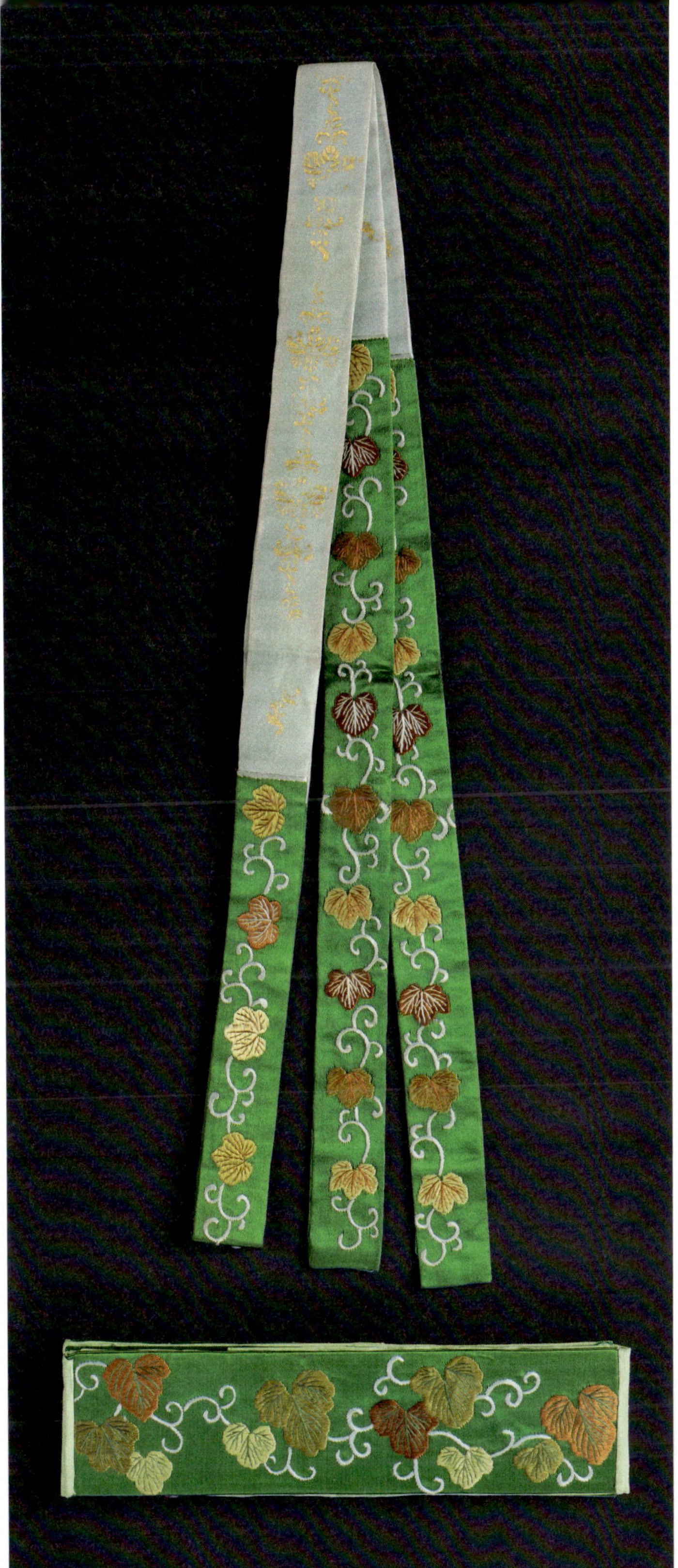

4 緑地蔦唐草模様鬘帯と腰帯
Headband (*kazura-obi*) and sash (*koshi-obi*) with ivy.
Edo period (1615–1868), late 18th–early 19th century.
Satin-weave silk with silk embroidery and plain-weave ramie with gold-leaf application; headband: 1½ × 90 in. (3.8 × 228.6 cm); sash: 2¾ × 106 in. (7 × 269.2 cm).
Lent by John C. Weber Collection

Headbands, such as this one with a pattern of ivy and stylized arabesques (*karakusa*), are used to hold wigs for female roles in place with a decorative effect. The band is tied in a knot at the back of the head, leaving the long ends to trail. As with sashes, only the visible sections — the middle, which runs across the forehead, and the ends — are decorated. This elegant set has a deep green ground with rich silk embroidery in green and brown hues, using fixed stitches (*tome-nui*). The ramie sections connecting the decorated parts are embellished with stenciled gold-leaf patterns (*surihaku*) of paulownia flowers and leaves.

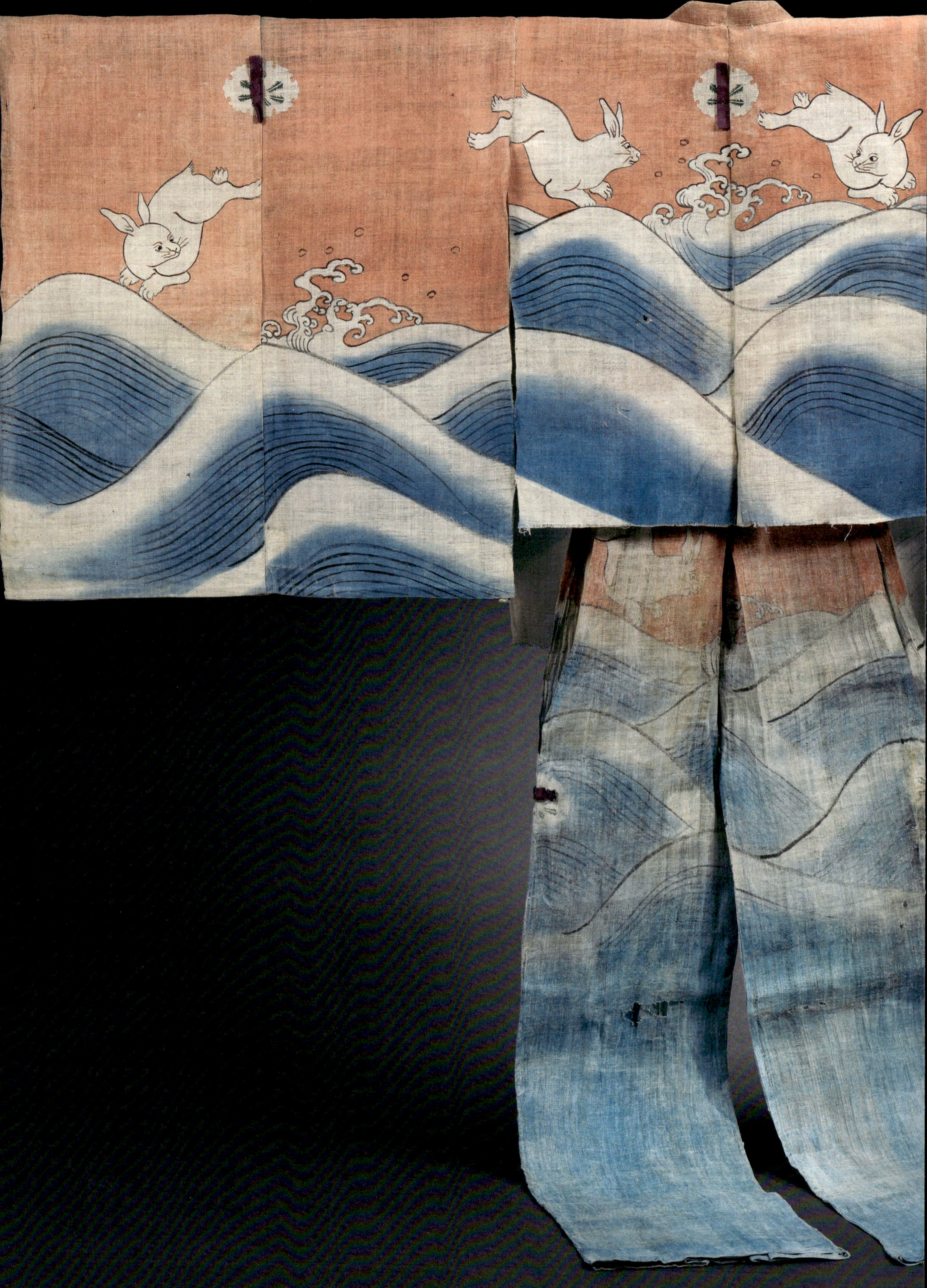

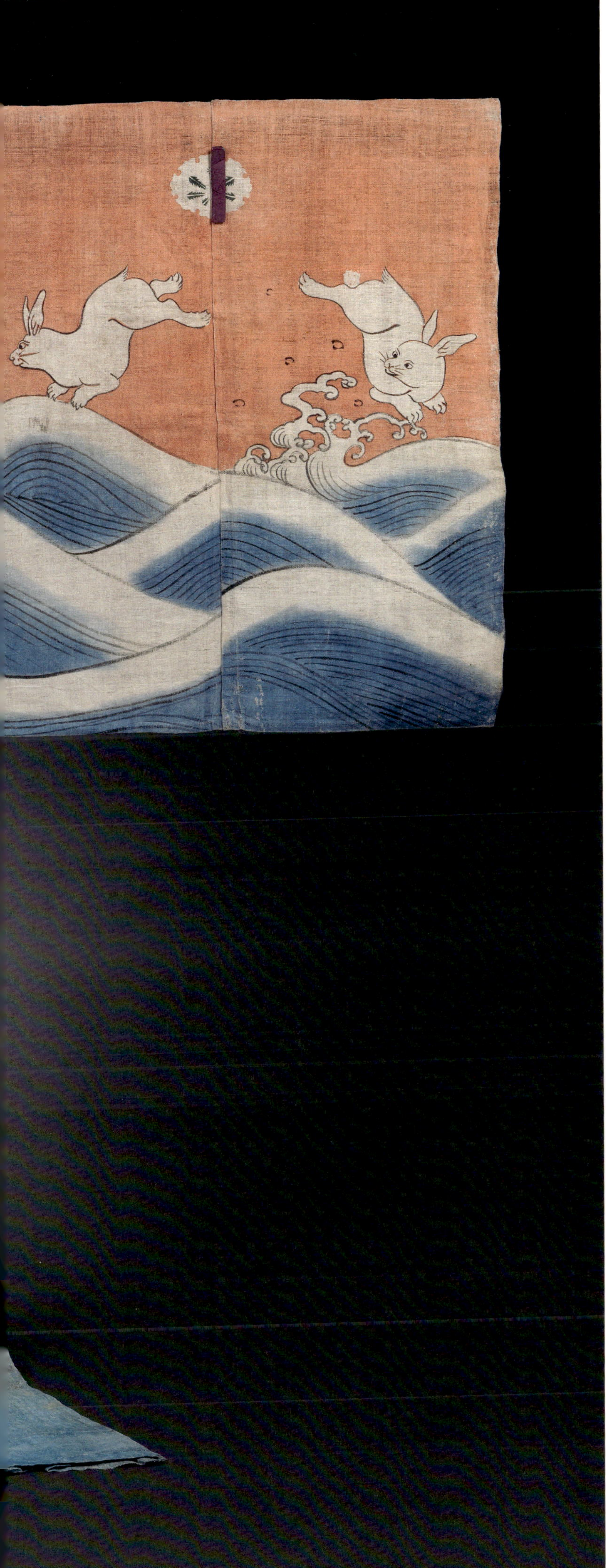

Kyōgen costumes are simple by comparison to the luxurious garments used in Noh theater and are typically made of dyed hemp. The *suō* — a suit made of hemp, with an unlined jacket with double-width sleeves and large sleeve openings (*ōsode*) and matching pleated *hakama* pants — was originally part of the samurai wardrobe and later adapted to Noh and Kyōgen, but for different roles.[6] In Kyōgen, the *suō* is worn by a successful person of some standing.

On the suit at left, white rabbits hop over blue-and-white waves. The playful motif refers to "The Hare of Inaba," a story in the *Records of Ancient Matters* (*Kojiki*, ca. 710), a sacred Shinto text, in which a clever rabbit tricks sharks into letting him hop across their backs so he can cross the sea. This story was later referenced in the Noh play *Chikubushima* (Chikubushima Island), which describes the moon's reflection in Lake Biwa as a rabbit (which legendarily inhabits the moon) running over the waves. The jacket is decorated with the crest of the Kyōgen schools — a shepherd's-purse flower within a snowflake; there are three on the back and two on the front. *Suō* with large patterns and bright colors were used for roles of amiable, benevolent characters, such as a bridegroom, a daimyo, or a wealthy man. The long pants (*naga-bakama*) indicate that this one was designed for the character of an influential figure. As the pants are subject to intense wear (the actor steps on the pants' long trains), it is rare to find a complete ensemble like this one. More typically, only the suit jacket survives, as did the one on the following pages, which is decorated with a stylized design of gourds, leaves, and vines.

5 波に兎模様素襖袴

Kyōgen suit (*suō*) with rabbits jumping over waves. Edo period (1615–1868), mid-19th century. Plain-weave hemp with tube-drawn paste-resist dyeing (*tsutsugaki*) with hand-painted details; jacket: 30½ × 72 in. (77.5 × 183 cm); pants length: 64½ in. (164 cm). Lent by John C. Weber Collection

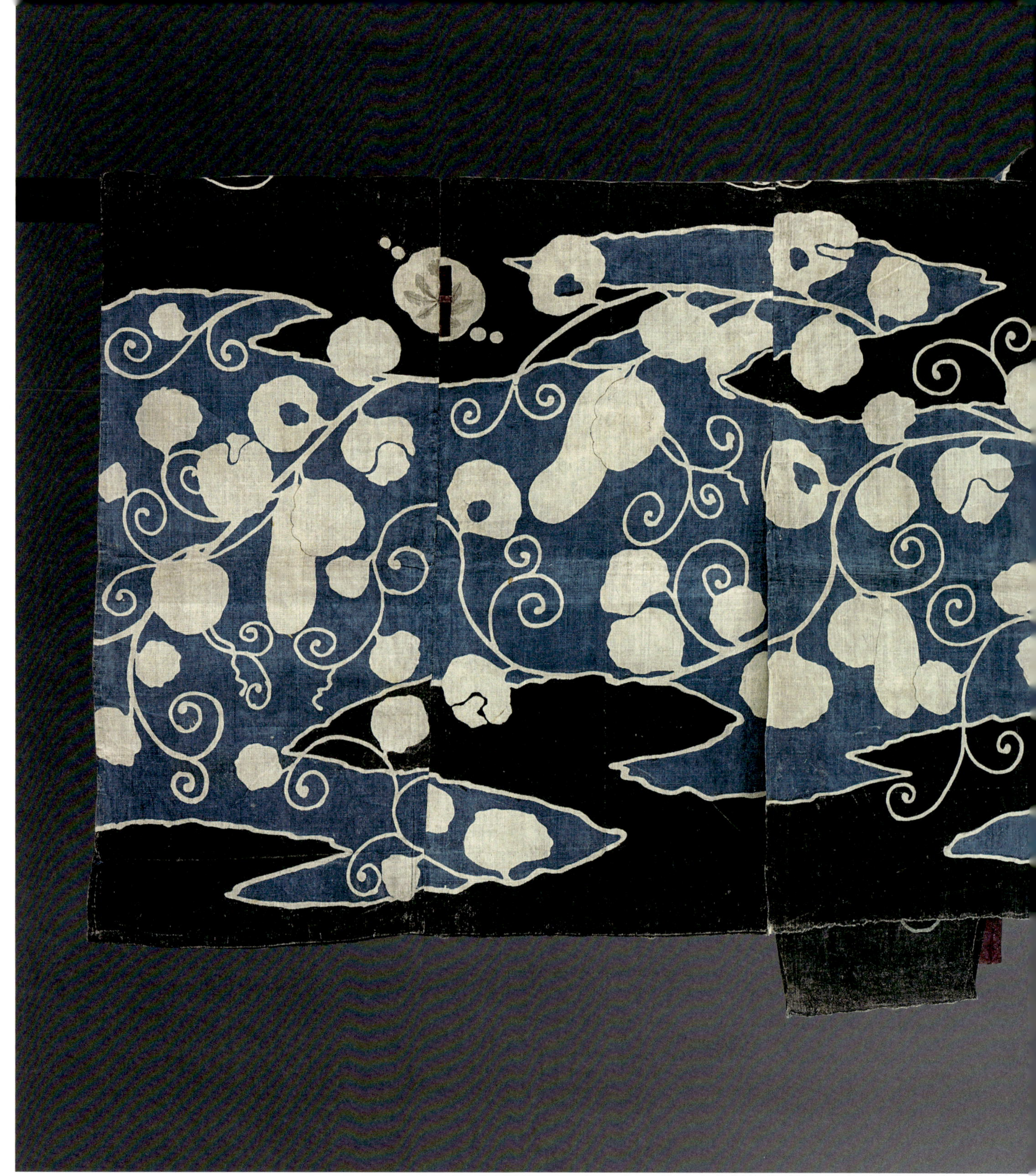

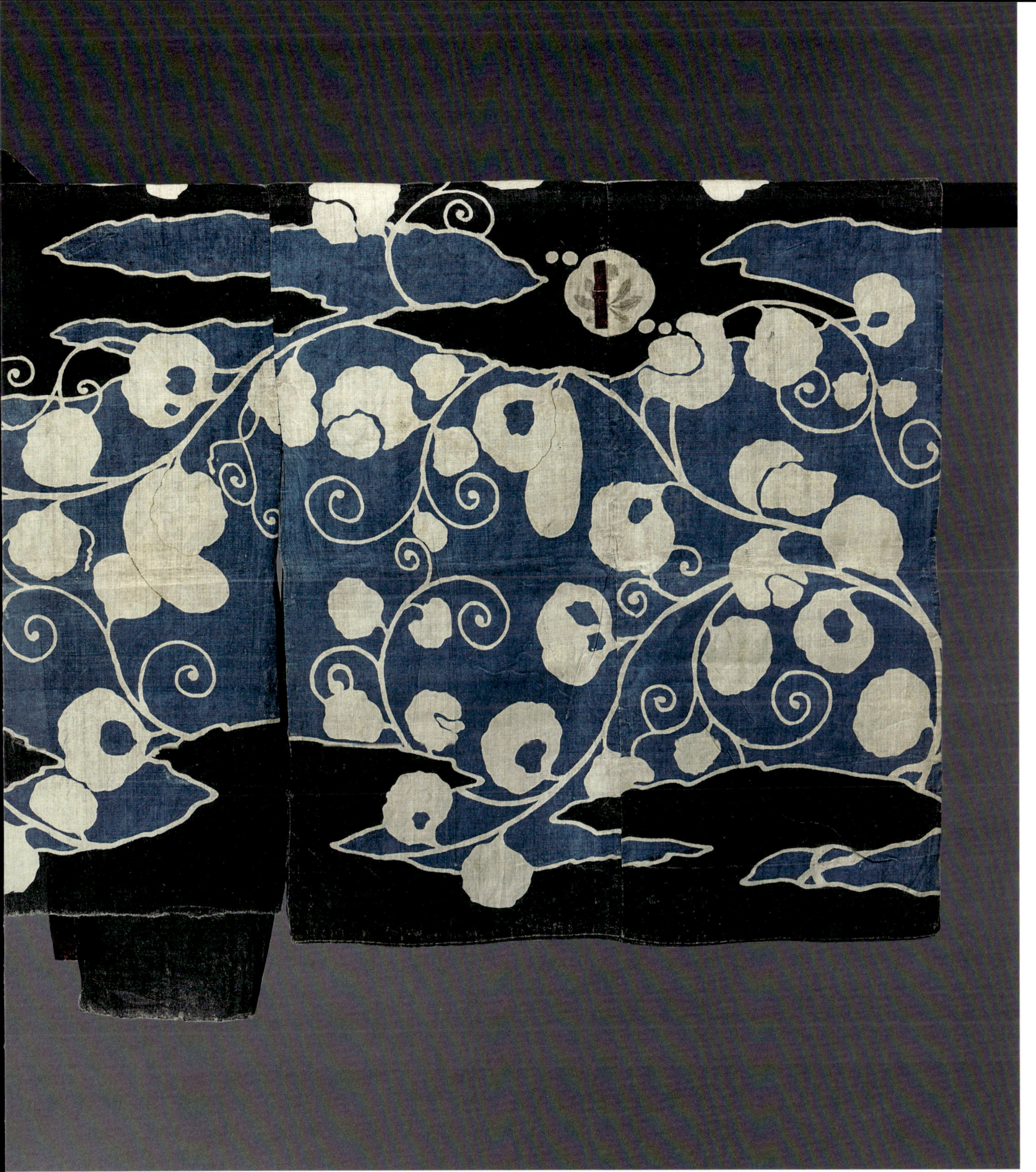

6 瓢箪模様素襖
Kyōgen suit (*suō*) jacket with gourd vines. Edo period (1615–1868), first half of 19th century. Plain-weave hemp with tube-drawn paste-resist dyeing (*tsutsugaki*), 41 × 82½ in. (104.1 × 209.6 cm). Lent by John C. Weber Collection

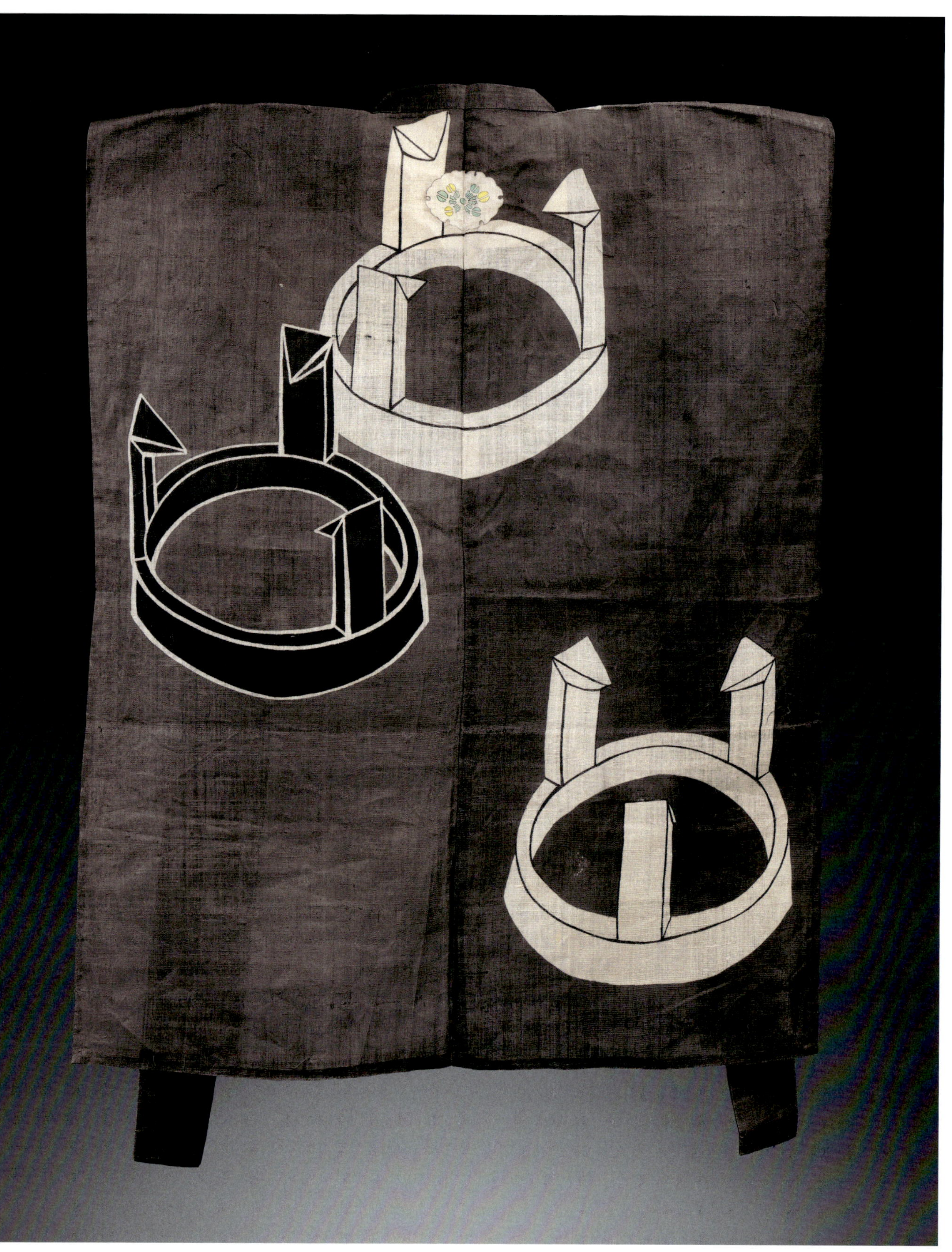

7 五徳模様肩衣

Vest (*kataginu*) ensemble with trivets. Edo period (1615–1868), first half of 19th century. Plain-weave hemp with stencil paste-resist dyeing (*kata-zome*); vest: 33 × 26½ in. (83.8 × 67.3 cm); pants length: 33 in. (83.8 cm). Lent by John C. Weber Collection

The most characteristic Kyōgen costume is probably the *kataginu*. This broad-shouldered, vestlike garment is usually decorated with large bold patterns related to the role being played. As most *kataginu* are worn by actors playing servants, typical patterns include animals, vegetables, and household items. The vest is worn over short *hakama* pants and a robe, with its front panels hanging in front of the pants, its back covering the hips, and the whole *kataginu* tied with a cotton sash.

The back of this *kataginu* (opposite) is decorated with three trivets on a dark gray ground, as well as with the shepherd's-purse-in-snowflake Kyōgen crest. Trivet patterns were likely favored for Kyōgen costumes because the word is written with the characters "five virtues." The Noh play *Iron Trivet* (*Kanawa*) may also have inspired the motif's development. The pants (below) are embellished with auspicious motifs and treasures in crest format on a green ground.

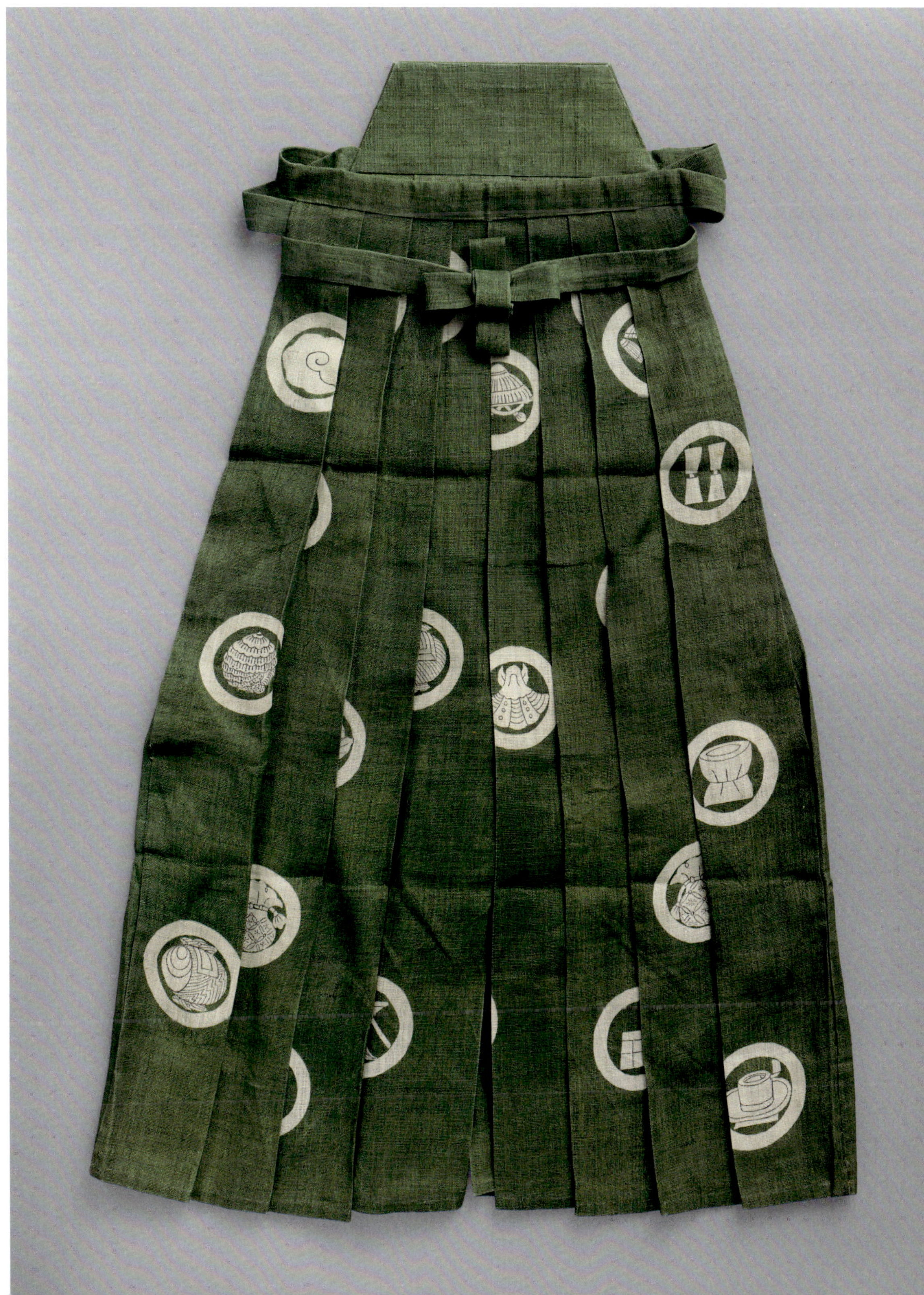

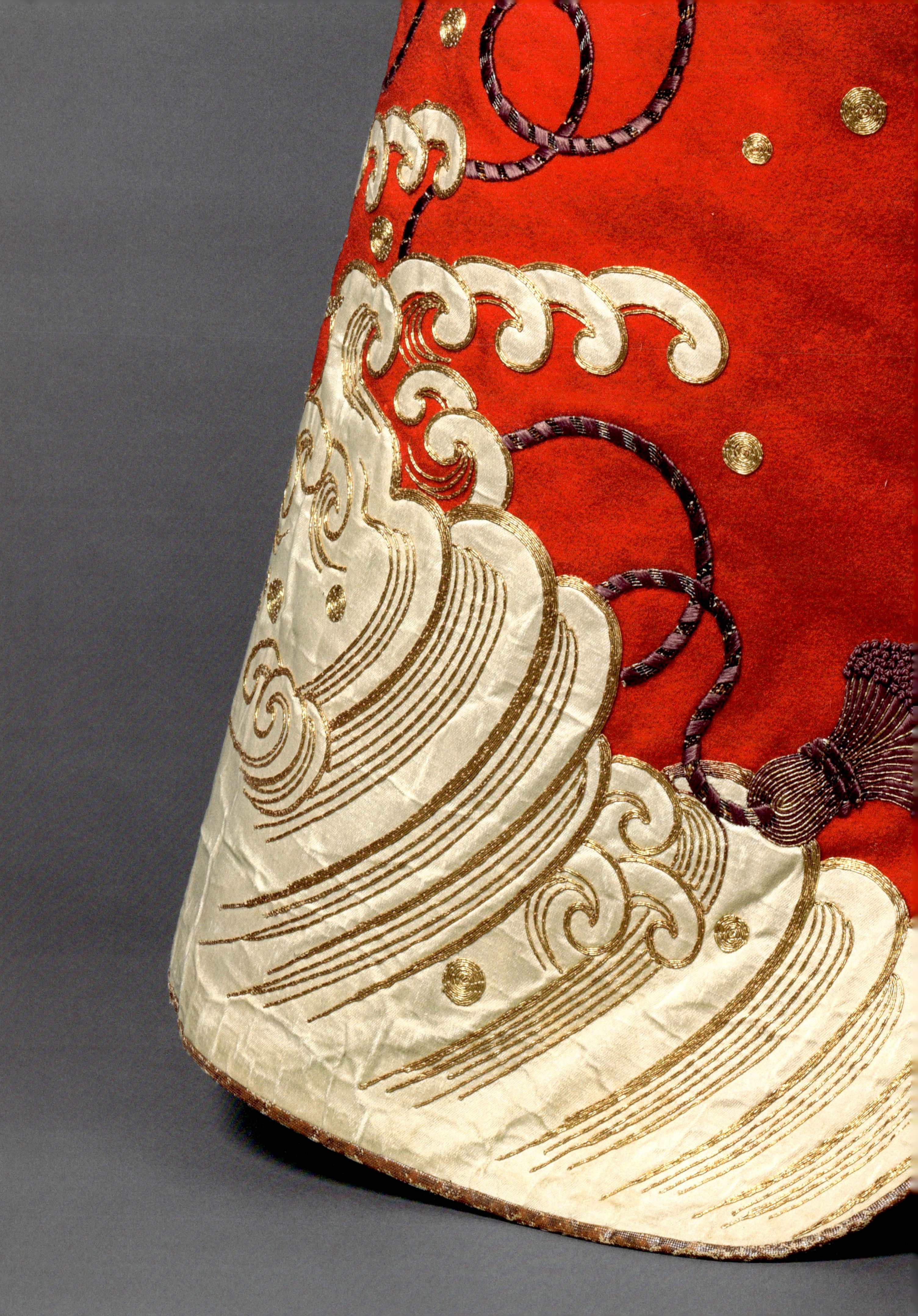

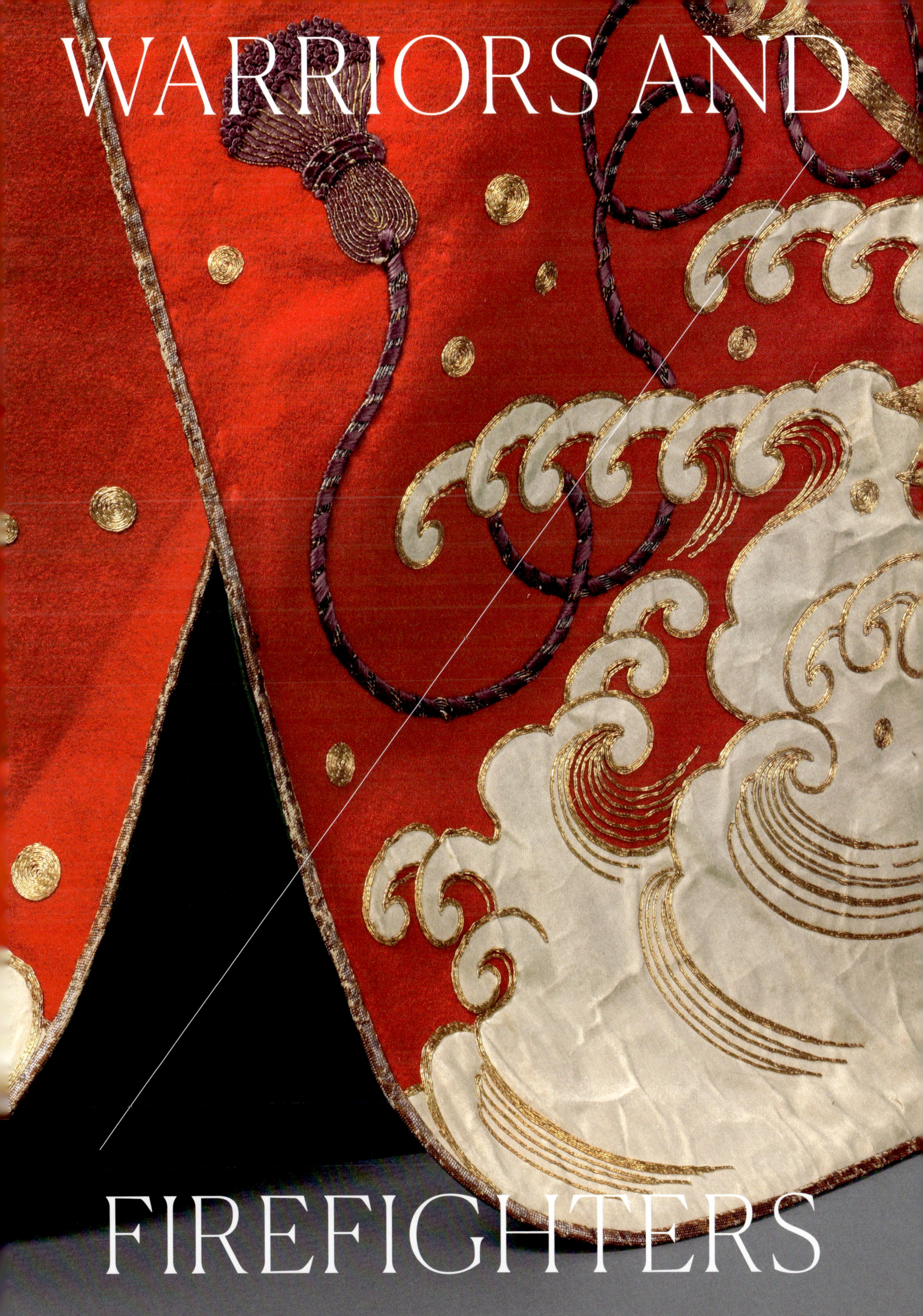

WARRIORS AND FIREFIGHTERS

SPECIALIZED APPAREL WORN TO CONDUCT dangerous tasks — whether fighting enemy soldiers or fighting fires — exemplifies the fusion of function and fashion in Japanese textiles. High-ranking samurai had access to the finest of materials, and they used battle surcoats (*jinbaori*) to project status and individual taste. *Jinbaori*, produced from about the fifteenth through the mid-nineteenth century, were sleeveless garments originally worn over armor as protection from the rain, wind, and cold; they eventually became ceremonial wear.

Most of the early surcoats were made of hemp or strong Japanese paper with persimmon tanning. They were decorated with flamboyant, boldly colored designs to increase visibility, facilitate identification, and express valor, and also with religious symbols to invoke divine protection and good outcomes. Samurai generally wore them when on a campaign and traveling by horse. In battle, the surcoat worn by the commander served as a proof for the troops that their leader was alive and confirmed his position.

The arrival of the Portuguese in 1543 brought significant changes to samurai battle wear, owing to both new forms of warfare and access to new materials and designs. Before the Portuguese introduced firearms to Japan, most warriors were mounted archers, and their armor (*ōyoroi*) was constructed of small rectangular slabs of lacquered leather or iron, laced together with cords of silk or leather. This armor gave archers easy arm movement while protecting them from enemy arrows. The use of European matchlock guns called for a more impenetrable armor. Modern armor (*tōseigusoku*) was made of large iron plates that closely followed the shape of the body. As the new armor more fully concealed the decorative undergarments, the surcoats became even more prominent than before.[1]

With the advent of global trade in 1543, expensive fabrics from faraway lands reached Japan, and *jinbaori* became increasingly luxurious. They were commonly made of thick, napped wool (*rasha*) imported from Europe (cat. 8), which proved to be warm and durable, and were often decorated with velvet, fine Chinese silk damask, and gold-brocaded silk.[2] Japan was unified at the end of the sixteenth century under three forceful warlords, Oda Nobunaga, Toyotomi Hideyoshi, and Tokugawa Ieyasu, each of whom expressed his unique character and flamboyant taste through lavish garments, including *jinbaori*, sometimes incorporating rare and precious imported materials, such as feathers, Indian calico (*sarasa* chintz), and Persian kilim.[3]

The forging of a new political system brought an overhaul of many long-standing conventions, including clothing styles for the military class. *Jinbaori* had developed from long-sleeved garments, such as the *dōbuku* (a coat worn by shoguns and high-ranking samurai), but in the Momoyama period (1573–1615) came to be influenced by Western garments such as mantles. The standing collar, rounded forms, buttons, and buttonholes are Western-style features of many *jinbaori*. As peace settled upon Japan in the Edo period, the *jinbaori* gradually lost its combat function and became a decorative symbol of power and bravery, often used in ceremonies and processions (cat. 9).[4]

Decoration was also important to firefighters' garments, which were far from purely utilitarian uniforms. Firefighters enjoyed respect and high status in urban Japan, especially in Edo, where wooden architecture and crowded living conditions led to frequent outbreaks of fire. The primary method of extinguishing a fire was to demolish the buildings surrounding those already ablaze to prevent the fire from spreading.

Firefighters and the areas for which they were responsible in Edo were classified according to social status, as samurai firefighters and *chōnin* firefighters. The samurai firefighters' garments were often made of expensive, imported wool, similar to the *jinbaori* (cat. 12). The commoners wore reversible coats (*hikeshi-banten*) made of several layers of thick, quilted cotton fabric, with a plain indigo-dyed exterior and an elaborately decorated interior. For fighting fires, these cotton coats were soaked in water and worn with the plain side facing out; they were worn inside out after the fire was extinguished or during festivals. Trousers, headgear, gloves, and socks of the same material completed the set.

Woodblock prints of warrior-heroes and mythical creatures, especially those by Utagawa Kuniyoshi (1798–1861), inspired many of the jackets' interior designs (cat. 15). Kuniyoshi, one of the most popular print artists of the time, came from a family of textile dyers, giving him a good sense for fashion trends. His compositions appealed to the vigorous young firefighters of the military capital, many of whom were tattooed with motifs similar to those inside their coats.[5]

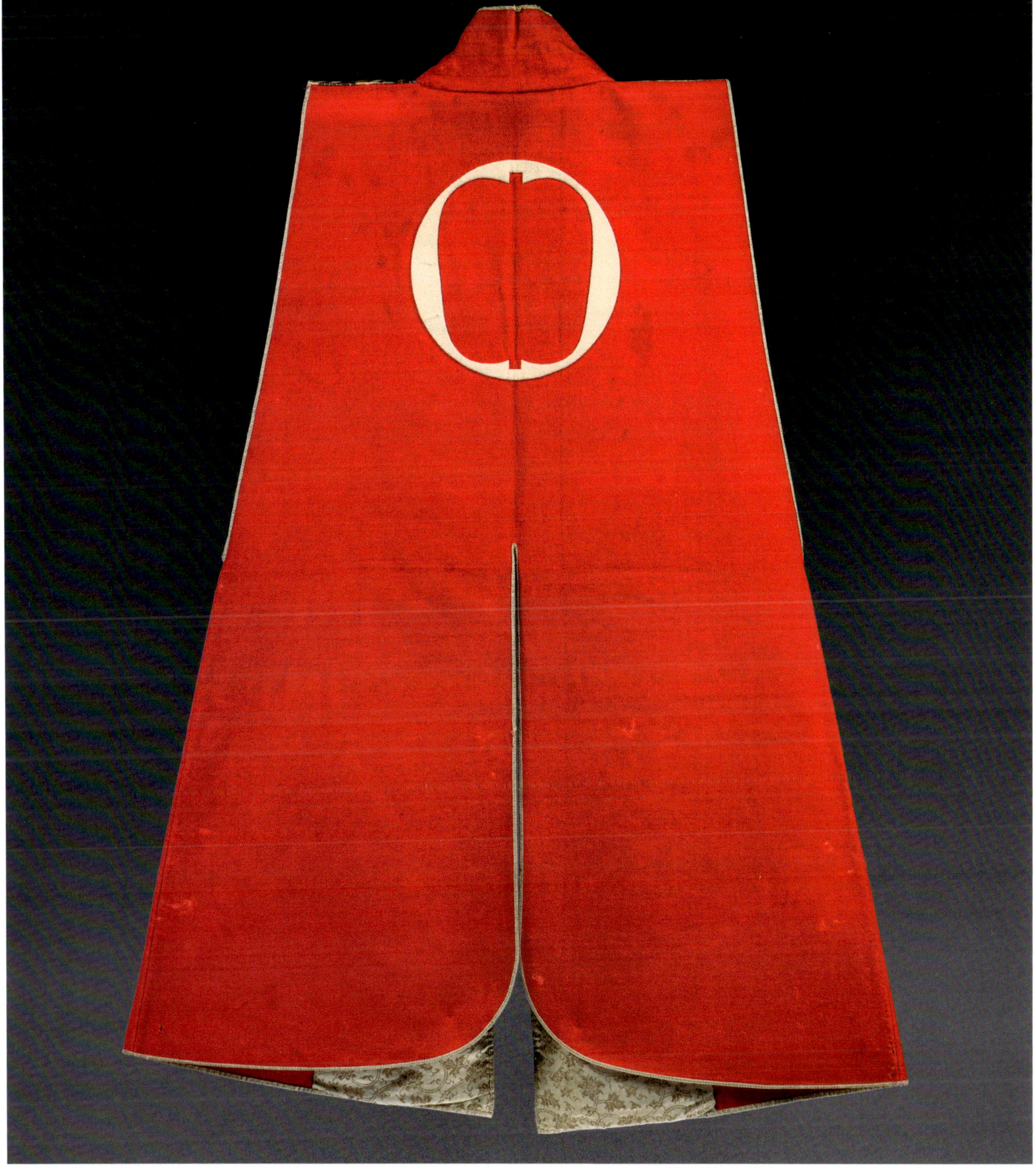

8 猩々緋羅紗地唐団扇模様陣羽織

Battle surcoat (*jinbaori*) with fan. Edo period (1615–1868), first half of 17th century. Wool (*rasha*), lining of twill-weave silk with supplementary metal thread, 42½ x 38¼ in. (108 x 97 cm). Lent by John C. Weber Collection

The most suitable material for a durable, visibly striking, and warm battle surcoat was wool, which in the seventeenth century could not be produced in Japan and had to be imported from Portugal and the Netherlands. *Rasha* (from the Portuguese *raxa*) is a thick, plain-weave wool fabric with a napped surface. It arrived predyed, most popularly in a deep scarlet derived from cochineal and tin mordant. The fabric was often requested by high-ranking samurai in that color, probably for its associations with fire, blood, fierceness, and talismanic qualities against evil. For this *jinbaori*, cochineal from the Americas, most likely Mexico, was used.[6]

The surcoat has an elongated shape and a decorative epaulet-like strip called a "sword support" (*tachi-uke*) sewn to the upper shoulder. The position of the shoulder piece here indicates that this example is an early *jinbaori*, but the use of mid-eighteenth-century European silk reveals the piece to be a replacement, possibly to conceal use. At the center of the back is a cut-out and finely stitched white *rasha* appliqué in the shape of a Chinese-style military signal fan (*tōuchiwa* or *gunbai*). It appears to be only a decorative pattern, not a family crest. The lining of the *jinbaori* is white silk brocaded with a gold peony arabesque; when the coat was worn with the collar folded back, the white lapels enhanced the garment's elegance.[7]

9 黒羅紗地破れ扇模様陣羽織
Battle surcoat (*jinbaori*) with tattered fan. Edo period (1615–1868), early 19th century. Wool (*rasha*), lining of twill-weave silk with supplementary metal thread, 34½ × 28½ in. (87.6 × 72.4 cm). Lent by John C. Weber Collection

The *jinbaori* ceased to be battle wear during the peaceful Edo period. The collar, originally designed to be closed against the cold, evolved into the open collar on this example, indicating a decorative, ceremonial use. The "sword support" shoulder piece (*tachi-uke*) was rotated toward the front, so it was no longer functional.

This thick wool fabric was dyed black with logwood. The lining is a brocaded red silk with silver threads (*ginran*) woven in a paulownia arabesque pattern. At the back of the *jinbaori*, directly above the slit, is the pattern of a tattered fan in white wool appliqué and gold embroidery. Battle fans had crucial roles in giving signals on the battlefield and were believed to have the ability to summon deities, good luck, and spiritual powers. This unusual tattered-fan motif might signify a military commander's determination to keep fighting and never to retreat, no matter how injured. It also suggests the fragility of life and the inevitability of decay.[8]

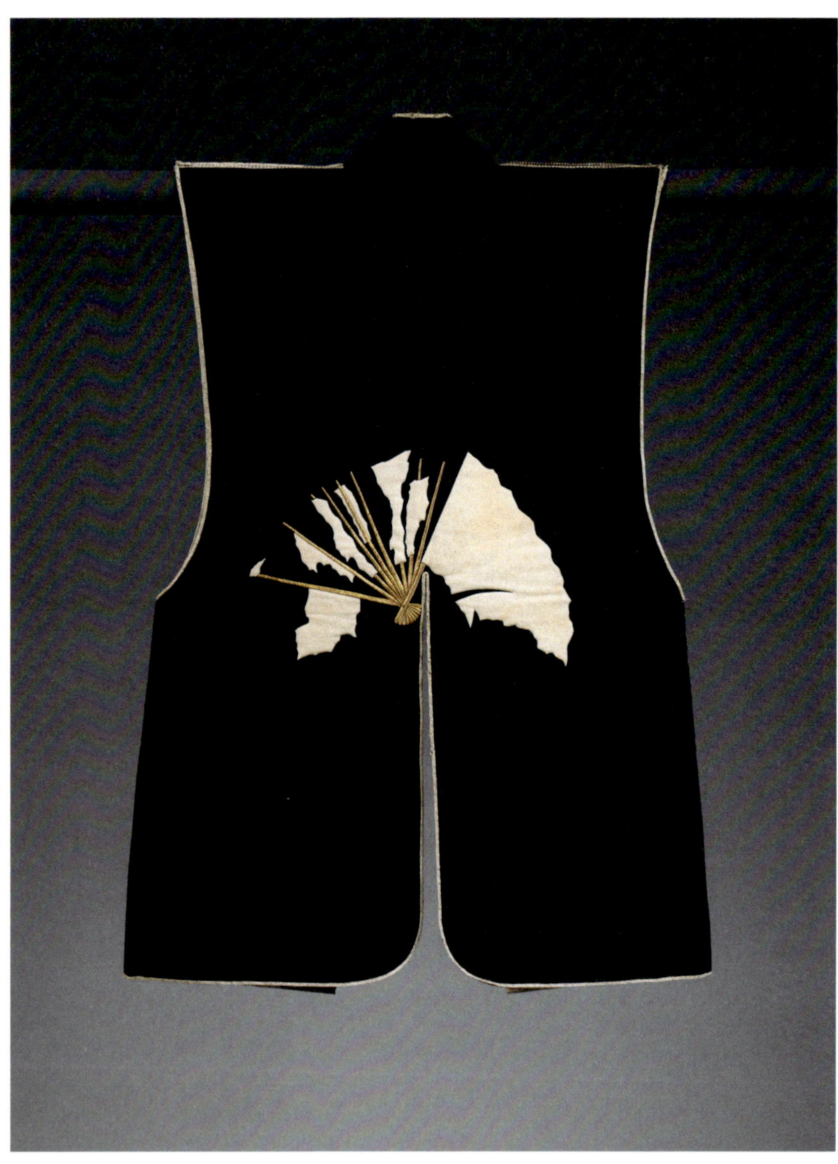

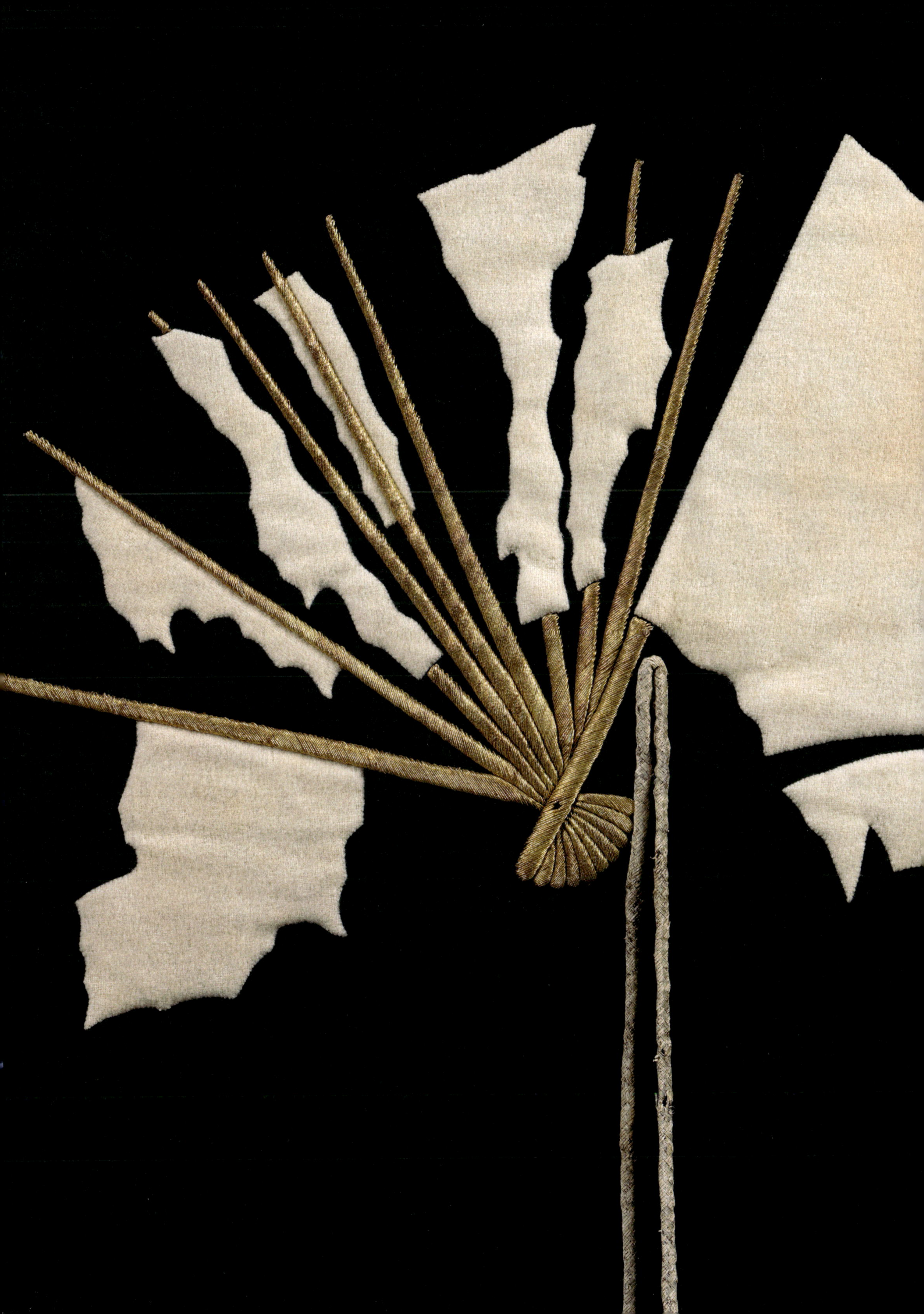

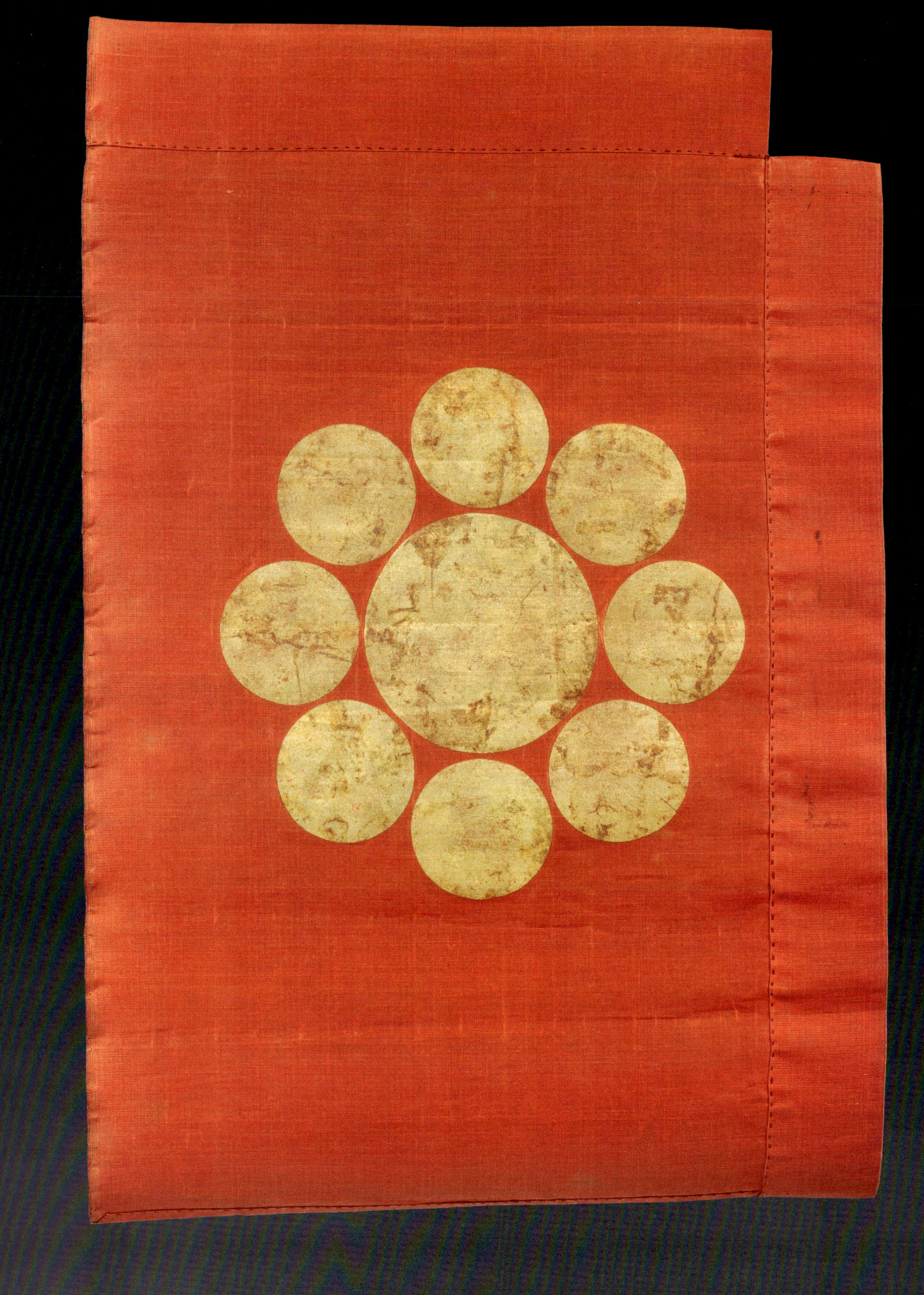

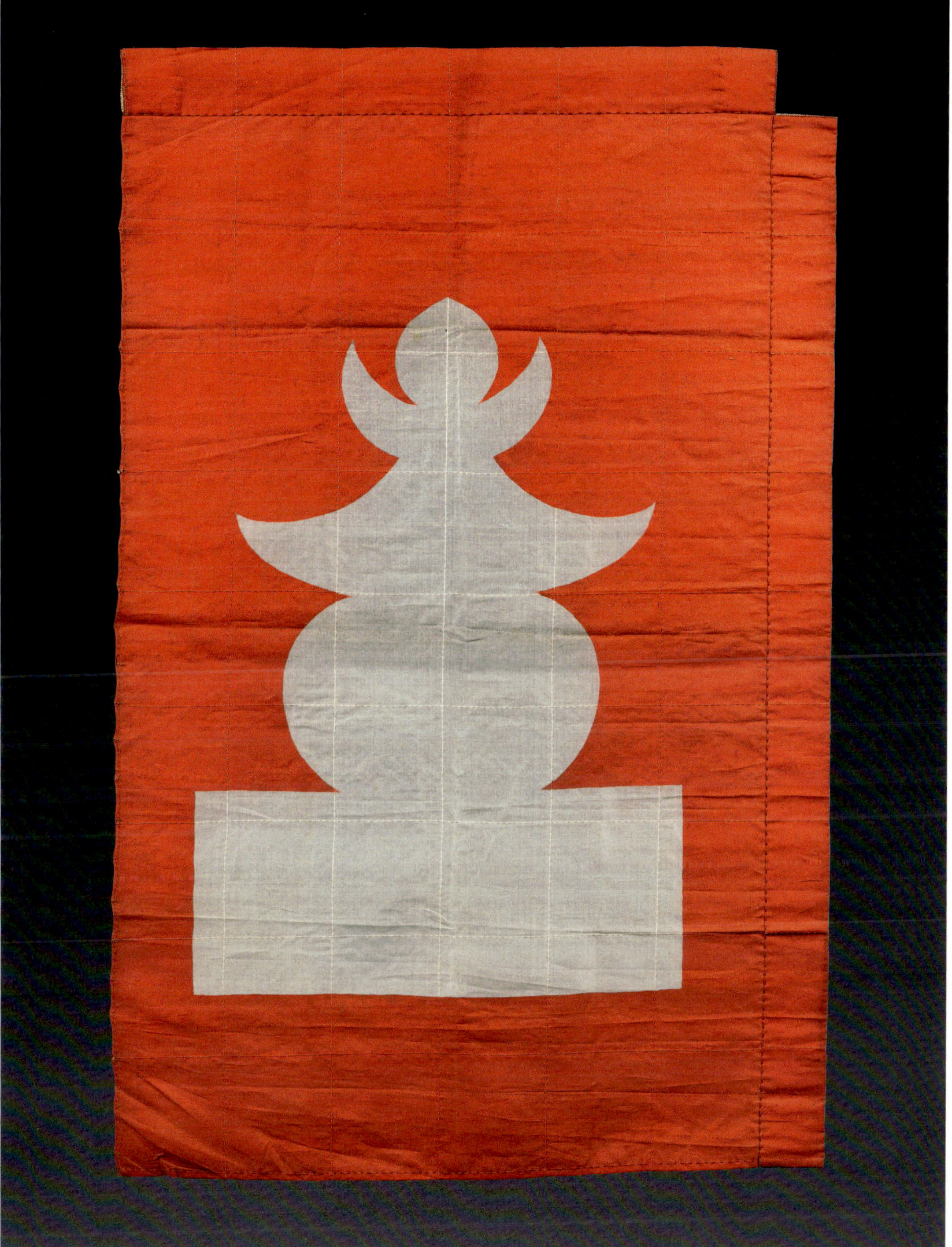

10 赤地九曜紋指物
Battle flag (*sashimono*) with nine-circle crest. Edo period (1615–1868), first half of 19th century. Plain-weave silk with gold-leaf application, 22½ × 15 in. (57.2 × 38.1 cm). Lent by John C. Weber Collection

11 赤地五輪塔紋指物
Battle flag (*sashimono*) with five-element stupa. Edo period (1615–1868), first half of 19th century. Plain-weave silk with stencil paste-resist dyeing (*kata-zome*), 20½ × 20 in. (74.9 × 50.8 cm). Lent by John C. Weber Collection

The dramatic combination of red and gold was popular on *jinbaori* as well as on armor, and this warrior aesthetic was also reflected on battle flags. At left, a crest executed in thin gold leaf shines against a vivid red ground. The crest's large circle surrounded by eight smaller ones refers to the nine planets and is associated with the Hosokawa family, a prominent samurai clan. This type of small banner (*sashimono*) with the daimyo's crest was worn for identification, mounted on a pole and attached to the back of the warrior's armor.

The other flag has a stencil-dyed crest representing a five-element stupa. This kind of stupa served as a grave marker or cenotaph, a function originating from a similar stupa that contained relics of the historical Buddha. Made of five pieces of stone, it also represents the five elements: from bottom to top, earth, water, fire, wind, and space. This insignia is often seen on samurai flags.

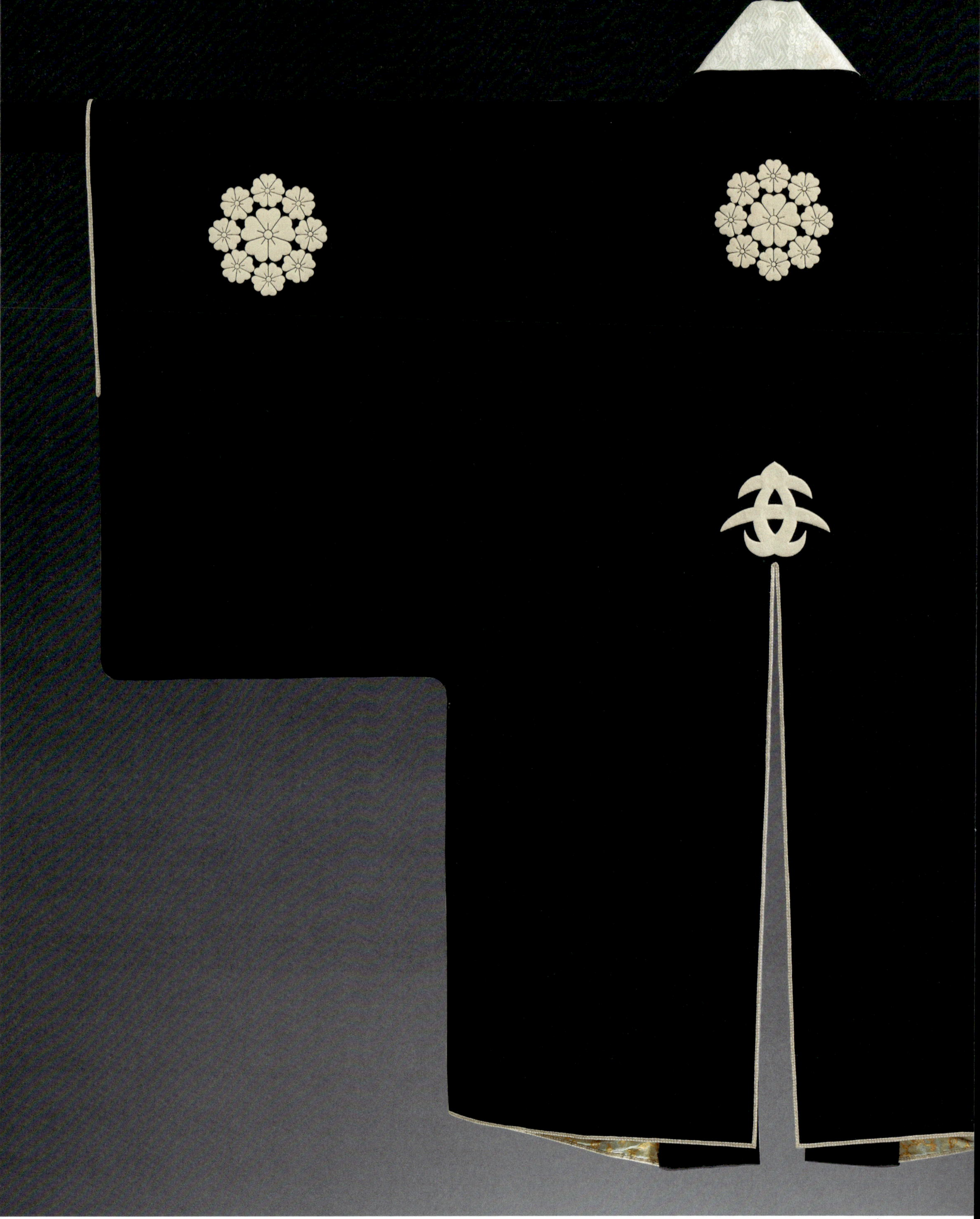

12 大名火事装束

Daimyo firefighter's ensemble (*kaji shōzoku*). Edo period (1615–1868), first half of 19th century. Jacket, plastron, sash: wool (*rasha*); jacket lining and pants: twill-weave silk with supplementary weft patterning in silk; jacket: 40 × 48 in. (101.6 × 121.9 cm); pants length: 38½ in. (97.8 cm); plastron: 23 × 11¼ in. (58.4 × 28.6 cm); sash: 2¾ × 60½ in. (7 × 153.7 cm). Lent by John C. Weber Collection

After 1643 samurai firefighters were responsible for protecting important government locations, such as Edo Castle, shrines and rice storehouses, certain public areas of Edo, and their daimyo's residence and surroundings. This rare and elegant ensemble of a jacket (*kaji-haori*), a plastron or breastplate (*muneate*), a sash, and *hakama* pants would not have been worn to extinguish fires. Rather, this set was made for a samurai who — on fire duty in service of his daimyo — safeguarded the area to prevent looting, supervised the scene, evacuated people, and perhaps gave instructions to firefighters.[9] The jacket's use of expensive imported wool (*rasha*) signifies the importance of this role and the wearer's high social rank. The black jacket is embellished across the back with three family crests in white *rasha* appliqué; each crest has eight flowers arranged around a larger central flower. The lining is light blue brocaded silk with golden-brown peonies and phoenix roundels. The collar and lapels, lined with white satin-weave silk figured with fretwork and flowers, are embellished with a pair of stylized dragons, one on each side, in raised gold embroidery. The refined embroidery indicates the set's high quality. The matching plastron is also black *rasha* and decorated with the white crest. The *fungomi-hakama* pants with narrow hems are made of expensive, Nishijin-made brocaded silk with brown, light blue, and gold patterns depicting auspicious treasures, pine-bamboo-plum motifs, and tortoiseshell patterns.

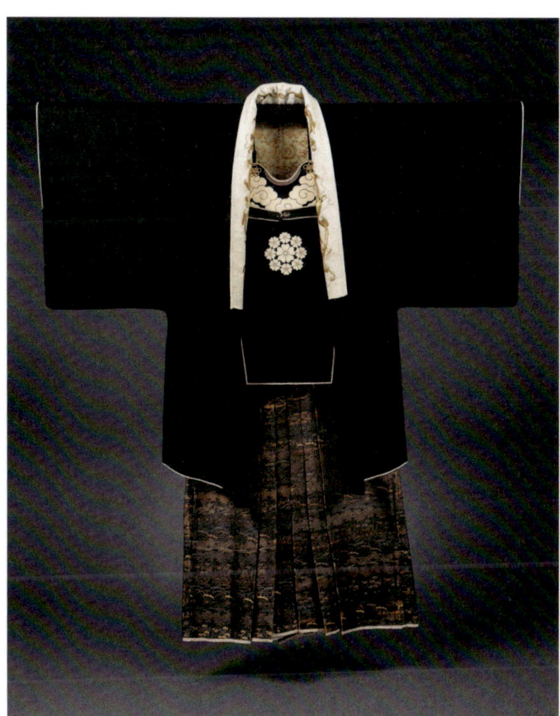

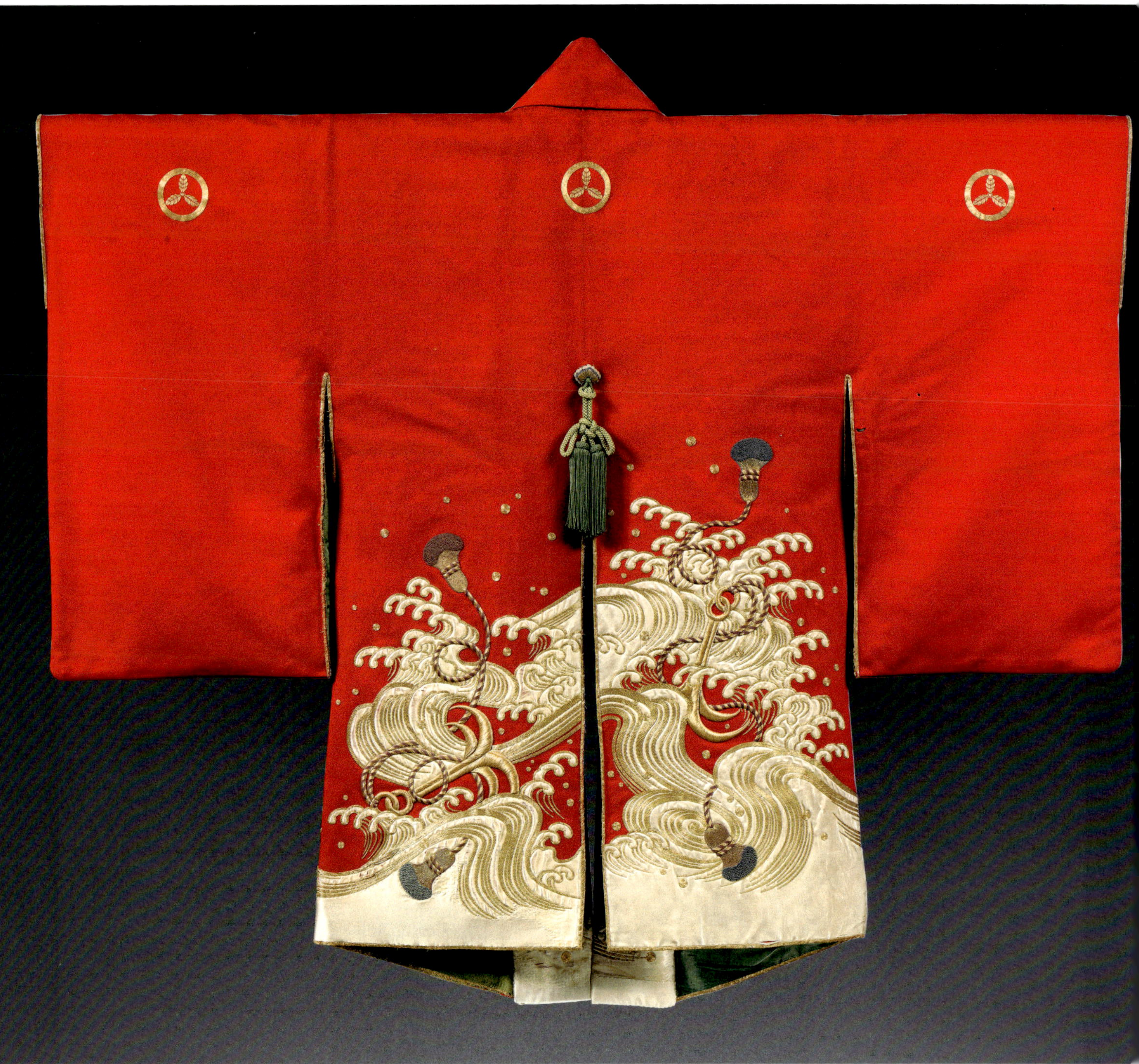

13 大名奥方火事装束

Daimyo firefighter's ensemble (*kaji shōzoku*) for samurai woman. Edo period (1615–1868), first half of 19th century. Wool (*rasha*) with satin-weave silk appliqué and silk- and gold-thread embroidery, lining of satin-weave silk; jacket: 38 × 48 in. (96.5 × 121.9 cm); hood: 36½ × 23 in. (92.7 × 58.4 cm). Lent by John C. Weber Collection

The luxurious red wool (*rasha*) jacket worn by a high-ranking samurai woman on fire duty is extravagantly decorated with crashing waves, water droplets, and anchors in embroidery on white satin-weave silk appliqué. The dynamic composition refers to the process of extinguishing a fire and pulling down smoldering buildings but also symbolizes security. The quality of the gold-thread embroidery is excellent, with various gold couching techniques and French knots on the tassels, which are attached to the cords of the anchors.

Five crests with a motif of three oak leaves, possibly the Yamauchi family crest, are depicted in gold thread on the jacket, which is lined with green satin-weave silk. The hood (*zukin*), embellished with the same patterns, testifies that this set was made for a woman, as male firefighters wore helmets. A matching plastron and *hakama* pants would have completed the ensemble. High-ranking samurai women, especially those living in the women's quarter of Edo Castle, were trained to evacuate and assist people during fires. They carried spears (*naginata*) to defend the fleeing occupants (mainly other women) and patrolled the grounds.

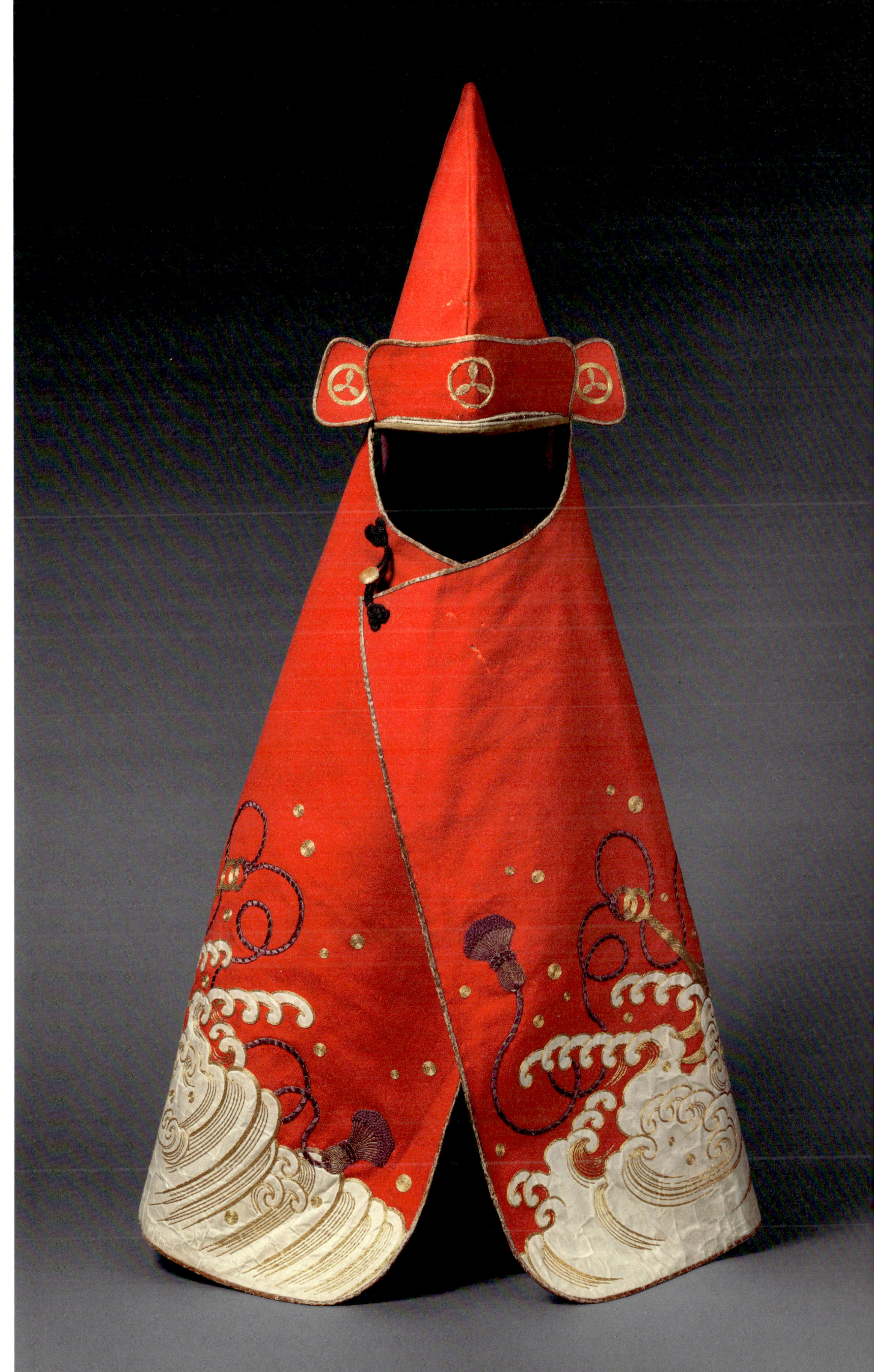

14 紺木綿地太郎良門模様火消半纏
Fireman's jacket (*hikeshi-banten*) with Tarō Yoshikado. Edo period (1615–1868), mid-19th century. Quilted cotton with tube-drawn paste-resist dyeing (*tsutsugaki*) with hand-painted details, 36 × 49 in. (91.4 × 124.5 cm). Lent by John C. Weber Collection

The *chōnin* firefighters were in charge of Edo's business and residential areas. Their reversible coats were made of several layers of thick, quilted cotton fabric with *sashiko* stitching (a running stitch of "small stabs," typically in white cotton thread but here in blue, to blend in).[10] The insides of these jackets were decorated with elaborate designs, often inspired by popular contemporary woodblock prints; they usually depicted warrior-heroes and mythical creatures that instill bravery or are related to water. This jacket's interior (shown reversed to the outside, opposite) features a scene popular in Kabuki and based on a print by Utagawa Kunisada (1786–1865) (Minneapolis Institute of Art, 2016.137.2): the warrior Yoshikado asks a frog sage for magical powers so he can avenge the murder of his father. Yoshikado holds his family banner, with its pattern of a tethered black steed. The theme signifies a heroic and honorable confrontation with death, suitable for such a garment. Inscriptions on the outside of the coat reveal that the wearer belonged to the "first group" of firefighters on the "Ki" team, which was responsible for the Shinagawa-Shirogane district.

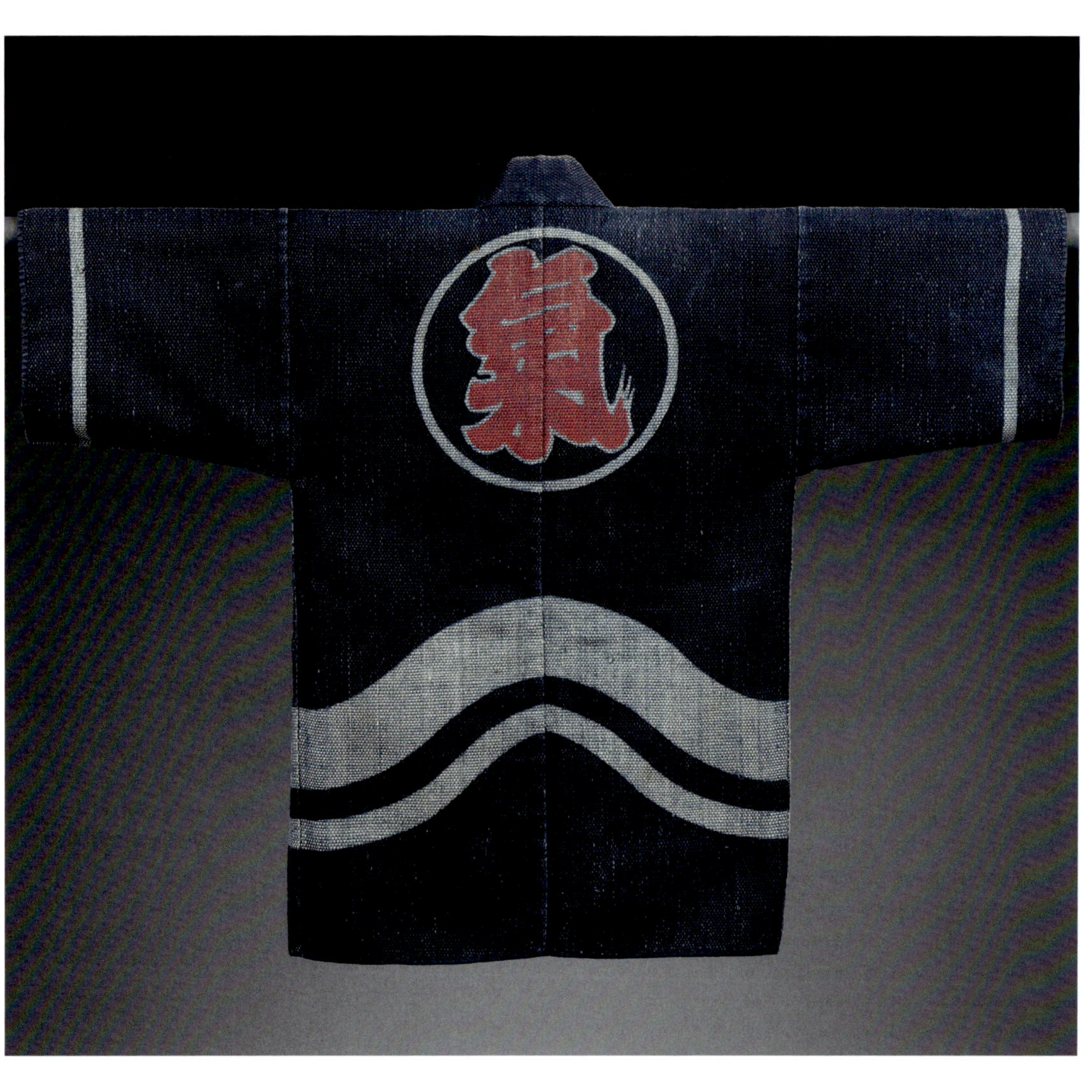

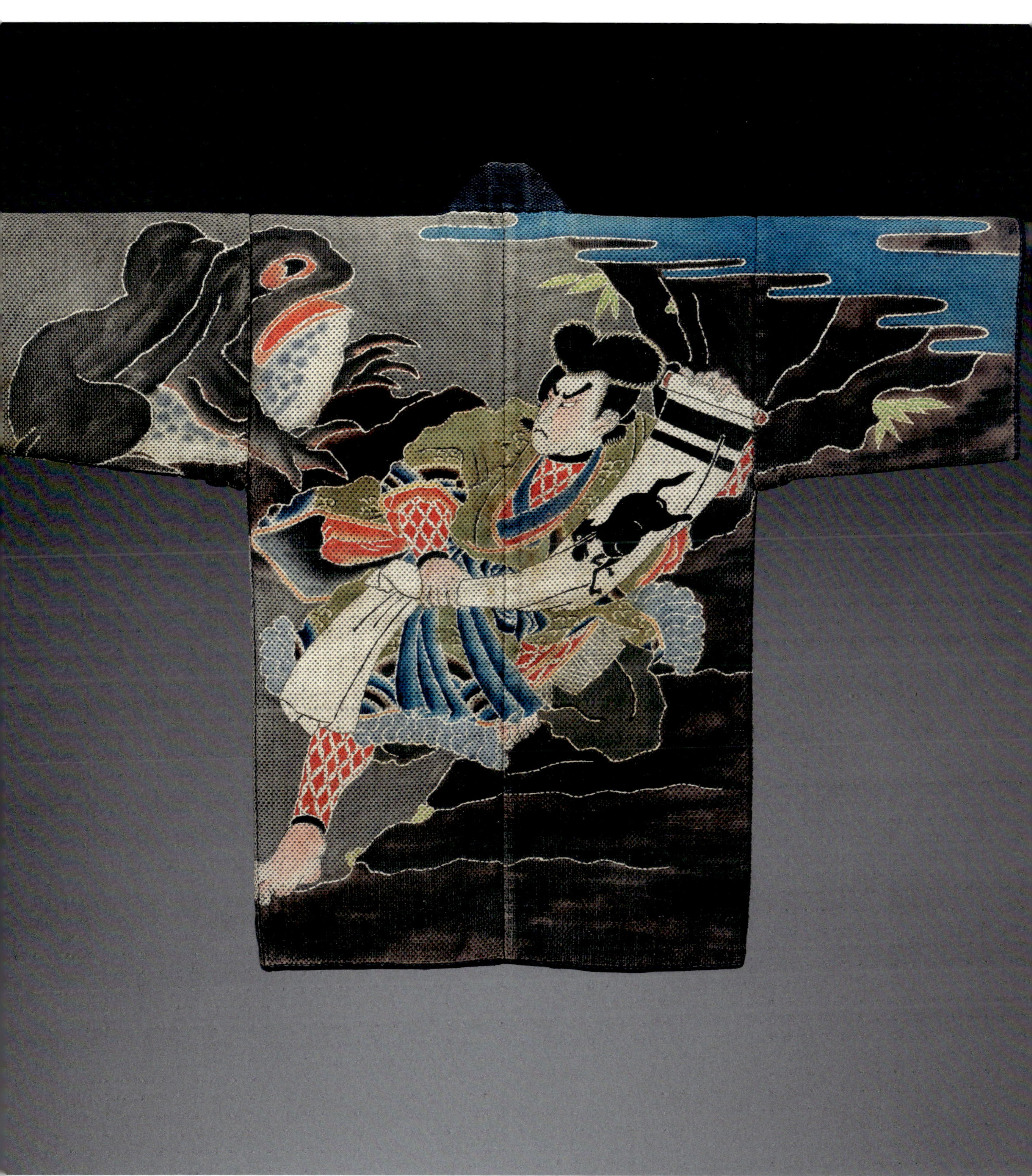

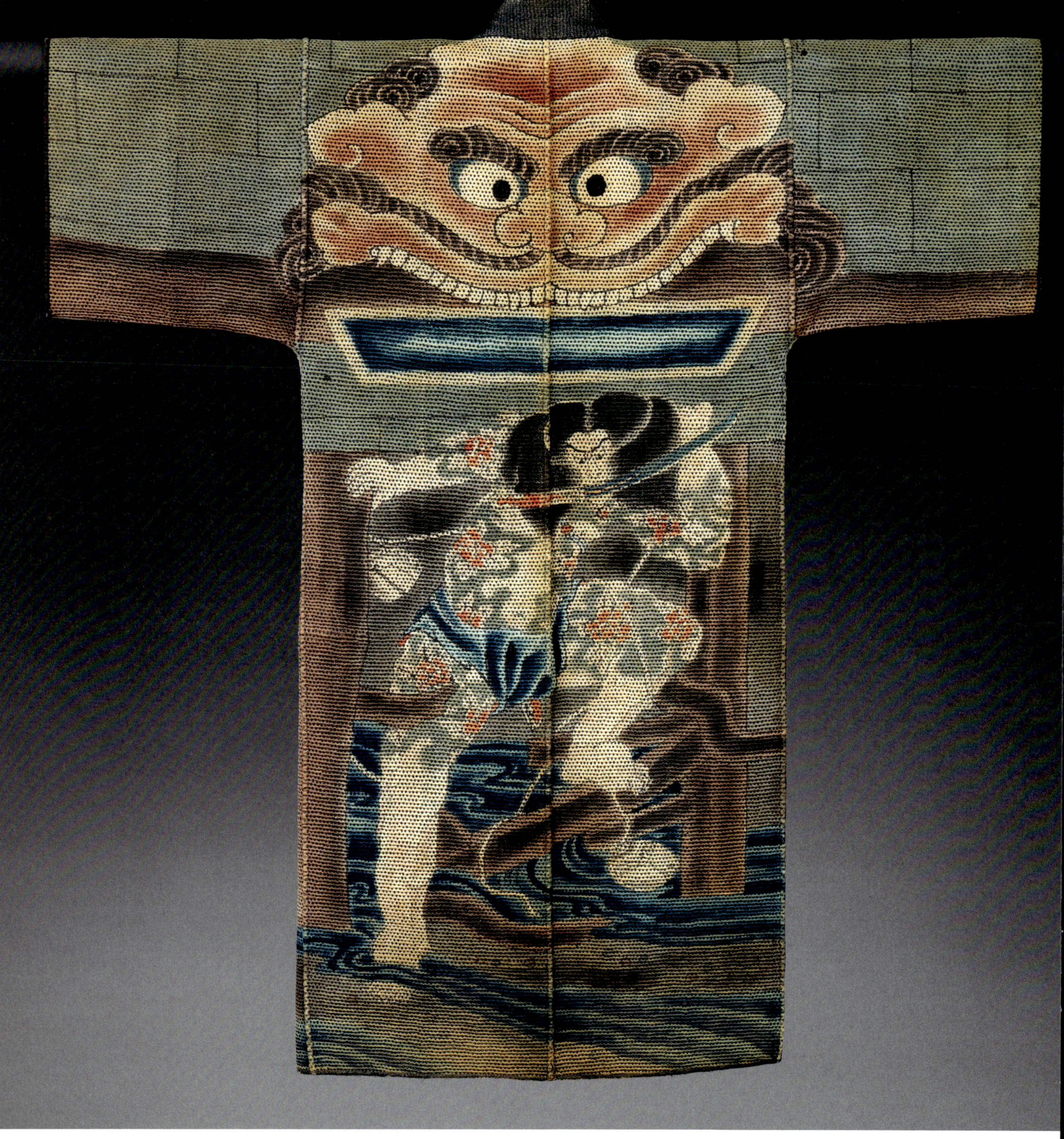

15 紺木綿地浪里白條張順模様火消半纏

Fireman's jacket (*hikeshi-banten*) with Chinese warrior. Edo period (1615–1868), mid-19th century. Quilted cotton with tube-drawn paste-resist dyeing (*tsutsugaki*) with hand-painted details, 49 × 46¼ in. (124.5 × 117.5 cm). Lent by John C. Weber Collection

The interior of this thickly layered, quilted cotton jacket is decorated with the image of Rōrihakucho Chō Jun (Zhang Shun), a character revered in nineteenth-century Japan for his courage. Chō Jun, one of the 108 heroes of the *Water Margin*, a novel translated from Chinese (*Shui hu zhuan*) into Japanese (*Suikoden*) during the second half of the Edo period, became the subject of works by celebrated print artists, prominently Utagawa Kuniyoshi (1798–1861). This composition is based on a print by Kuniyoshi published in 1827–30 (The British Museum, London; 2008.3037.10043). The righteous rebel is shown clenching a sword between his teeth as his characteristically pale, muscular, and tattooed body forcefully emerges from a destroyed water gate. He undauntedly faces the enemy soldiers anticipating his arrival, who will slay him in an attack of arrows. Embroidered on the jacket's lapels is a family name, Saitō, most likely the garment's owner.

16 歌川(五雲亭)貞秀筆　鍾馗図絵のぼり

Banner with Shōki, the Demon Queller. Utagawa (Gountei) Sadahide (1807–1878/79). Edo period (1615–1868), 1840s. Ink and color on cotton, 68⅛ x 37⅜ in. (173 x 95 cm). Lent by John C. Weber Collection

This large hand-painted banner depicts the legendary seventh-century scholar-physician Shōki holding a sword and wearing a scholar's robes and hat. The large eyes, bulbous nose, and fierce expression are his characteristic features. After being denied first rank in civil service to the emperor, Shōki (Chinese: Zhong Kui) committed suicide, but he was buried with honors after the emperor heard the tragic tale. In gratitude, Shōki appeared to the emperor in a dream vowing to quell demons of illness and evil. Shōki's popularity peaked in Japan during the Edo period, when people began to hang his image outside their homes to ward off evil spirits and disease. Such banners were originally used in battle, but ornamental use was common in the Edo period. This powerful ink painting is signed "Gyokuransai Sadahide ga" and has a red seal. The artist, also known as Hashimoto Sadahide, a member of the Utagawa school, is best known for his prints depicting foreigners in Yokohama in the 1860s. In the 1840s, when this banner was made, he created numerous warrior prints (*musha-e*).

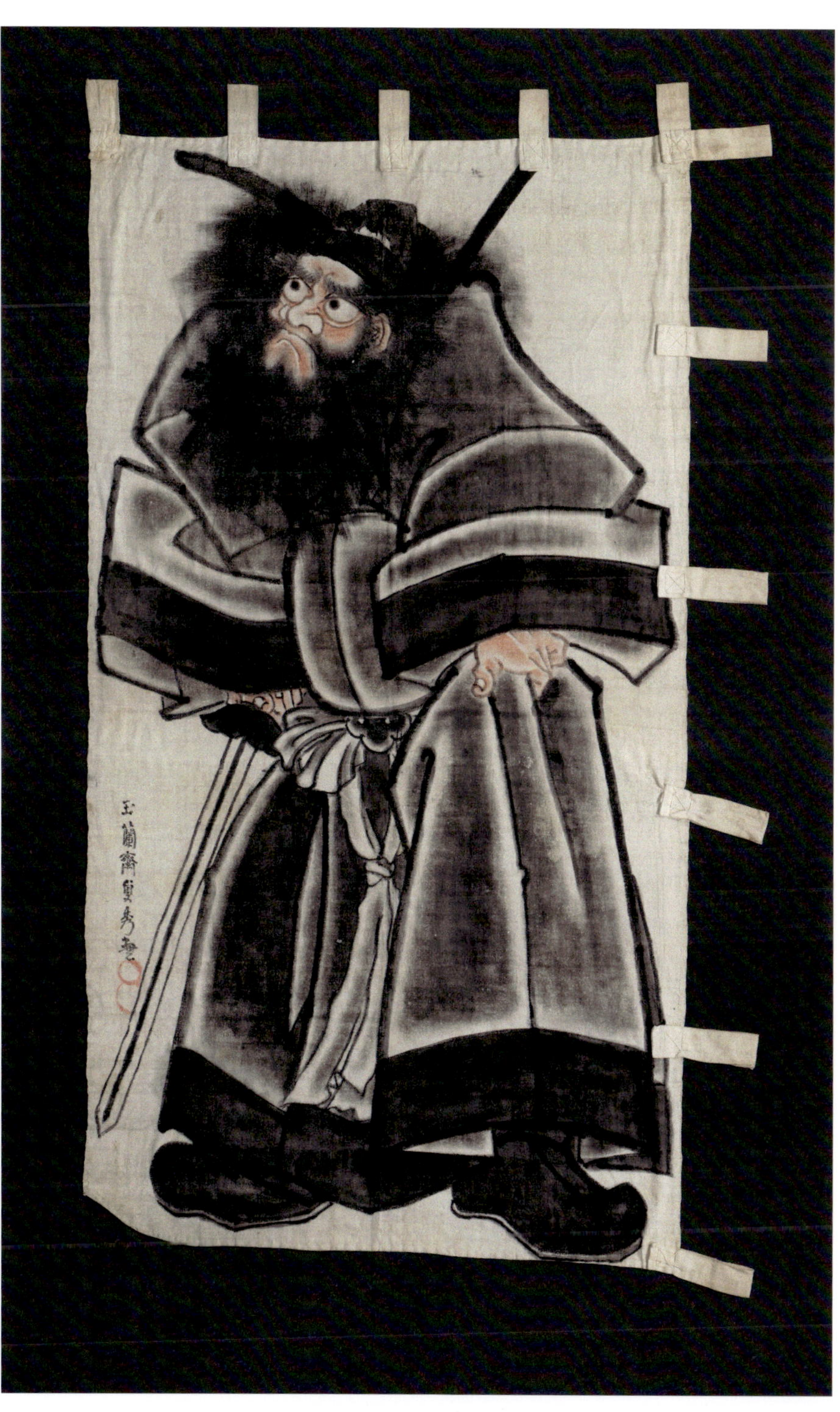

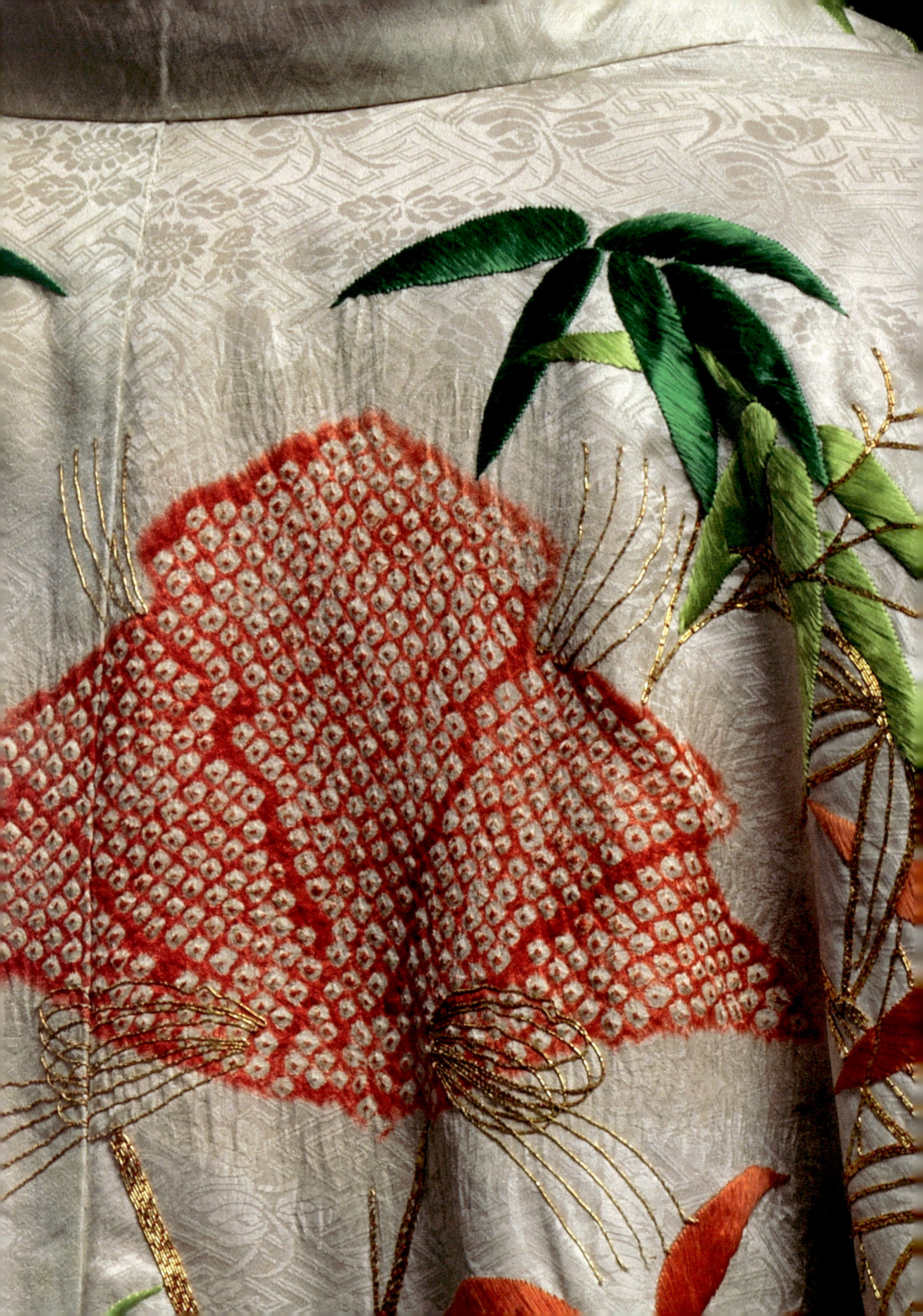

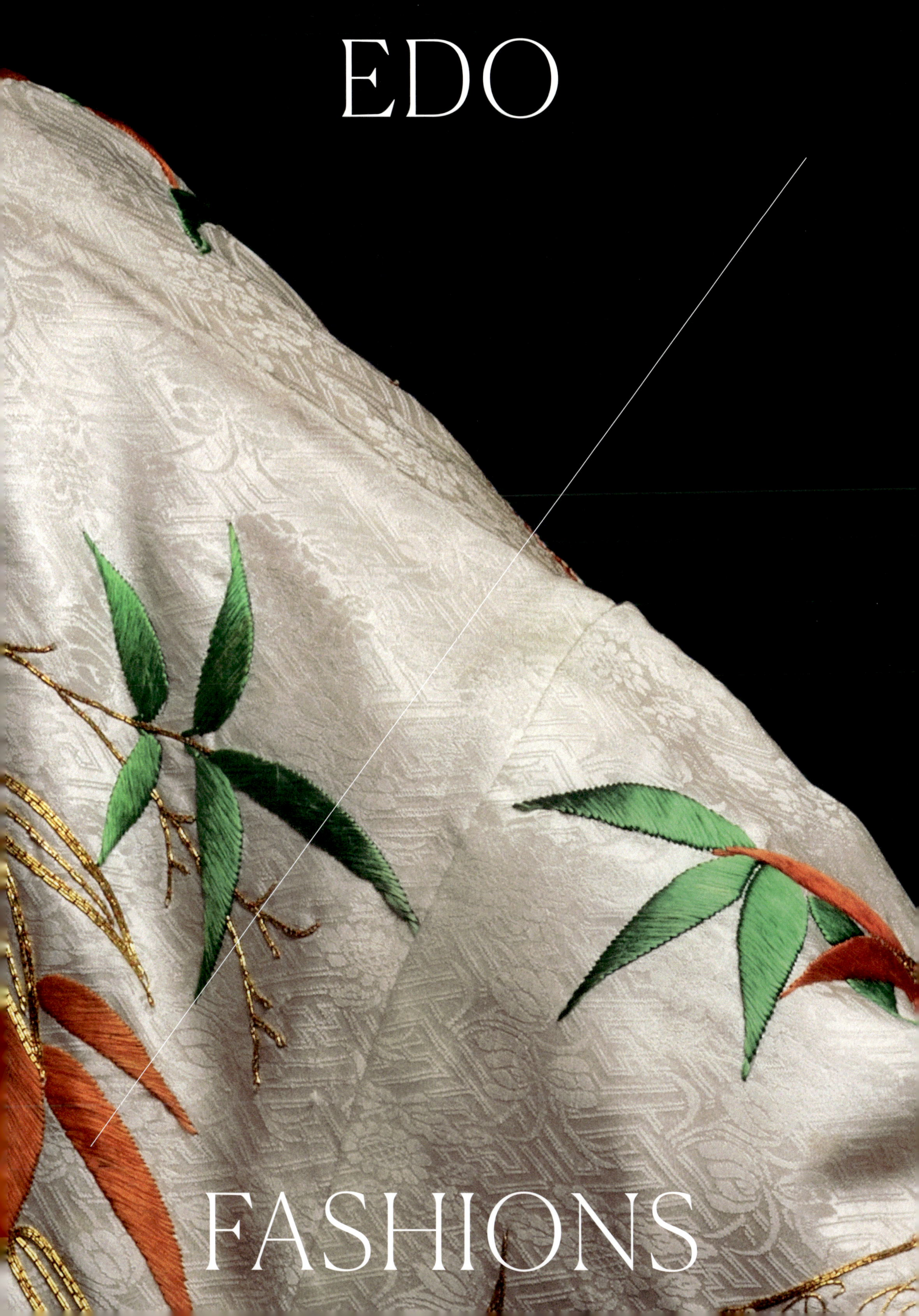
EDO
FASHIONS

THE *KOSODE* (A ROBE WITH SMALL OPENINGS AT the wrist) was the most common garment throughout the Edo period (1615–1868), and its most important accessory was the obi, a sash that was carefully coordinated with the rest of the ensemble (cat. 27). Elaborate obi-tying methods had their own distinct fashions, and the *kosode* itself appeared in several variations. The *uchikake*, for example, was worn over a *kosode* and without a sash (so that it was open in the front and fabric pooled at the hem) for special occasions (cat. 19). Beginning in the late Edo period, thick padding was added to the hem of the *uchikake*, creating a pleasing shape on the ground as the robe trailed behind the wearer. *Furisode*, literally "swinging sleeves," were lined silk robes with long sleeves and narrow wrist openings; the eye-catching, swaying sleeves were meant to accentuate the graceful movements of the young, unmarried women who wore them. A *furisode*-style *uchikake* was often used as a wedding garment, representing the bride's last youthful appearance as she transitioned to married life (cat. 26). *Katabira*, unlined, light robes of finely woven ramie or hemp, were worn in the summertime (cat. 25). The variation made from silk, beginning in the nineteenth century, was called *hito-e* (cat. 18). Not only the materials but also the robe's patterns and colors would change to reflect the four seasons.

Color played an important role in Edo fashion. The hundreds of color names recorded in pattern books (*hinagata-bon*), with a wide range of purples, pinks, reds, yellows, greens, blues, browns, and grays, demonstrate the continuously changing trends. Dye recipes were the closely guarded secrets of the dye houses, as creating new colors from the limited number of natural materials required ingenuity. Most colors were named after and identified with the plant or mineral from which their dyes were originally made. As many of these were age-old medicinals, the ensuing colors were associated with spiritual and talismanic powers based on literary references. According to ancient Chinese theories, the five primary colors were related to both the five basic elements and the seasons: blue, wood and spring; red, fire and summer; yellow, earth and late summer; white, metal and autumn; and black, water and winter. Color suggested deeper meaning and emotion in classical literature. For example, in the *Manyōshū* (*Collection of Ten Thousand Leaves*, eighth century), subtle brown hues made from acorns, unfading and long-lasting, signified a wife's constant love. By contrast, because the striking red produced from safflower petals (*benibana*) was fugitive and short-lived, it was compared to a fleeting love affair.[1] With its connotations of youth and beauty, red was a highly coveted hue (cat. 20).

Indigo was another important plant-based dye, but a widely available and inexpensive one that colored most farmers' work clothes and many folk textiles made of cotton and bast fibers (cat. 29). As the plant was also used to relieve stomach disorders, lower fevers, and treat snakebites, indigo-dyed fabrics were believed to have beneficial medicinal properties.

By contrast to indigo, the safflower's brilliant red was costly to produce, so innovative dyers made inexpensive imitations with madder or sappanwood and experimented with top-dyeing techniques and mordants. Still, the sumptuary laws issued in 1683 barred the merchant class from using red, as well as from numerous luxurious decorative techniques, such as "fawn spot" tie-dyeing. An alternative arrived at the end of the seventeenth century, when the celebrated fan painter Miyazaki Yūzen (1654–1736) developed the paste-resist dyeing technique (*yūzen-zome*). Miyazaki applied a resist of rice paste directly to silk through a fine tube.[2] Dye could not color the fabric where the resist was placed, leaving fine lines (*shiro-age*) or larger areas white (cat. 18). This technique, which also prevented colors from running, made it possible to create complex, precise, painterly compositions with freehand drawing and the refined application of colors by brush. As *yūzen*-dyeing looked best on matte crepe silk (*chirimen*), the number of *kosode* made of that material soon increased (cat. 23).[3]

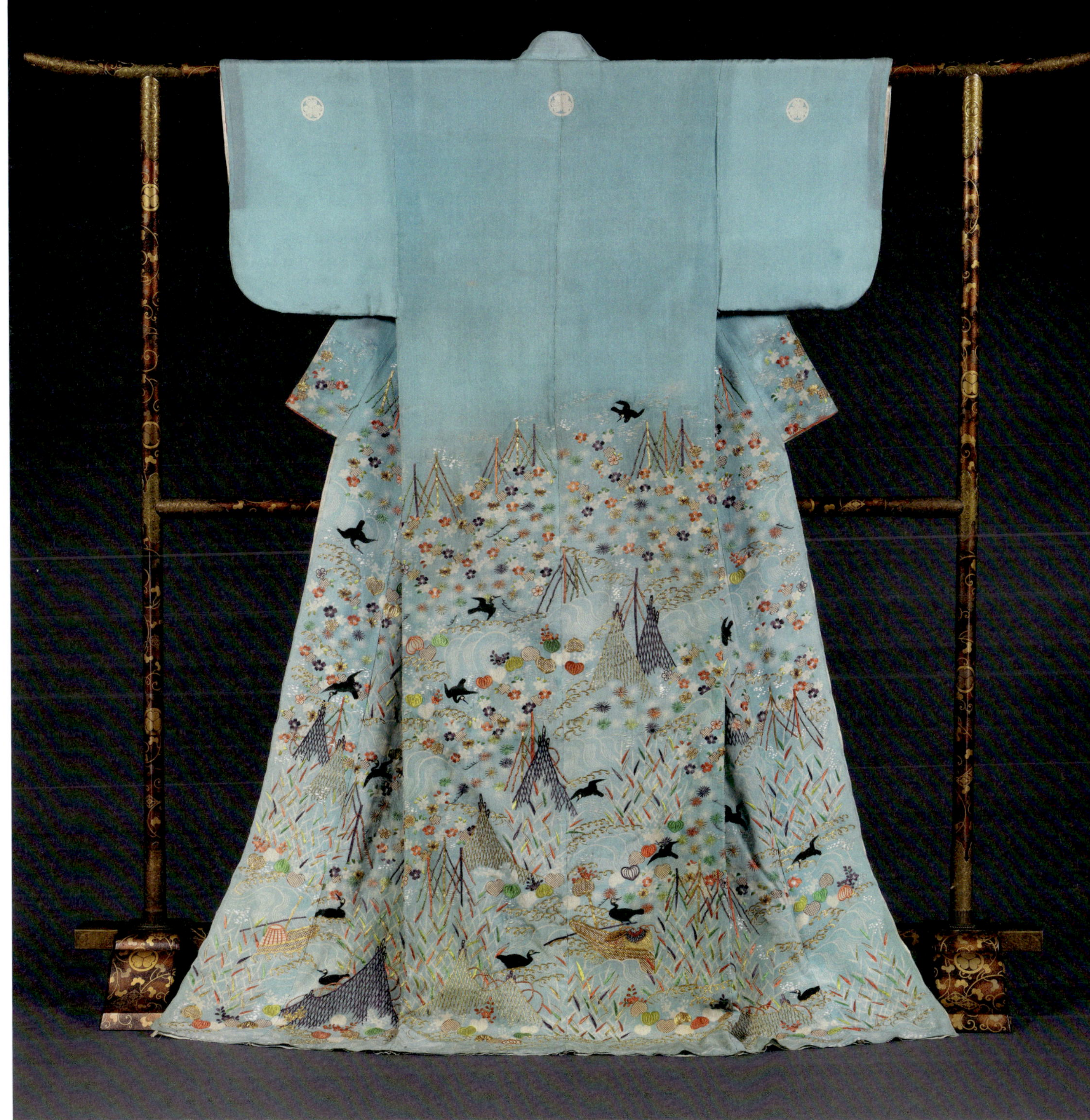

17 浅葱絹縮地葵桜水辺に鵜飼い模様単衣

Summer robe (*hito-e*) with cormorant-fishing scene. Edo period (1615–1868), late 18th–early 19th century. Thin crepe silk (*chijimi*) with paste-resist dyeing, stencil-dyed dots (*suri-bitta*), hand-painted details, silk embroidery, and couched gold thread, 70⅛ × 47½ in. (178.1 × 120.7 cm). The Metropolitan Museum of Art, New York, Gift of John C. Weber, 2019 (2019.16.1)

Unlined summer robes made from fine crepe silk were worn as the weather turned warm and humid, beginning in May. This light blue robe's meticulous decoration—with cormorants swimming among reeds, drying fishing nets, and a fisherman's straw raincoat and hat on one boat—refers to the Noh play *The Cormorant Fisher* (*Ukai*). It represents the *goshodoki* (courtly) style, which typically combined seasonal elements, such as the scattered wild ginger leaves, cherry blossoms, and water scene on this robe, with literary motifs that would be recognized by a well-educated upper-class woman. The crests of wild ginger across the shoulders of this sophisticated robe indicate that the owner was a princess from the Tokugawa shogun family. The careful composition and delicate embroidery reflect the expensive tastes of high-ranking samurai women, but simple stencil-dyed dots stood in for the labor-intensive "fawn spot" tie-dye technique (*kanoko shibori*), as required by the sumptuary laws.

18 萌黄絽地桜菊松御所車屋形水辺模様単衣

Summer robe (*hito-e*) with court carriage and waterside scene. Edo period (1615–1868), early 19th century. Gauze-weave silk with stencil paste-resist dyeing, stencil-dyed dots (*suri-bitta*), hand-painted details, silk embroidery, and couched gold thread, 72¾ × 48¾ in. (184.6 × 123.8 cm). Lent by John C. Weber Collection

This elegant *goshodoki* (court-style) robe is made of chartreuse silk gauze (*ro*), a transparent, open-weave fabric well suited for summer attire. The three basic styles of gauze weave in Japan—*ra*, *sha*, and *ro*—are collectively called *usumono* (thin fabric). The complex patterns on this robe are expressed in fine embroidery and white-resist details (*shiro-age*). Among pine trees, cherry blossoms, chrysanthemums, and reeds, representing the four seasons, are references to literary classics. The brushwood fence with a gate in the center of the lower section and the court carriage partly hidden by pines on the left might allude to different chapters from *The Tale of Genji*, while the beach and the drying fishing nets suggest a Noh play, *The Reed Cutter* (*Ashikari*). However, by the late Edo period, when this robe was made, such motifs had become formalized and generally conveyed the aesthetic of an idealized court culture from the past. The shoulder area is undecorated save for the Tokugawa family crest, which signals that the owner was from the shogun family.

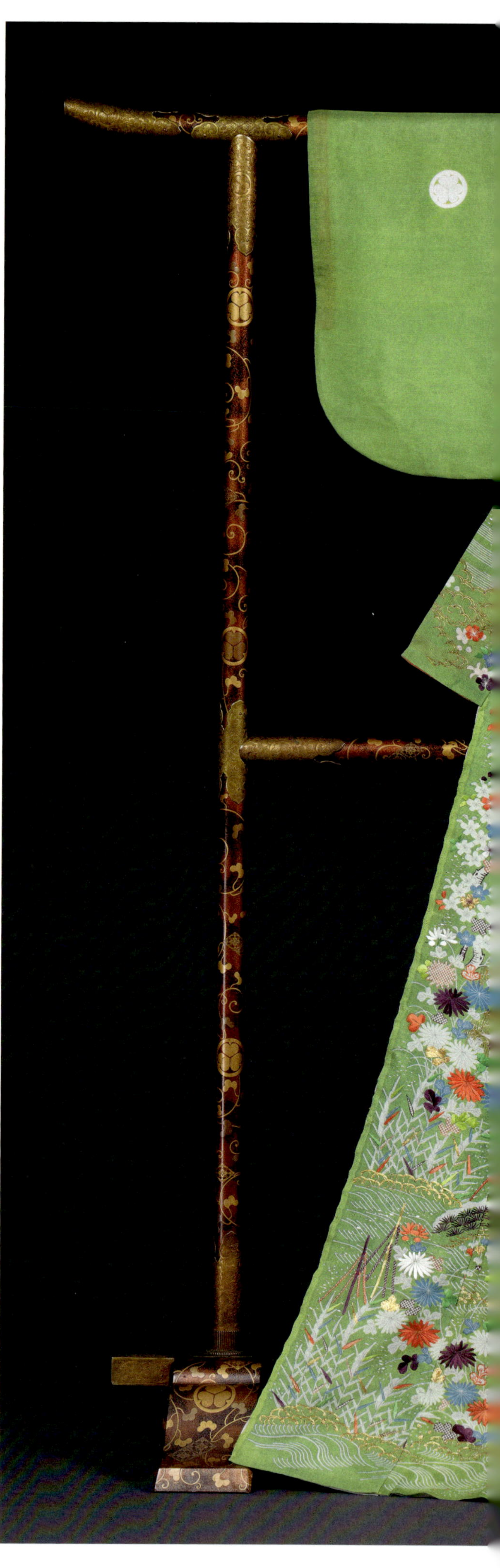

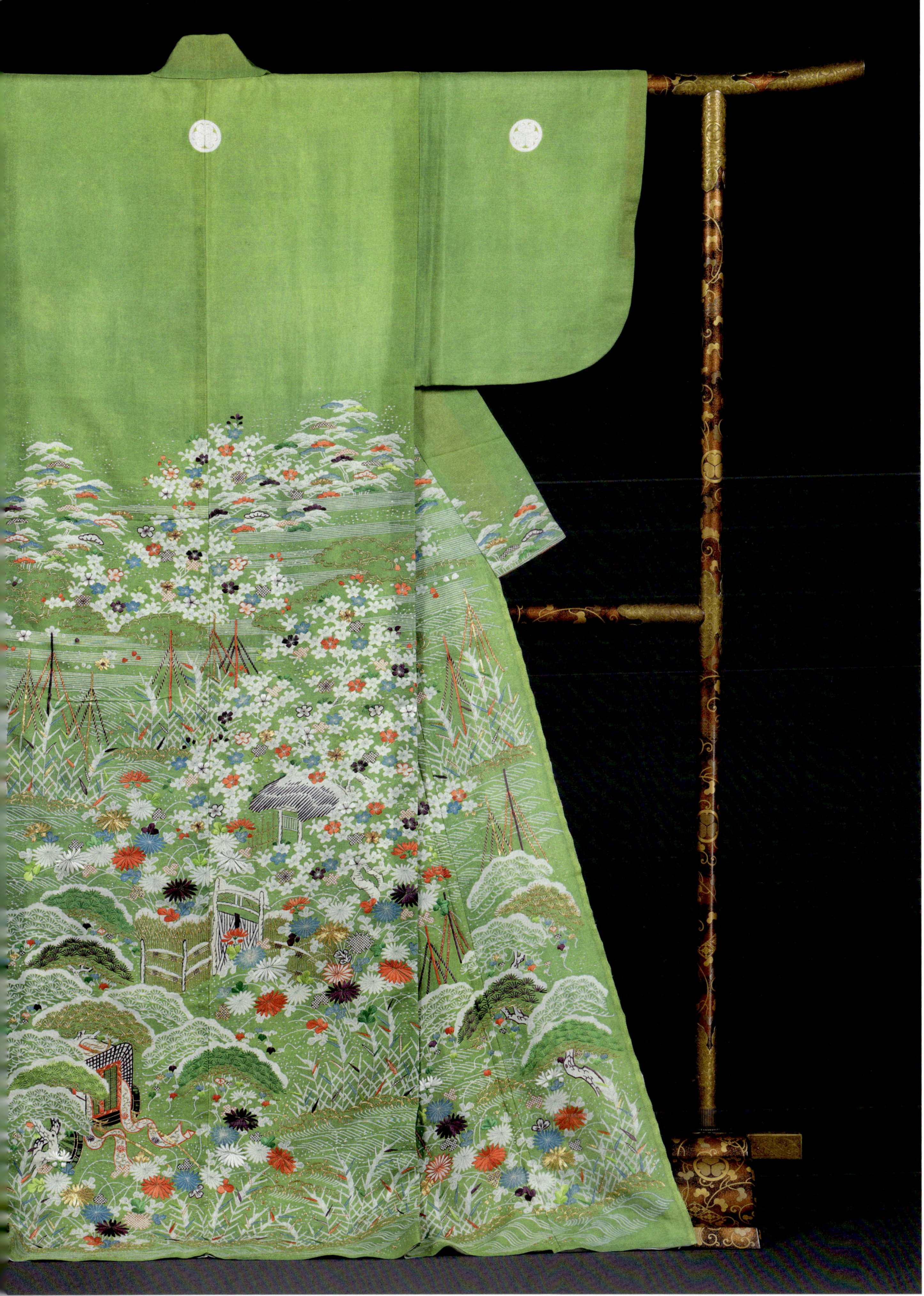

19 白綸子地源氏車葵模様打掛

Over robe (*uchikake*) with Genji wheels and wild ginger leaves. Edo period (1615–1868), early 19th century. Figured satin-weave silk (*rinzu*) with silk embroidery and couched gold thread, 68 × 46¼ in. (172.7 × 117.5 cm). Lent by John C. Weber Collection

The ground fabric of this elegant over robe for a samurai woman is lustrous white satin-weave silk patterned with large bamboo, an unusual motif that points to the early nineteenth century, as earlier woven ground patterns were smaller. The entire surface is decorated with embroidered wild ginger leaves in gold, green, light brown, and purple, as well as with purple lozenge-shaped crests. The main design is the wheels of an imperial ox-drawn carriage, or *Gosho-guruma*. Court carriages, which were often depicted in paintings associated with *The Tale of Genji*, are sometimes referred to as *Genji-guruma*, a term that came to be used for the wheels as well. Combined with the wild ginger, the cartwheel imagery refers to Lady Aoi, Prince Genji's wife, and might allude to the tale's ninth chapter, "Leaves of Wild Ginger" (*Aoi*), in which Aoi's attendants obstructed and damaged the carriage of Genji's lover during a grand procession. A similar composition was published in *Hinagata yoshino-yama*, a woodblock-printed pattern book from 1765.

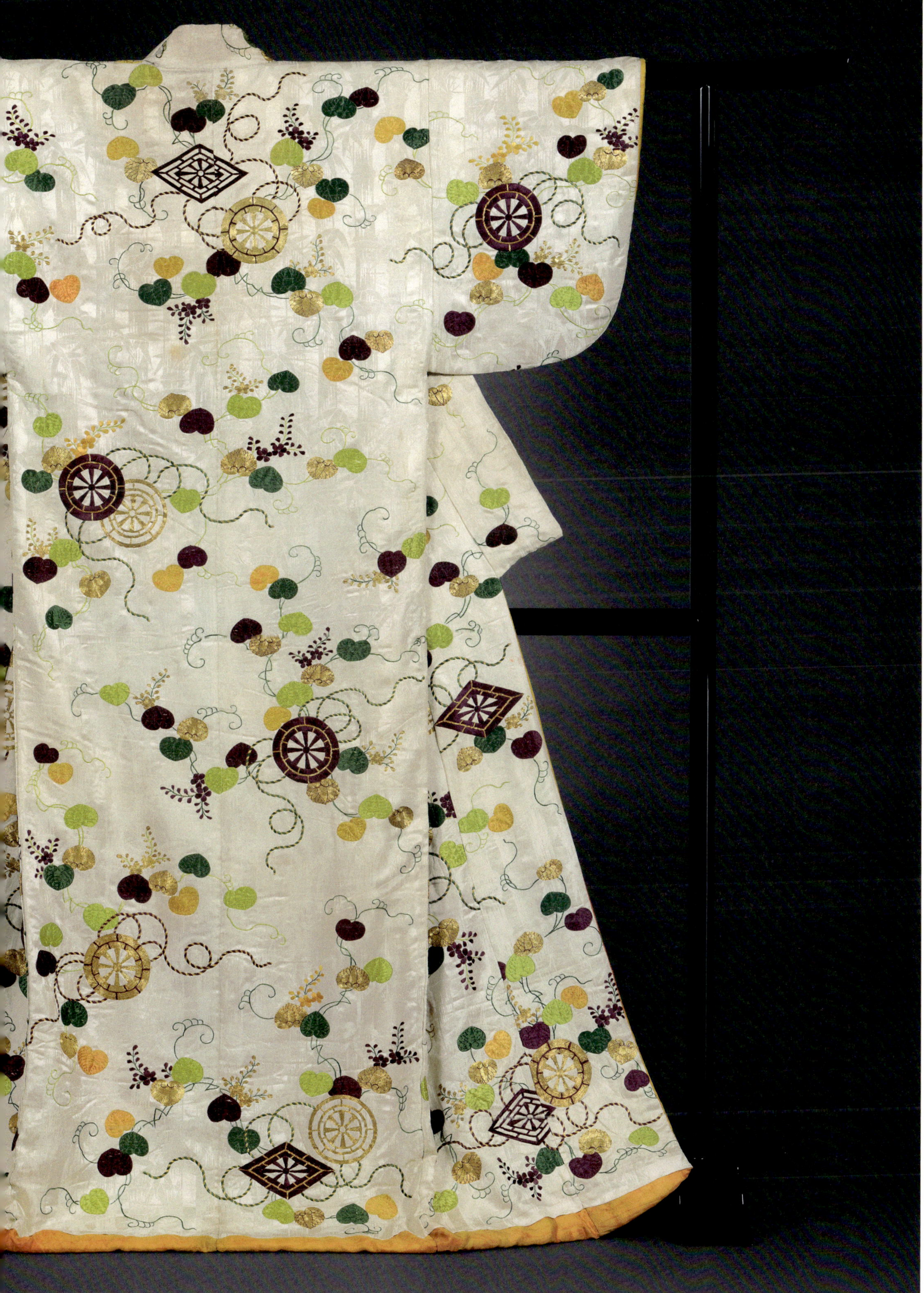

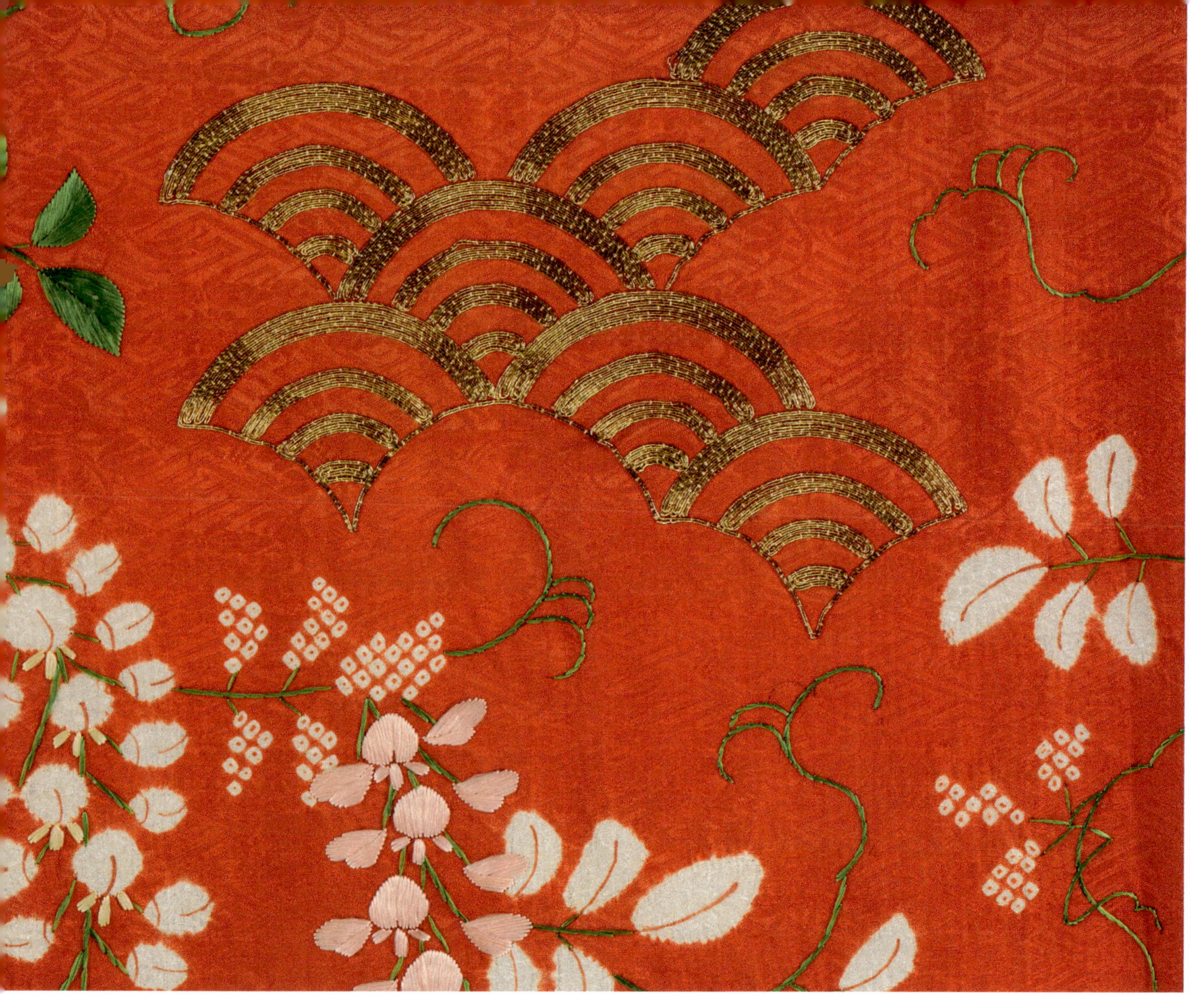

20 赤綸子地藤青海波模様打掛
Over robe (*uchikake*) with wisteria and waves. Edo period (1615–1868), early 19th century. Figured satin-weave silk (*rinzu*) with tie-dyeing, silk embroidery, and couched gold thread, 64⅝ × 48⅜ in. (164.1 × 122.9 cm). Lent by John C. Weber Collection

This beautifully preserved over robe might have been a young samurai bride's wedding garment. Its exceptional condition suggests that it was worn only for a special occasion. The robe's most spectacular feature is the vivid red of its silk ground, achieved with dye obtained from safflower petals (*benibana*). Such natural dyes are typically sensitive to light, but safflower is especially fugitive, and most *beni*-dyed fabrics have faded. This silk's woven motifs are a key-fret pattern, chrysanthemums, and orchids. Embroidered trailing wisteria and stylized wave motifs in varied colors are evenly distributed on the surface. Some of the leaves and petals are expressed in precise tie-dyeing (*shibori*) that reveals the undyed white ground. "Fawn spot" *kanoko shibori* is also used.

Wisteria, which is associated with longevity, resilience, and love, is treasured for the fragrance that fills the air when it blooms in the late spring. Its white and purple petals inspired poems as early as the Heian period (794–1185). The combination of wisteria and wave motifs suggests a well-known figure of speech in *waka* poetry: *fuji-nami* (wisteria waves), which evokes the swaying of the flowers.

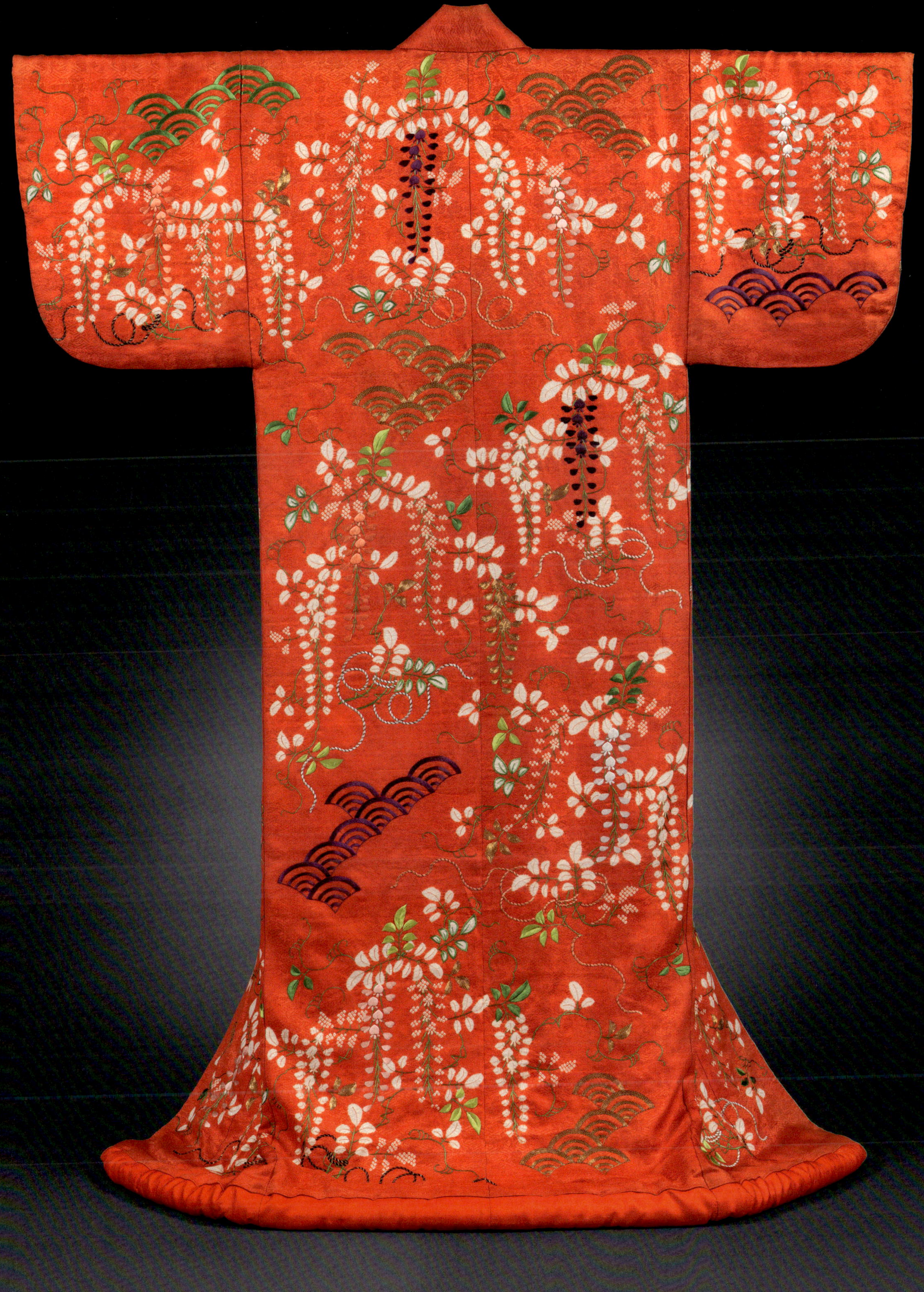

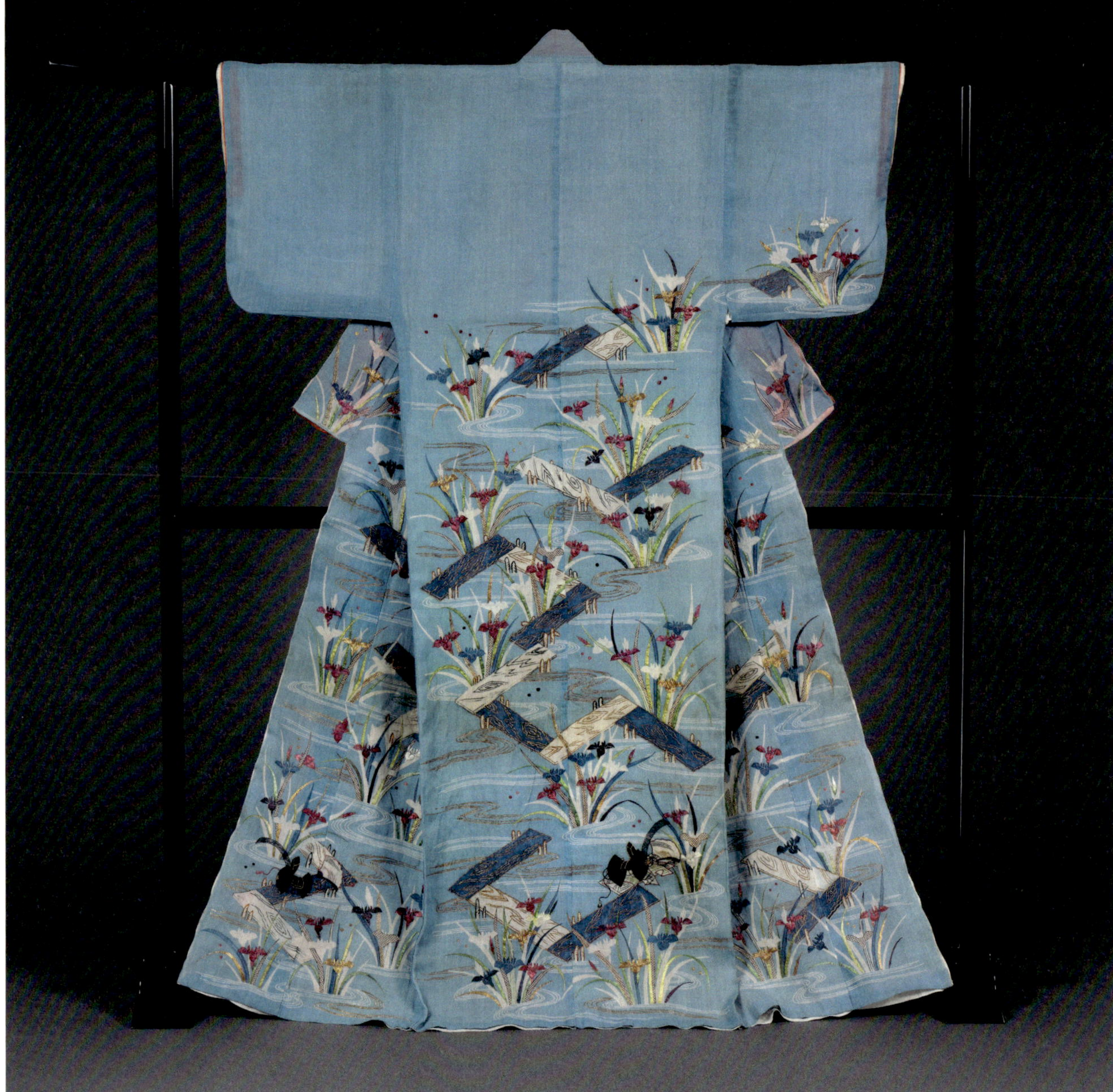

21 浅葱麻地八橋模様帷子

Summer robe (*katabira*) with irises at Yatsuhashi (Eight Bridges). Edo period (1615–1868), mid-19th century. Plain-weave ramie with paste-resist dyeing, stencil-dyed dots (*suri-bitta*), hand-painted details, silk embroidery, and couched gold thread, 67 × 47 in. (170.2 × 119.4 cm). The Metropolitan Museum of Art, New York, Gift of John C. Weber, 2019 (2019.16.2)

This samurai woman's summer robe evokes water, from its light blue fabric with wavy motifs reserved in white (*shiro-age*) to its embroidered pattern of irises blooming by a river crossed by zigzagging plank bridges. The composition refers to an episode from the tenth-century classic *The Tales of Ise* (*Ise monogatari*) and to the Noh play derived from it, *Irises* (*Kakitsubata*). In episode nine from the tales, a famous ninth-century poet and his friends leave the capital in exile. (The play signifies the poet, Ariwara no Narihira, by his headdress, alluded to on this robe by a black courtier's hat and a fan near the hem.[4]) Pausing at Yatsuhashi, where bridges cross eight channels of a river, they admire the irises growing in the marshy riverbank. Inspired by the blossoms, the poet composes a poem that begins each line with one of the five syllables of the word for "iris," *ka-ki-tsu-ba-ta*.

Karagoromo
kitsutsu narenishi
tsuma shi areba
harubaru kinuru
tabi o shi zo omou

I wear robes with well-worn hems,
Reminding me of my dear wife
I fondly think of always,
So as my sojourn stretches on
Ever farther from home
Sadness fills my thoughts.[5]

22 浅葱麻地梅流水模様帷子

Summer robe (*katabira*) with stream and plum trees. Edo period (1615–1868), first half of 19th century. Plain-weave ramie with paste-resist dyeing, stencil-dyed dots (*suri-bitta*), and hand-painting, 66 × 48 in. (167.6 × 121.9 cm). Lent by John C. Weber Collection

Fine white lines (*shiro-age*) create a graceful, painterly composition on this samurai woman's pale blue summer robe. Playful butterflies and delicate plum blossoms are depicted among a stream's rushing waters. No coded motifs indicate a specific location or scene, so this delightful garment seems dedicated only to the pleasures of the mild seasons. Some of the details are stencil-dyed, but there is no embroidery. The robe bears the crest of the Nabeshima clan, but close examination reveals the Tokugawa family crest underneath it, indicating a change of ownership.

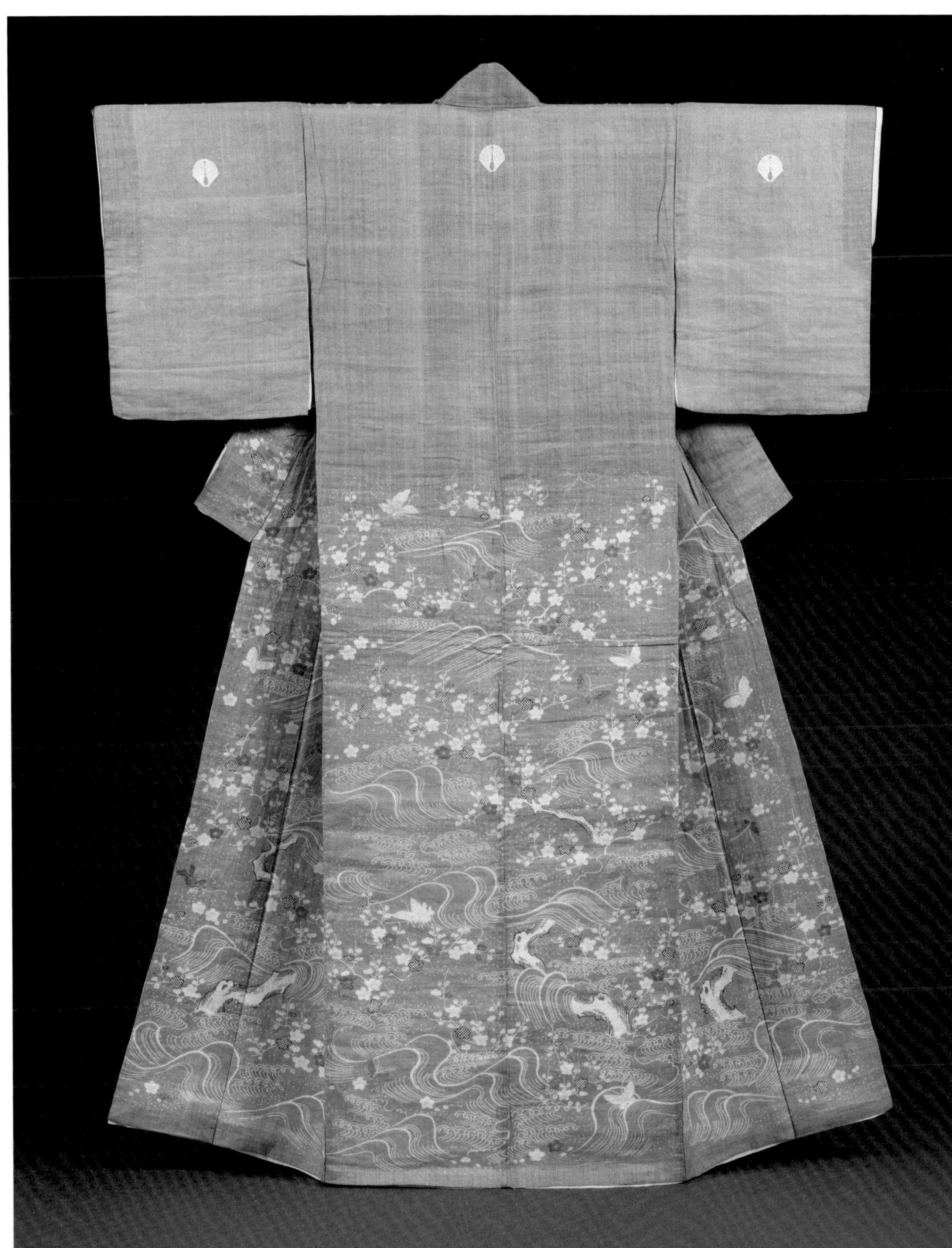

23 紺縮緬地柳文字模様打掛
Over robe (*uchikake*) with willow and poem. Edo period (1615–1868), second half of 18th century. Crepe silk with paste-resist dyeing, stencil-dyed dots (*suri-bitta*), silk embroidery, and couched gold thread, 59⅞ × 46⅛ in. (152 × 117 cm). Lent by John C. Weber Collection

Embroidered and stencil-dyed branches of a tall willow bursting into leaf trail down this over robe, originally a *kosode* designed for a wealthy *chōnin* woman. The curved tree trunk is depicted in finely stenciled dots (*suri-bitta*); the leaves are in white reserve (*shiro-age*), embroidery, and *suri-bitta*, creating variety. Semicursive Chinese characters are rendered in orange-red silk embroidery and couched gold threads. On the front of the garment are 梳 (*kushi-kezuri*, to comb), 柳 (*ryū*, willow), and 気 (*ki*, weather). On the back, from right to left: 鬚 (*hige*, whiskers), 霽 (*harete*, to clear), 風 (*kaze*, wind), and 新 (*shin*, new). Before this *kosode* was altered, with padding added to the hem and the sleeves inverted, the characters were correctly ordered to present a ninth-century poem written in Chinese by a Japanese courtier, Miyako no Yoshika.

Ki harete wa kaze shinryū no kami o kushikezuri,
kōri kiete wa nami kyūtai no hige o arau.

The weather clears, breezes comb the
hair of the young willows;
The ice is melting, wavelets wash the whiskers
of the old bog moss.[6]

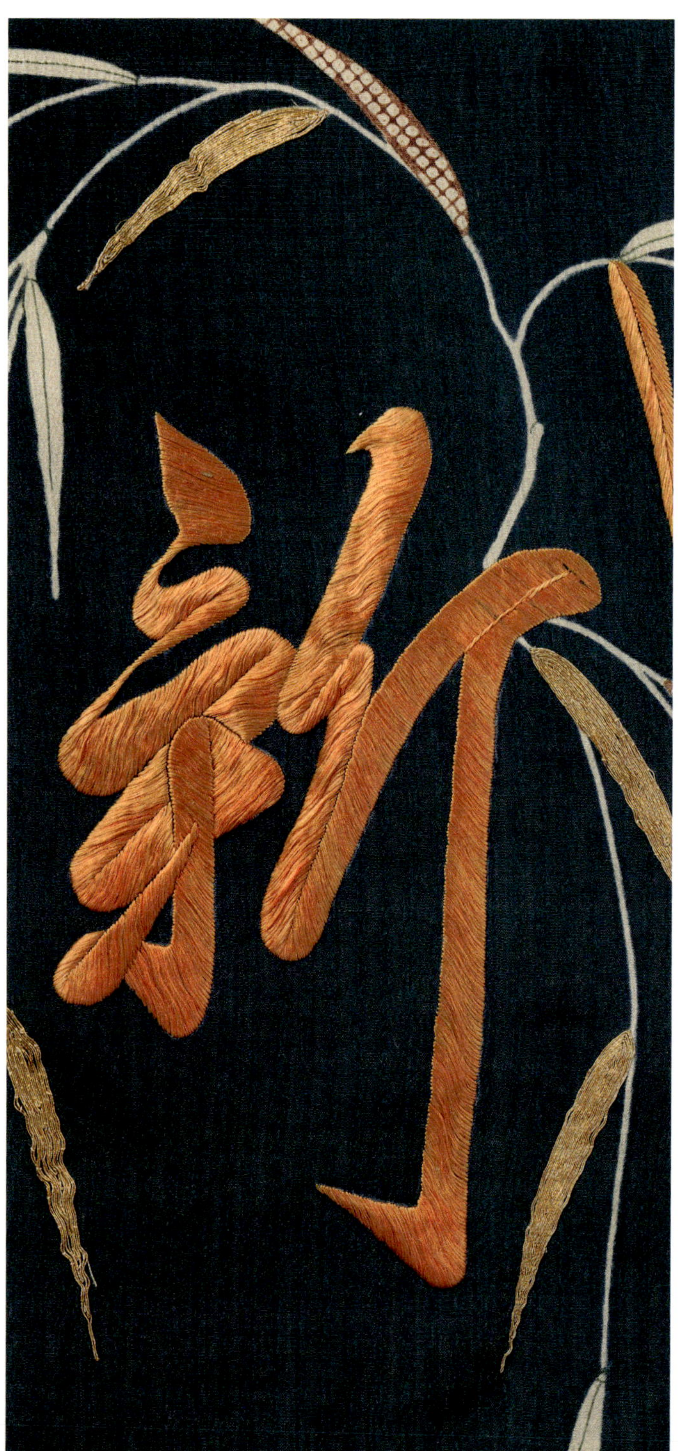

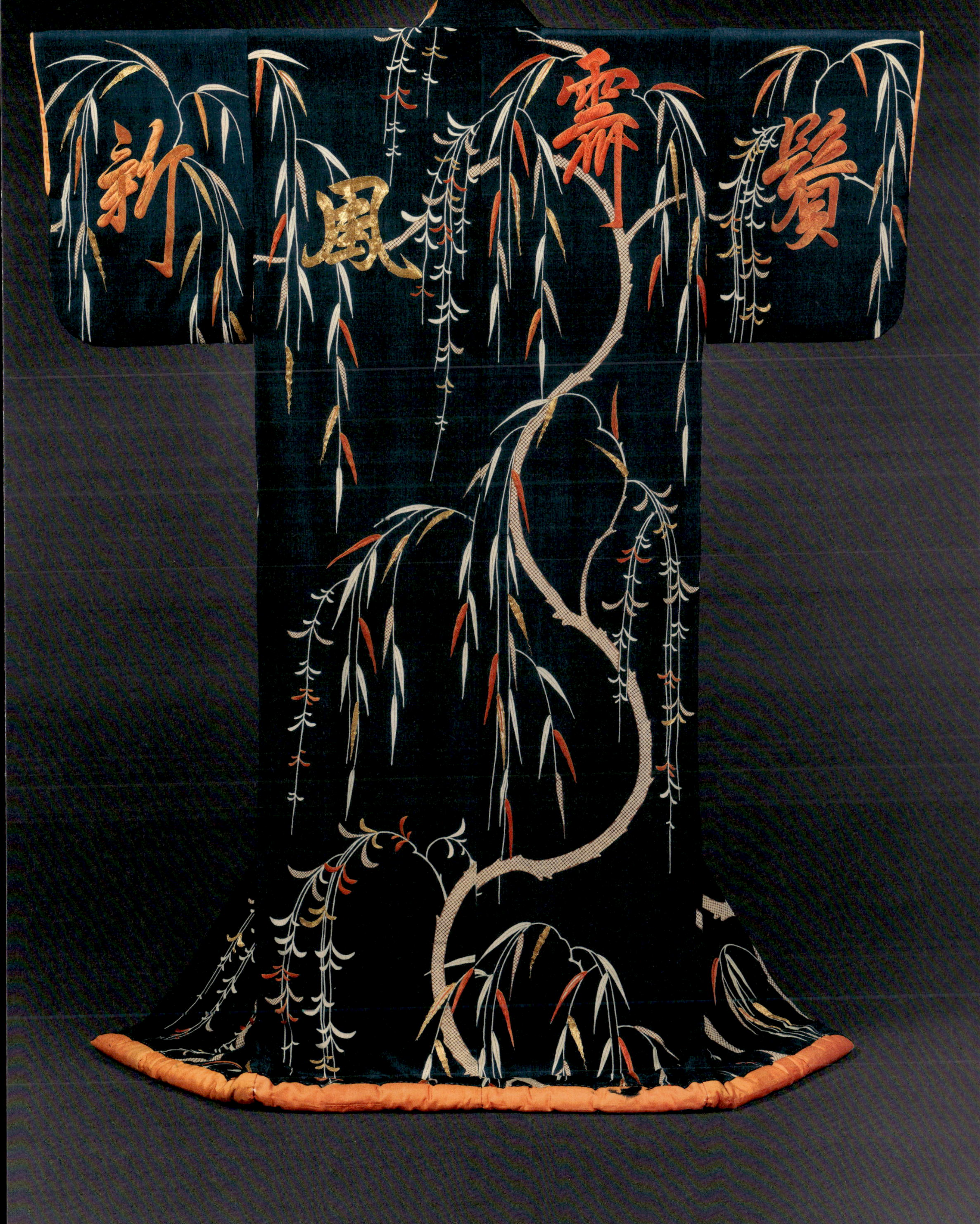
新
風
霽
鬢

24 白麻地蹴鞠柳菊鉄線模様帷子

Summer robe (*katabira*) with *kemari* balls and willow. Edo period (1615–1868), late 18th–early 19th century. Plain-weave ramie with paste-resist dyeing, stencil-dyed dots (*suri-bitta*), hand-painted details, and couched gold thread, 57 × 48 in. (144.8 × 121.9 cm). Lent by John C. Weber Collection

Light garments of bast fibers were most suitable for summer. This unlined robe was designed with long sleeves for a young, unmarried *chōnin* woman, probably in Kyoto. The cascading branches of a weeping willow provide the structure of the composition, to which scattered chrysanthemums and clematis flowers were added, along with *kemari* balls that appear to be suspended in the air. Accents of couched gold thread add highlights that suggest sunshine.

Courtiers played *kemari*, a game somewhat like soccer, beginning in the Heian period (794–1185); the aim is to keep the soft leather ball aloft only by kicking. The game was usually played within a large square marked by a cherry tree on the southeast, a maple on the southwest, pine and bamboo in the northwest, and a willow in the northeast.

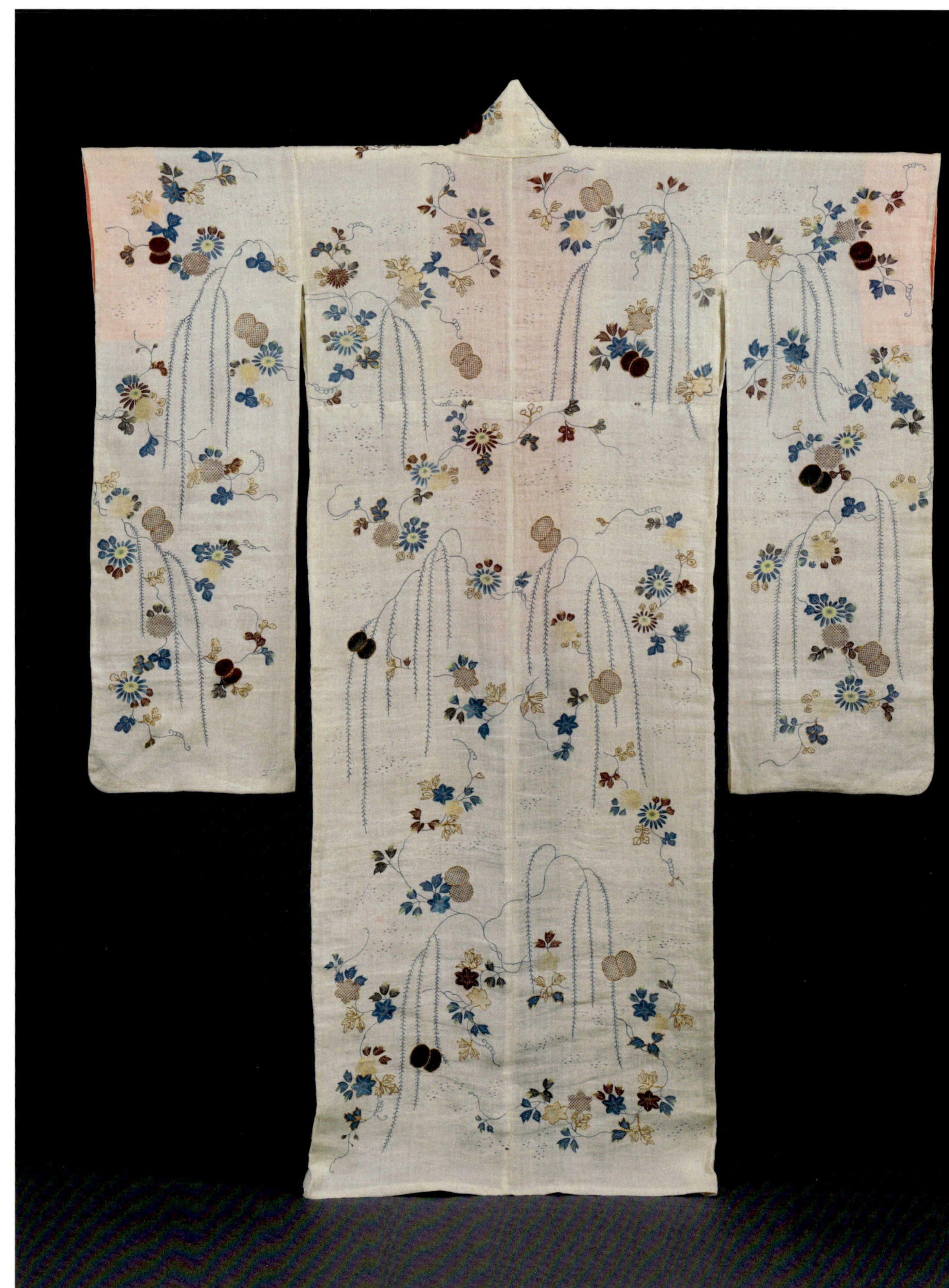

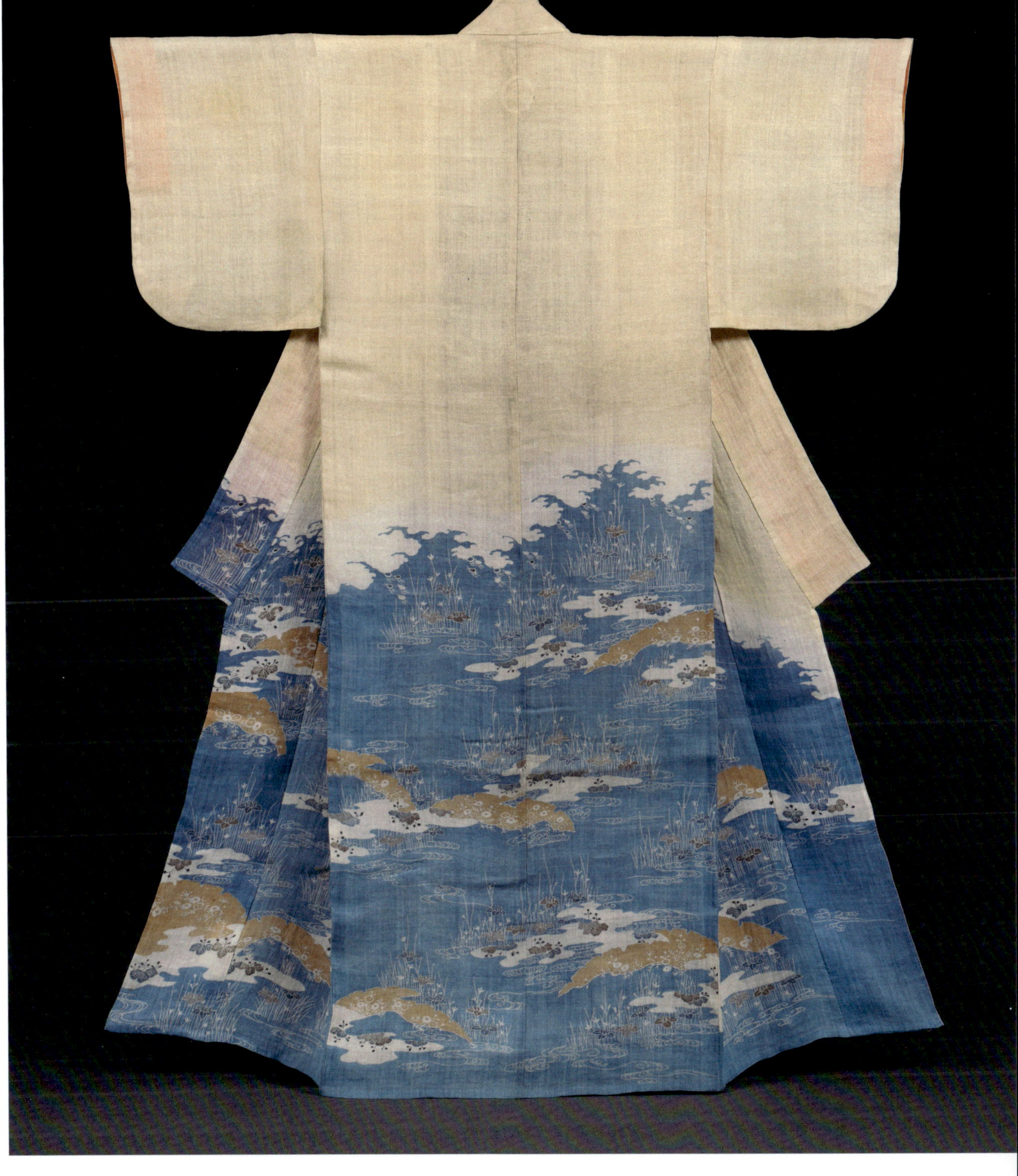

25 白麻地水辺千鳥杜若菊桐模様帷子
Summer robe (*katabira*) with plovers above sandbars and flowering plants. Edo period (1615–1868), 18th century. Plain-weave hemp with stencil paste-resist dyeing, 59⅛ × 44½ in. (150 × 113 cm). Lent by John C. Weber Collection

Conjuring a shoreline, the surface of this robe is divided into upper and lower sections of light beige and light blue respectively, divided by a white border resembling a sandbar. As was common in the first half of the eighteenth century, the pattern is concentrated on the lower half of the garment. The fine white lines of the waves and plants are reserved in white (*shiro-age*). The patterns represent early summer (iris), autumn (chrysanthemum), and late fall (paulownia); the plovers too are associated with fall. Motifs evoking cooler months are prevalent on summer garments. These stylized examples were based on Kōrin patterns, textile designs developed by the painter Ogata Kōrin (1658–1716) and popularized by woodblock-printed pattern books.[7] On the inside of the collar of this robe is a piece of paper with an inscription: "number 766, very fine unlined hemp fabric *katabira* with embroidered crest." The crest was likely added sometime after the robe was made for a merchant-class woman, since the garment is not otherwise embroidered. Only traces remain of the crest, which was probably removed when the owners had to part with the robe.

26 白綸子地竹蝶熨斗模様打掛
Over robe (*uchikake*) with bamboo and folded-paper butterflies. Edo period (1615–1868), first half of 19th century. Figured satin-weave silk (*rinzu*) with tie-dyeing, silk embroidery, and couched gold thread, 63¾ × 51¼ in. (162 × 130 cm). Lent by John C. Weber Collection

Fretwork, chrysanthemums, and orchids decorate the white figured satin-weave silk of this over robe, which was worn by a wealthy merchant-class bride. It is embroidered with bamboo stalks — a symbol of resilience and vitality — reaching from the hem to the neck. The other embroidered motif is the folded paper decoration known as *noshi*, a token of good luck traditionally attached to gifts and sake bottles. The *noshi* here are in the shape of butterflies, which allude to a long marriage. They are folded so as to distinguish them as male and female, symbolizing the new couple. They are accompanied by other symbols of longevity, such as turtles, pines, cranes, and plum blossoms. Several *noshi* are executed in *kanoko* tie-dyeing, an expensive, labor-intensive technique.

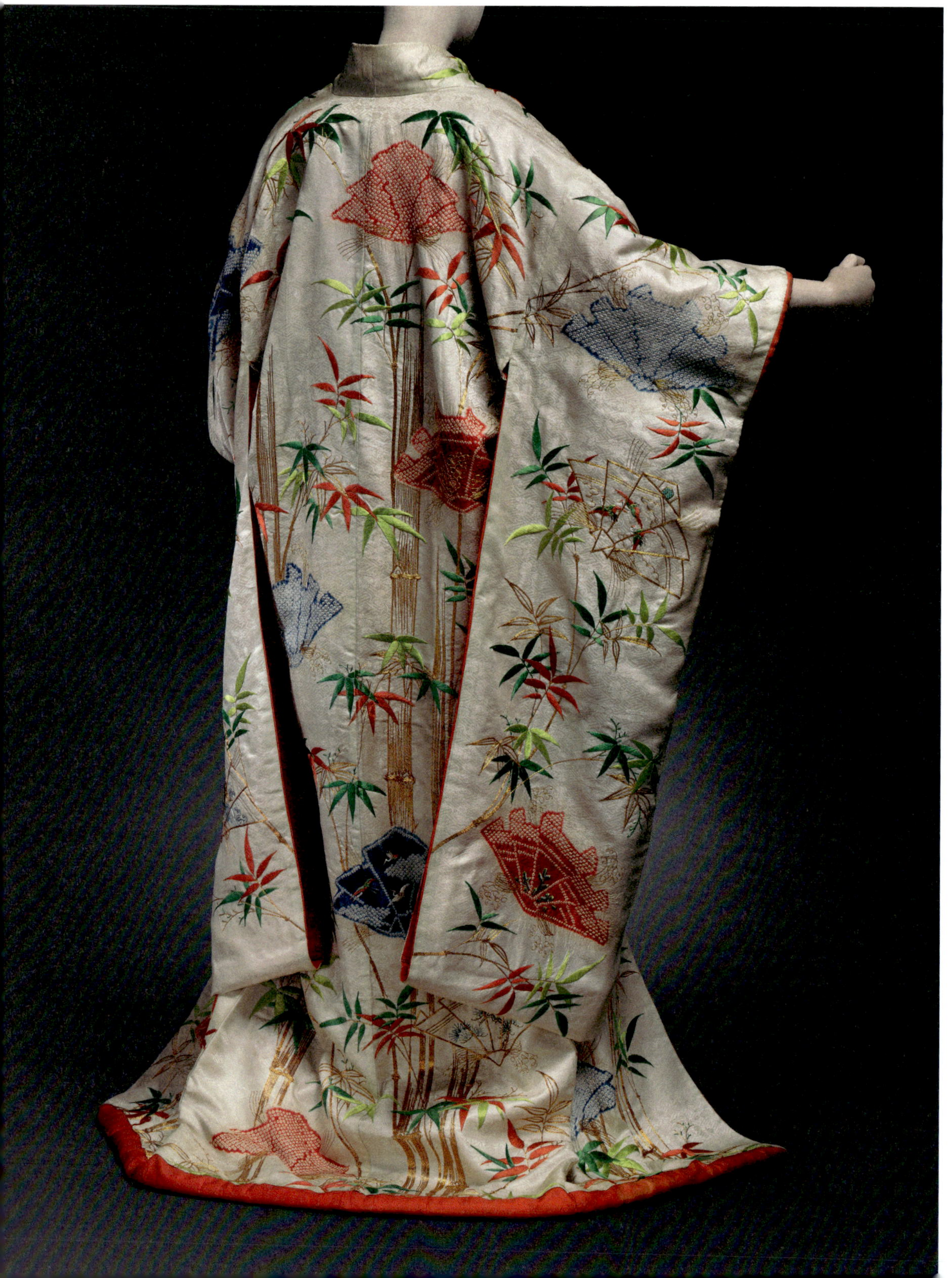

27 浅葱織地貝桶模様掛下帯

Obi (*kakeshita-obi*) with shell-matching-game boxes. Edo period (1615–1868), late 18th century. Satin-weave silk with silk embroidery and couched gold thread, 10 in. × 12 ft. 6 in. (25.4 × 381 cm). Lent by John C. Weber Collection

This type of ceremonial, formal obi would have been coordinated with a robe with long sleeves (*furisode*) worn beneath an over robe (*uchikake*) for a merchant-class bride's wedding. It would have been tied to emphasize the beauty of the *uchikake*'s draping.

The underside of this light blue sash has auspicious crane and cloud patterns, while the front depicts accoutrements of the shell-matching game, which was closely associated with weddings. The goal of the game, which became a popular courtly pastime in the late Heian period (794–1185), was to pair as many matching halves of clamshells as possible.[8] In its most elaborate form, the game was played with 360 paired clamshells, a number reflecting the average number of days in a year, according to the astronomical almanac. The shells' left halves — the "male" sides — would be spread out in concentric circles at the start of the game; the "female" sides were pulled one by one to be matched with their male counterparts. From the late Muromachi period (1392–1573), pairs of decorative, polygonal lacquer boxes with felicitous patterns in gold and silver were made to hold the shells. The shells and the boxes came to be linked to weddings, as they represented a perfect match.

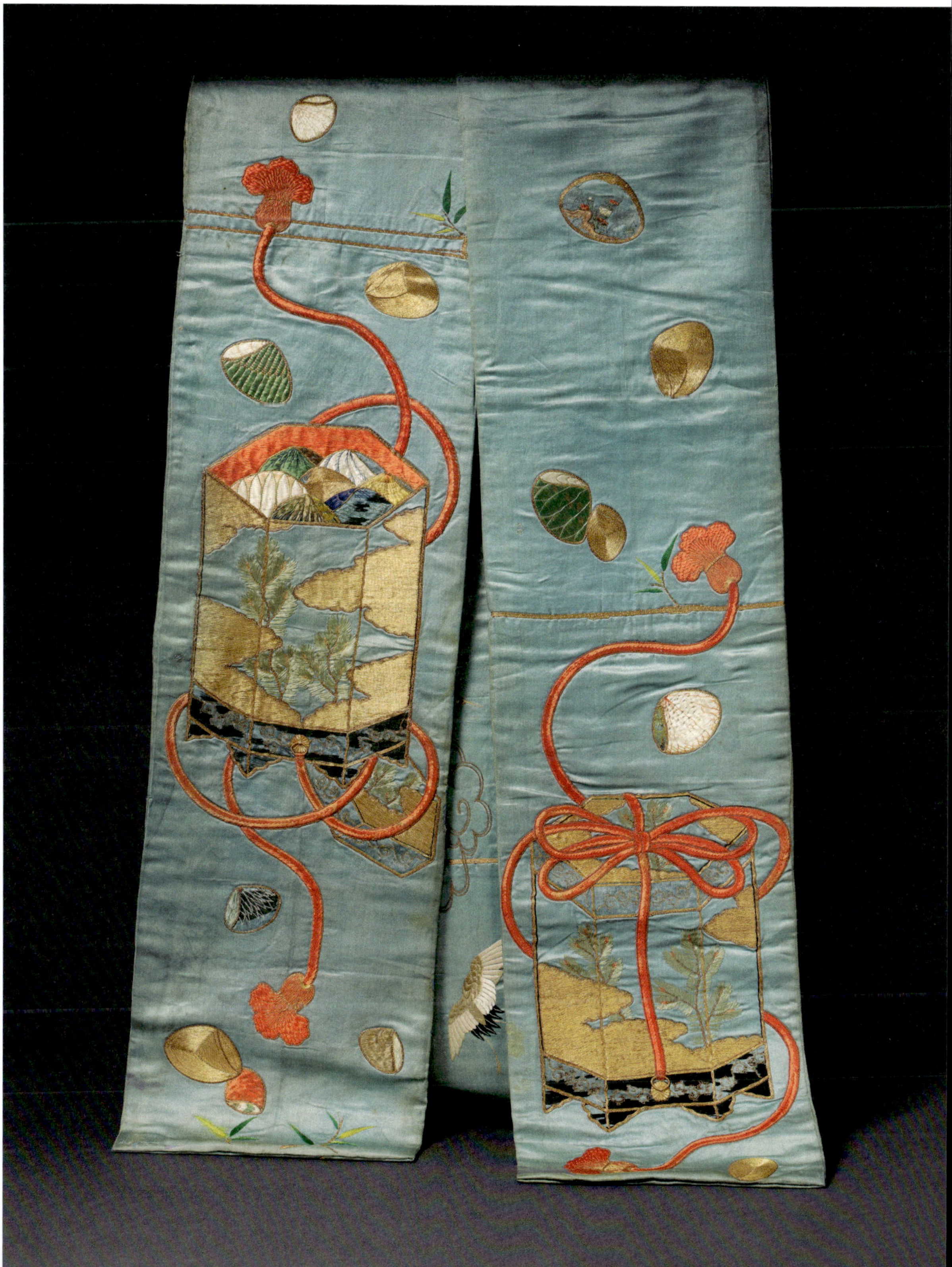

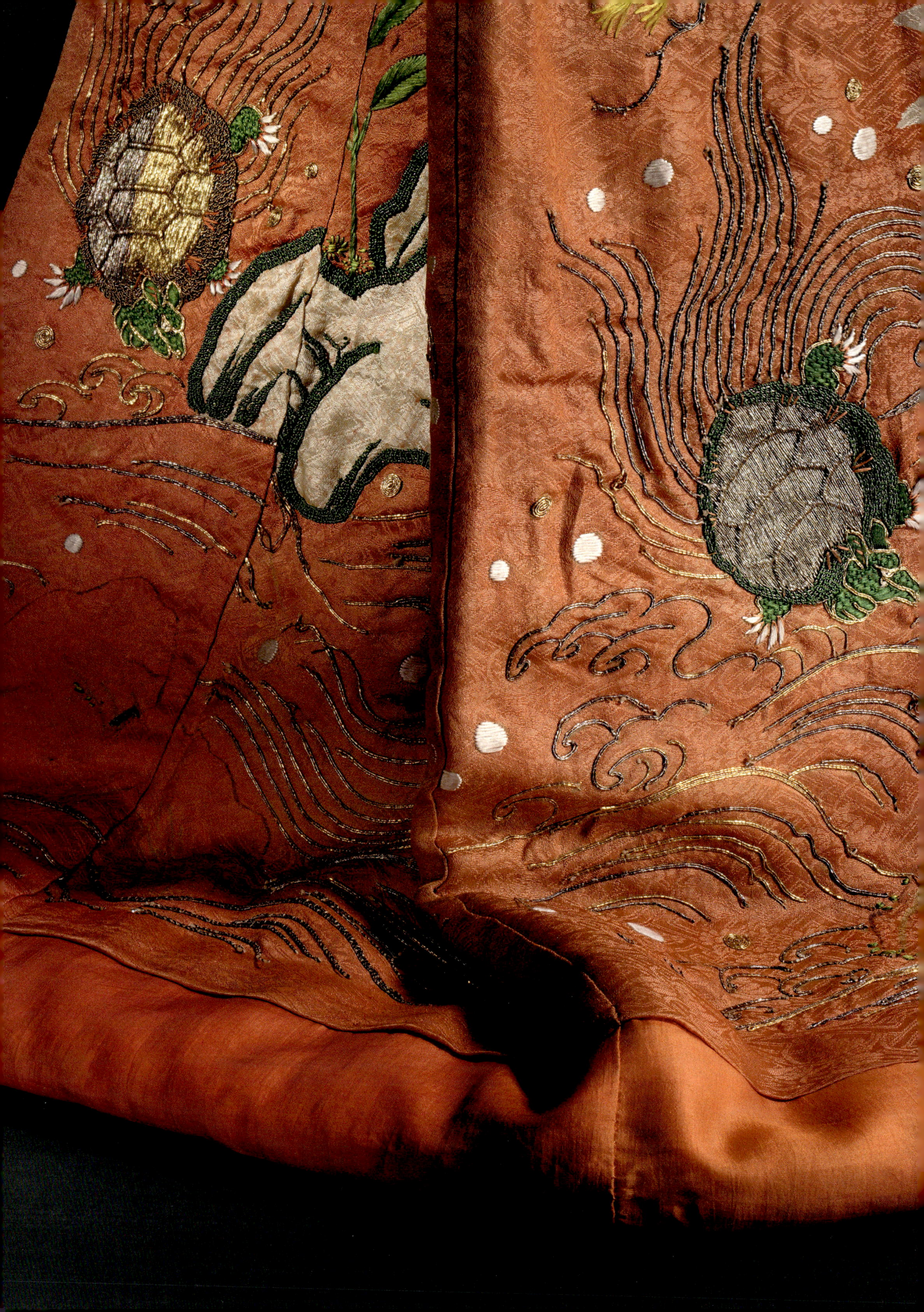

28 赤綸子地松竹梅鶴亀模様打掛

Over robe (*uchikake*) with Mount Hōrai. Edo period (1615–1868), mid-19th century. Figured satin-weave silk (*rinzu*) with paste-resist dyeing, stencil-dyed dots (*suri-bitta*), silk embroidery, and couched gold and silver thread, 66 × 49 in. (167.6 × 124.5 cm). Lent by John C. Weber Collection

This was one of a set of three luxurious over robes—white, red, and black *uchikake*, all with matching designs—worn by a samurai bride. Such sets were specially ordered for the wedding and typically worn only for that occasion. For the ceremony, the bride wore an all-white *kosode* and *uchikake* with a white silk headdress, symbolizing her resolve to be a gentle and obedient wife. After the ritual drinking of sake, the bride changed into colorful garments (*ironaoshi*) presented by the groom for the celebratory banquet. Eventually a convention was established that the bride had to change three times, giving rise to the creation of *uchikake* sets.[9]

The matching over robes were decorated with auspicious patterns, summoning both good fortune and a long and happy married life. This red robe evokes Penglai, the mythological Chinese mountain of eternal life, known in Japan as Mount Hōrai. Japanese depictions of the legendary site became stylized as a gathering of cranes and long-tailed tortoises in a bright landscape dominated, like this one, by pine, plum, and bamboo. The white mate to this robe is in the Weber Collection, but the black is lost. Black robes rarely survive, as the iron mordanting deteriorates the fabric over time.

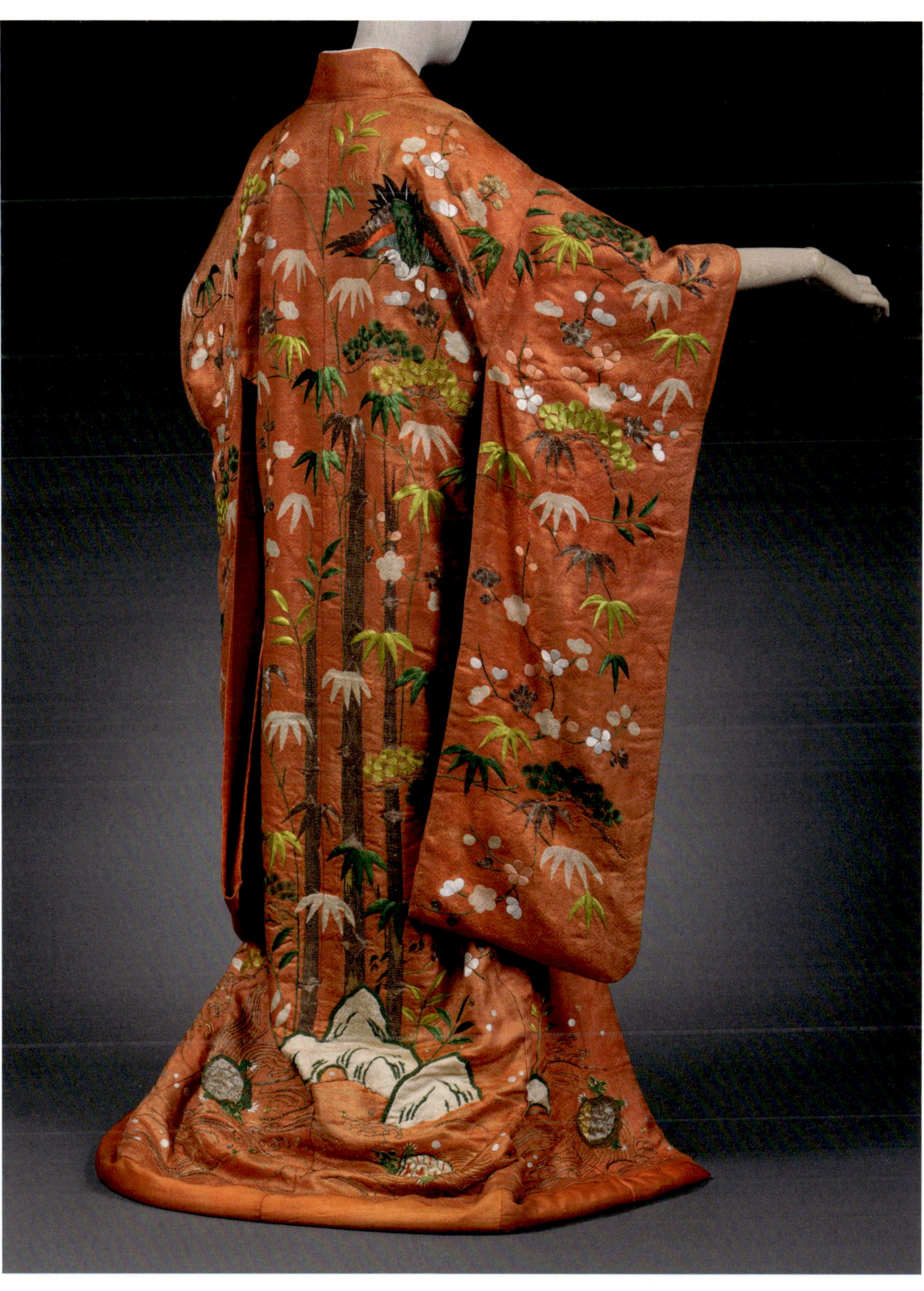

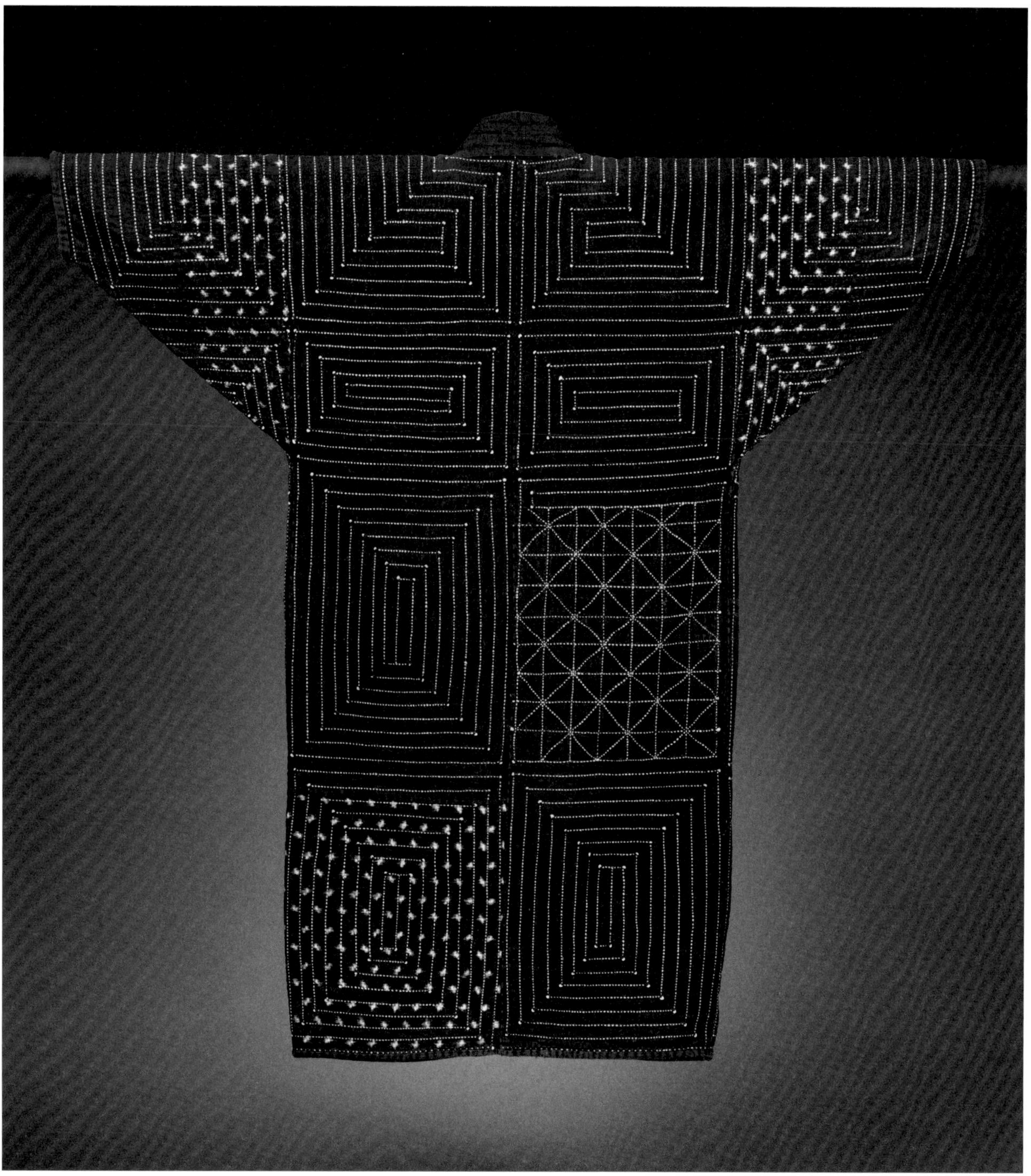

29 藍木綿刺子どんざ
Fisherman's jacket (*donza*) with geometric patterns. Meiji period (1868–1912), early 20th century. Cotton with quilting, 46 ½ × 45 ¼ in. (118.1 x 114.9 cm). Promised Gift of John C. Weber

The geometric patterns enlivening this sturdy fisherman's jacket were produced with *sashiko* stitching in white cotton thread and, in some sections, *kasuri* (ikat) dyeing. *Sashiko* is a quilting technique: a simple running stitch is used to reinforce or patch textiles or, as for this jacket of indigo-dyed cotton, to join layers of cloth. The technique produces garments that are as decorative as they are warm and durable. They were typically made at home by women in fishing and farming communities, and the intricate needlework took several months to complete. As a result, *sashiko* jackets were considered precious; they were worn when the fishermen went into port to sell their catch or for festive occasions.

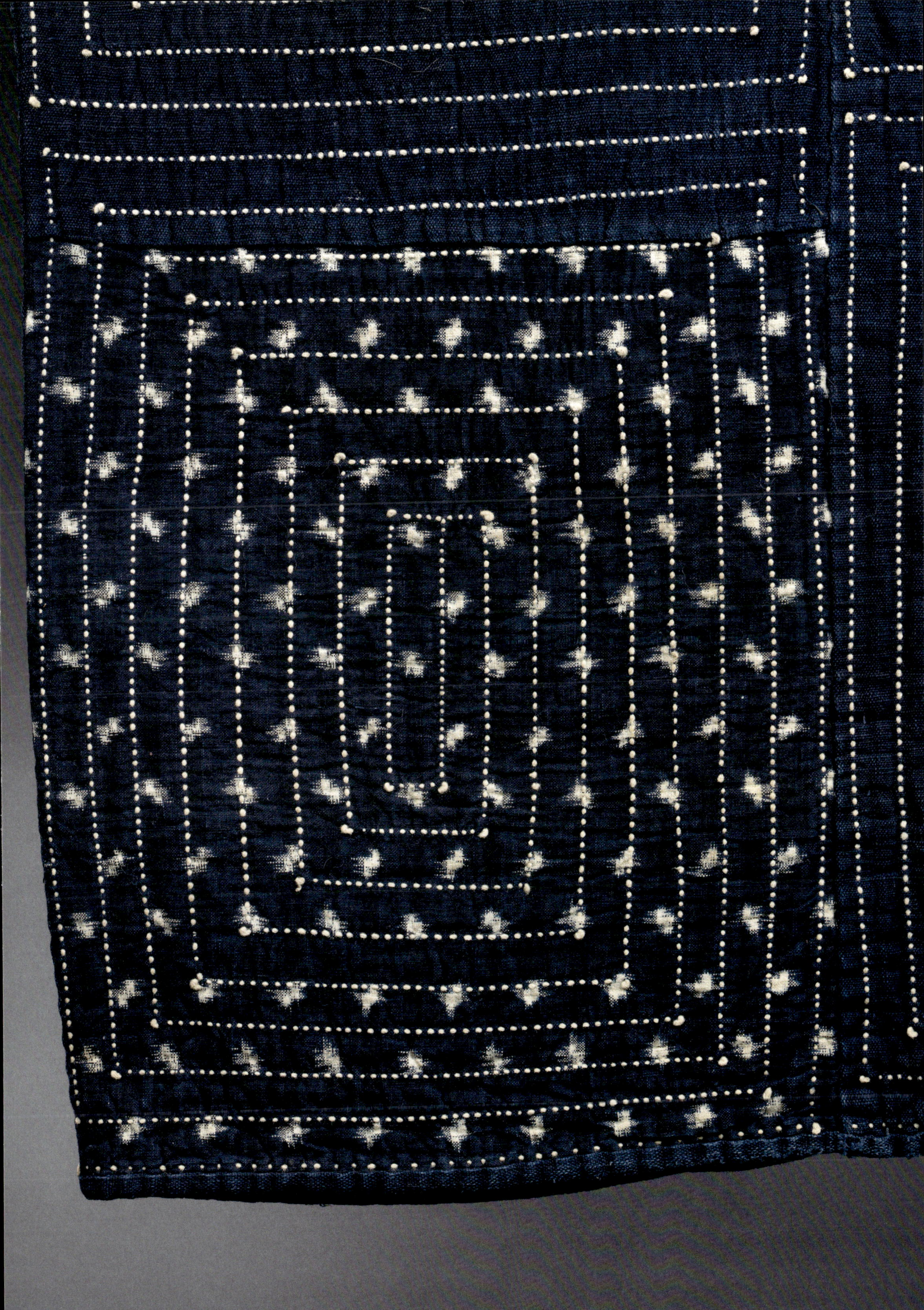

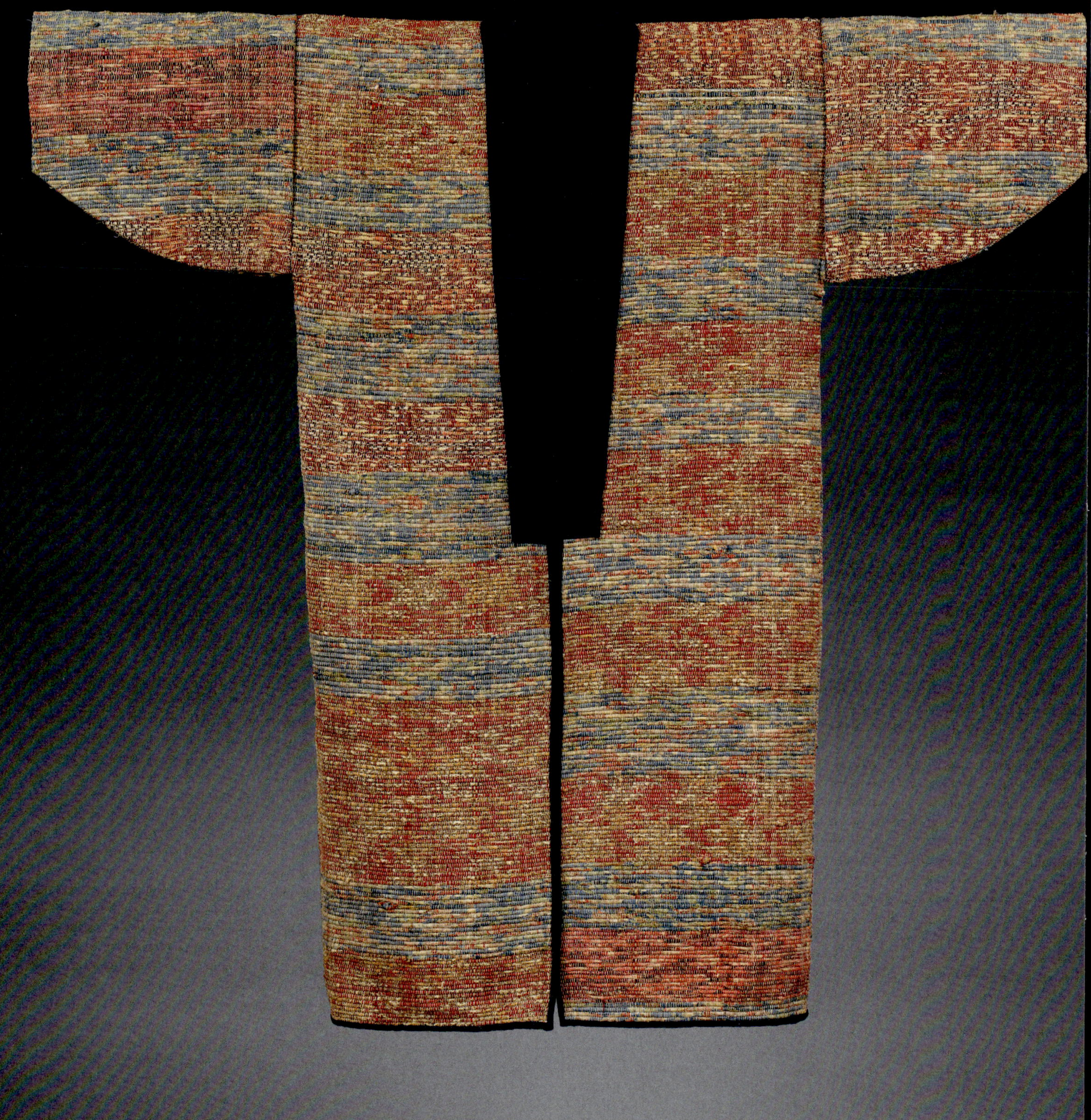

30 裂織仕事着

Farmer's jacket (*shigotogi*). Shōwa period (1926–89), second quarter of 20th century. Plain-weave cotton scraps with mountain-wisteria fiber, 47½ × 51 in. (120.7 × 129.5 cm). Promised Gift of John C. Weber

Probably once owned by a well-to-do farmer, this stylish and sturdy jacket is made with alternating blue, green, pink, red, and orange scraps of fabric of various widths. Strips of cotton were reused as wefts, woven together with warps of mountain wisteria (tree-bast fiber, *yamafuji*) in a plain-weave technique known as *sakiori*. This method began as a means of recycling old textiles, mainly cotton, which were too valuable to discard. Often women wove *sakiori* textiles on a traditional backstrap loom, using a heavy batten to beat down the thick weft. This jacket's pristine condition suggests that it was never worn. Very few antique farmer's jackets survive.

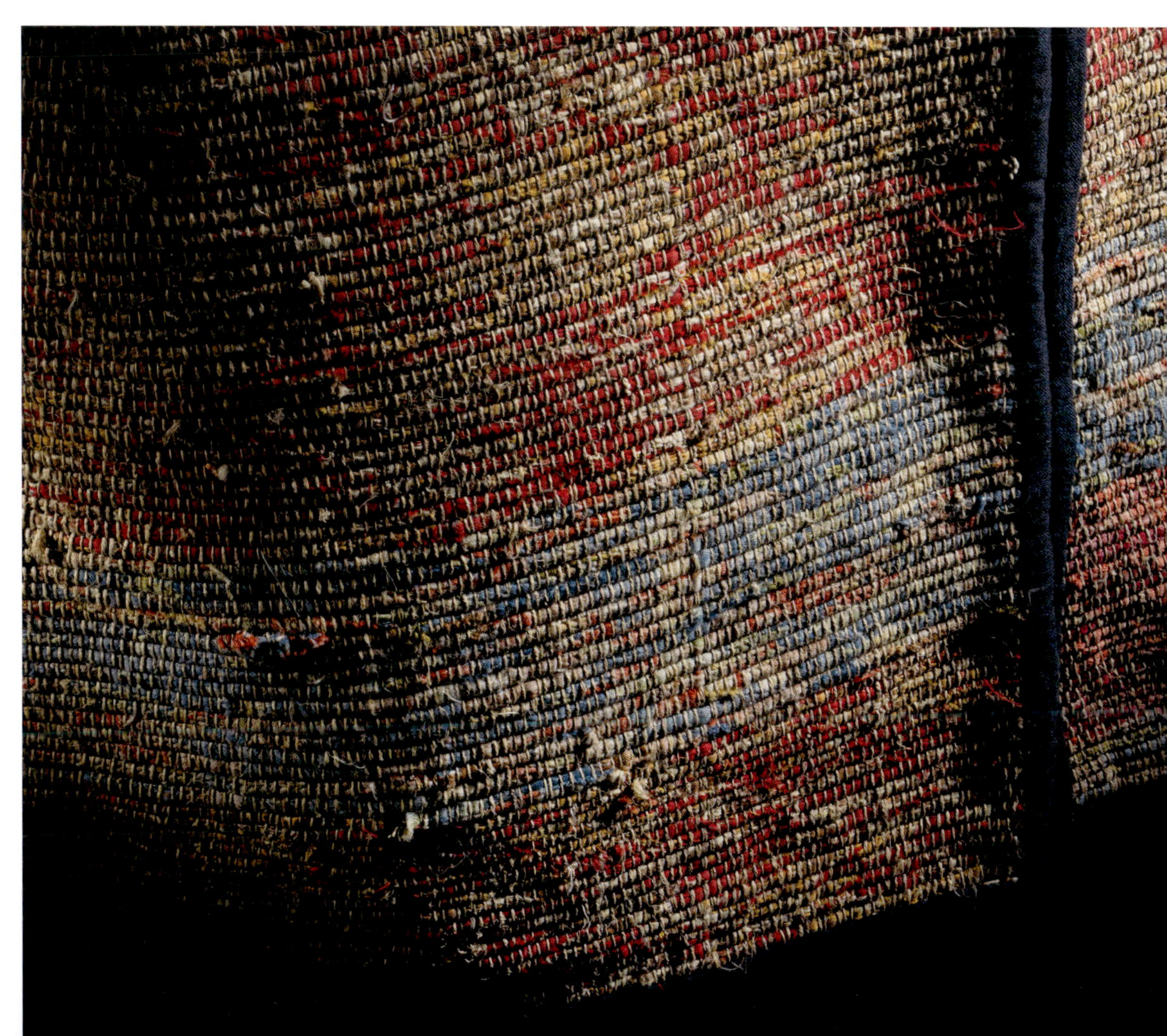

31 寄裂袖なし胴着

Vest. Edo period (1615–1868), first half of 19th century. Patchwork of various fabrics, 34 x 23 in. (86.4 x 58.4 cm). Promised Gift of John C. Weber

This stylish vest was made of swatches from more than thirty types of fabric, including velvet and silk with gold and silver embroidery, resulting in a colorful and playful composition. Patchwork had connotations of longevity, since stitching together the scraps extended their use.

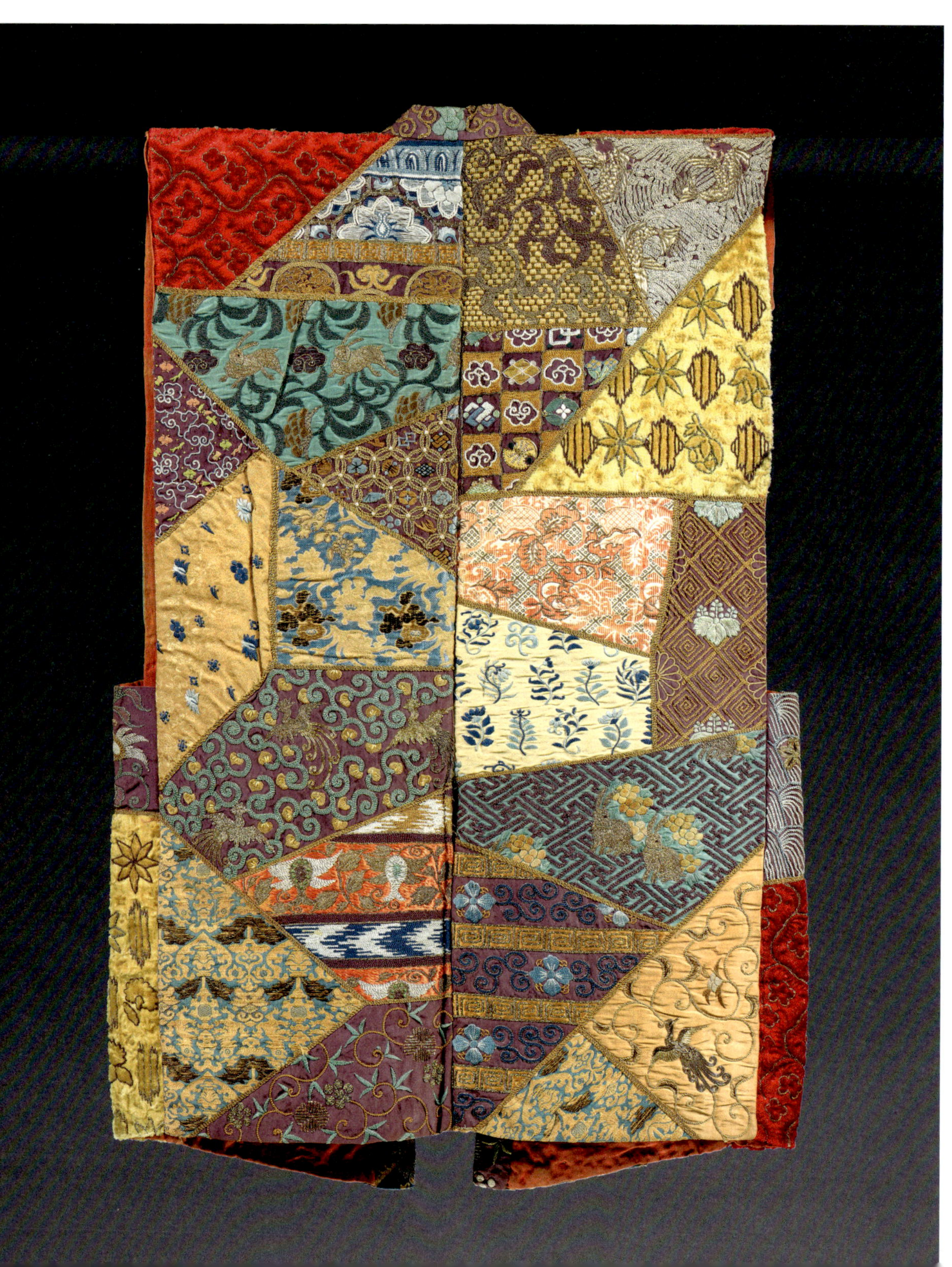

32 藍木綿地菊紋小紋模様被衣

Outer robe (*katsugi*) with chrysanthemum crest. Edo period (1615–1868), first half of 19th century. Plain-weave cotton with stencil paste-resist dyeing, 48 × 46 in. (121.9 × 116.8 cm). Promised Gift of John C. Weber

A *katsugi* is a woman's mantle or coatlike veil, usually in the shape of a *kosode*, worn pulled over the head with the sleeves unused. Some *katsugi* were made of silk, but most were hemp with indigo-dyed patterns. The garment dates to the Heian period (794–1185), but by the early Edo period at least three distinct types had developed, with different pattern vocabularies.[10] This example represents the type that was embellished with a large flower motif, here a chrysanthemum crest, where the garment covered the head. Stencil-dyeing and tube-drawn paste-resist dyeing (*tsutsugaki*) created the patterns on this robe in white reserve. From shoulder to hem, the patterns are: chrysanthemums and stylized concentric motifs among small dots against an indigo ground; plum blossoms on a green ground; stylized hemp leaves against an indigo ground; and bracken fern fiddleheads on a blue-black ground. As the chrysanthemum crest is placed lower than usual and the patterns are relatively simple, this could be a regional variation of *katsugi* made for a commoner in Kyoto, where it remained popular throughout the Edo period.

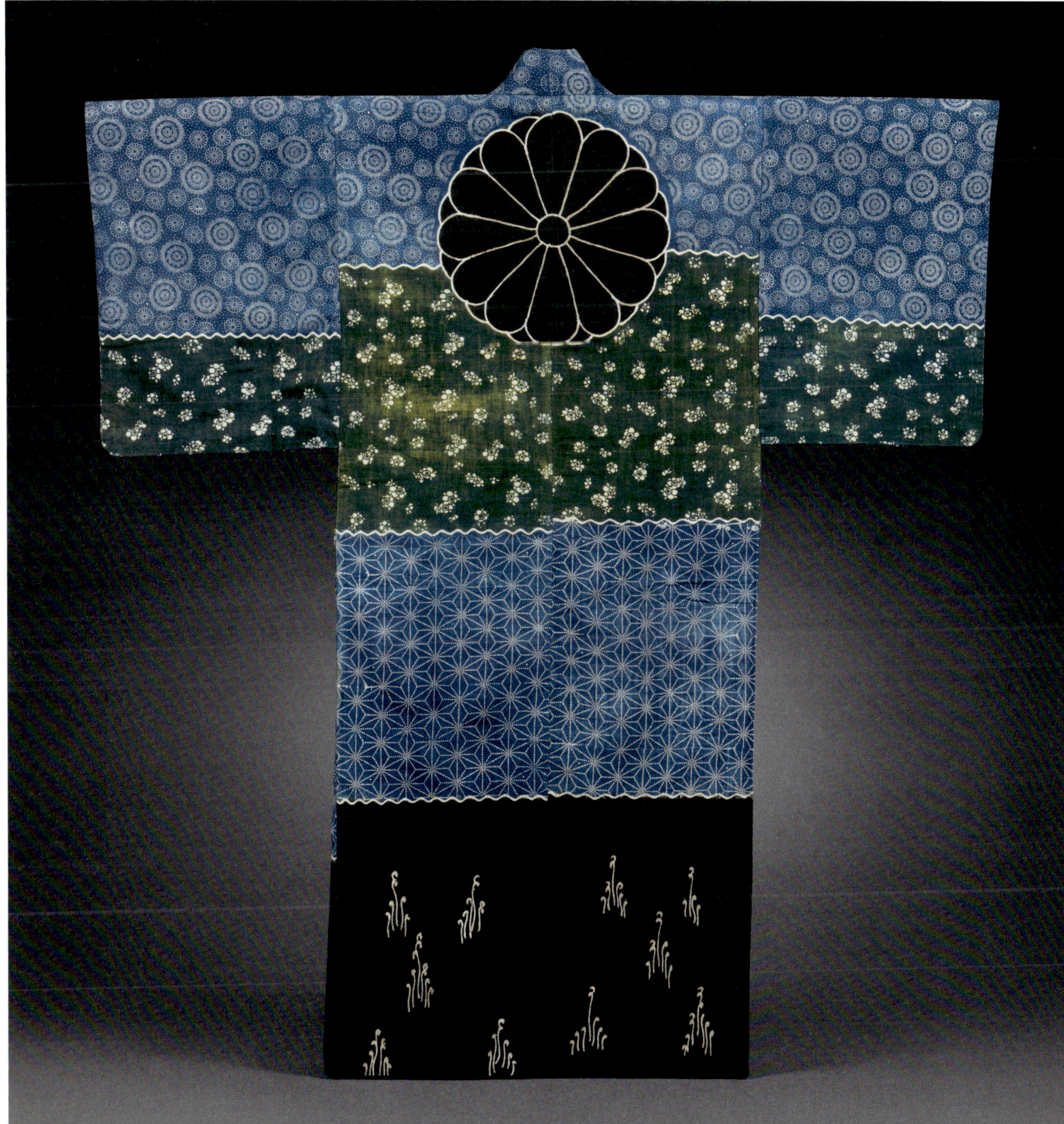

33 浅葱木綿地松皮菱桜模様着物

Summer kimono with pine lozenge and cherry blossoms. Meiji period (1868–1912), early 20th century. Ramie with stencil paste-resist dyeing, 57⅛ × 46¼ in. (145.1 × 117.5 cm). Promised Gift of John C. Weber

This summer kimono only looks as if it were composed of three different fabrics, an effect created by skillful dyeing. On the back, the shoulder area has a vertical stripe combined with a pattern of straight bamboo stalks, while the lower section features horizontal stripes. A large pine-lozenge motif with scattered cherry blossoms occupies the center. After the application of the patterns with stencils, the ramie ground was dyed with indigo with white-reserve motifs. Ramie, also called "China grass," is a fiber-yielding plant of the nettle family (Urticaceae). Known for its high quality and soft touch, ramie fabric (*karamushi*) is often used for summer clothing. It is produced primarily in Fukushima prefecture.

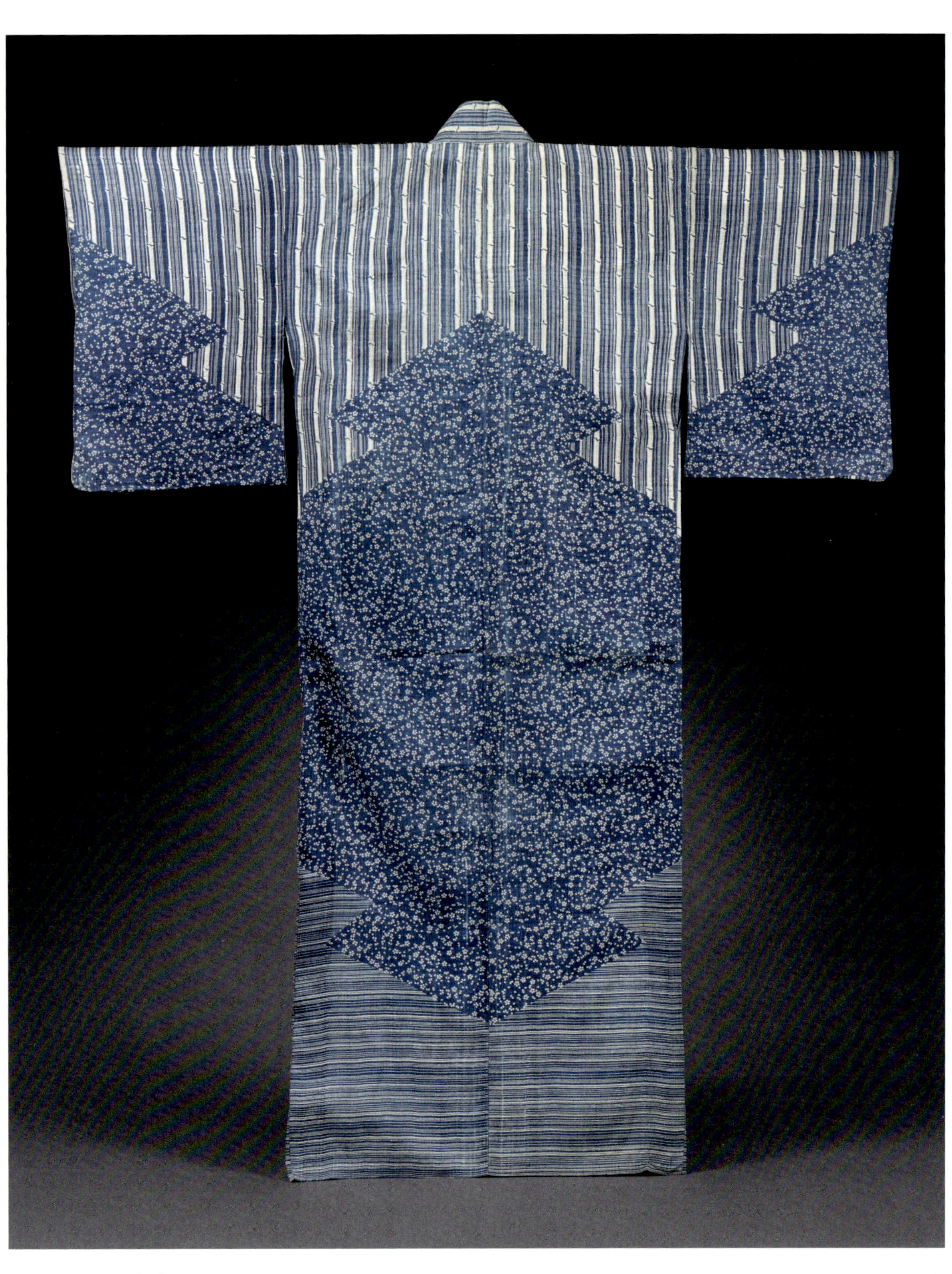

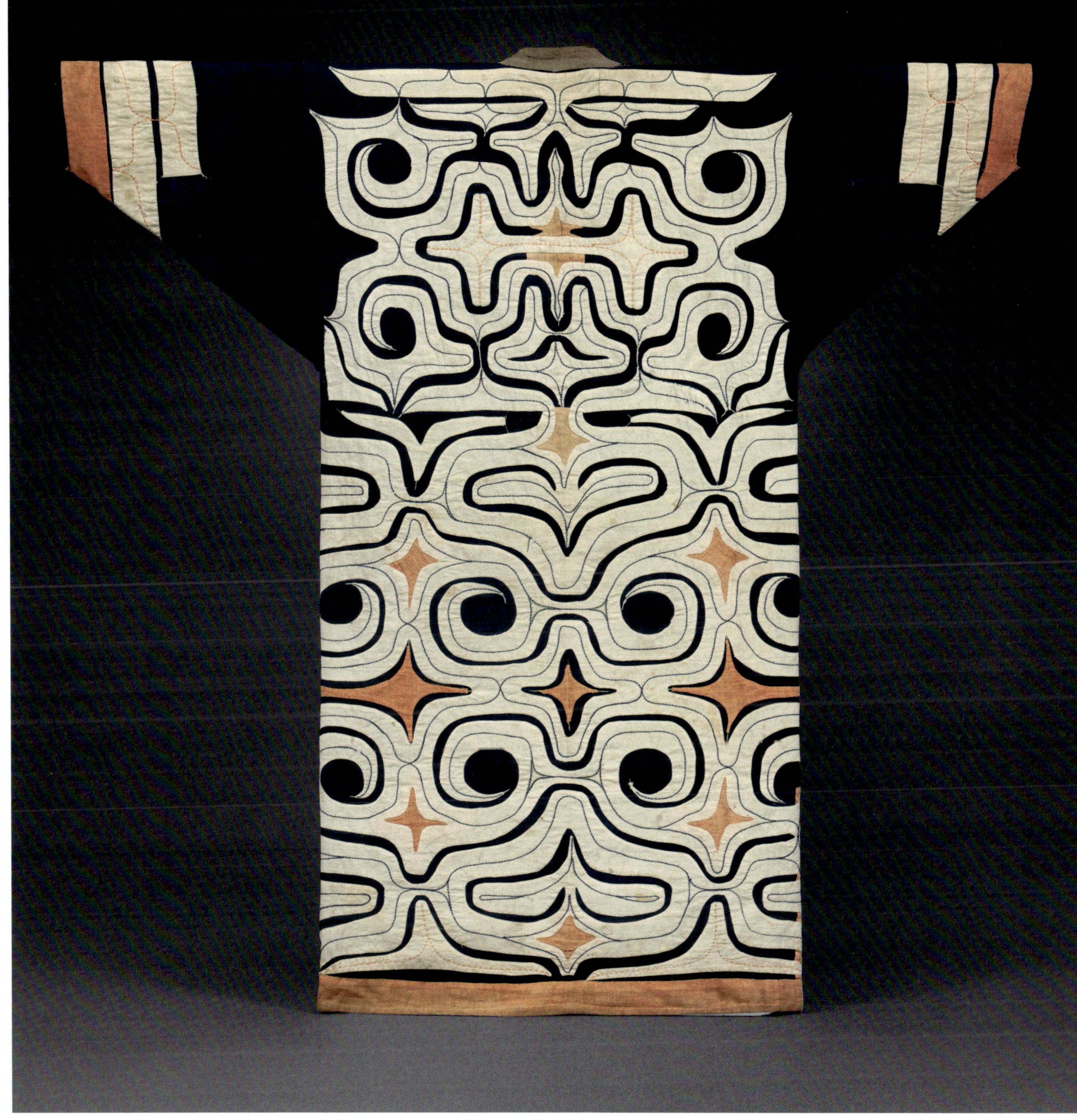

34 色裂置紋木綿衣　ルウンペ
Ainu coat (*ruunpe*). Meiji period (1868–1912), early 20th century. Cotton, appliqué, and decorative stitches, 48 × 50 in. (121.9 × 127 cm). Promised Gift of John C. Weber

The clothing culture of northern Japan's native Ainu people was transformed by the development of an extensive trade in cotton and used clothing, which introduced the fabric to places where cotton could not be grown. The Ainu's traditional garments were made from the fur and skin of deer, bear, and other animals, as well as from salmon skin, but eventually used plant fibers such as elm bark, grass, and finally cotton. Creatively and economically recycling used fabrics, the Ainu developed a distinctive and attractive style. One of the most striking types of Ainu robe is the cotton *ruunpe*.[11] The cotton ground fabric, typically dyed a dark indigo, was embellished with additional cotton pieces, usually taken from old Japanese clothing whose patterns and colors often remained distinct. These now-faded cutouts of bright red and white were appliquéd onto the *ruunpe* robes with vividly colored decorative stitches. The easily worn-out areas around the neck, cuffs, and hem were reinforced with appliqué as well. The robe's complex geometric patterns were thought to have talismanic qualities that protected the wearer.

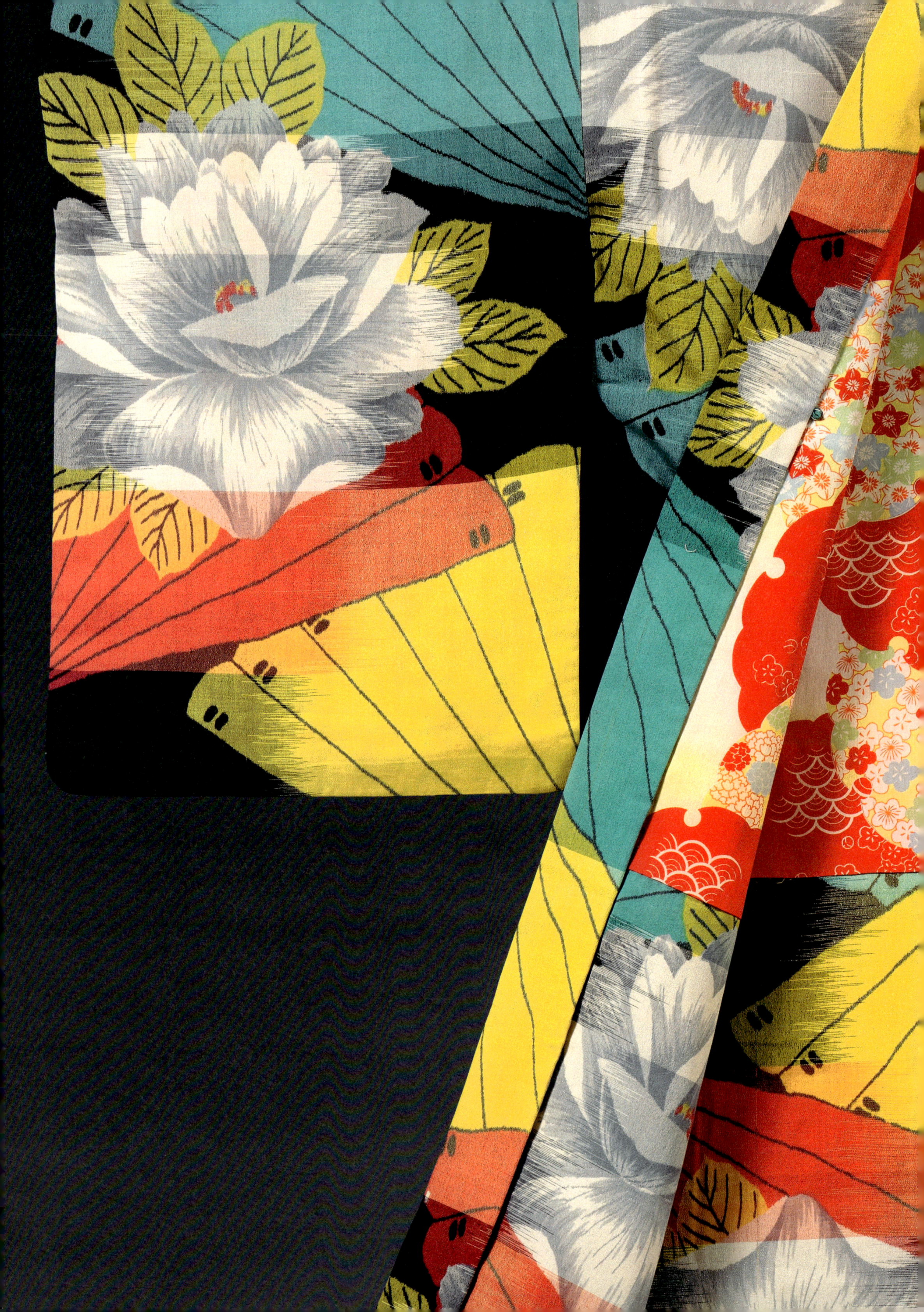

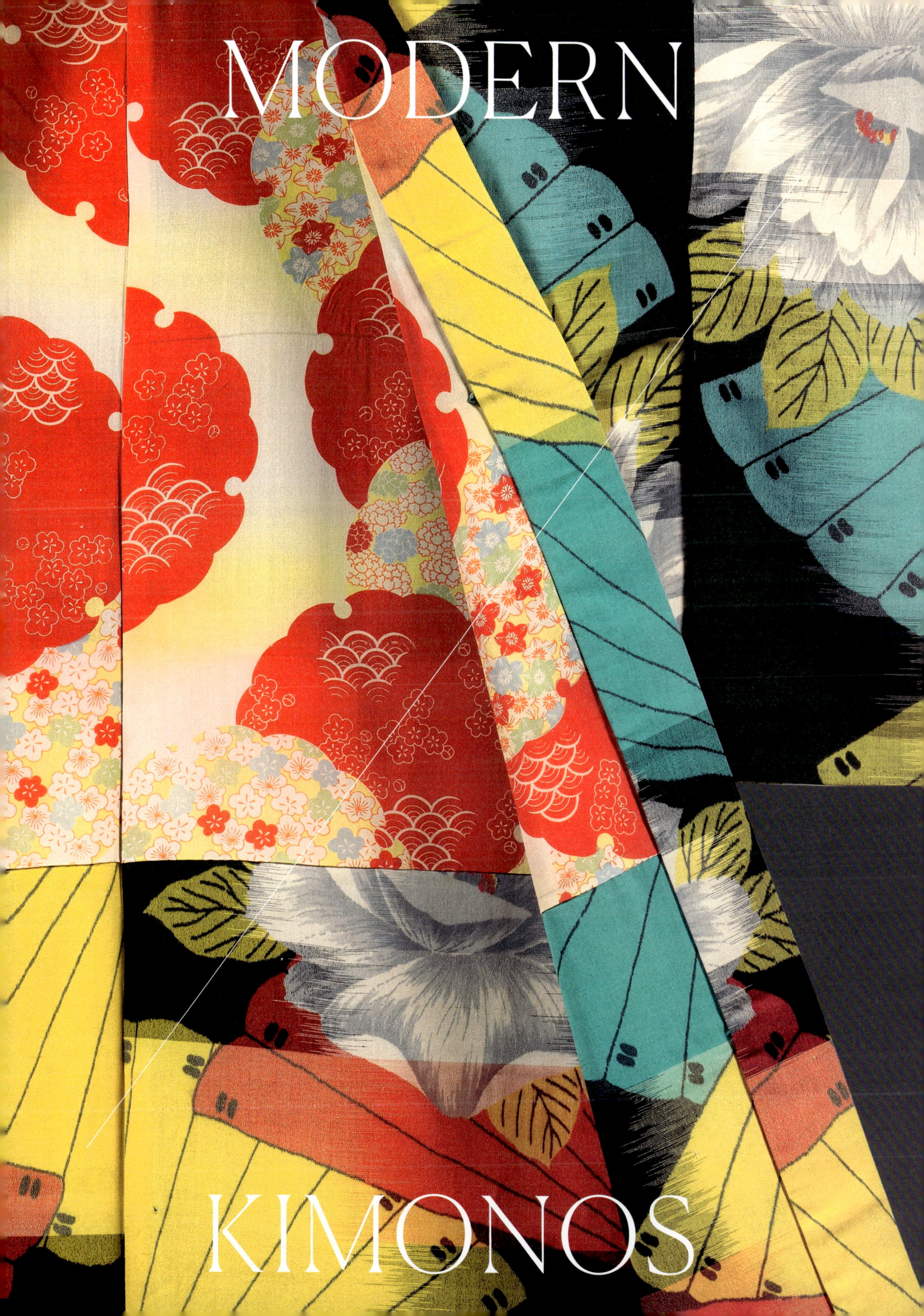
MODERN
KIMONOS

THE MODERNIZATION OF THE JAPANESE FASHION system did not manifest first in the widespread adoption of new or Western styles but rather in the field of textile production. Global trade and industrialization in the second half of the nineteenth century vastly expanded Japan's access to previously expensive or restricted wool, cotton, and machine-spun silk. The importation of European aniline dyes led to a powerful and novel palette, including vivid violets, deep reds, and bright greens. A fresh design vocabulary encompassed realistic depictions of flowers and landscapes as well as traditional, auspicious motifs — autumn grasses, dragonflies — presented in modern, vibrant compositions (cats. 41, 55). Even as Edo-period designs enjoyed a revival, kimono patterns increasingly drew from Western imagery, including European flowers and art movements such as Art Nouveau, Art Deco, and, eventually, abstraction; oversize, repeating patterns superseded intricate iconography based primarily on literature (cats. 65–68). And while kimonos continued to be worn with obis — both traditional, formal silk versions for festive occasions (cat. 47) and affordable, informal ones to update everyday robes — they were also accessorized with Western-style handbags, parasols, shawls, gloves, and hats.

The Western influence was pervasive, even if Western wear itself caught on only gradually. While many women routinely wore kimonos until the mid-twentieth century, they became familiar with Western design, as clothes were paraded on the streets, displayed in department stores, and modeled in fashion magazines, all conveying modernity. The introduction of Western furniture and dining habits encouraged the use of garments that were better suited to tall tables and chairs than was traditional Japanese attire. A sartorial dualism characterized the early twentieth century, with Western-style clothes increasingly worn in the public sphere and kimonos, comfortable for sitting on the tatami, worn in the privacy of home. Men, in particular, adopted Western clothing for work and relaxed among family in informal under kimonos (*nagajuban*) (cats. 35–37).

Kimonos were still highly customized into the early twentieth century, with the wearer selecting the ground fabric and picking favored motifs. However, Western clothing, all made of predyed fabrics, introduced the idea of separating tailoring from patterns, contributing to the development of ready-to-wear kimonos in the early 1900s. Textile manufacturers and retailers realized that a fashion system based on regularly changing, widely available, mass-produced styles could reap significant profits.[1] Adapting the lesson to Japanese fashion, they promoted ready-made kimonos of *meisen*, a low-cost silk that conveyed a sense of luxury to the "modern girls" (*moga*) joining the workforce in the 1920s (cats. 52–68).

Mirroring Japan's democratization, what had been a luxurious, bespoke tradition for affluent merchant-class ladies in the Edo period gave way to affordable kimonos sold in Japanese department stores. Decorative techniques were simplified: time-consuming, special-order hand-painting and tie-dyeing were replaced by stencil-dyeing and *kasuri*, the weaving of predyed yarns (cat. 52); instead of rich, three-dimensional embroidery and gold-leaf application, kimonos presented flat surfaces with vibrant, synthetic colors and a wide variety of patterns, some derived from Edo-period fashions (cat. 54) and some inspired by Western art (cat. 67). At the same time, affluent women from conservative households kept alive the tradition of elaborately decorated haute couture kimonos made with time-honored techniques.

"Fast-fashion" *meisen* robes for the "new woman" were among the first commodities that helped build Japan's capitalist economy. However, modern and *meisen* kimonos tended to be overlooked by aficionados of Japanese art until recently, in contrast to Noh costumes, *kesa*, *kosode*, and *uchikake*, all of which have long been coveted as collectibles. One of the first *meisen* collectors was John C. Weber, who started to buy them as early as 1996. He gradually assembled a significant group representing the garment's history, from the 1920s through the 1950s, a pivotal time when Japan's engagement with the West changed Japanese fashion and laid the foundations of contemporary styles, both for kimonos and for Western designs inspired by them.

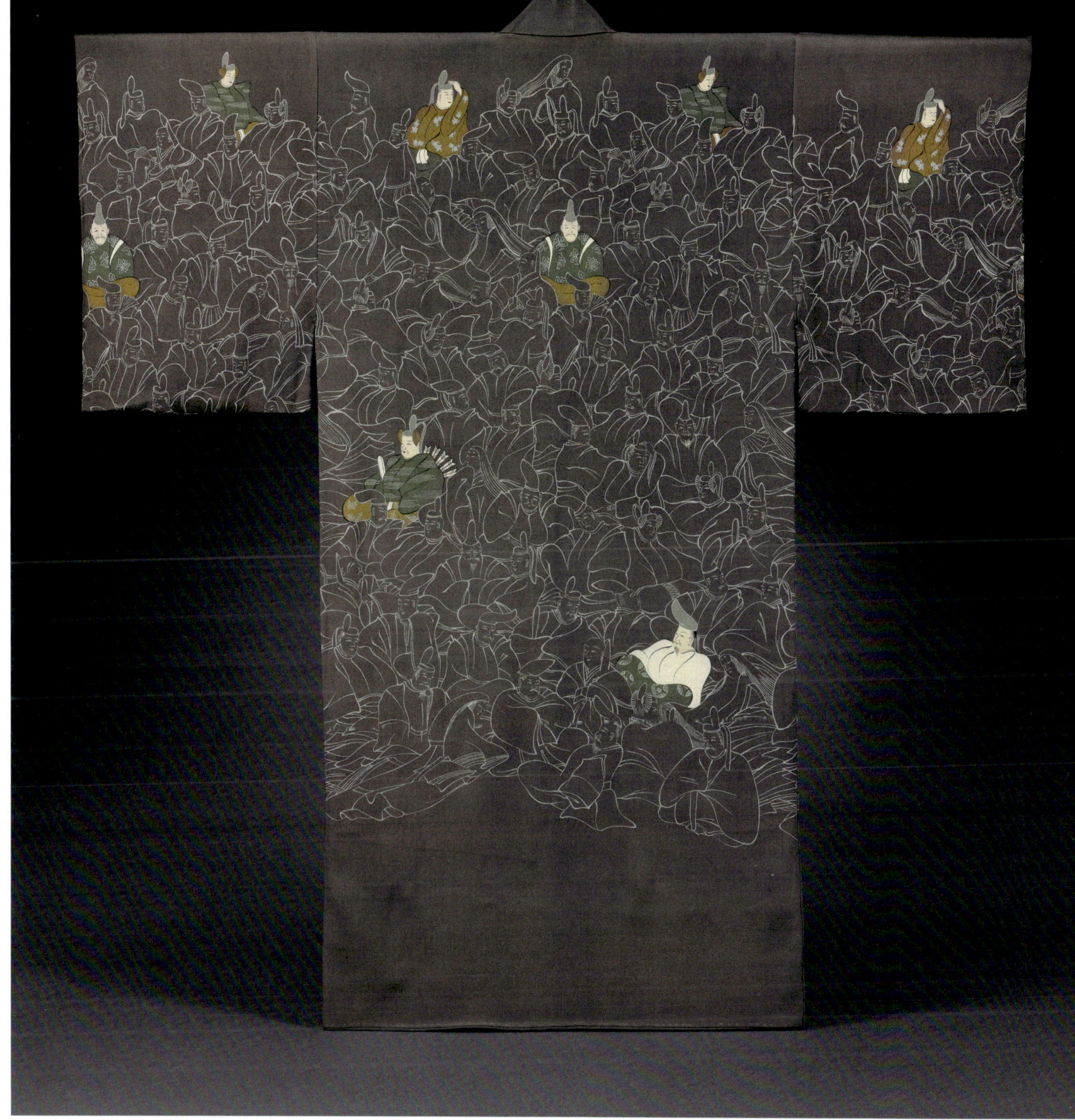

35 薄緑色縮緬地三十六歌仙模様男物長襦袢

Man's under kimono (*nagajuban*) with the Thirty-Six Immortal Poets (*Sanjūrokkasen*). Late Meiji (1868–1912)–Taishō (1912–26) period, first quarter of 20th century. Crepe silk (*chirimen*) with stencil paste-resist dyeing and hand-painted details, 50⅜ × 49⅝ in. (128 × 126 cm). Promised Gift of John C. Weber

A *nagajuban* is an informal garment worn under an outer kimono or at home, among family members. This example's complex composition depicts the thirty-six famous poets, including five women, whose works were anthologized by Fujiwara no Kintō in the early eleventh century. Throughout medieval times these "immortals of poetry" were depicted in handscroll format. Later followers of the painter Ogata Kōrin, such as Sakai Hōitsu (1761–1828), Ikeda Koson (1802–1867), and Kamisaka Sekka (1866–1942), revived and modernized this traditional subject by combining all the poets in a single scene—a composition that inspired this *nagajuban*. Here, most of the poets are depicted in a simple white outline, while a few are emphasized by hand-painted details added to their faces, hats, and garments. Kakinomoto no Hitomaru stands out in his white attire with a flower-crest pattern. It appears that one large stencil (*kata-zome*) was used to create the composition on the back, which is made of a single panel of silk instead of the usual two.

36 璃寛茶縮緬地蜘蛛模様男物長襦袢

Man's under kimono (*nagajuban*) with spider and spiderweb. Taishō (1912–26)–Shōwa (1926–89) period, 1920s–30s. Crepe silk (*chirimen*) with freehand paste-resist dyeing (*yūzen*), 52½ × 50¾ in. (133.4 × 128.9 cm). Promised Gift of John C. Weber

Worn under an outer garment or at home, the *nagajuban* frequently bore eye-catching designs that would be seen only by family and friends. The large spider perched on the right shoulder of the crepe silk robe below, whose back is covered with a web against gray clouds, exemplifies such a decoration. The pattern could be a reference to Tsuchigumo, a monstrous, shape-shifting spider featured in Japanese myths and legends as well as in Noh and Kabuki plays. The dramatic, supernatural subject was also featured in ukiyo-e prints, which might have inspired this *nagajuban*'s composition.

A snow-covered Mount Fuji adorns the fashionable *nagajuban* shown opposite, which is made of a soft, lightweight plain-weave silk (habutai) similar to taffeta. The large stylized design of the sacred mountain was rendered against a dark blue ground in stitch-and-bind resist technique (*nuishime-shibori*), with a painstakingly executed gradation from white to deep gray. The dark hue delicately contrasts with the deep blue ground. Mount Fuji is one of the most represented subjects in Japanese art, depicted on hanging scrolls, folding screens, woodblock prints, ceramics, and lacquerware, and it is prominently featured in Japanese literature. On this robe, the perfectly shaped mountain, revered in Shinto and Buddhism, was a symbol of good fortune.

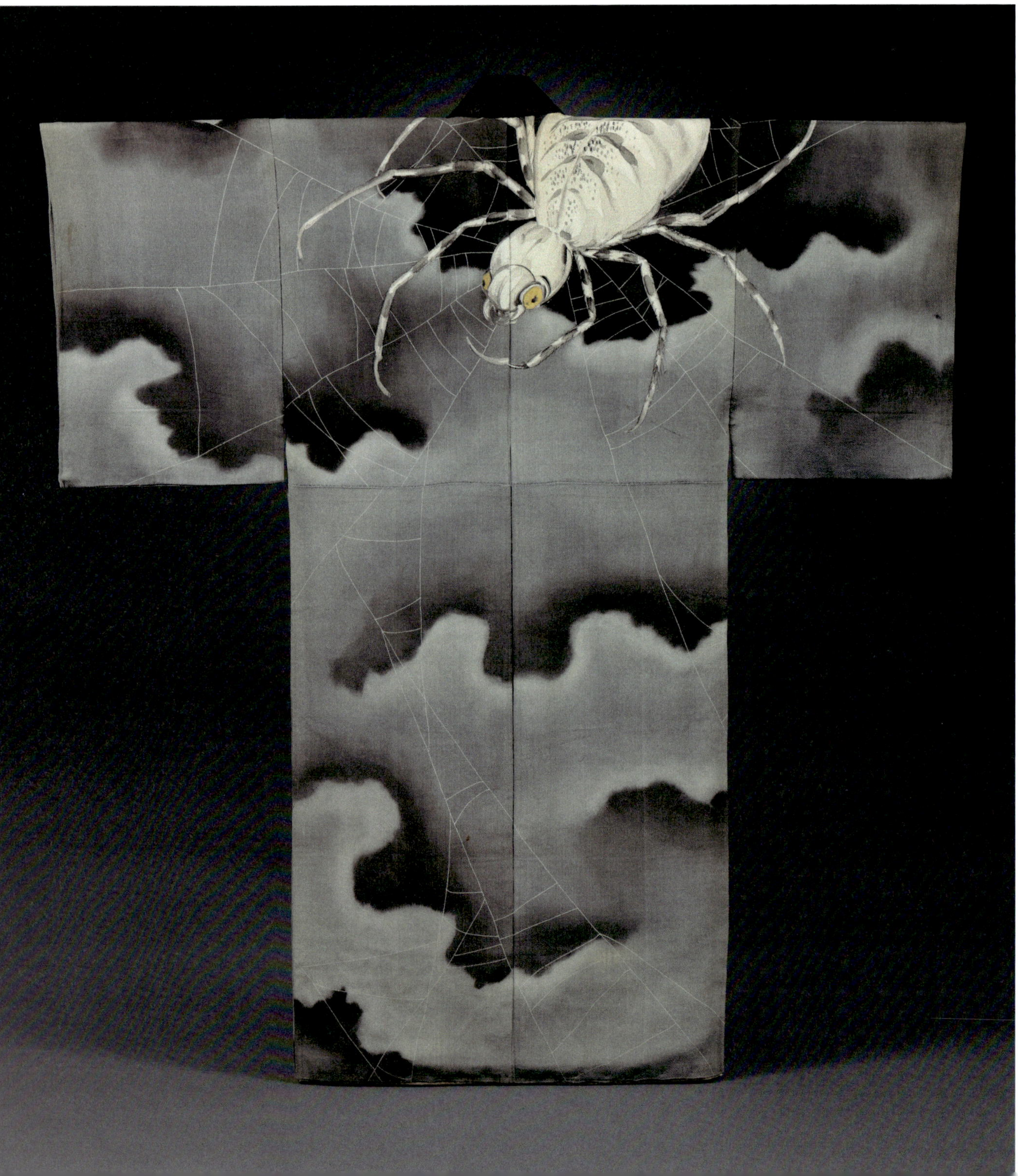

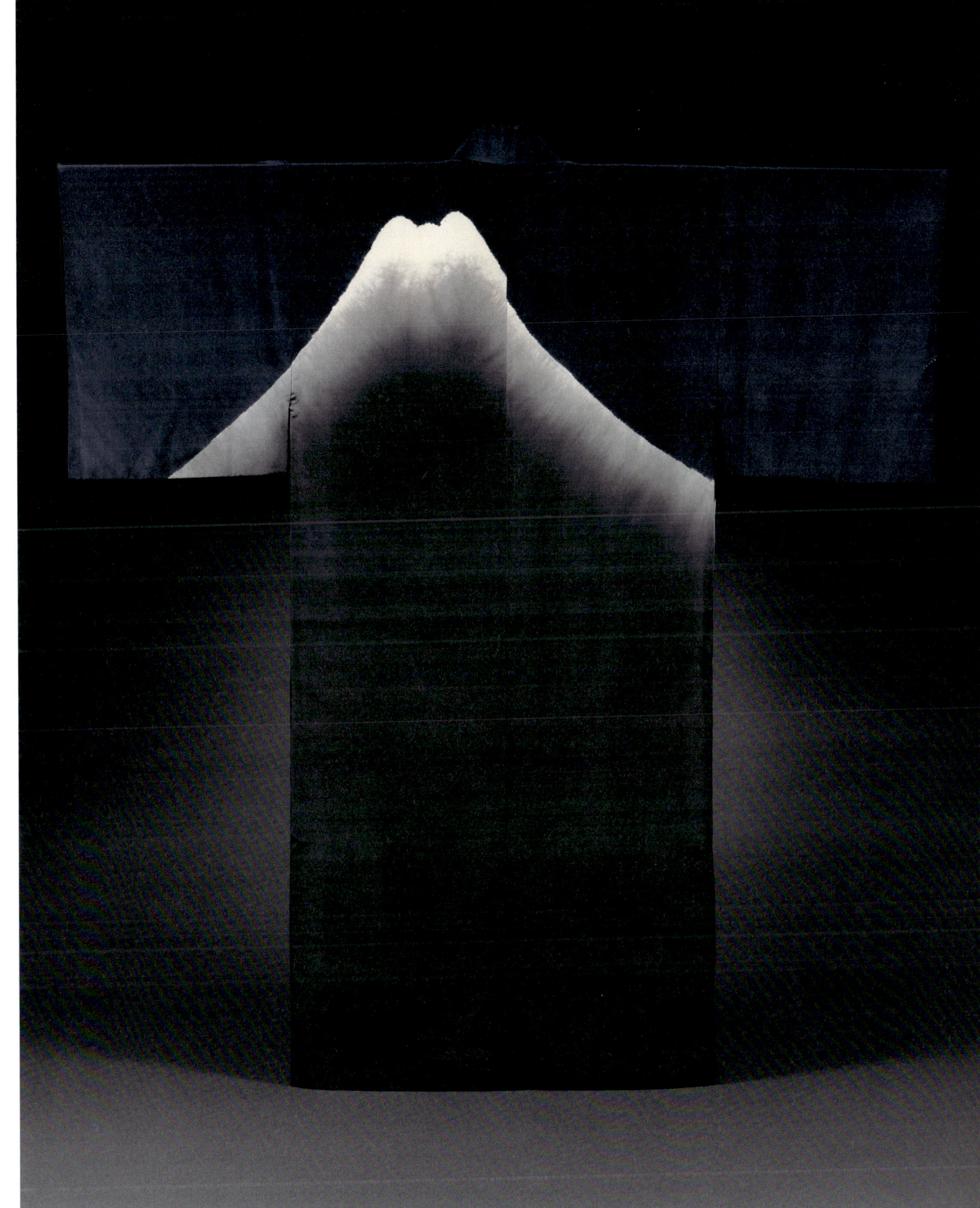

37 藍羽二重地富士山模様男物長襦袢
Man's under kimono (*nagajuban*) with Mount Fuji. Shōwa period (1926–89), second quarter of 20th century. Plain-weave silk with stitched tie-dyeing, 53⅝ × 52¾ in. (136.5 × 134 cm). Promised Gift of John C. Weber

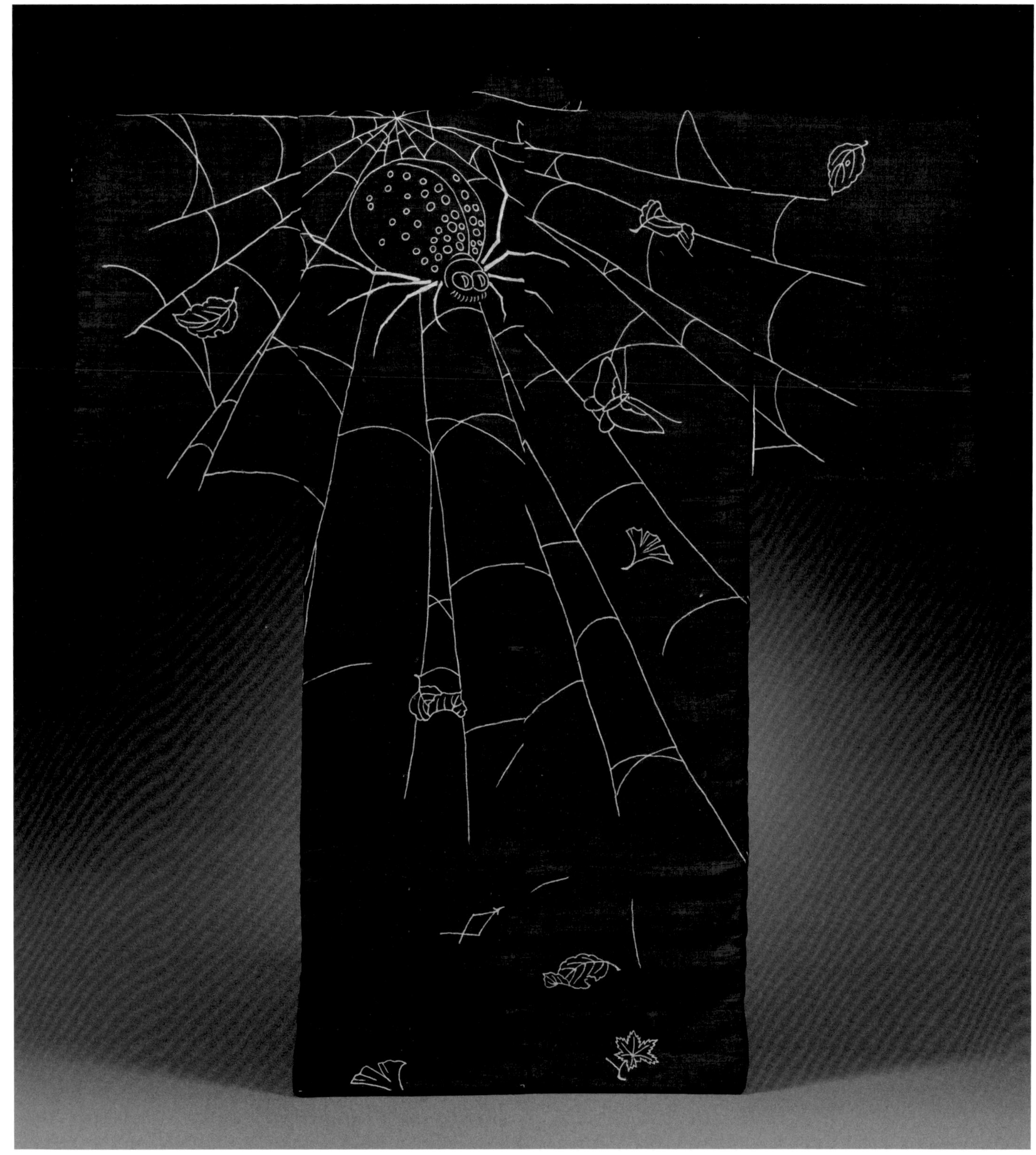

38 藍紬地蜘蛛蝶蜻蛉模様男物冬着物
Man's padded winter kimono. Late Meiji (1868–1912)–Taishō (1912–26) period, ca. 1910s–20s. Plain-weave pongee silk with tube-drawn paste-resist dyeing (*tsutsugaki*), 52¾ × 50 in. (134 × 127 cm). Promised Gift of John C. Weber

A spider and the insects trapped in its web — a butterfly and, on the garment's front, a dragonfly — are traced in white reserve against a deep indigo ground of pongee silk (*tsumugi*). As further decoration, pine needles and leaves including ginkgo and maple are scattered across the ground, suggesting the chilly season when this outerwear was worn. The fabric is heavily repaired, indicating protracted use.

39 紫麻絽地矢羽根模様帷子

Summer kimono (*katabira*) with arrow feathers. Taishō period (1912–26), first quarter of 20th century. Gauze-weave, warp-dyed bast fiber with silk threads, 57 × 48 in. (144.8 × 121.9 cm). Promised Gift of John C. Weber

This vivid, unlined, gauze (*ro*) summer kimono features a vertical arrow-feather design. The warp-dyed fabric of bast fiber was enriched with silk threads of turquoise, a popular color in the Taishō period that provided a striking contrast with the purple-and-white ground. The arrow-feather pattern, referencing samurai bravery, was in use from the late Edo period (1615–1868) but over time became both increasingly popular and increasingly large; it came to be called *yagasuri*, "*kasuri* arrow feathers." In the 1920s–30s, purple kimonos with this pattern were common school uniforms for girls, often combined with *hakama* pants. The feather pattern became favored for *meisen* and *omeshi* kimonos as well.

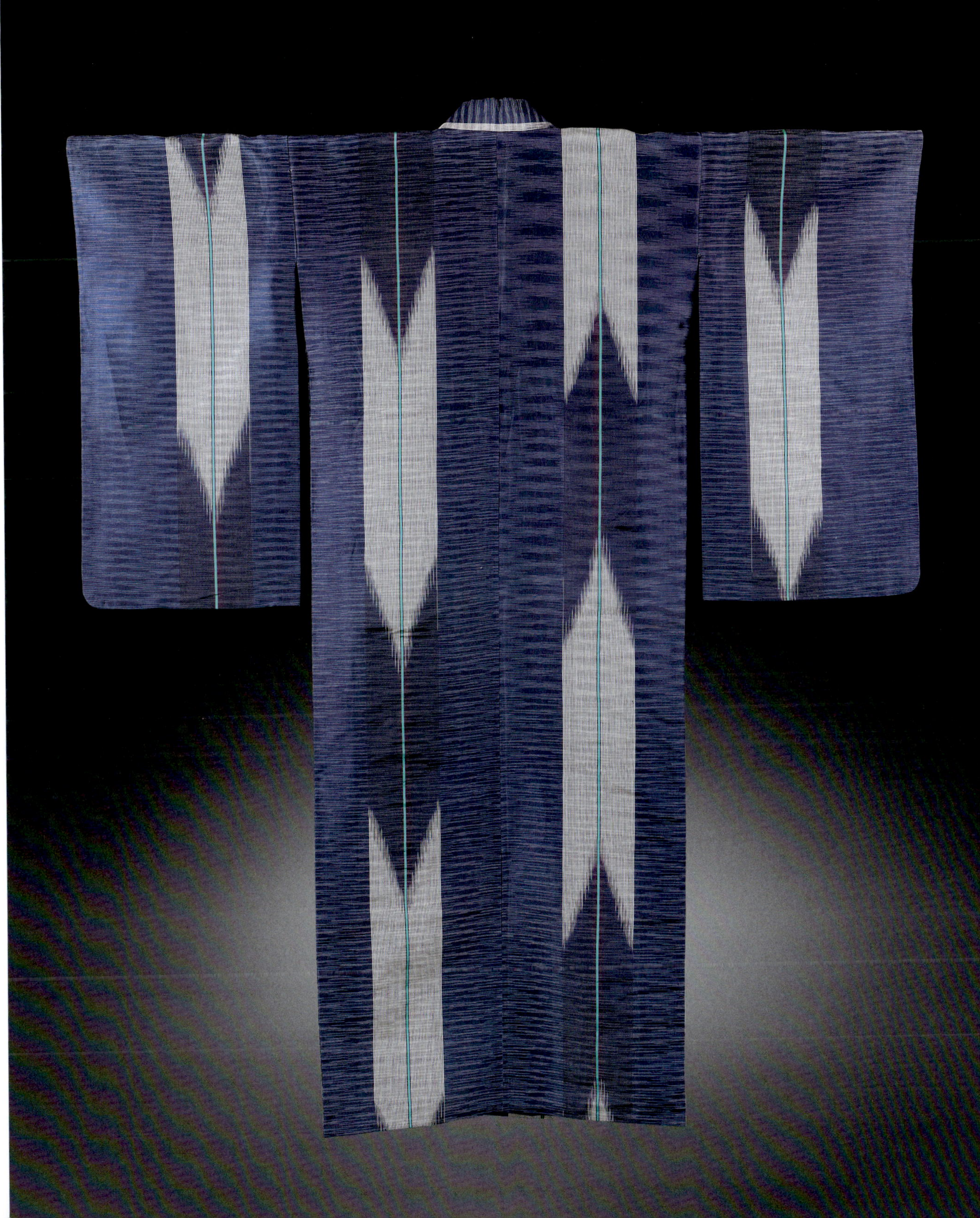

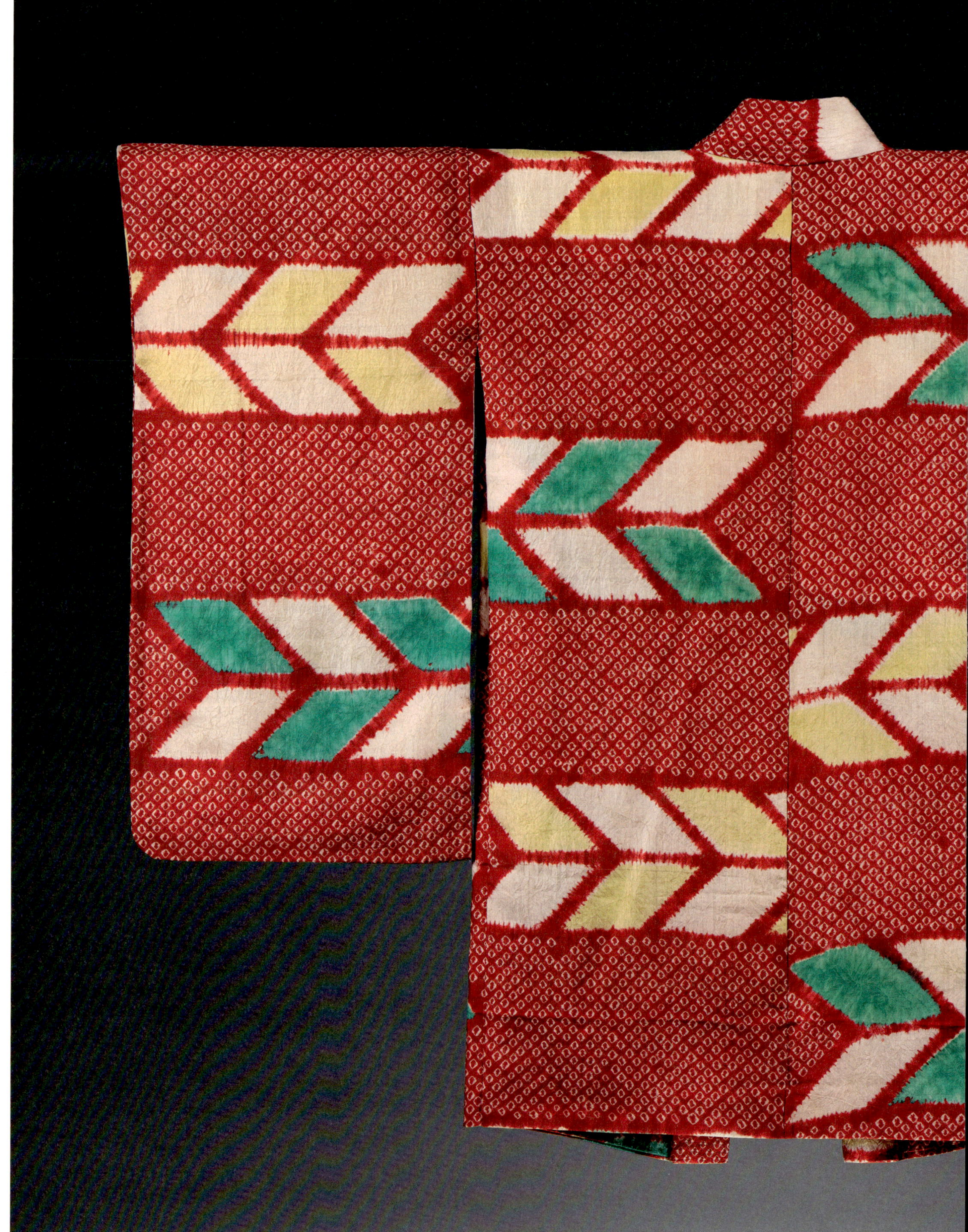

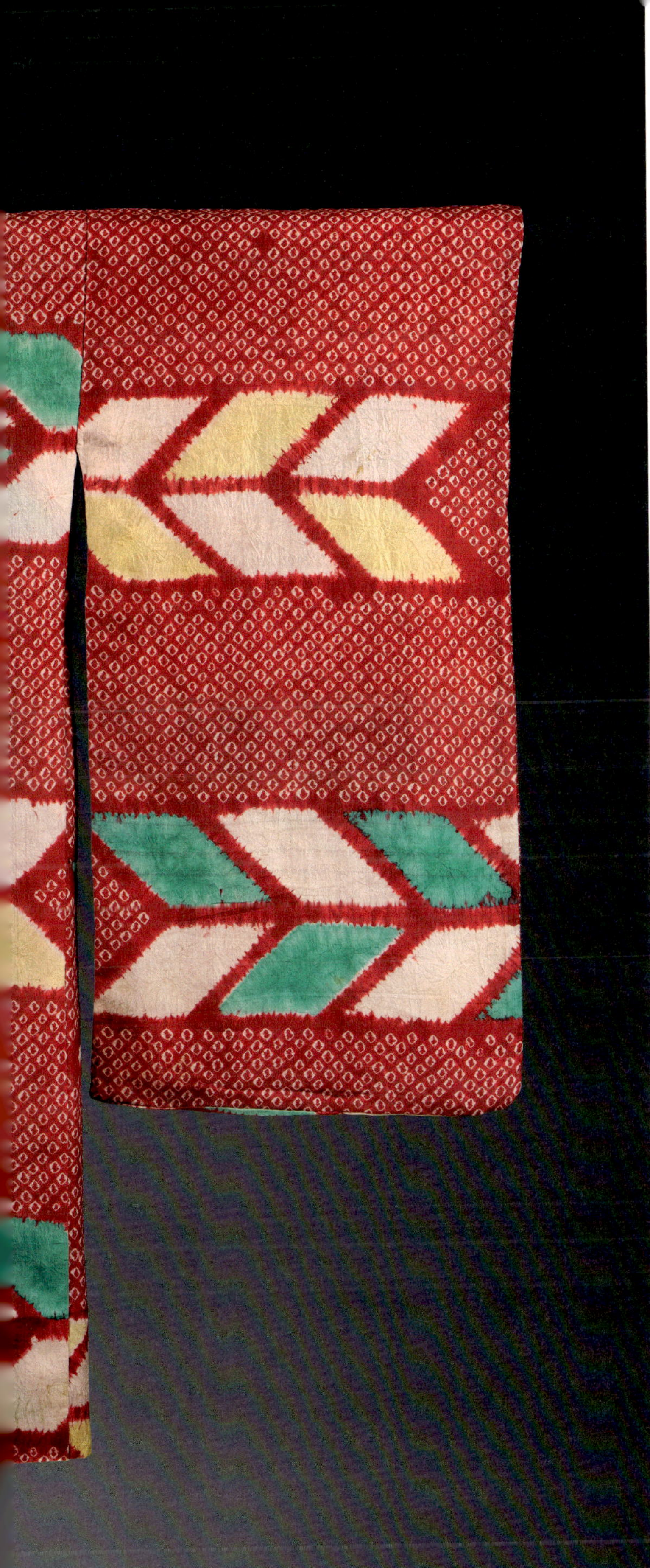

40 赤地矢羽根模様羽織
Jacket (*haori*) with arrow feathers. Taishō (1912–26)–Shōwa (1926–89) period, 1920s–30s. Plain-weave silk with tie-dyeing, 50 × 36 in. (127 × 91.4 cm). Promised Gift of John C. Weber

This *haori* jacket is embellished with *kanoko shibori* tie-dyeing and capped-and-stitched (*oboshi*) resist-dyeing. In the latter method, the motif to be dyed was outlined in small stitches. Then the outline was placed around the side of a solid form (in this case a rhomboid), and the thread was pulled tight around it and secured with a string. Here, the feathers are formed of dyed areas in yellow and teal blue and undyed white areas, all against a red ground. Arrow-feather motifs were typically vertical in the 1920s, but this jacket's runs horizontally.

The designs of these unlined summer kimonos reflect the move toward abstraction in art of the early twentieth century. In the first example (below), dewdrops sparkle amid highly stylized purple and orange blades of grass, which seem to sway. The lightweight hemp fabric with a crepelike texture, the subtle pastel hues, and the dewdrops of couched silver threads all recall the cool of the early morning, making this kimono perfectly suited for summertime wear.

The abstract design of overlapping books on the blue-and-white robe (opposite) is a modern rendering of a traditional motif dating to the Edo period (1615–1868), when it referred to woodblock-printed books and women's education.

41 白麻地草露模様帷子
Summer kimono (*katabira*) with blades of grass and dewdrops. Taishō (1912–26)–Shōwa (1926–89) period, 1920s–30s. Printed plain-weave hemp with twisted wefts, couched silver thread, 59⅛ × 49¼ in. (150 × 125 cm). Promised Gift of John C. Weber

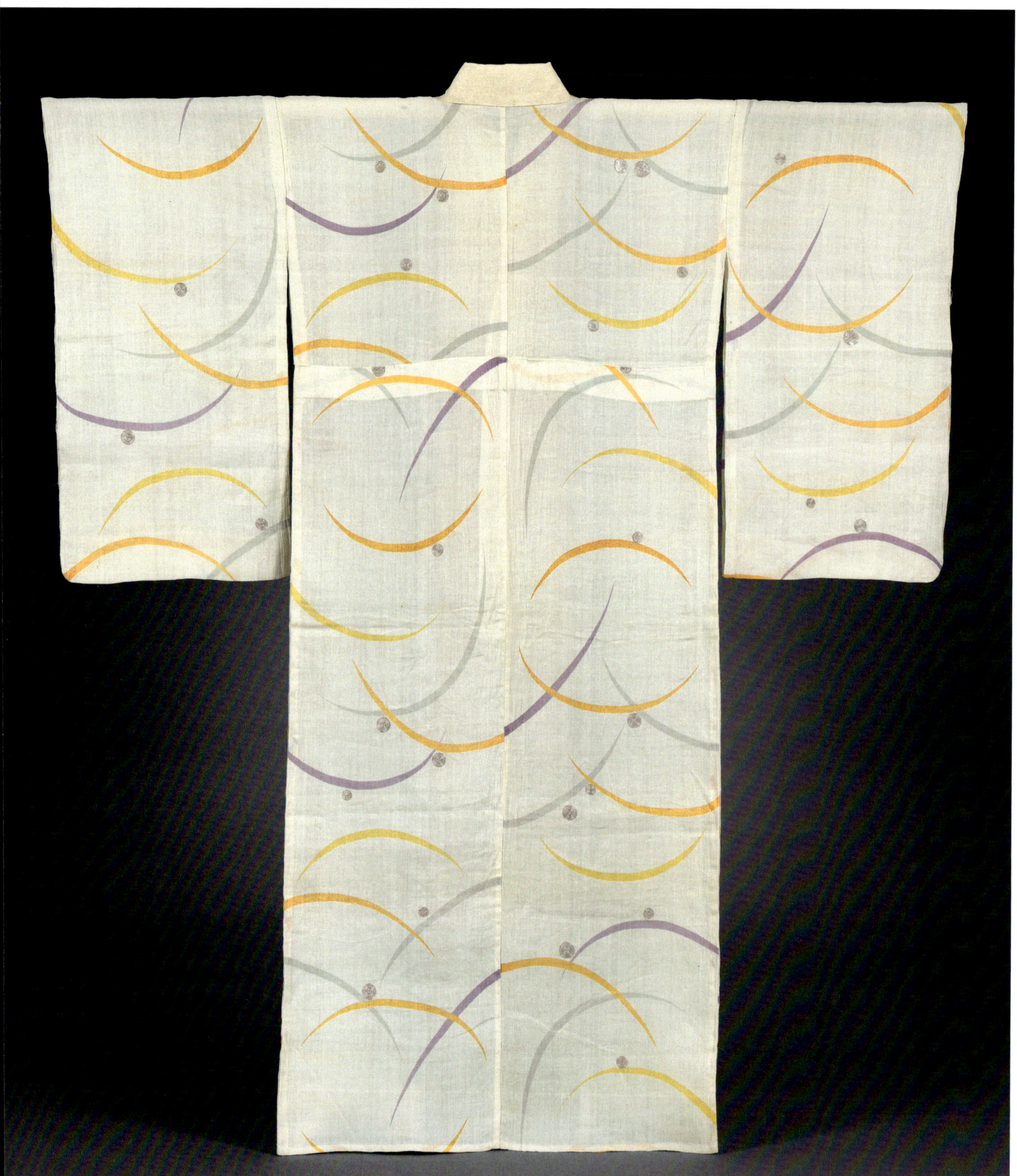

42 白麻地書物模様帷子
Summer kimono (*katabira*) with books. Shōwa period (1926–89), 1930s. Printed plain-weave hemp, 62 × 48 in. (157.5 x 121.9 cm). Promised Gift of John C. Weber

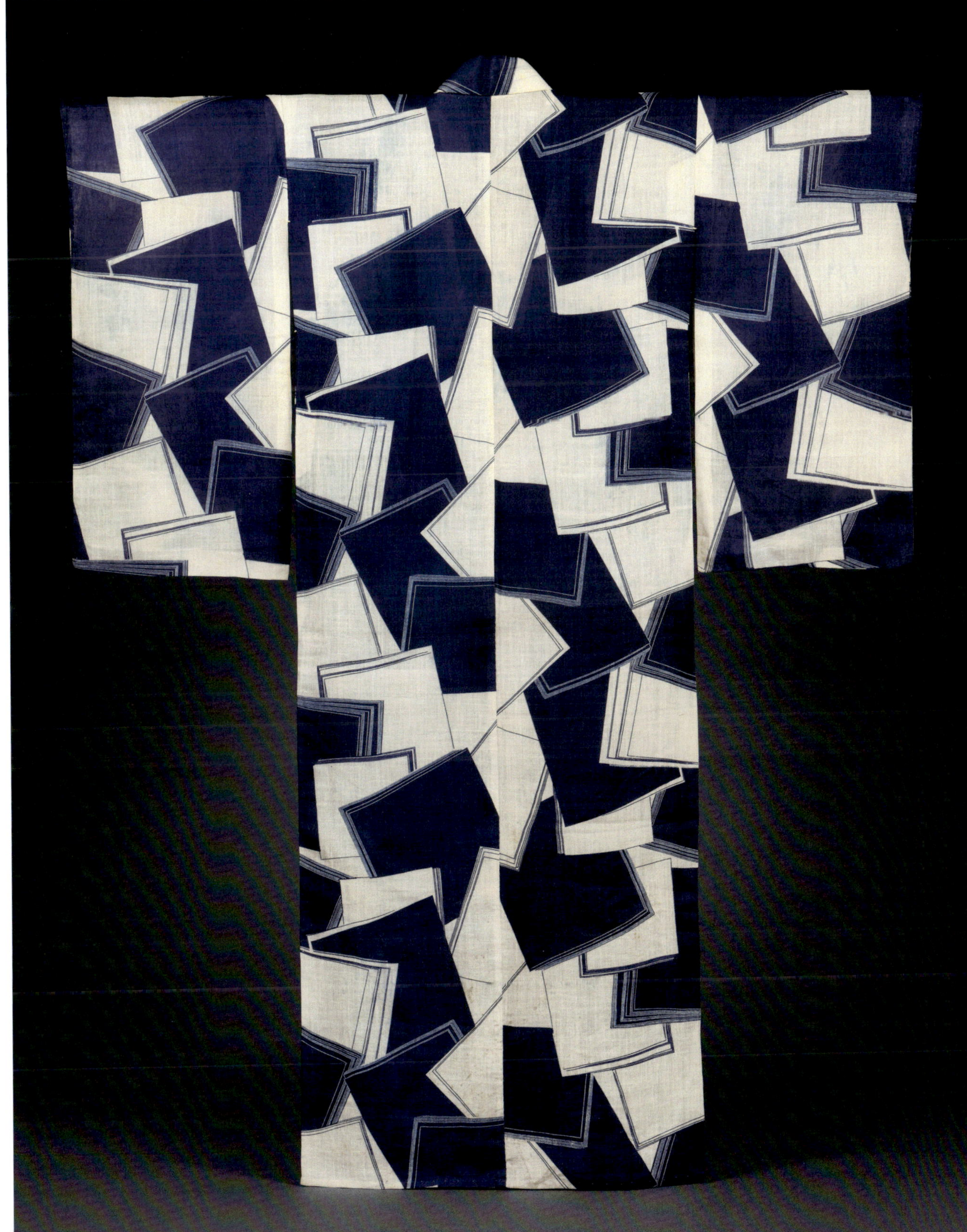

43 薄緑地流水模様着物

Summer kimono (*hito-e*) with waves. Taishō (1912–26)–Shōwa (1926–89) period, 1920s–30s. Printed plain-weave crepe silk, 60 × 49 in. (152.4 × 124.5 cm). Promised Gift of John C. Weber

This unlined summer kimono is made of a stiff, crimped fabric with a stylized wave pattern on an olive-green ground. Purple outlines the unprinted white waves. The swirls of water convey the simplicity of a characteristic Kyoto style developed by the artist Ogata Kōrin (1658–1716), an aesthetic that enjoyed a revival in the early twentieth century owing to its similarity to Art Nouveau.[2] A swirling ornamental water pattern called "Kanze water" was among Kōrin's signature motifs. It was prominently featured in his textile designs, as well as in the *hinagata* pattern books of Kōrin motifs published in the Edo period.

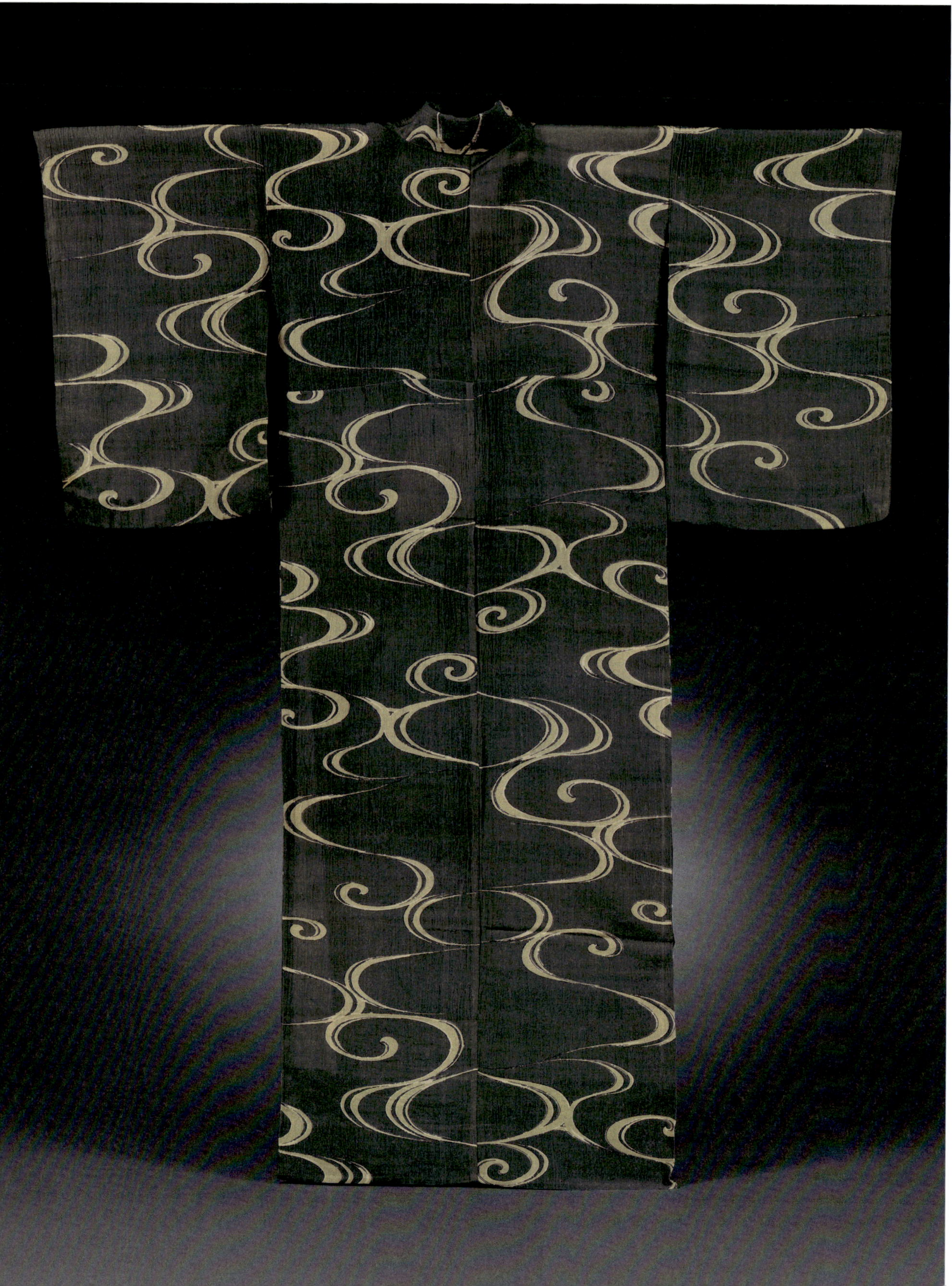

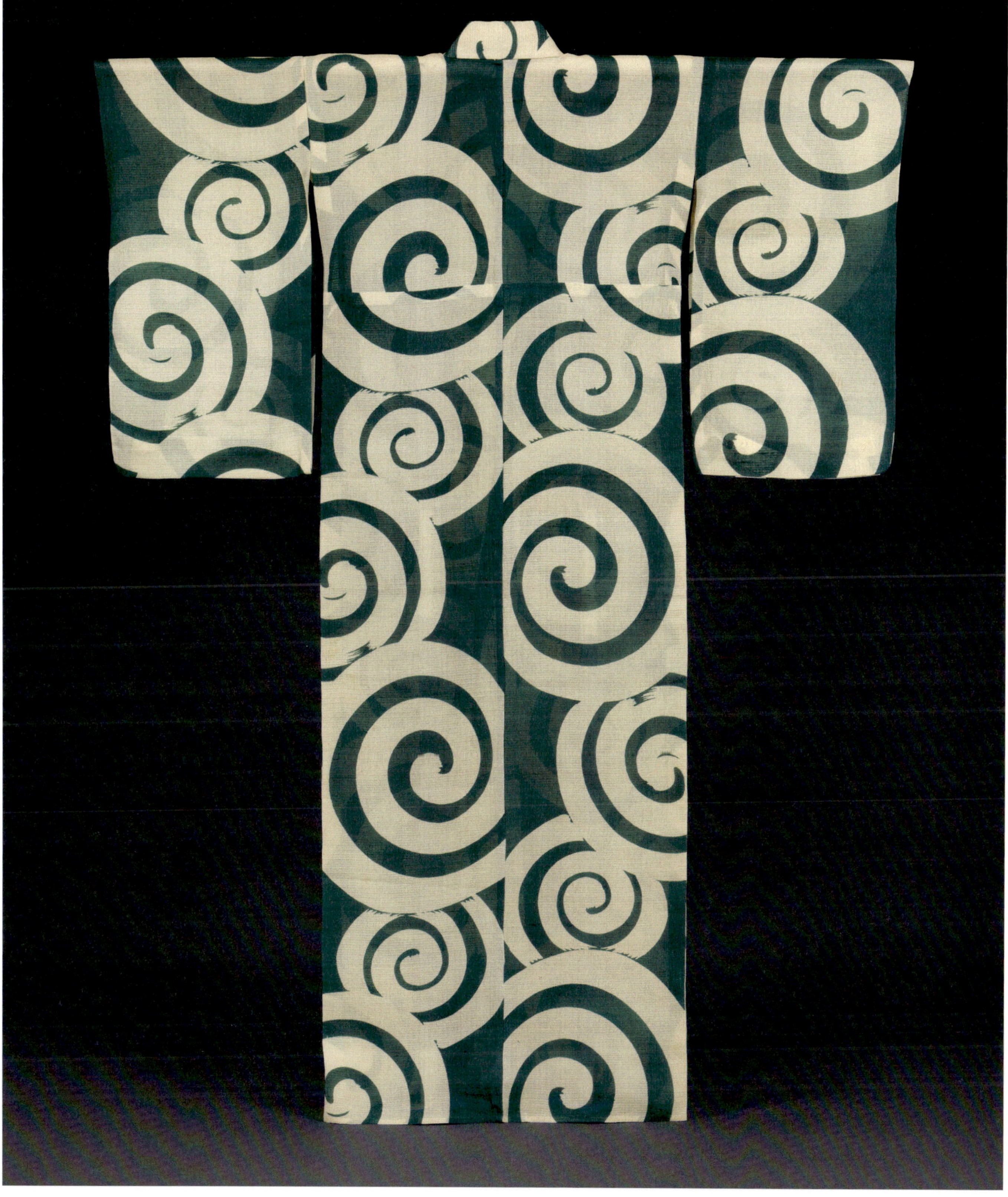

44 白絽地渦巻模様単衣

Summer kimono (*hito-e*) with swirls. Taishō (1912–26)–Shōwa (1926–89) period, 1920s–30s. Printed gauze-weave (*ro*) silk with twisted wefts, 60⅞ × 45 in. (154.5 × 114.3 cm). Promised Gift of John C. Weber

While the rendering of the swirl (*uzumaki*) motif on this unlined kimono with a crepelike texture is very modern, the spiral or vortex pattern has a long history in Japan. It appears on ancient Jōmon pottery (ca. 10,500–ca. 300 B.C.) and was carved into the stone walls outside A.D. sixth-century burial sites, most likely as a talismanic symbol. In the Heian period (794–1185), swirl patterns embellished the robes in depictions of certain Buddhist deities, especially Yakushi Nyorai (Medicine Master Buddha). In the Edo period (1615–1868) small swirl motifs were often used in the background as part of complex compositions depicting rivers. This summer kimono's large swirls of white on a dark green ground are a blown-up, stylized version of the motif, reflecting the influence of Western art and the contemporary Art Deco aesthetic.

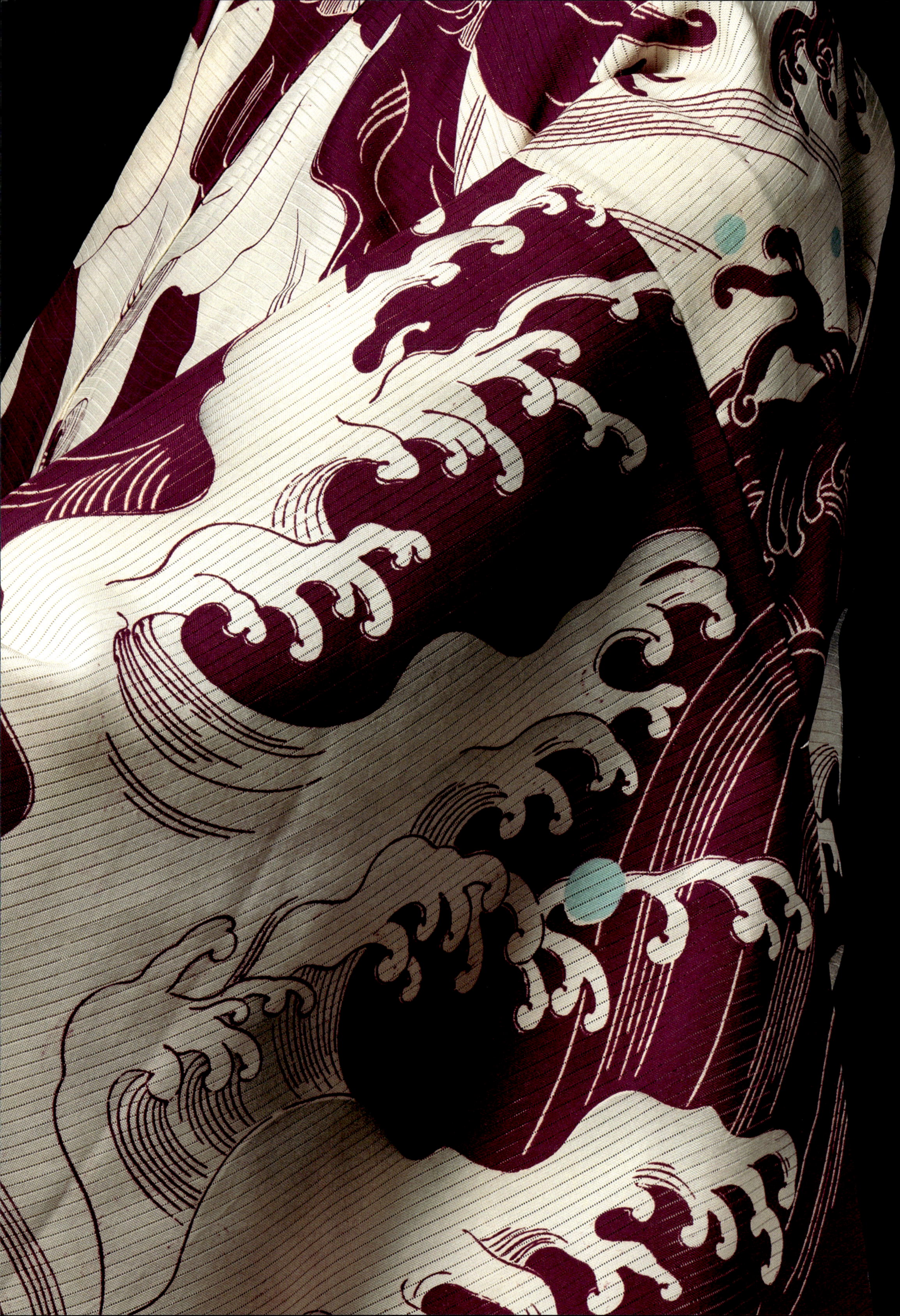

45 白絹レノ地波水玉模様単衣

Summer kimono (*hito-e*) with waves and waterdrops. Taishō (1912–26)–Shōwa (1926–89) period, 1920s–30s. Printed gauze-weave (*ro*) silk, 59⅛ × 49¼ in. (150 × 125 cm). Promised Gift of John C. Weber

Waves were a major theme in the archipelago's painting and prints and the subject of Japan's most iconic artwork, *The Great Wave*, by Katsushika Hokusai (1760–1849). The playful design on this unlined gauze- or leno-weave summer kimono updates that print's turbulent waters in a modernized form, depicting only the foaming swells and the splashing blue droplets. The weaving technique creates an airy fabric with fine stripes of openwork.

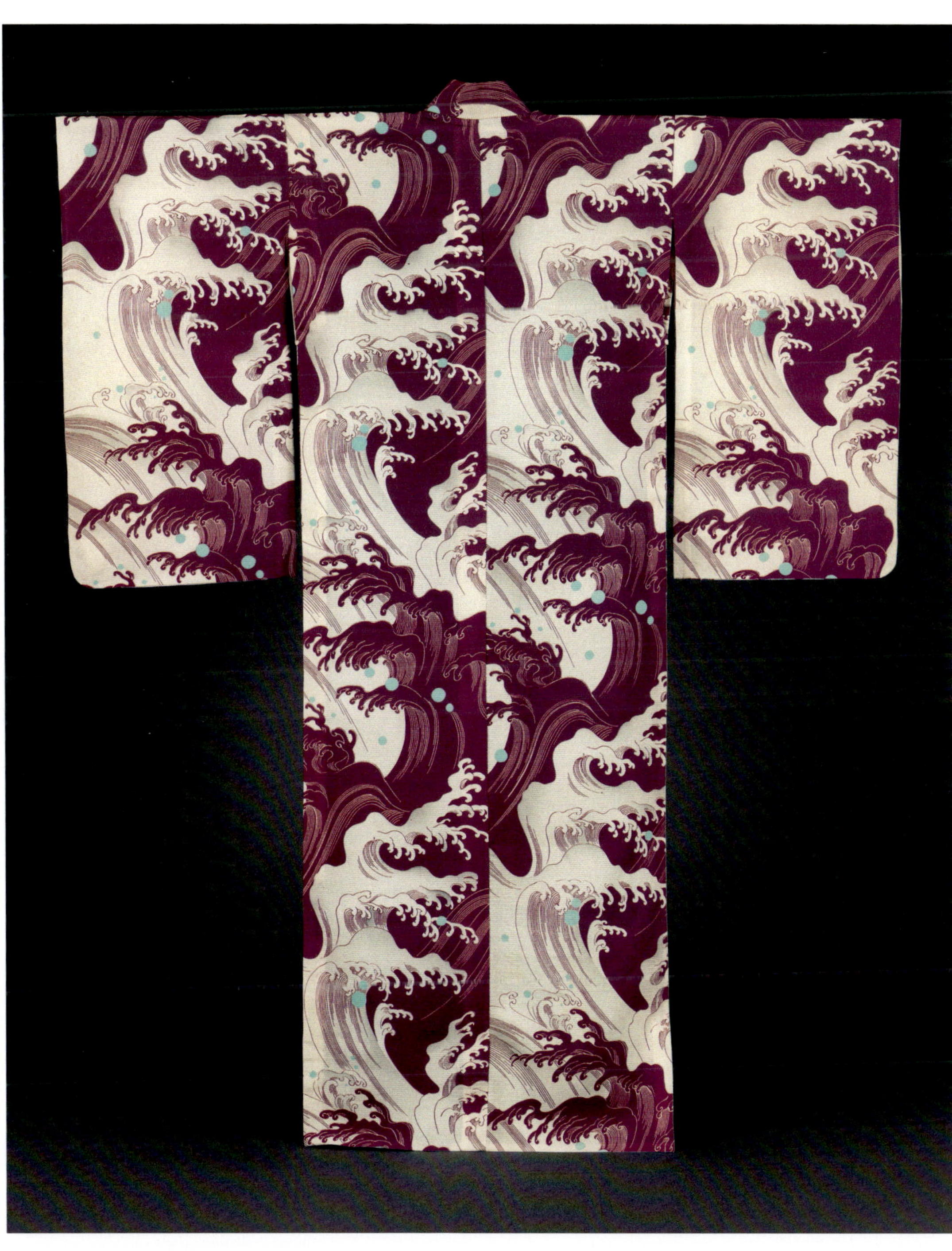

46 綿紅梅地芭蕉模様着物

Summer kimono with banana leaves. Shōwa period (1926–89), 1920s–30s. *Kōbai* silk with stitch-resist dyeing, 59 × 51 in. (149.9 × 129.5 cm). Promised Gift of John C. Weber

Boldly simple patterns rendered at a large scale and seeming to burst from the garment's confines are typical of early Shōwa-period kimonos. The motif of swaying banana leaves evokes a cooling breeze appropriate for a summer garment. This example is similar to a *yukata*, a casual kimono much like a bathrobe. The latticelike, diagonal positioning of the leaves enhances the sense of movement. The ground is *kōbai*, a fine fabric of silk and cotton with a waffled texture, which does not adhere to the skin and is cool to wear. The pattern was executed by a stitch-resist method called *tritik*, whereby the design is outlined with thread that is then gathered up tightly to keep the ground areas from being dyed, a variation of the *shibori* technique. The fabric has also been bound up within each part of the blue pattern, creating a double row of small dots that delineates the veins of the leaves.[3]

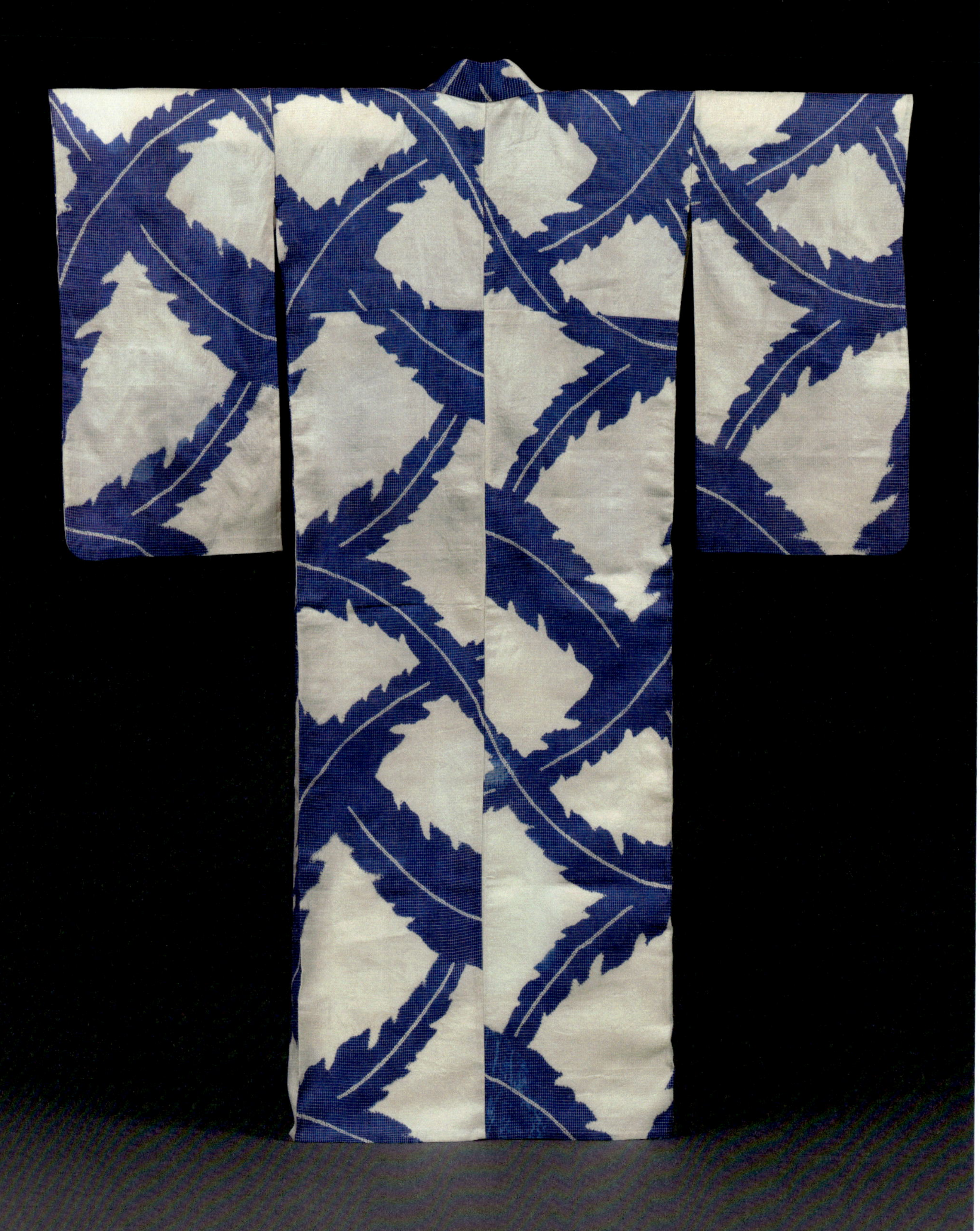

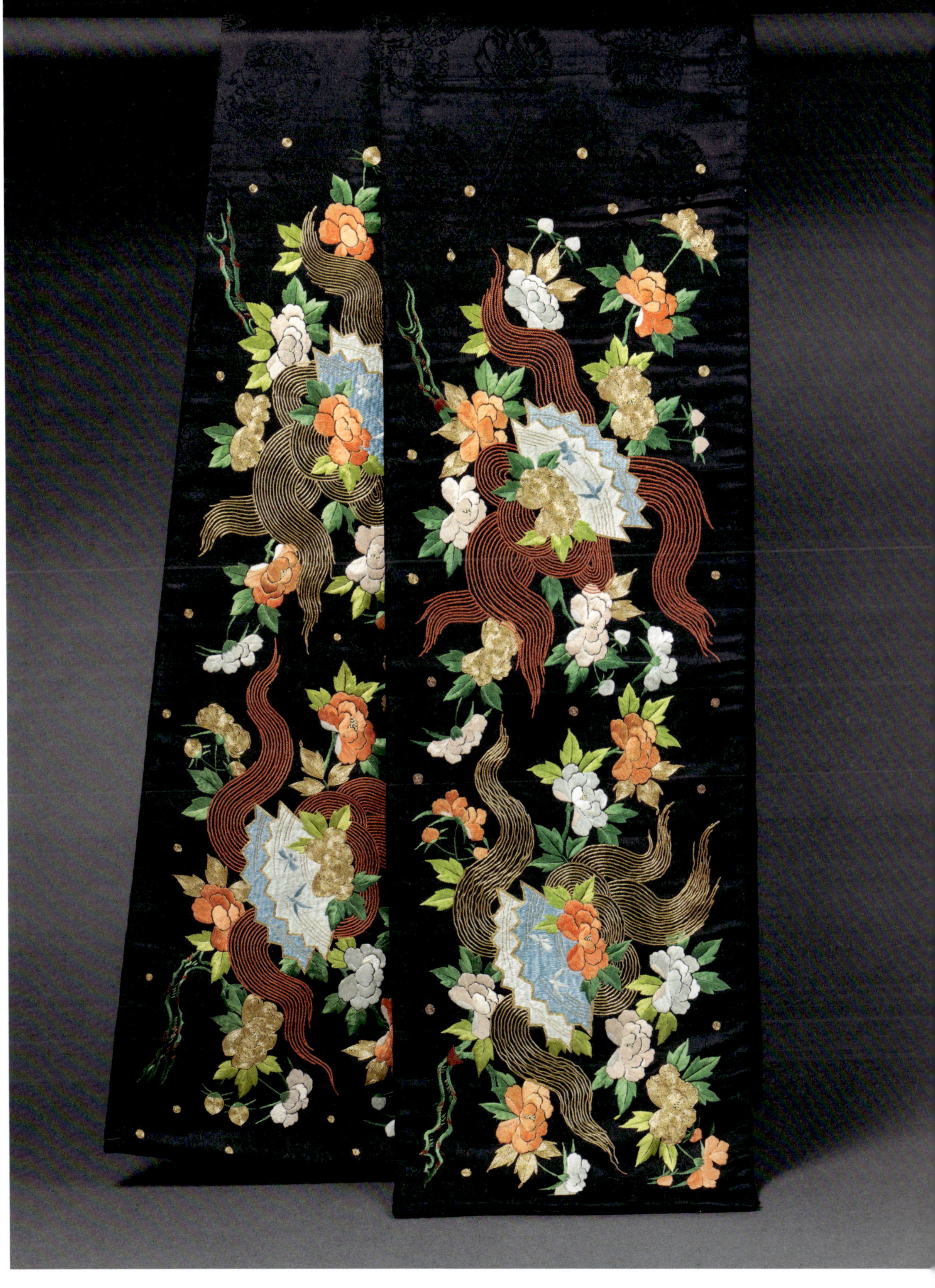

47 黒緞子地牡丹露扇子模様帯
Obi with peonies, fans, and dewdrops. Meiji period (1868–1912), mid-19th century. Figured damask-weave silk with silk embroidery and couched gold thread, 12 in. x 12 ft. 7½ in. (30.5 x 384.8 cm). Lent by John C. Weber Collection

On this high-quality and luxurious sash, embroidered bouquets of peonies decorate a ground fabric of figured damask (*donsu*), likely imported from China.

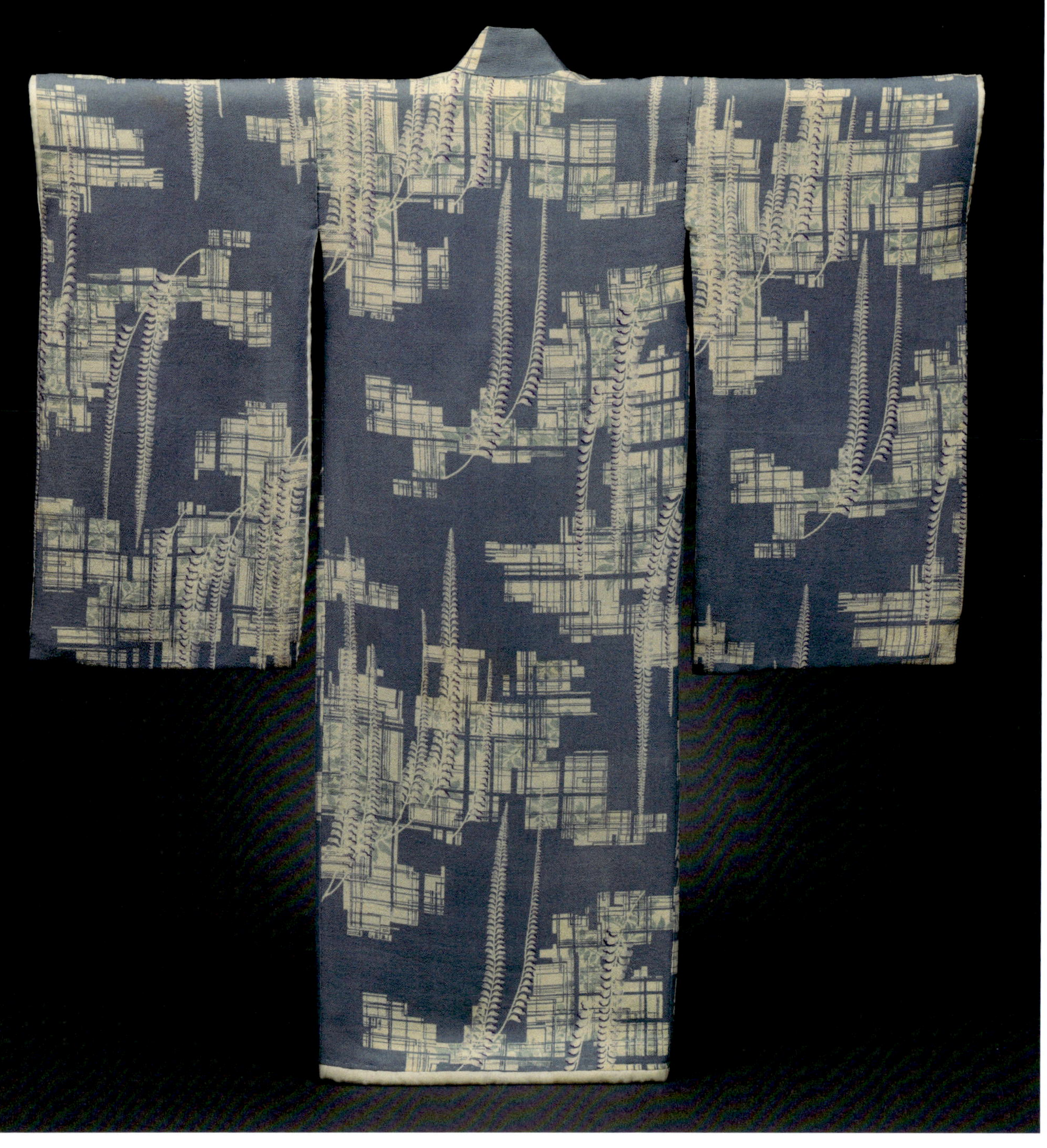

48 楝縮緬地藤棚模様子供用着物
Girl's kimono with wisteria and trellis. Meiji period (1868–1912), early 20th century. Crepe silk (*kabe chirimen*) with stencil paste-resist dyeing, 35½ × 33½ in. (90.2 × 85.1 cm). Promised Gift of John C. Weber

49 ミッキーマウス模様子供用着物
Child's winter kimono with Mickey Mouse. Shōwa period (1926–89), ca. 1930s. Plain-weave cotton with roller printing, 35½ × 35½ in. (90 × 90 cm). Promised Gift of John C. Weber

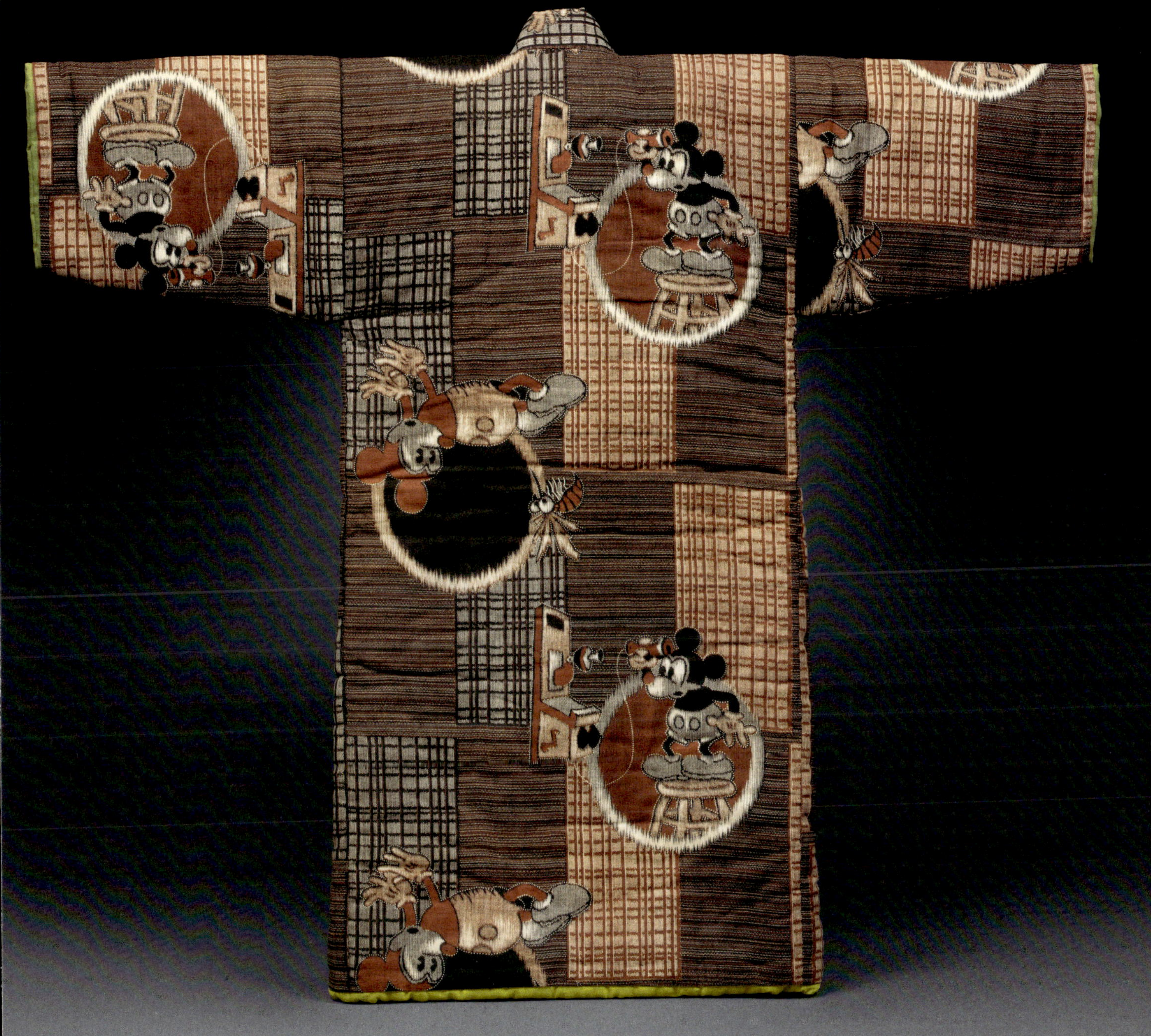

Children's clothing was traditionally decorated with auspicious patterns and talismanic motifs to keep the wearer safe. Kimonos for both boys and girls had long sleeves (*furisode*), and the patterns reflected their social status and gender. The patterns became more varied in the Meiji period, ranging from traditional auspicious motifs and those inspired by literature and Noh plays to animals and, from the late Meiji to the Taishō–Shōwa period, flowers and Art Nouveau–inspired motifs in vivid colors. The fresh, modern design of this girl's kimono with wisteria and an abstractly rendered trellis (opposite) sparked the admiration of Frank Lloyd Wright (1867–1959). An avid collector of Japanese art, the American architect purchased this piece in Japan, perhaps in 1905.

The Mickey Mouse design on a child's thickly padded winter garment (above) evidences twentieth-century Japan's appropriation of Western popular culture and its adaptability in a changing world. In one repeating element, Mickey's pal is on the verge of being stung by a mosquito, a reference to the 1934 Disney film *Camping Out*, in which the cartoon characters battle a swarm of angry insects. The motif, set against a checked, patchwork-patterned cotton ground, was produced by roller printing: copper rollers — one for each color — are carved with the design in small dots and fine lines and used to press colored paste into the fabric. The technique facilitated the mass production of textiles reminiscent of *kasuri* and was often used to make inexpensive cotton clothing for children.

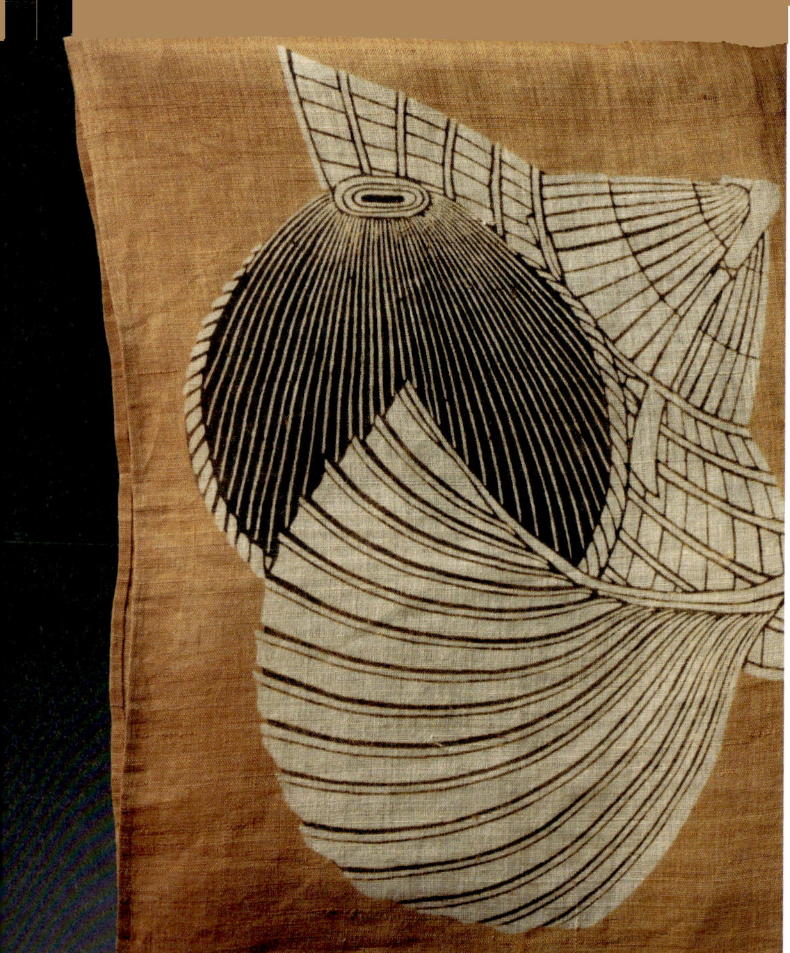

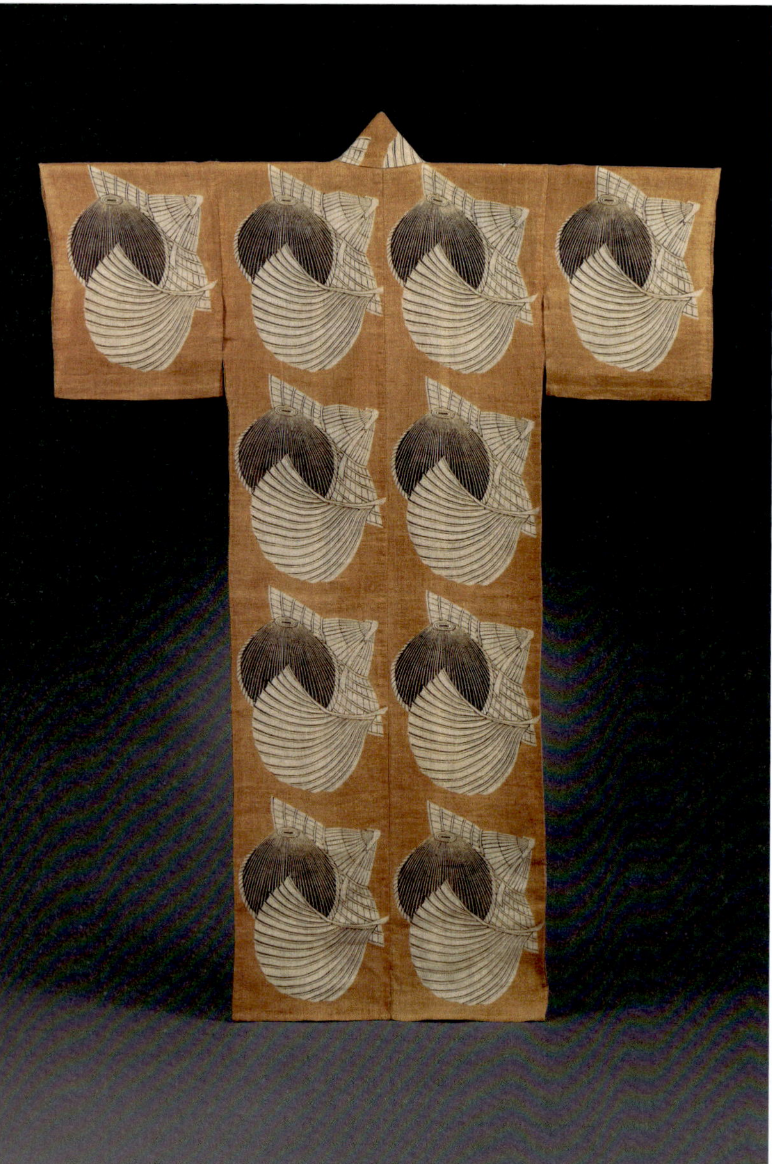

50 芭蕉布地沖縄笠団扇文部屋着
Kimono with Okinawan hats and fans. Serizawa Keisuke (1895–1984). Shōwa period (1926–89), 1960. Plain-weave banana fiber with stencil-dyeing, 69 × 48 in. (175.3 × 121.9 cm). Promised Gift of John C. Weber

51 藍絹紬地松竹刈込みヒイラギ模様着物
Kimono with pine, bamboo, and topiary holly trees. Serizawa Keisuke (1895–1984). Shōwa period (1926–89), ca. 1962. Plain-weave pongee silk with stencil-dyeing, 59½ × 48⅛ in. (151 × 122 cm). Promised Gift of John C. Weber

Serizawa Keisuke emerged from the 1930s Japanese folk crafts (*mingei*) movement to become a towering figure of textile arts, honored in 1956 as a Living National Treasure. He developed his own *kata-zome* stencil-dyeing technique after studying Okinawan *bingata*, a similar technique with a colorful dye palette. As in the *bingata* process he so admired, Serizawa poured equal effort into the pattern, the stencil, and the color.

The depiction of pine, bamboo, and topiary holly on the kimono with a deep indigo ground (opposite) is emblematic of Serizawa's — and the *mingei* movement's — revival of traditional forms and techniques. Rhythmic repetitions of motifs and brilliant colors, such as the bright yellow on the kimono with Okinawan hats and fans (at left), became characteristic of his work. The latter kimono's Okinawa references extend to its fabric, which is made of thread banana (*basho*) plants native to the Ryukyu Islands. The cloth made from the plants' fibrous stems has long been favored for summer kimonos because of its lightness and crisp, nonclingy surface.

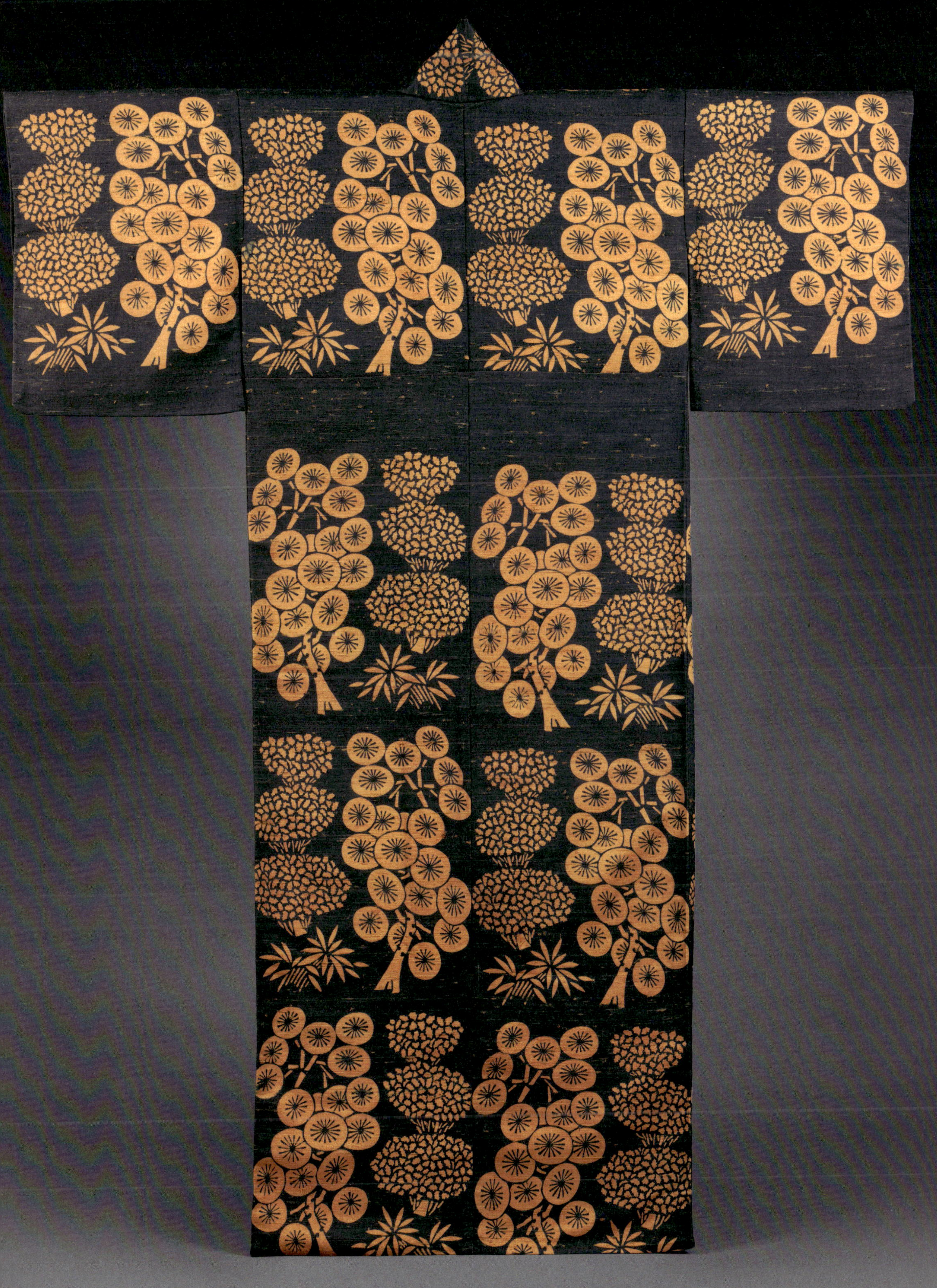

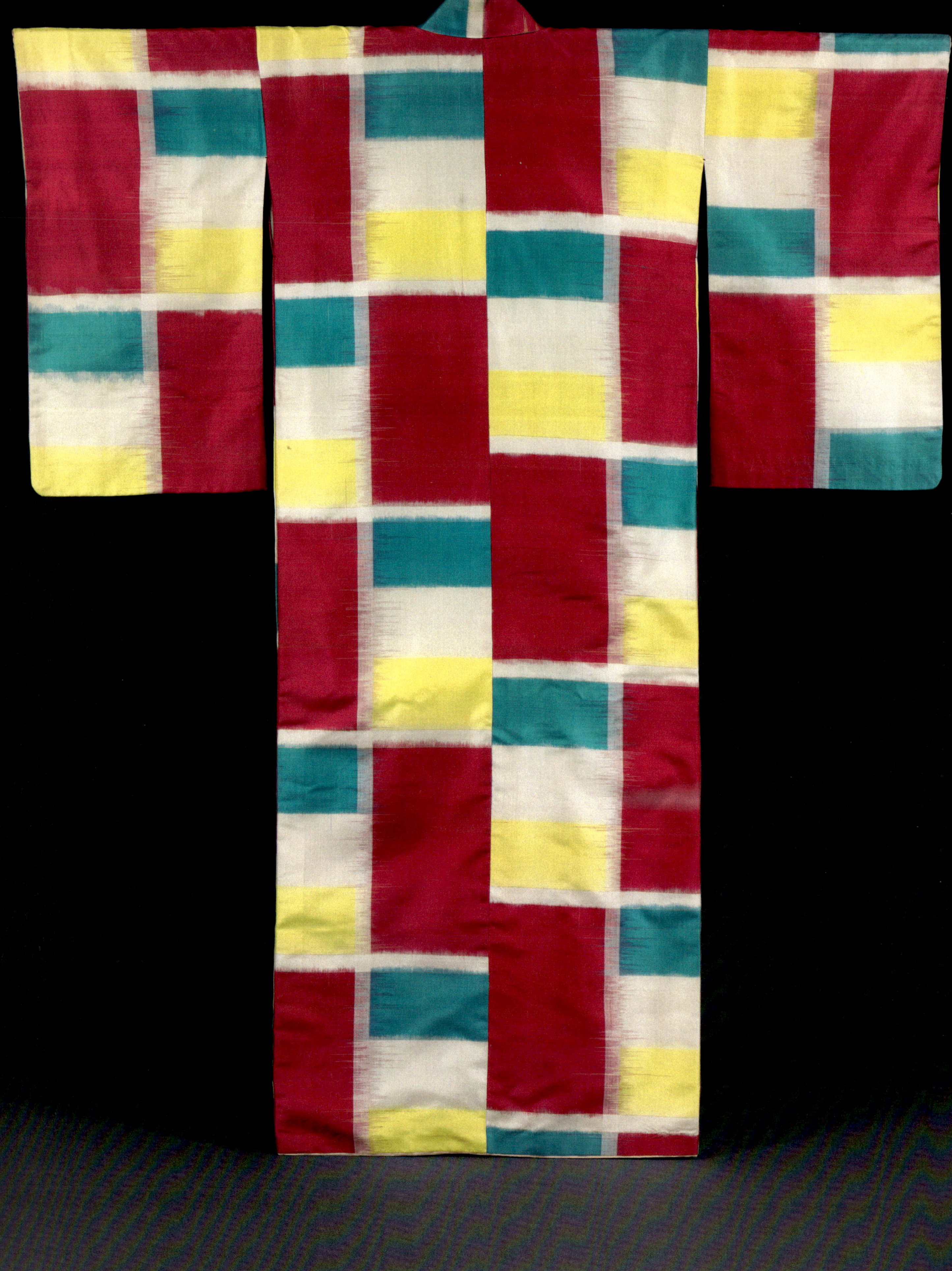

52 変り大格子模様銘仙着物
Meisen kimono with large checkered pattern. Shōwa period (1926–89), ca. 1930s. Plain-weave machine-spun silk in resist-dyed large ikat (*ōgasuri*) with gold-thread weft, 57 × 47 in. (144.8 × 119.4 cm). Promised Gift of John C. Weber

53 変り市松格子模様銘仙着物
Meisen kimono with checkered pattern. Shōwa period (1926–89), ca. 1930s. Plain-weave machine-spun silk in resist-dyed large ikat (*ōgasuri*), 59 × 49 in. (150 × 124.5 cm). Promised Gift of John C. Weber

These garments are characteristic examples of the *ōgasuri* technique from the 1930s, in which both the warp and weft yarns were bound and dyed before being woven. This method could produce only straight lines, such as stripes, blocks, and checks. The blurry edges are typical of the *kasuri* technique, as the patterns dyed into the yarns could not be perfectly aligned on the loom.

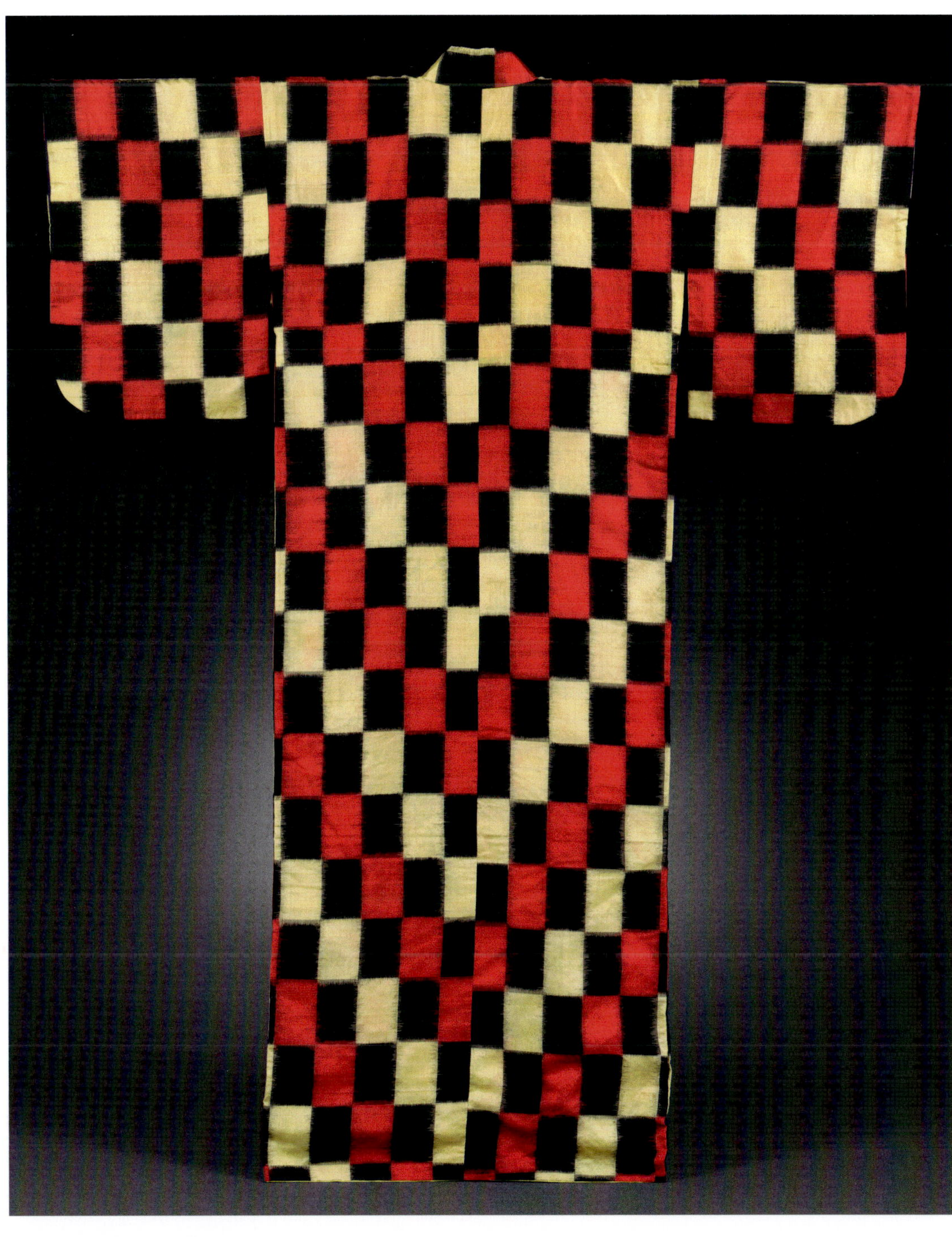

54 赤紫地兎木賊模様銘仙単衣

Meisen summer kimono with rabbits and scouring rushes. Shōwa period (1926–89), ca. 1930s. Plain-weave machine-spun silk in unraveled ikat (*hogushi-gasuri*), 58 × 47 in. (147.3 × 119.4 cm). Promised Gift of John C. Weber

This playful pattern of white rabbits and scouring rushes, stiff plants used for polishing, has a long history in Japanese art. Suggesting that the rabbits are polishing their teeth with the rush, it symbolizes self-improvement and industriousness. Here, however, the classical composition has been modernized and stylized. This kimono might have been created in 1939, the Year of the Rabbit. It was likely made as a young girl's ceremonial garment for the New Year's celebration, then retailored into a summer kimono.

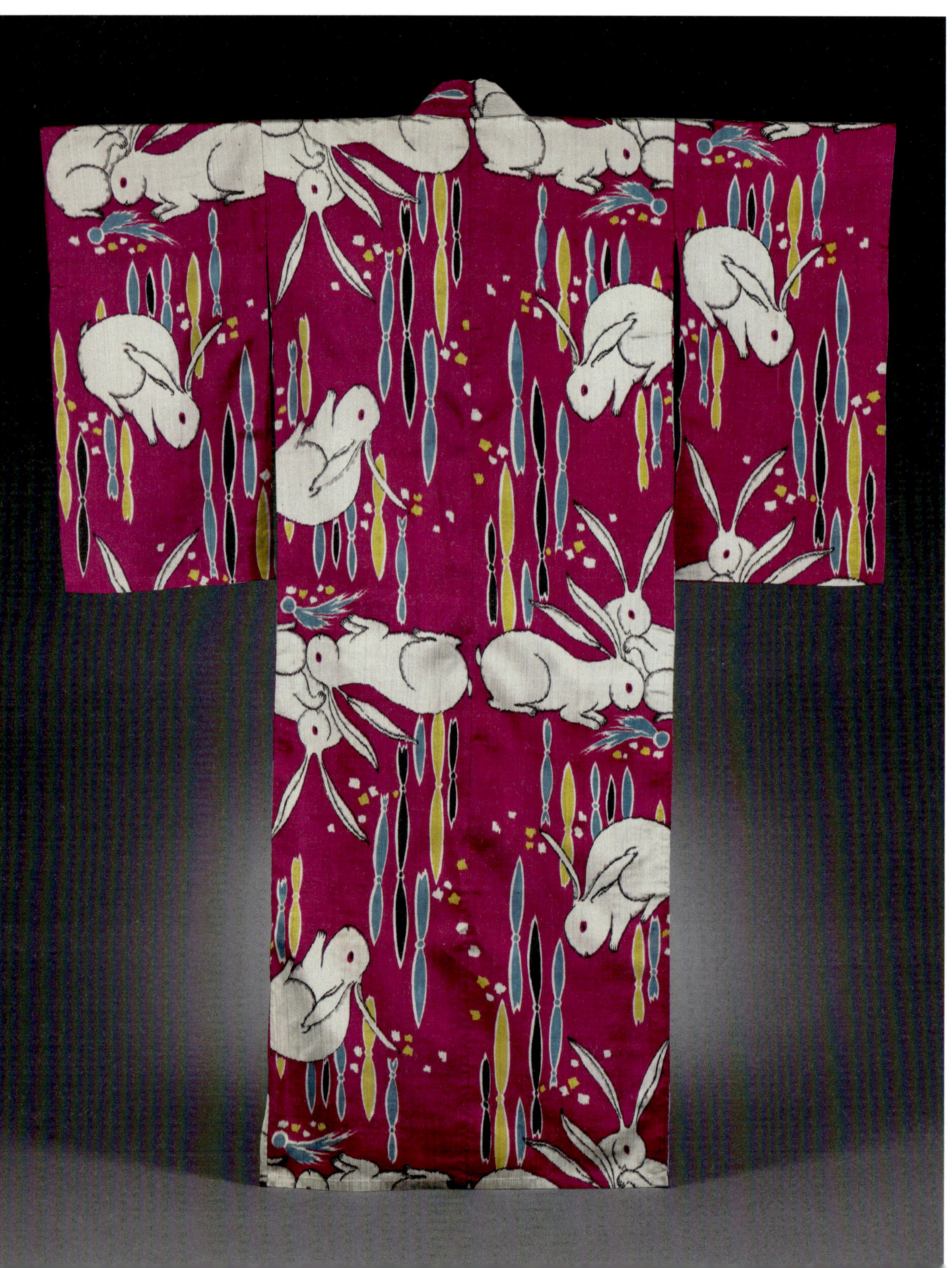

55 紺地蜻蛉模様銘仙単衣
Meisen summer kimono with dragonflies. Shōwa period (1926–89), ca. 1940–45. Plain-weave silk warps with twisted dupioni silk wefts in unraveled ikat (*hogushi-gasuri*), 61 × 47 in. (154.9 × 119.4 cm). Promised Gift of John C. Weber

The dragonfly (*tonbo*) featured on this unlined summer robe is one of the oldest motifs in Japan, symbolic of patriotism, courage, and good fortune. Samurai warriors considered the dragonfly the victory insect because of its agility and perceived fearlessness. Thriving in the watery rice fields, it portended a good harvest. Dragonflies appear in various art forms but became particularly prominent in the bold designs of early twentieth-century kimonos, reflecting the influence of Art Nouveau. Their seasonal associations made dragonflies appropriate for summer kimonos such as this one.

The design was created by dyeing the warp threads with three stencils in three colors before weaving. The wefts are tightly twisted to create texture. The contrast of the very dark blue ground, the teal, and the undyed sections gives the image depth, as does the overlapping of the insects' tails and wings. The dragonflies appear to fly beyond the boundaries of the garment's form, a sense of movement emphasized by the alternating direction of each panel of fabric.[4]

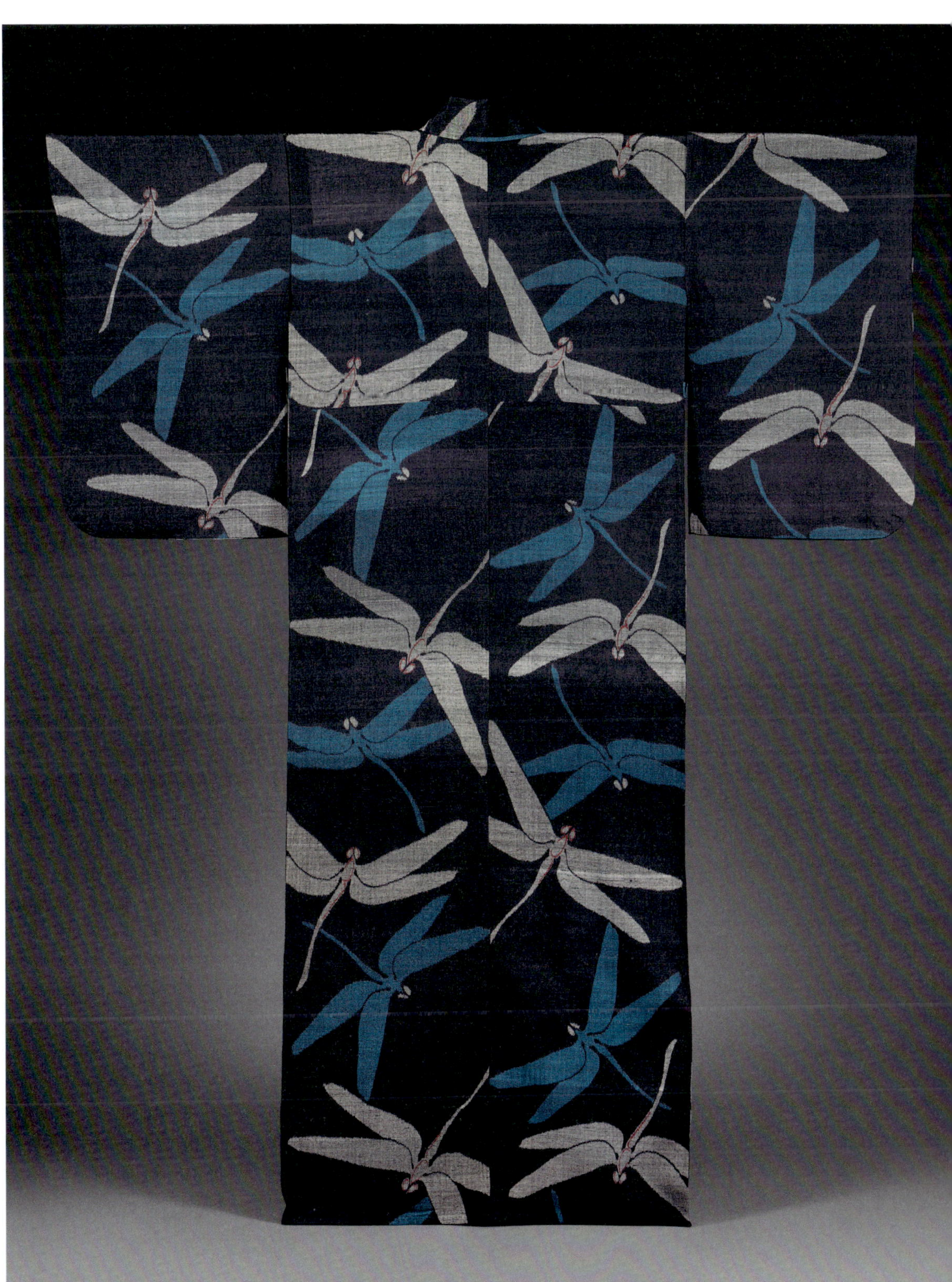

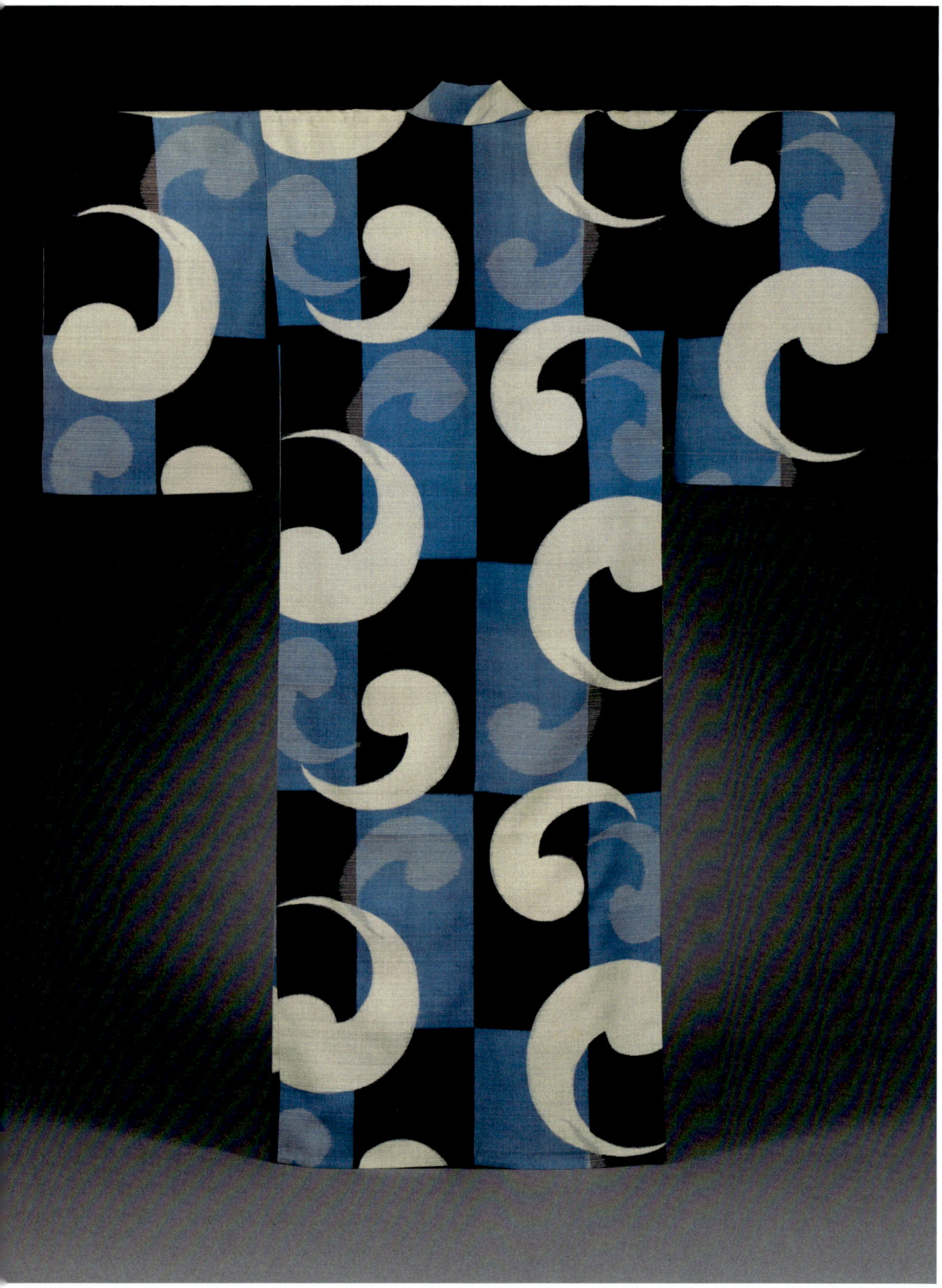

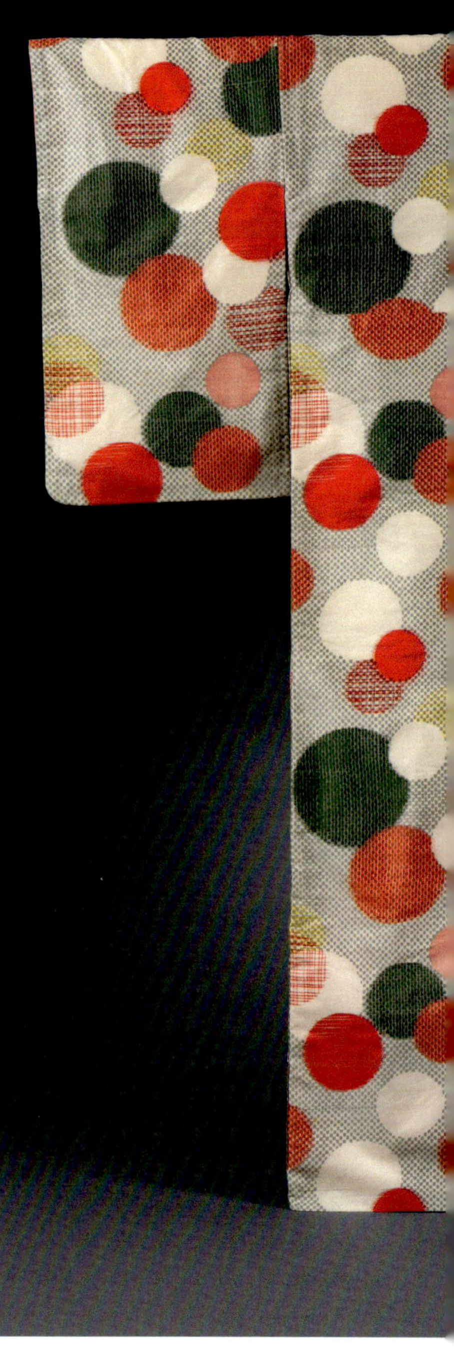

56 紺青市松格子地巴模様御召銘仙単衣
Meisen summer kimono with comma (*tomoe*) patterns. Shōwa period (1926–89), ca. 1930s. Plain-weave machine-spun silk warps with twisted silk and rayon wefts in double ikat (*heiyō-gasuri*), 62 × 50 in. (157.5 × 127 cm). Promised Gift of John C. Weber

57 白地水玉模様銘仙着物
Meisen kimono with water droplets. Shōwa period (1926–89), ca. 1930–40. Plain-weave reeled-silk warps with machine-spun silk wefts in double ikat (*heiyō-gasuri*), 59 × 49¼ in. (149.9 × 125.1 cm). Promised Gift of John C. Weber

58 黒地冊子糸巻模様銘仙着物
Meisen kimono with books and yarn spools. Shōwa period (1926–89), ca. 1935–40. Plain-weave machine-spun silk with silver-thread wefts in double ikat (*heiyō-gasuri*), 57 × 47 in. (144.8 × 119.4 cm). Promised Gift of John C. Weber

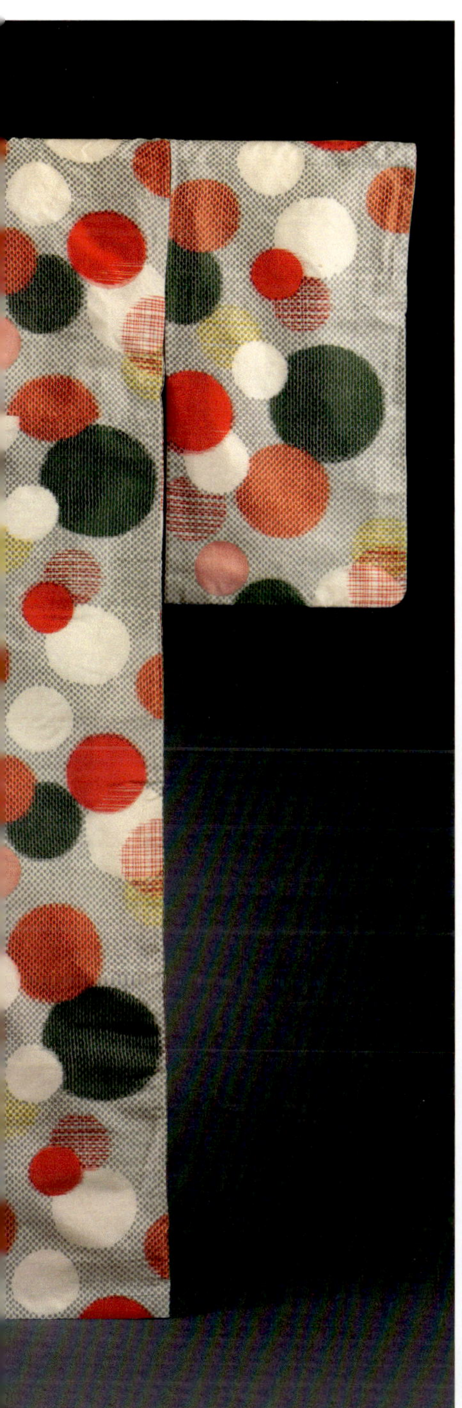

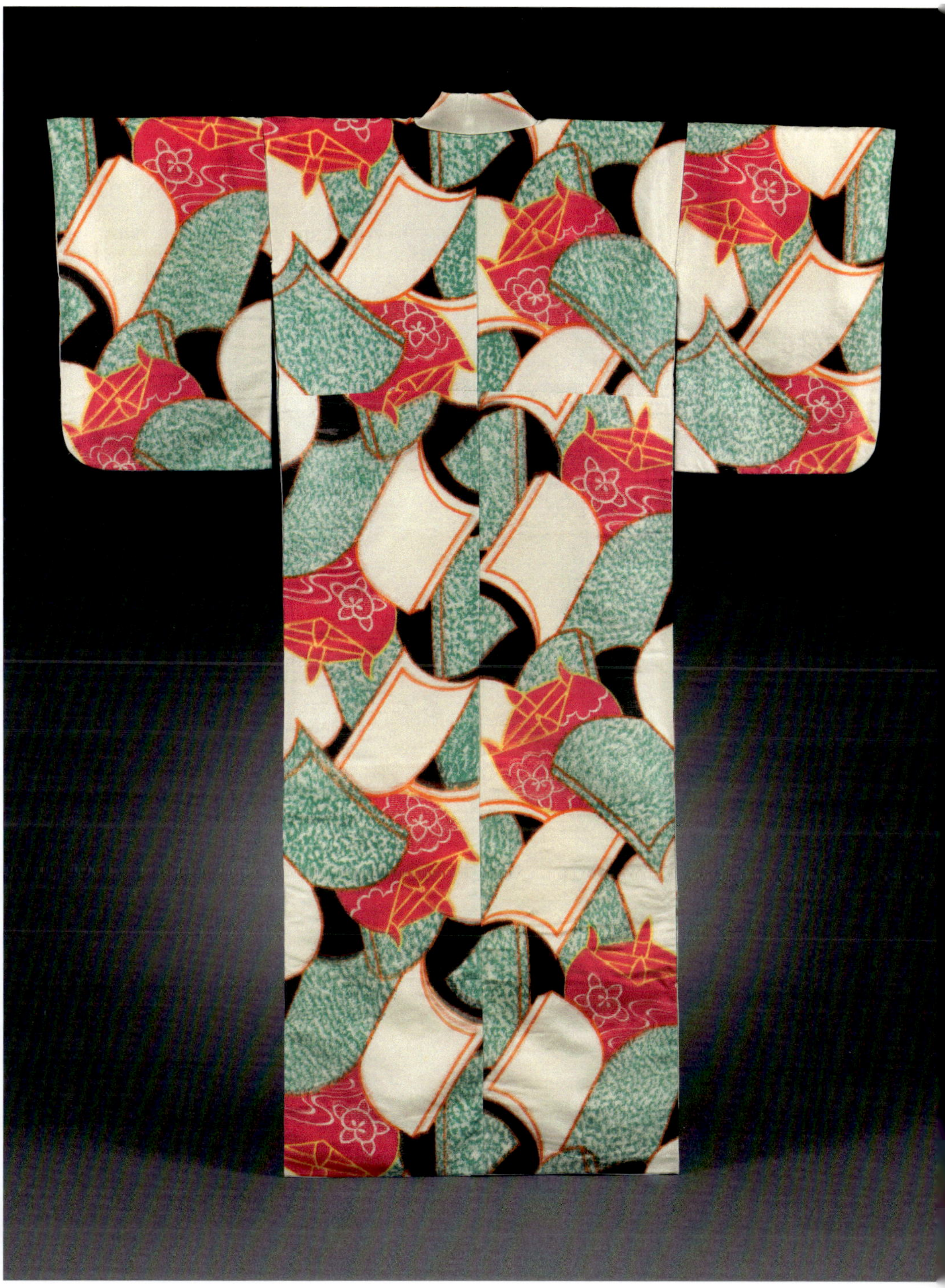

These three kimonos exemplify the *heiyō-gasuri* technique, which uses stencil-printed warps and wefts to produce complex double-ikat patterns with curves and flowing lines. All were made in Isesaki, the *meisen* production center where this technique was developed and refined. The first features a modern rendering of a traditional comma (*tomoe*) pattern, which was associated with samurai culture and also used as a family crest in the Edo period (1615–1868). Here, large commas boldly punctuate a background of rectangles. The fabric, which was promoted as Chiyoda *omeshi*, has a slightly ribbed texture similar to crepe, the result of strongly twisted silk and rayon wefts. The use of inexpensive rayon was common in Isesaki in the 1930s, when the demand for *meisen* was at its peak.

The finely dotted ground of the second *meisen* kimono here is overlaid with overlapping orange, red, green, white, yellow, and pink discs of various sizes and varying transparency—a striking visual effect that required unusually complex techniques. Simple compositions used the same stencils for the warps and wefts, but this one required three stencils to dye the warps and four for the wefts.

The design of the third *meisen* kimono was created with six stencils to dye six colors. Large green-and-white open books and red yarn spools decorated with mandarin oranges and streams are arranged in an allover design that minimizes the black ground. Although books and bobbins were favored motifs in the Edo period, their combination reflects contemporary ideas, such as women's increasing access to education and their increasing role in the textile industry.

59 紺地扇子白花模様御召銘仙羽織

Meisen jacket (*haori*) with fans and white flowers. Shōwa period (1926–89), ca. 1935–45. Plain-weave silk warps with twisted rayon and silk wefts in partial double ikat (*hanheiyō-gasuri*), 32 × 47 in. (83 × 119.4 cm). Promised Gift of John C. Weber

A stylized, almost abstract rendering of a pattern of large fans and flowers lends a modern feel to this lined jacket. It is made of a textured, crepelike silk called *omeshi chirimen*. The white flowers are depicted in full bloom with rich gradation, displaying the fine detail and depth produced by the *hanheiyō-gasuri* technique.

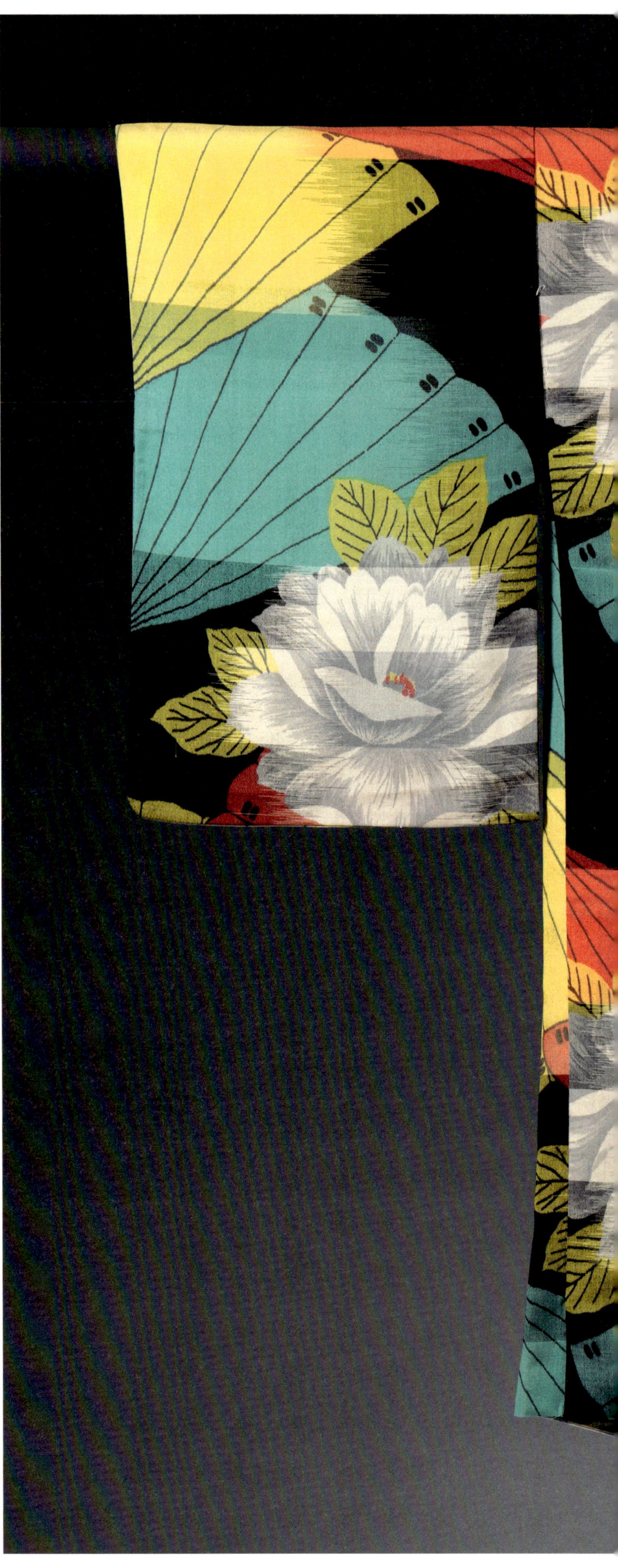

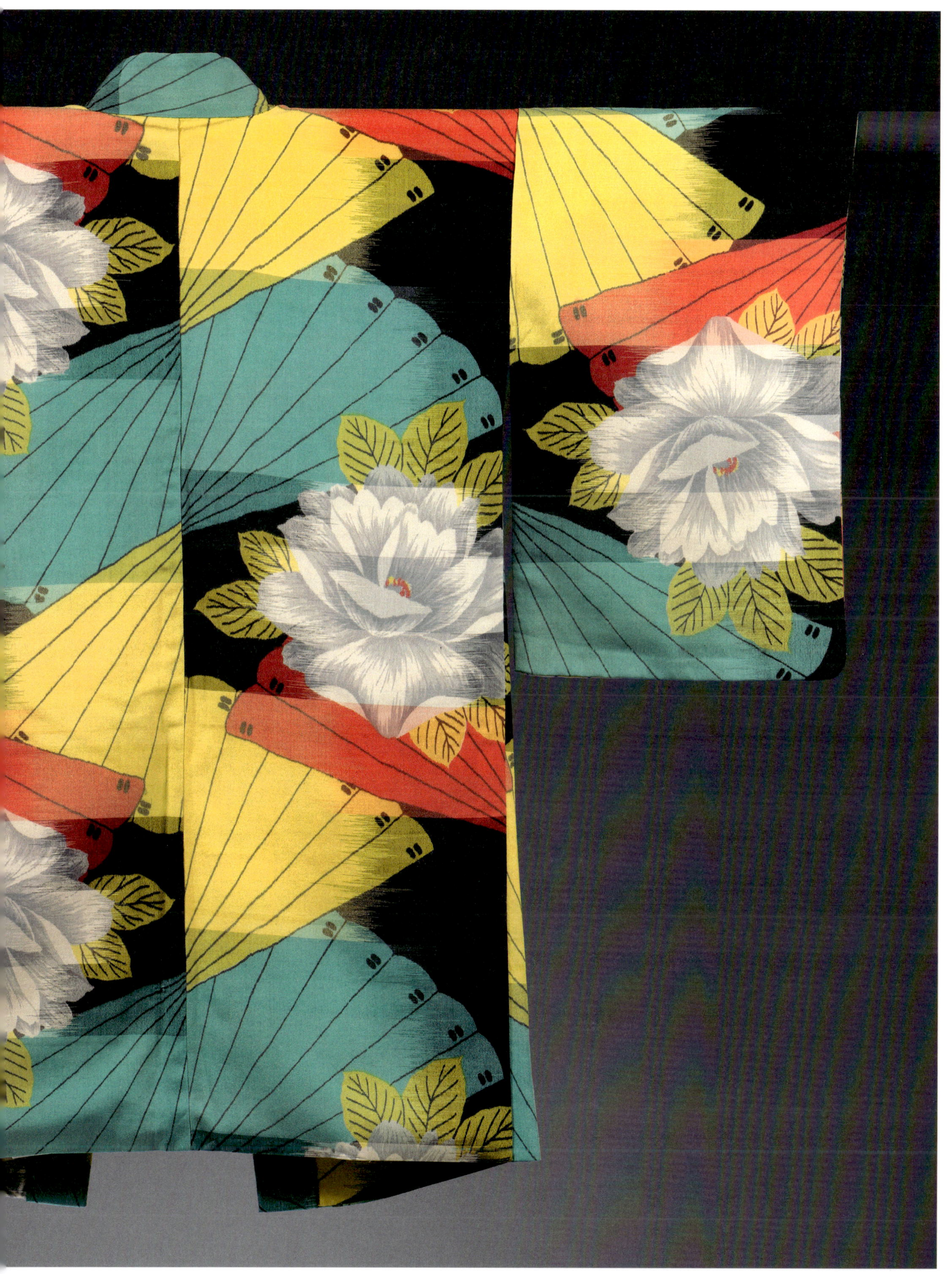

60 紺地芭蕉雪模様銘仙単衣
Meisen summer kimono with banana leaves and snowflakes. Shōwa period (1926–89), ca. 1940–45. Plain-weave silk warps with twisted silk wefts in all-weft ikat (*yokosō-gasuri*), 59½ × 50½ in. (151.1 × 128.3 cm). Promised Gift of John C. Weber

The snow falling on banana leaves lends a chill to this light, unlined kimono. The fabric (Akashi *chijimi*), similar to crepe in texture, was made with wefts with residual sericin (a gelatinous protein produced by the silkworm), which created a crisp, nonclingy drape suitable for summer robes.

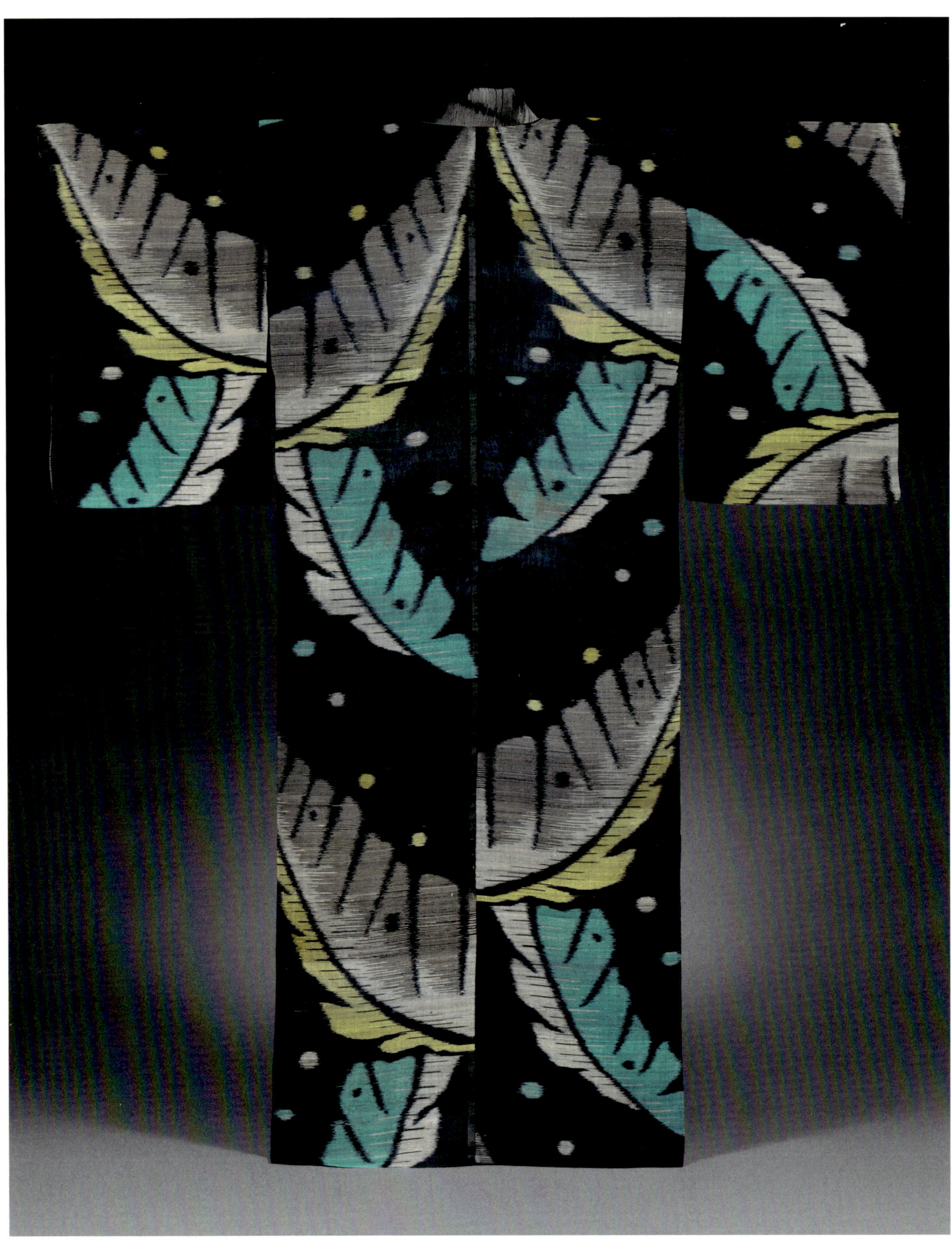

61 オレンジ赤地折り鶴模様銘仙着物

Meisen kimono with origami cranes (*orizuru*). Shōwa period (1926–89), ca. 1945–55. Plain-weave silk in all-weft ikat (*yokosō-gasuri*), 60 × 48 in. (152.4 × 121.9 cm). Promised Gift of John C. Weber

This vivid robe is embellished with a design of paper cranes in a rectangular, abstract composition. Cranes are symbols of longevity and good fortune, and folding a thousand paper cranes was supposed to make a wish come true.

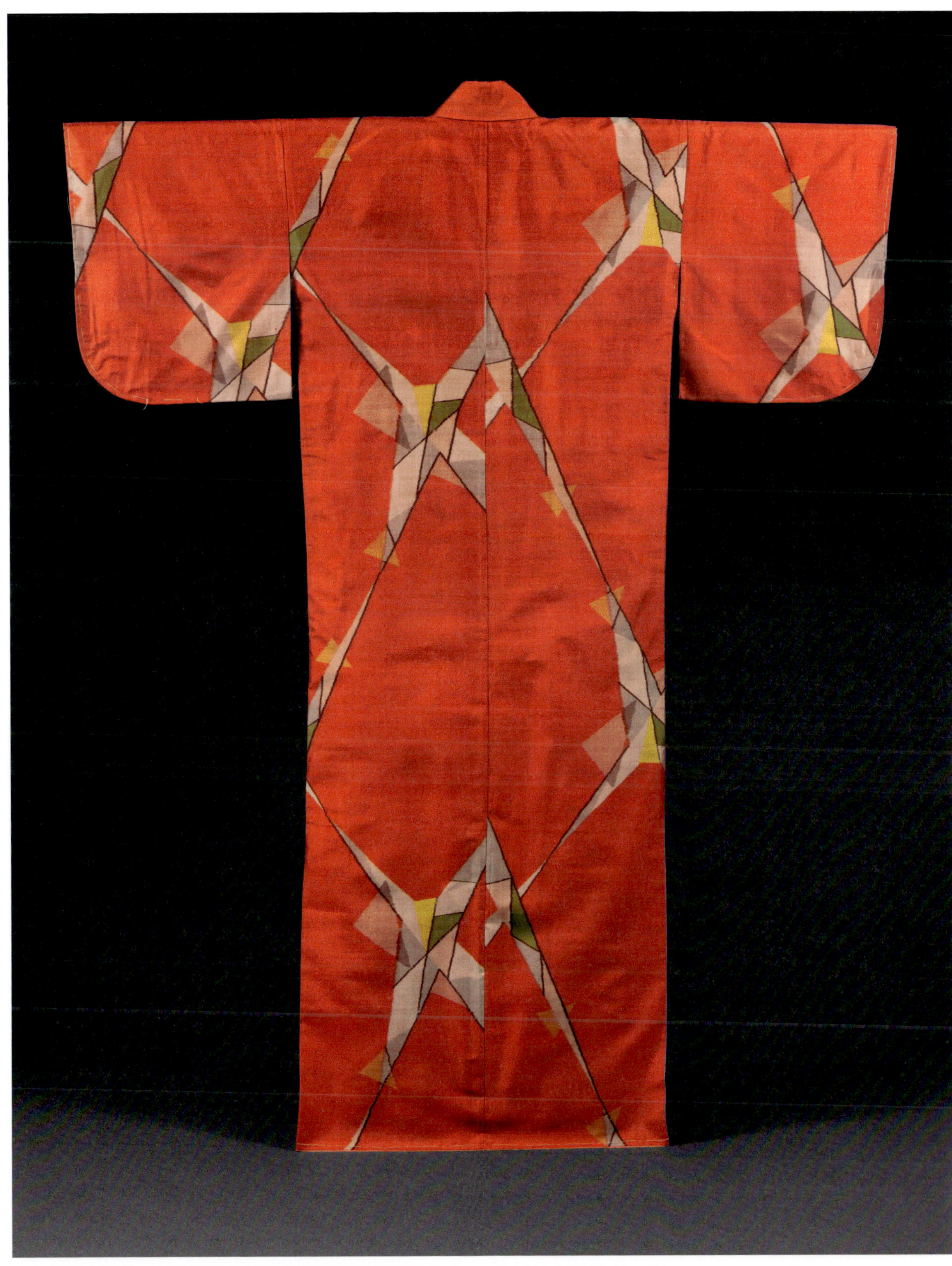

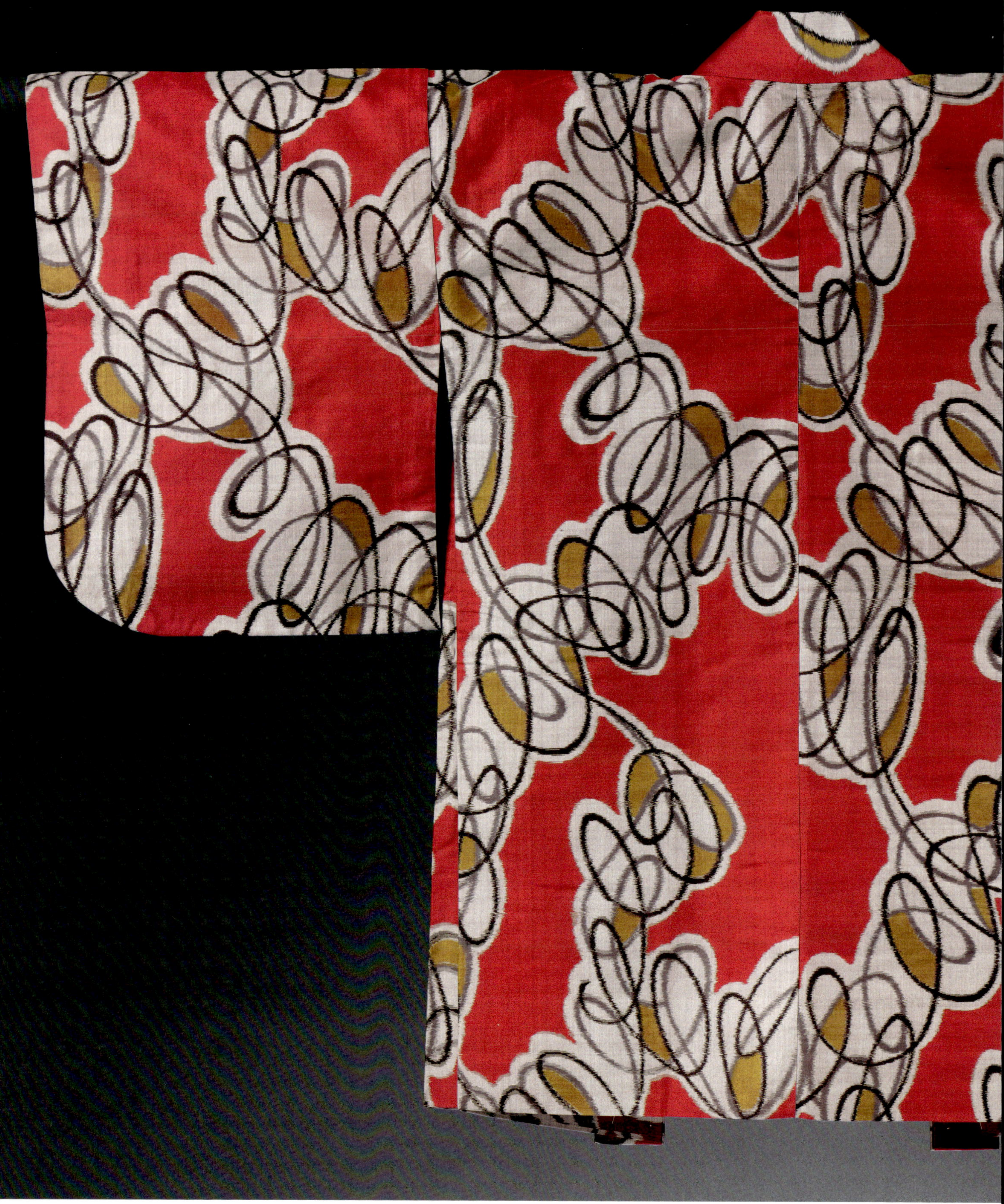

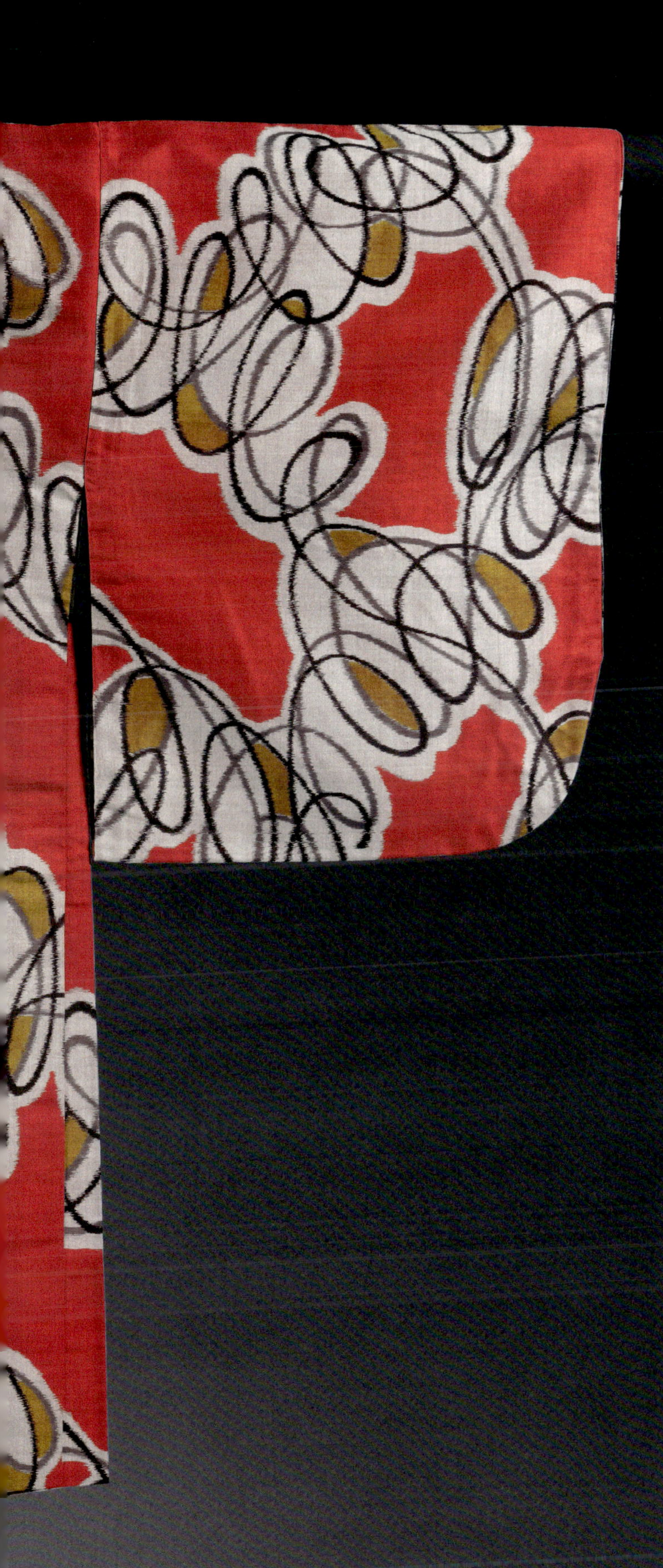

62 赤地曲線模様銘仙羽織
Meisen jacket (*haori*) with looped lines. Shōwa period (1926–89), ca. 1950–55. Plain-weave silk warps with machine-spun silk wefts in all-weft ikat (*yokosō-gasuri*), 33½ × 48 in. (85 × 121.9 cm). Promised Gift of John C. Weber

This abstract, stylized pattern was created using the all-weft ikat technique and four stencils to dye the wefts. The ground color, a dark strawberry red, was achieved by crossing plum-red wefts with dark red warps. This lined jacket was made in Isesaki.

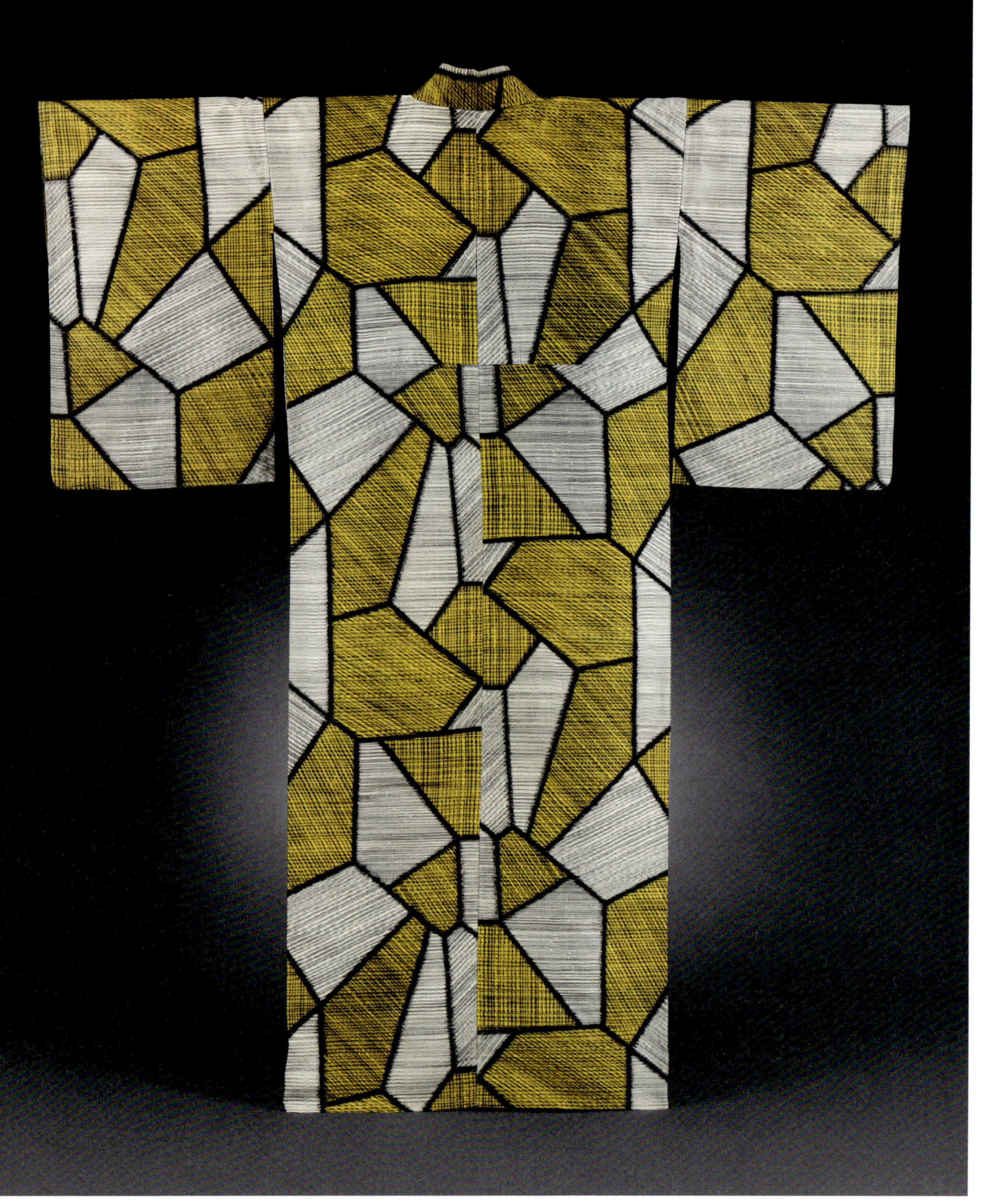

63 氷割模様銘仙単衣

Meisen summer kimono with cracked-ice pattern. Shōwa period (1926–89), ca. 1950–55. Plain-weave silk warps with machine-spun silk wefts in double ikat (*heiyō-gasuri*), 55½ × 50 in. (141 × 127 cm). Promised Gift of John C. Weber

A vivid design of golden-yellow and silver-gray polygons accented by thick black outlines adorns this unlined summer kimono. "Cracked-ice" patterning dates to the Edo period (1615–1868), but this large modern rendering of the motif resembles contemporary abstract painting.

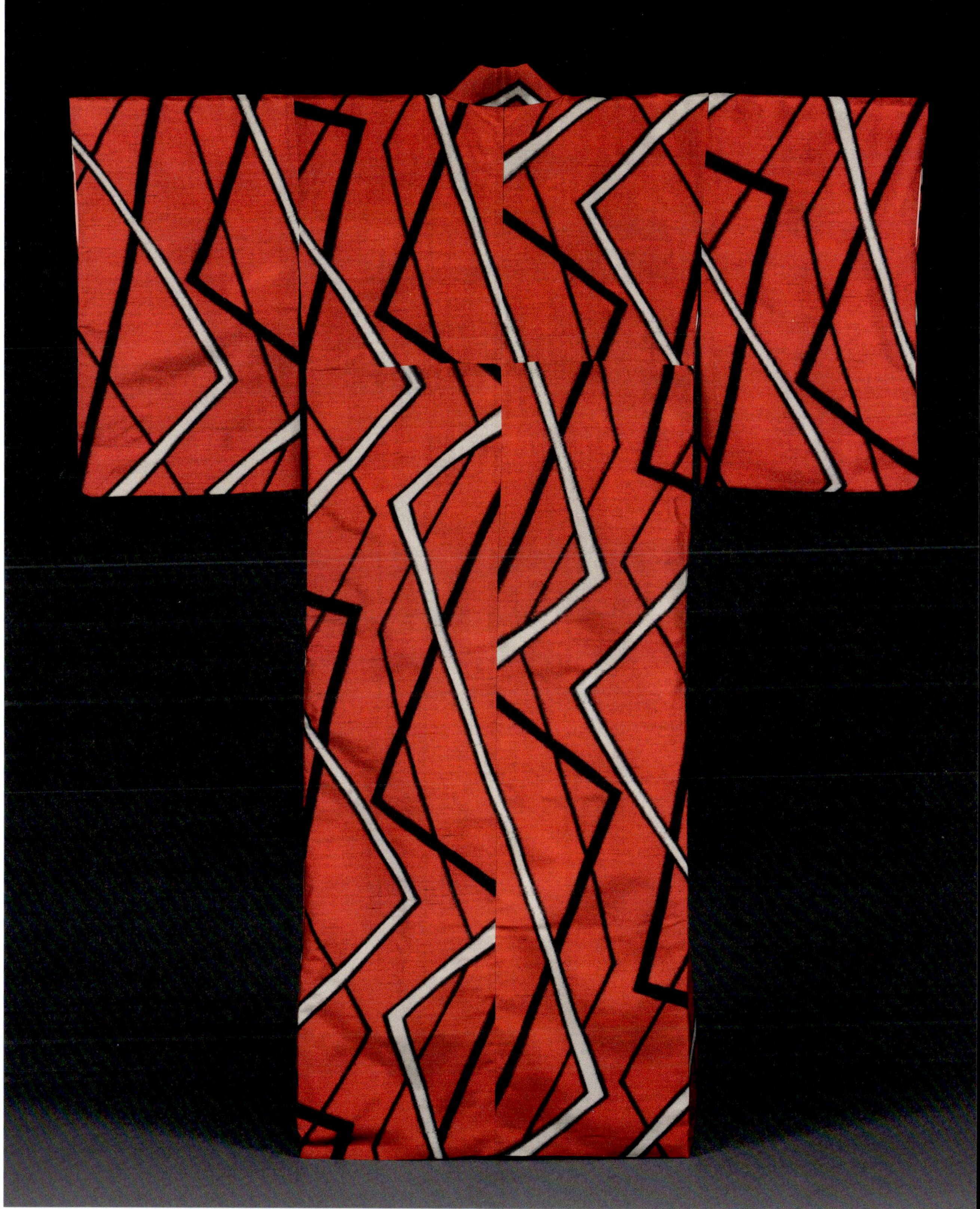

64 赤地落雷模様銘仙着物
Meisen kimono with thunderbolts. Shōwa period (1926–89), ca. 1950–55. Plain-weave silk in double ikat (*heiyō-gasuri*), 57½ × 49 in. (146 × 124 cm). Promised Gift of John C. Weber

The dazzling pattern of thunderbolts, rendered as white and black lines on a red ground, was made with the stenciled double-ikat technique. The wefts were dyed with three stencils and the warps with two. This lively composition was created in Isesaki.

The three *meisen* kimonos that follow, all made in Isesaki in the 1950s, demonstrate the enduring popularity of the abstract, geometric motifs that were favored in the 1920s and 1930s. Each was inspired by Western art: Pointillism (cat. 65), Cubism (cat. 66), and De Stijl (cat. 67).[5] They also represent the revival of the *heiyō-gasuri* technique from the 1930s, with stencil-printed warp and weft threads.

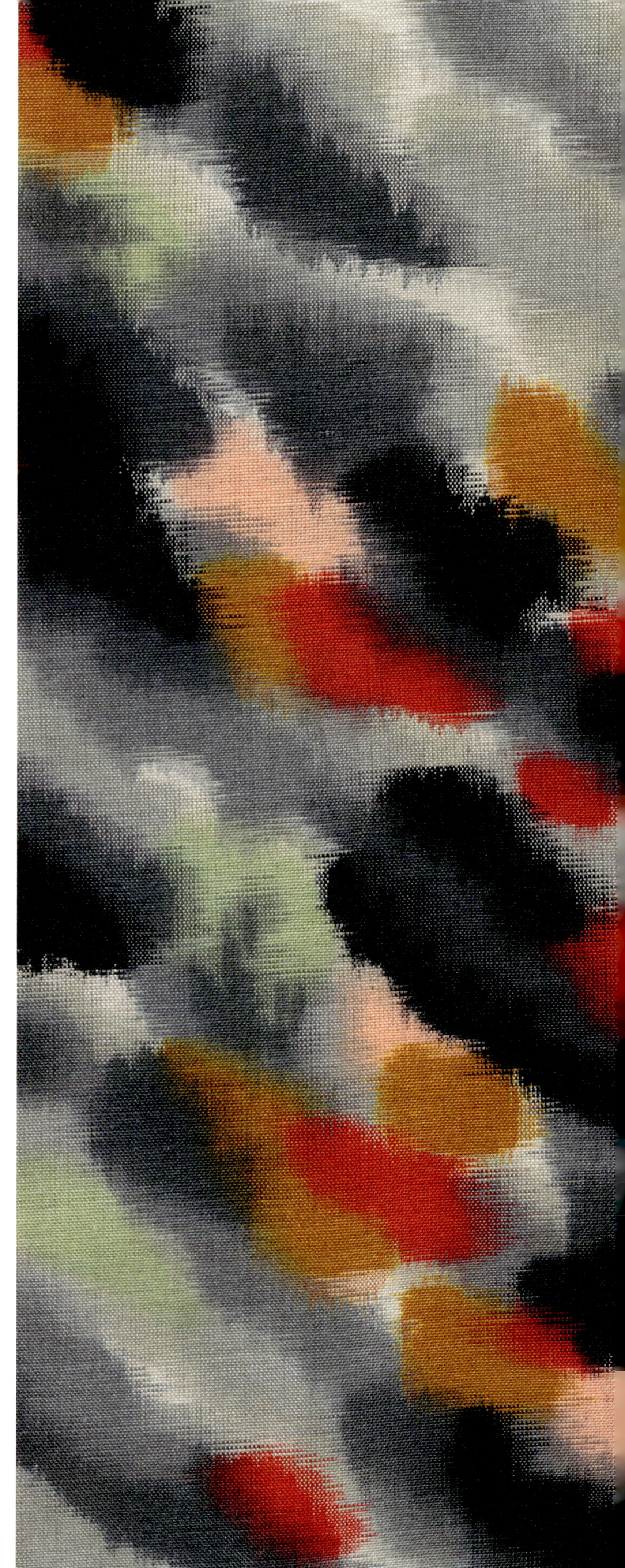

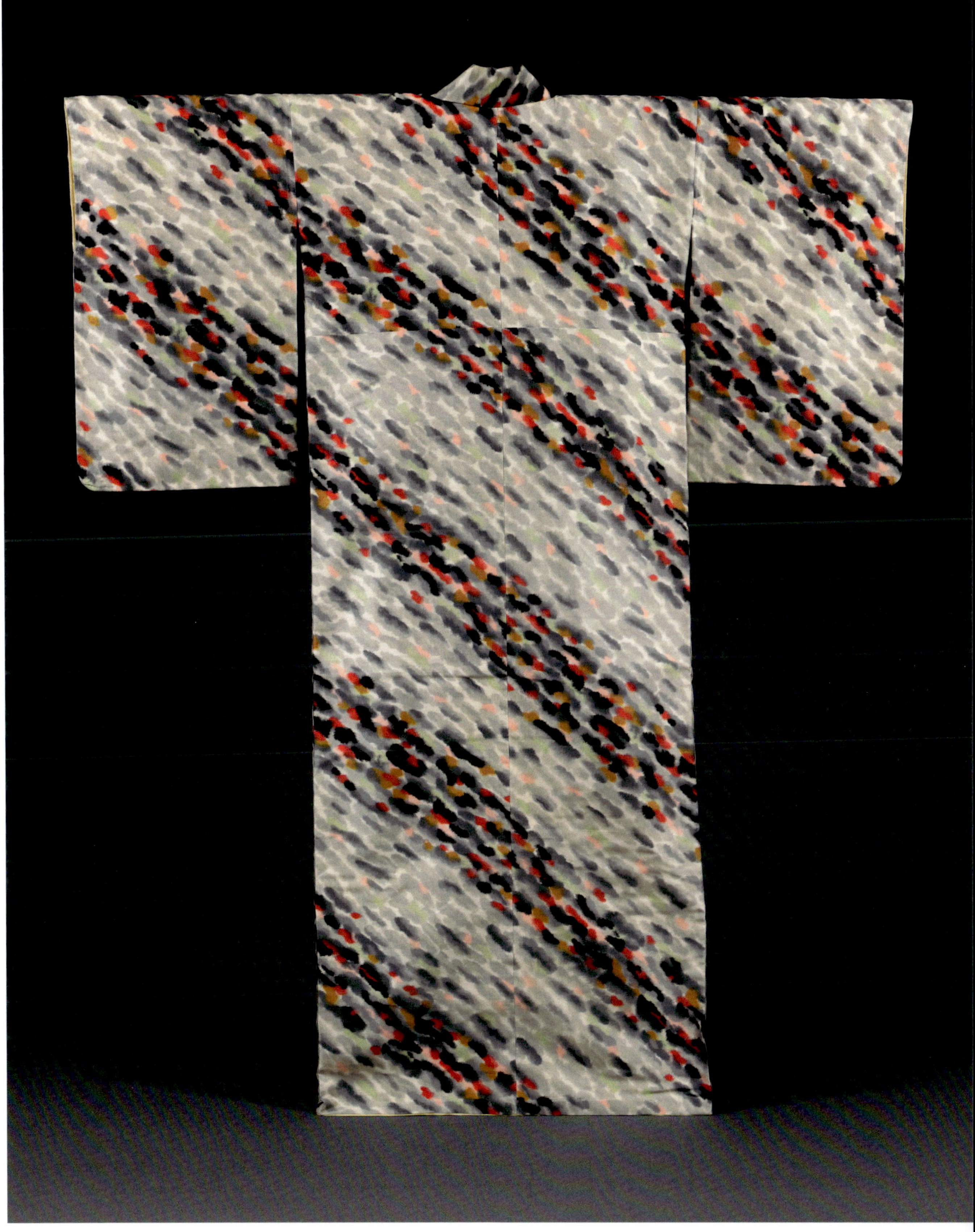

65 白地筆書き斜線模様銘仙着物
Meisen kimono with dotted diagonals. Shōwa period (1926–89), ca. 1955–60. Plain-weave silk warps with machine-spun silk wefts in double ikat (*heiyō-gasuri*), 56¾ × 48 in. (144 × 122 cm). Promised Gift of John C. Weber

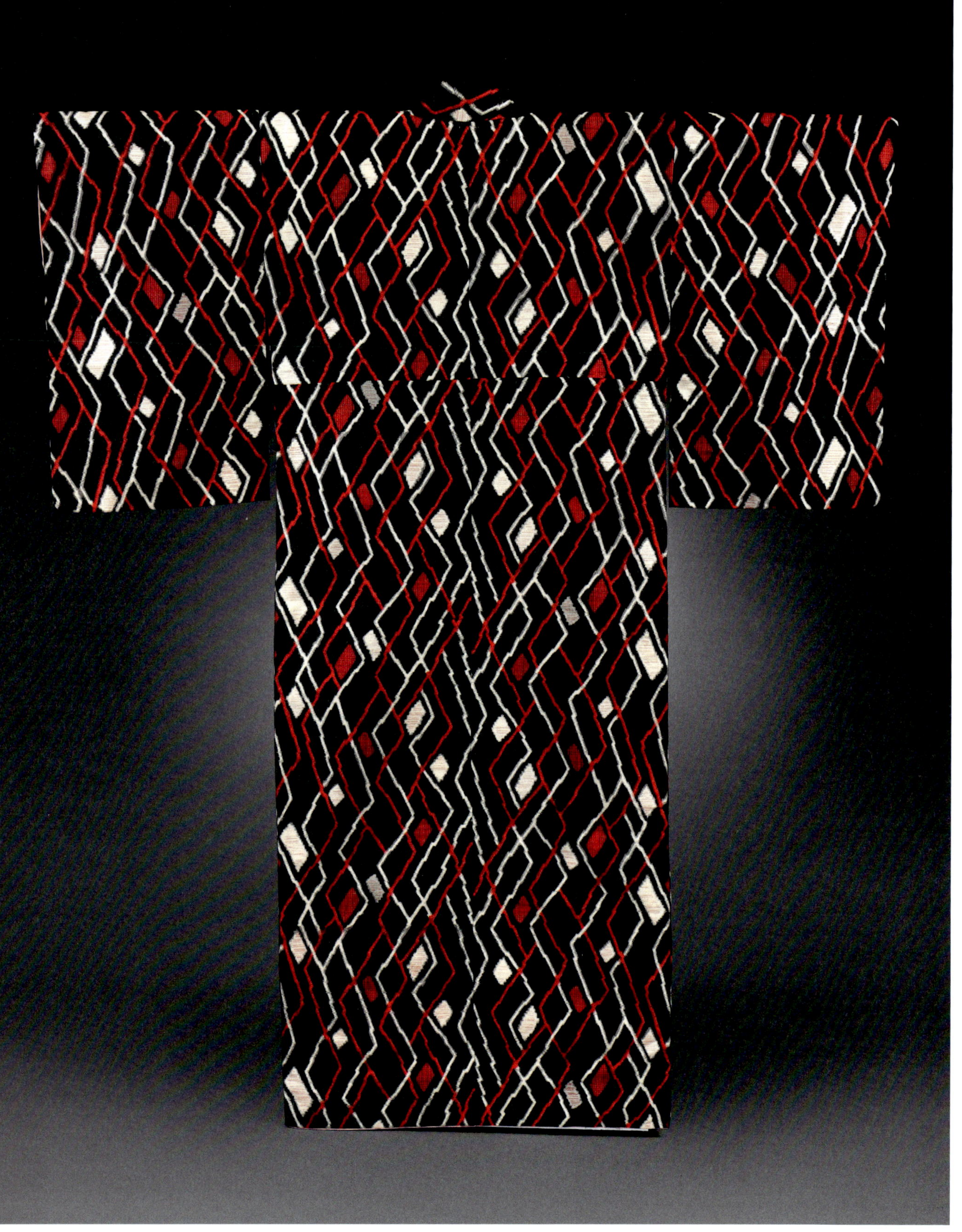

66 黒地変り菱格子模様銘仙着物
Meisen kimono with diamond patterns. Shōwa period (1926–89), ca. 1950–55. Plain-weave silk warps with machine-spun silk wefts in double ikat (*heiyō-gasuri*), 56¼ × 48⅞ in. (143 × 124 cm). Promised Gift of John C. Weber

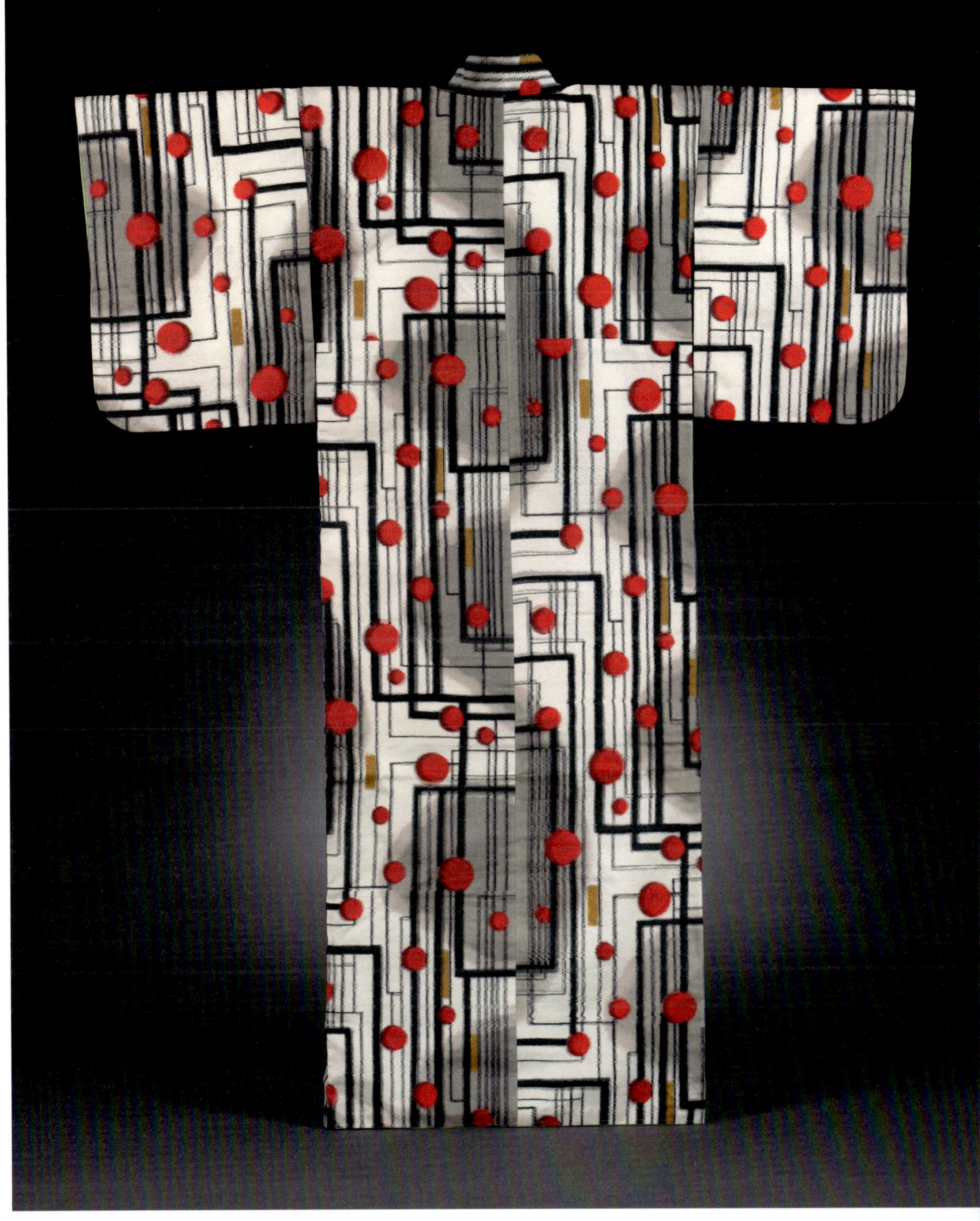

67 白地変り格子赤玉模様銘仙着物
Meisen kimono with geometric patterns. Shōwa period (1926–89), ca. 1950–55. Plain-weave machine-spun silk in double ikat (*heiyō-gasuri*), 58¼ × 48½ in. (148 × 123 cm). Promised Gift of John C. Weber

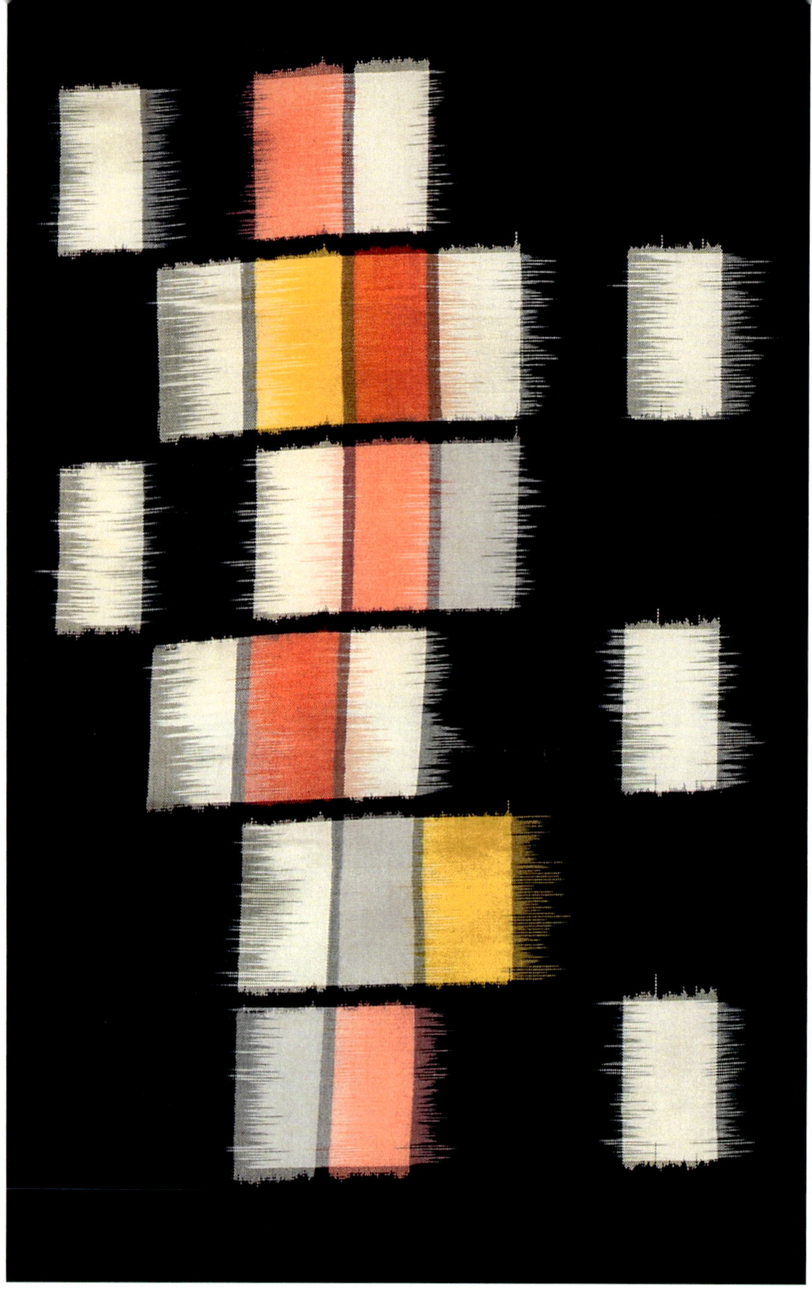

68 黒地窓格子模様銘仙着物
Meisen kimono with stylized windows. Shōwa period (1926–89), ca. 1950–55. Plain-weave silk warps with machine-spun silk wefts in partial double ikat (*hanheiyō-gasuri*), 54 × 48 in. (137.2 × 121.9 cm). Promised Gift of John C. Weber

This composition of small colorful rectangles on a black ground recalls the illuminated windows of high-rise buildings at night; it also suggests works of Piet Mondrian (1872–1944). It was made in Ashikaga, where many *meisen* kimonos were designed with modern, abstract patterns. The warps were dyed with five stencils and the wefts tied-resist dyed.

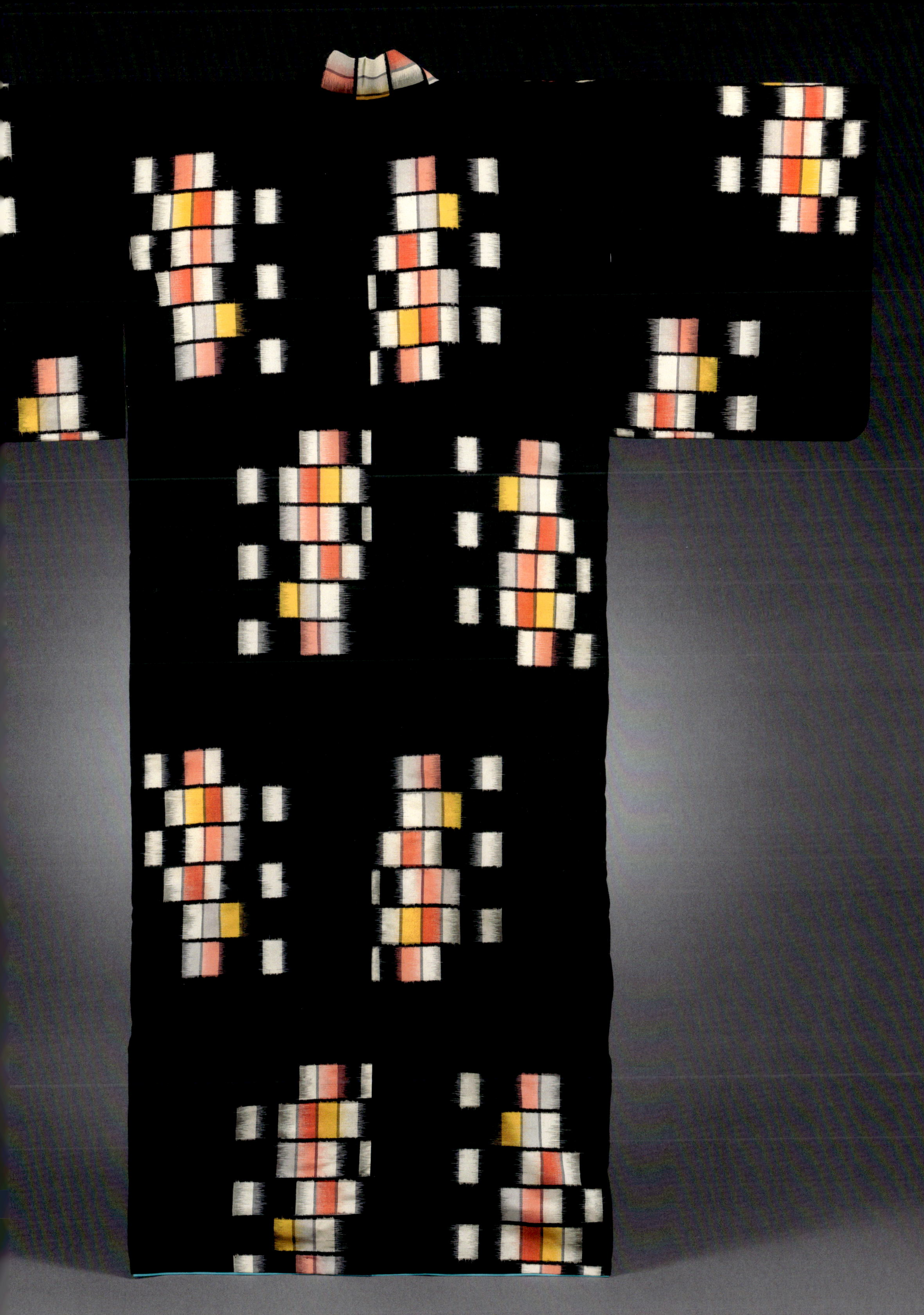

TEXTILES AND

IN THE

KRISTINE M. KAMIYA

WEBER COLLECTION

TECHNIQUES

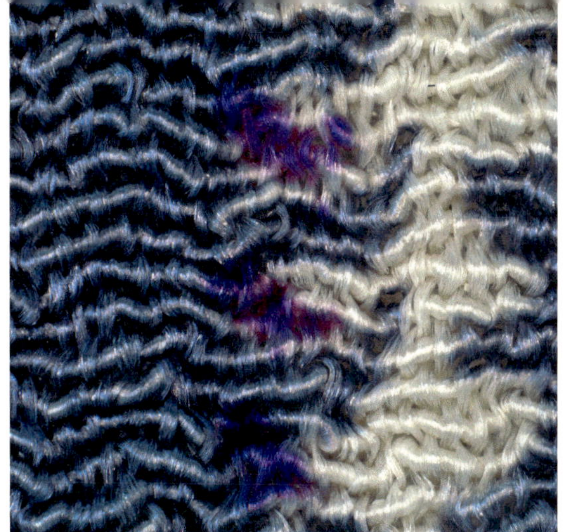
1

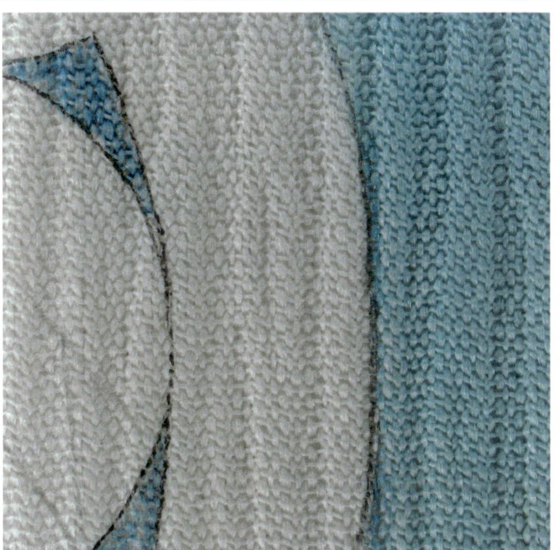
2

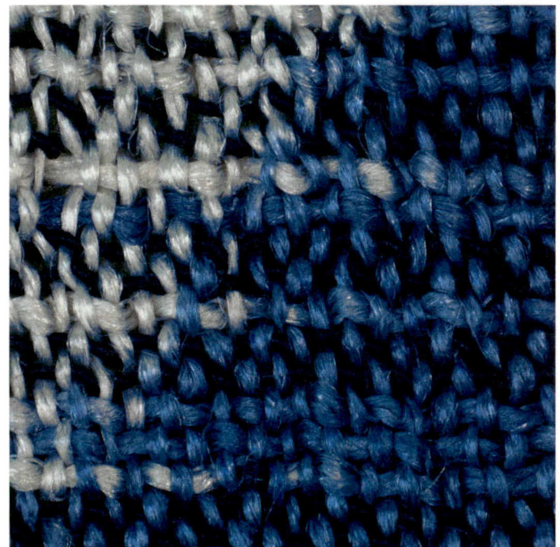
3

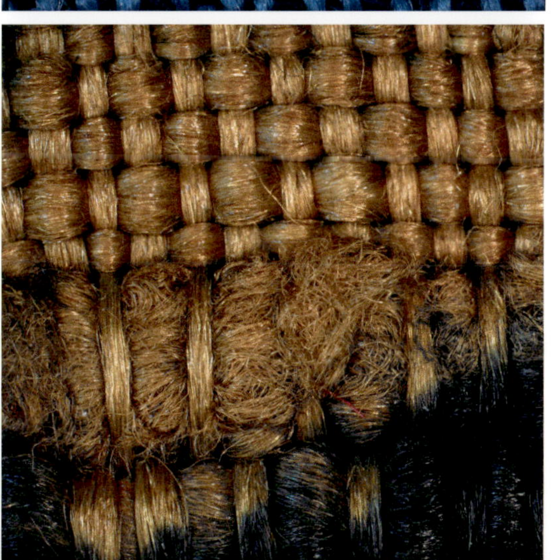
4

FABRICS

1. *CHIRIMEN*: JAPANESE CREPE SILK

Detail (20x) of cat. 48. A plain-weave, textured, matte fabric produced with threads of raw silk (fibers that have not been boiled and thus retain a gummed, or sericin, coating). Thick, highly twisted wefts (starched to retain their twist) are woven with thin, smooth, untwisted warps, creating tension that results in a crimped surface with horizontal ribs. The fabric is washed to remove the sericin and starch, further crinkling the textile. There are many varieties of *chirimen* with different textures, as well as slight differences between Edo-period and modern production techniques. It resists creasing and drapes beautifully. The preferred fabric for paste-resist dyeing because the texture prevents the dyes from running. See *chijimi*.

2. *CHIJIMI*: JAPANESE CREPE SILK WITH VERTICAL RIBS

Detail (10x) of cat. 17. A type of *chirimen* in which untwisted warps are plain-woven with either S- or Z-twist wefts—meaning the threads were spun either counterclockwise or clockwise. In the standard *chirimen*, by contrast, S- and Z-twist wefts alternate. The one-directional pull of *chijimi*'s weft creates a vertically ribbed surface texture. *Chijimi*, thinner and with a finer texture than the standard *chirimen*, was used for luxurious Edo-period summer garments.

3. *OMESHI*: CREPE SILK WITH PREDYED THREADS

Detail (20x) of cat. 56. Similar to *chirimen*, a heavy, good-quality, plain-weave silk fabric in which the warps are slightly twisted and the wefts are highly twisted. The threads are degummed and dyed (usually by the *kasuri* technique) prior to weaving. Sometimes inexpensive yarns of rayon or rayon wrapped around a silk core (*kabe-ito*) were used as wefts. *Omeshi meisen* was especially popular in the first half of the twentieth century.

4. *TSUMUGI*: PONGEE SILK

Detail (20x) of cat. 51. Fabric made from thick, handspun, floss-silk threads produced from fibers that are broken, stained, or uneven in thickness. The imperfections create a dull, nubby texture in the resulting fabrics, which are usually handwoven. New *tsumugi* is quite stiff but softens with use. This durable fabric is often used for casual kimonos. During the Edo period, farmers made it for their own use.

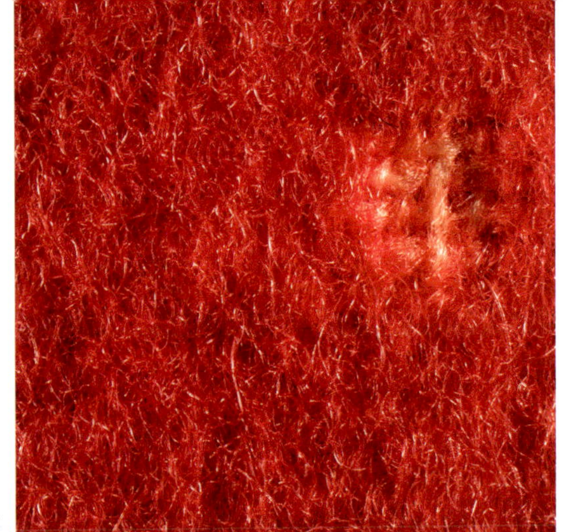
5

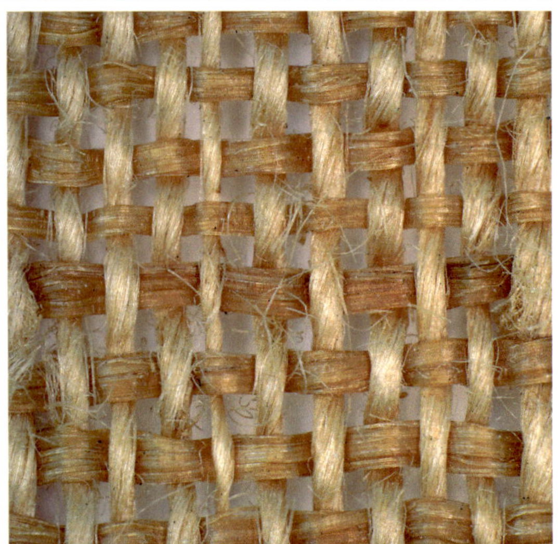
6

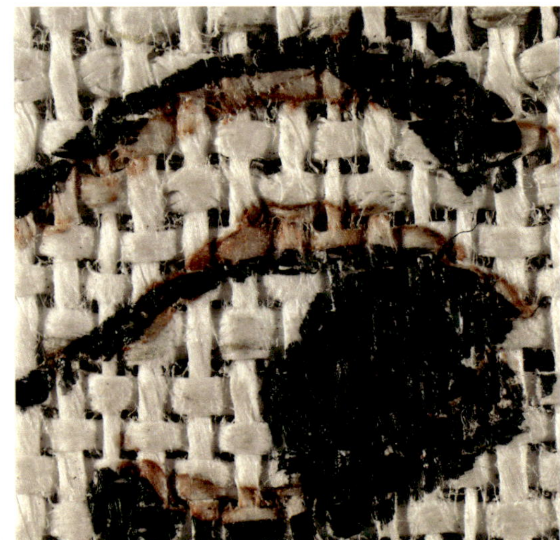
7

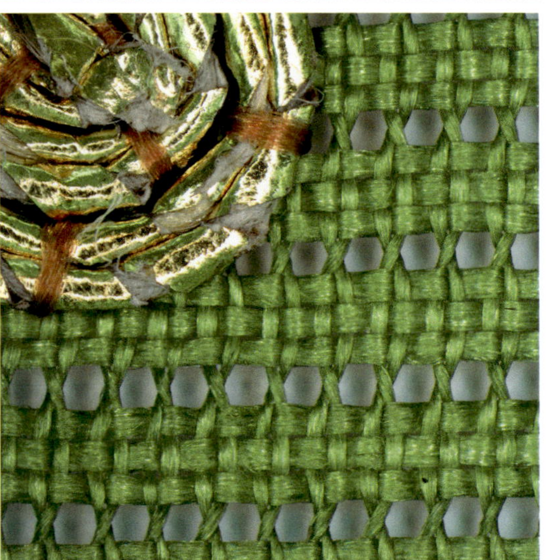
8

5. *RASHA*: WOOL WITH A NAPPED SURFACE
Detail (20x) of cat. 8. A plain-weave fabric made from thick wool yarns, it has a napped or brushed surface resembling felt. Imported from Europe as a woven and dyed cloth prior to the mid-nineteenth century, its use indicated high status. It was used for *jinbaori*, coats (*dōbuku*), samurai firefighters' jackets, and ceremonial wear.

6. *BASHŌFU*: BANANA-FIBER CLOTH
Detail (20x) of cat. 50. Made from the fibers of the tree-like plantain or "thread banana" plant (*Musa balbisiana* var. *liukiuensis*), a non-fruit-bearing variety introduced from southern China to Okinawa (previously the Ryukyu Islands). The fibers are knotted and/or spliced to create lengths of thread. The fiber's texture is similar to that of bast fibers and can be used to produce a range of fabrics, from very fine to coarse.

WEAVES

7. *HIRA-ORI*: PLAIN WEAVE
Detail (10x) of cat. 5. The most basic of weave structures consists of one warp thread (vertical) and one weft thread (horizontal), with the weft passing over and under the warp so that the two cross, or bind, in an over-one, under-one rhythm. It produces a strong and durable fabric. This example, which is embellished by hand-painting (*kaki-e*), illustrates the weave's simplicity.

8. *RO*: GAUZE, LENO
Detail (20x) of cat. 18. A light and airy fabric produced by interlacing pairs of warps: warp yarns cross over adjacent warps and then, held in place by wefts, cross back to their original position, creating small visible openings. Variations on the complex warp crossings and weft bindings create a range of patterns. In the example here, silk warps cross over each other between three rows of plain-weave weft. *Ro*, *ra*, and *sha*, the basic Japanese gauze weaves, are collectively called *usumono* (thin fabric). They were used for expensive, elegant summer garments and certain Noh costumes.

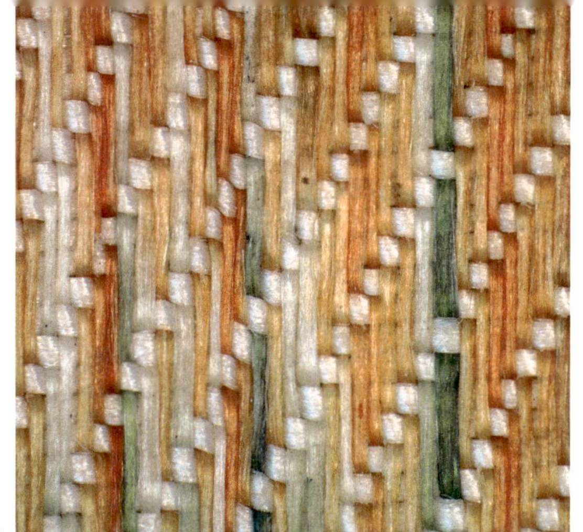
9

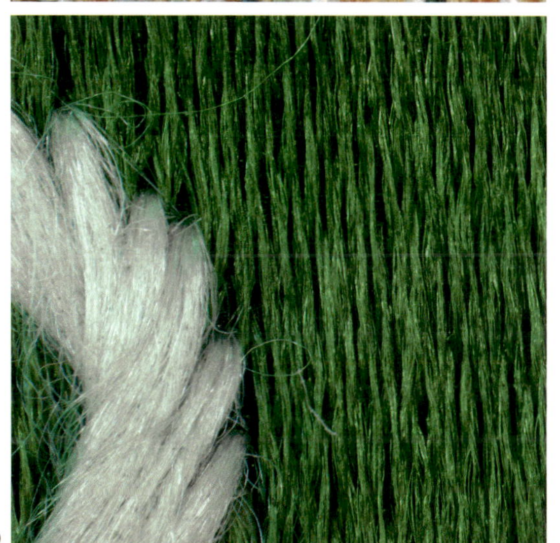
10

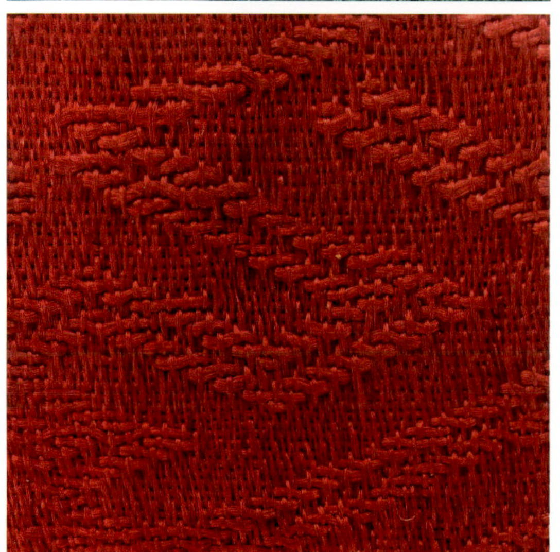
11

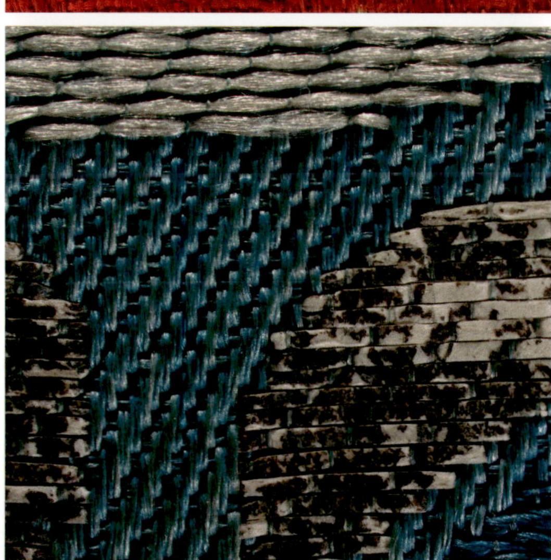
12

9. *AYA-ORI*: TWILL
Detail (20x) of cat. 2. Another of the basic weave structures, in which the weft thread floats over a group of warp threads before binding under the next warp thread (weft-faced twill) or the warp thread floats over a group of weft threads before binding over the next weft thread (warp-faced twill, illustrated here). It can be identified by its diagonal pattern, which is created by offsetting the pass on each successive row. The weave produces a relatively thick, durable, and wrinkle-resistant fabric with a light-reflecting sheen. This example, a 5/1 twill (meaning the warp floats over five wefts, then binds under one), has *kasuri*-dyed warps.

10. *SHUSU*: SATIN
Detail (20x) of cat. 4. One of the three basic weave structures. Its warps and wefts bind at regular intervals, with warps floating over at least four wefts and binding under only one weft. The result of the long warp floats is a smooth and lustrous surface. Satin-weave fabrics were often embellished with elegant embroidery or gold-leaf application.

11. *RINZU*: FIGURED SATIN-WEAVE SILK (SATIN DAMASK)
Detail (10x) of cat. 28. The use of two weaving techniques produces a monochrome, self-patterned fabric, or damask. The ground is a satin weave, and the figured or patterned design is created by a twill or plain weave. *Rinzu* is a soft, beautifully draping fabric that is as durable as it is lustrous. It became the standard ground fabric for samurai women's *kosode* in the seventeenth century and often featured chrysanthemums, orchids, or continuous key-fret patterns. Later it was favored among merchant-class women.

12. *NISHIKI*: JAPANESE BROCADED SILK WITH SILK AND METAL THREADS
Detail (10x) of fig. 13. *Nishiki* is a compound weave, using satin, twill, or plain weave for the ground and twill or plain weave for the pattern to create a lavish, decorative fabric. Its raised patterns are created with supplementary wefts of polychrome threads of silk and/or metal. These flat metal threads are made of gold or silver foil that is adhered with lacquer to a paper substrate. Depending on the threads used, the result may be known as *kinran* (gold-brocaded fabric) or *ginran* (silver-brocaded fabric). Though the fabric is often referred to as "brocade," the term should not be mistaken for the brocade weave structure, which creates a pattern with discontinuous supplementary wefts. *Nishiki* was typically used for Noh costumes and formal obis and is associated with Nishijin, Kyoto's famed weaving district.

DYEING TECHNIQUES

13

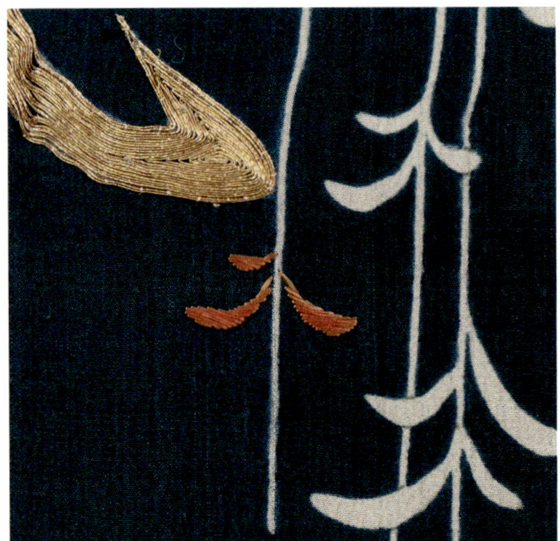

14

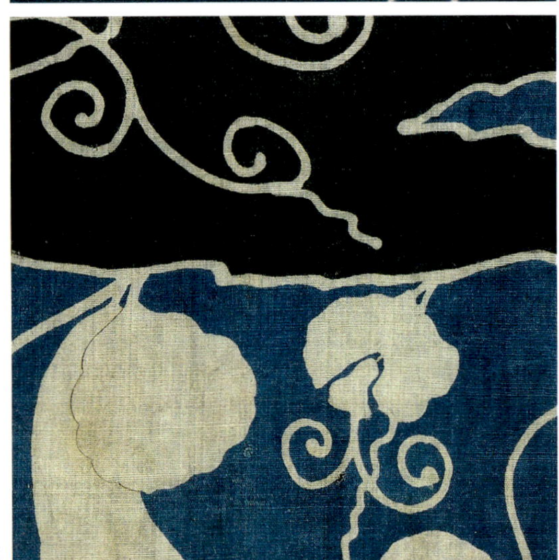

15

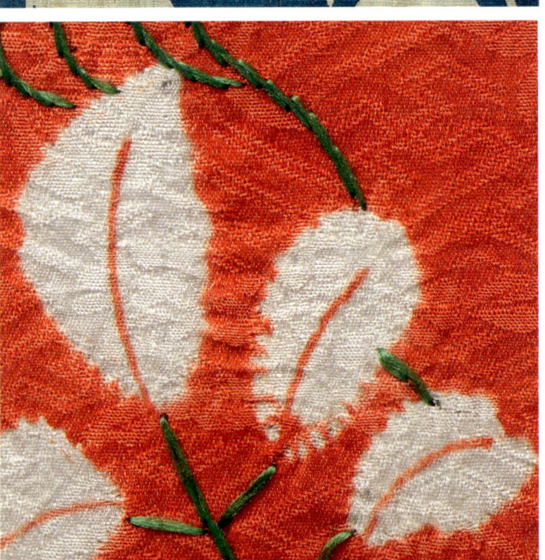

16

13. *YŪZEN-ZOME*: PASTE-RESIST DYEING

Detail (10x) of cat. 18. A surface resist-dyeing technique that uses a narrow-tipped tube to outline a design by hand on fabric with rice paste. Dyes are then brushed into the areas outlined by paste, often in multiple tones or gradation. The rice paste protects the designs where dyes are applied and defines the dyed areas, allowing for complex, painterly compositions with distinct contours. After the fabric is steamed to set the dyes, the rice paste is washed away, revealing the undyed ground fabric, or white reserve. The process can be repeated numerous times on one fabric with a variety of color applications. This genuine Japanese innovation revolutionized Edo-period fashion in the late seventeenth century by creating colorful patterns without expensive and time-consuming compound weaves (see *nishiki*). The pattern of fine white lines and contrasting colors on this gauze fabric demonstrates the potential of *yūzen-zome*.

14. *SHIRO-AGE*: WHITE-RESERVE PATTERNS

Detail of cat. 23. A *yūzen* paste-resist technique that produces a fine white design (revealing the undyed fabric) against a solid-color or patterned ground. Often delicate linear details, such as leaves and stems, are depicted in *shiro-age* freehand drawing.

15. *TSUTSUGAKI*: TUBE-DRAWN PASTE-RESIST DYEING

Detail of cat. 6. Similar to the more refined and complex *yūzen* technique, *tsutsugaki* uses a wide-nozzled tube of paste to draw large and bold designs onto fabric, typically cotton or bast fiber that would be dyed in an indigo bath. Colors, including shading, would often be applied to the undyed areas of fabric with a brush. This freehand drawing technique was widely used in towns and villages to decorate ceremonial, household, and commercial folk textiles.

16. *SHIBORI-ZOME*: TIE-DYEING

Detail of cat. 20. A resist-dyeing technique using tied thread or other methods (such as clamping, folding, and twisting) to prevent reserved areas of fabric from being penetrated when submerged into dye. A variation of this technique uses stitching to outline a design, then pulls the stitches tightly to prevent dye from penetrating the gathered fabric. Many kimonos were embellished with botanical or geometric patterns using this technique from about the late fifteenth century. See *kanoko shibori*.

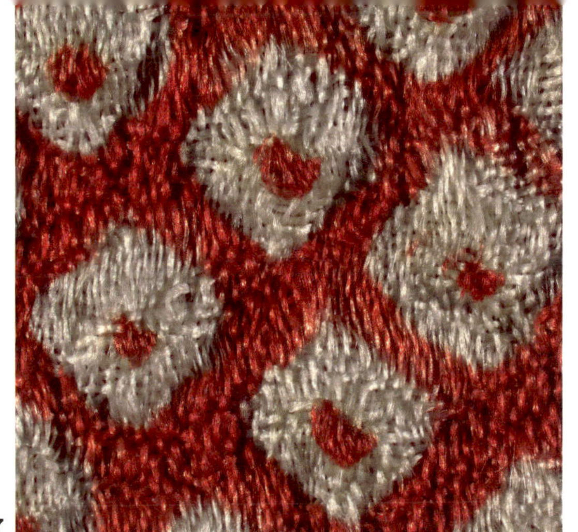

17

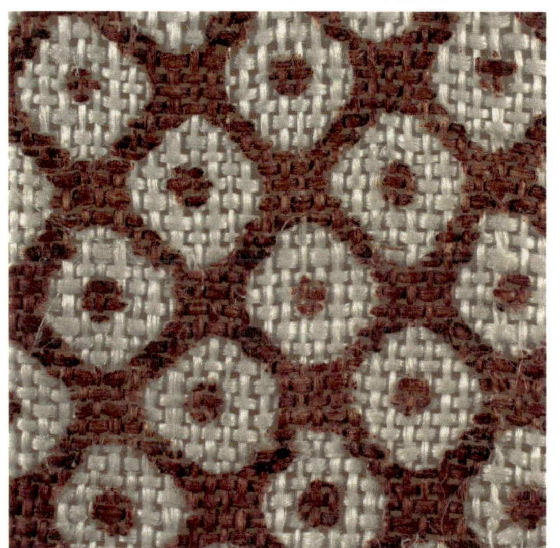

18

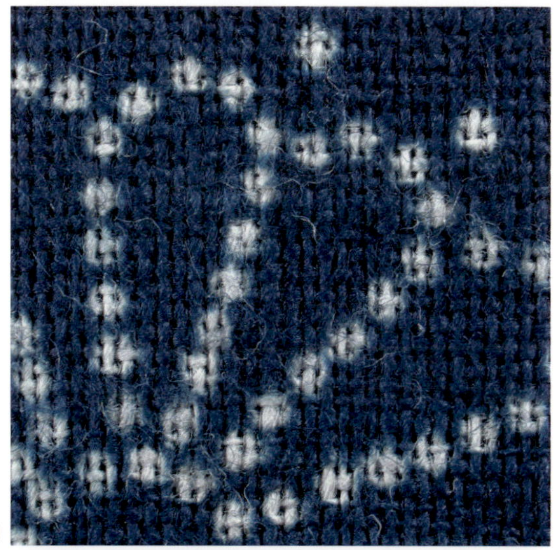

19

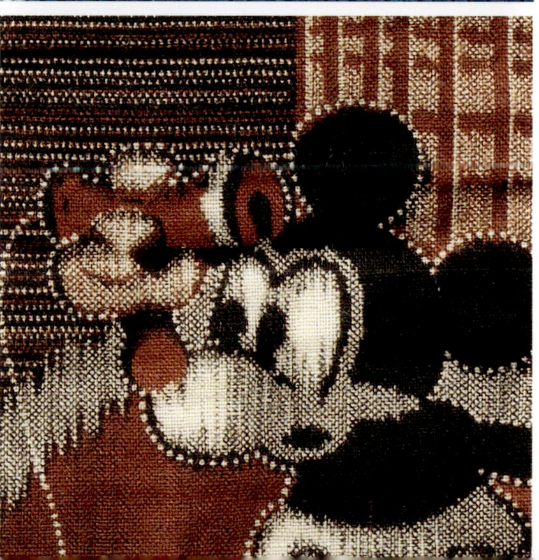

20

17. *KANOKO SHIBORI*: "FAWN SPOT" TIE-DYEING
Detail (10x) of cat. 26. A resist-dyeing technique whereby small areas of silk fabric are pinched or gathered and then tightly wrapped with silk or cotton thread, which keeps the dye from penetrating. The tiny tied bundles usually fill a motif or the entire ground. The threads are removed after the fabric is dyed, revealing both a repeat pattern of small dots or squares and a raised surface design. A garment with a full surface of *kanoko*, made by this intricate, time-consuming technique, was the ultimate luxury.

18. *SURI-BITTA* OR *KATA-KANOKO*: STENCIL-DYED *KANOKO SHIBORI* IMITATION
Detail (10x) of cat. 24. A resist-dyeing technique using a stencil to imitate a *kanoko shibori* pattern—a white square with a small dot of color at its center. This technique does not produce any surface texture and was less time-consuming and less expensive than the original *shibori* or tie-dyed version.

19. *KATA-ZOME*: STENCIL PASTE-RESIST DYEING
Detail (10x) of cat. 32. A paste-resist dyeing technique using a stencil to create repeat-pattern designs. Rice paste is spread thinly over a stencil of *shibugami* (a mulberry-fiber paper treated with persimmon tannin for strength and water resistance) with openwork patterns (in this example, a pattern of tiny dots). Dye is applied to the fabric by hand with a brush; the fabric is then steamed to set the dyes and washed to remove the rice-paste resist. This technique was used primarily on cotton and bast fibers to create small motifs (*komon*) in the Edo–Meiji period. Dyes can also be applied through stencils directly to the fabric. See *suri-bitta*.

20. *RŌRĀ NASSEN*: ROLLER PRINTING
Detail of cat. 49. Roller printing, developed in Scotland in 1783, is the oldest mechanized method of continuous printing. It was exported in the 1890s to Japan, where it was used to imitate *kasuri*, mainly for inexpensive garments of cotton and wool muslin. A dye paste is applied to the fabric by a copper roller that is incised with tiny dots and fine lines to create the design. The copper rollers, one for each color, are mounted against a large cylinder around which the fabric travels. The technique produces sharp outlines, which is important for printing small patterns.

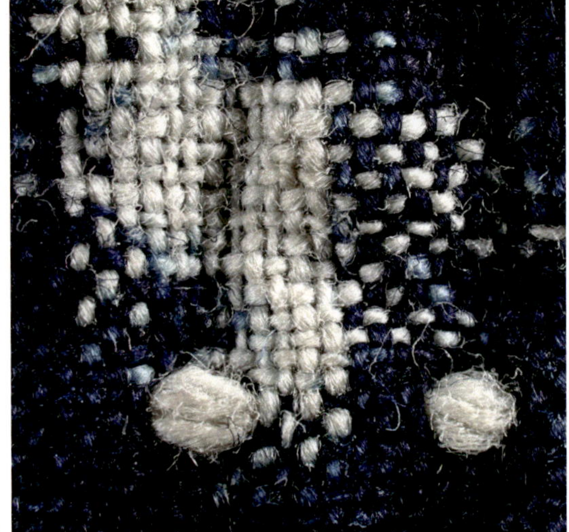
21

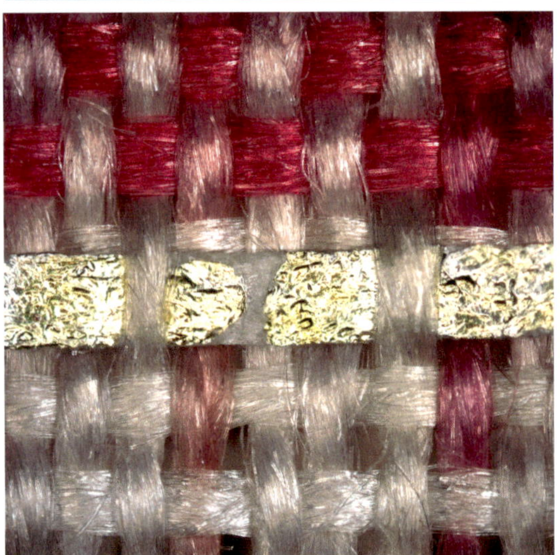
22

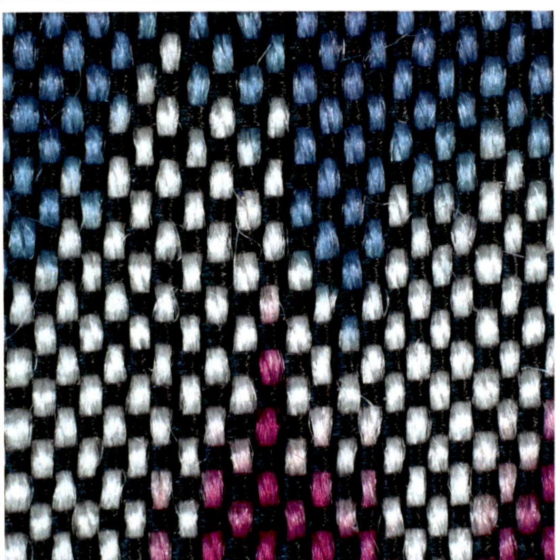
23

24

IKAT TECHNIQUES

21. *KASURI*: TIE-DYED IKAT
Detail (10x) of cat. 29. A resist-dyeing technique used to dye yarns before weaving. The yarns are tightly bound with cotton threads (*shibari*) at specific intervals along the warp and weft to prevent dye from penetrating, thus creating a pattern of undyed white yarns. As the resist-dyed areas cannot be precisely aligned on the loom, the resulting pattern has slightly blurred outlines, an artistic characteristic of *kasuri* fabric. The technique was typically used by farmers and commoners in the Edo period to create indigo-dyed garments with highly contrasting white geometric patterns.

22. *ŌGASURI*: LARGE IKAT
Detail (50x) of cat. 52. In *ōgasuri*, a version of the *kasuri* resist-dyeing technique used for *meisen* fabric, both the warp and weft threads are resist-dyed. The method, popular in about 1930–40, produces only rectilinear patterns, which were often embellished with wefts of metal thread. Like the following *meisen* techniques, it is now largely unused.

23. *HOGUSHI-GASURI*: UNRAVELED IKAT
Detail (20x) of cat. 54. To pattern only the warp yarns in this *meisen* fabric, temporary wefts, meant only to hold the warps in place, were loosely interwoven before dyeing. The fabric was printed by applying dyes suspended in a starchy paste over stencils. Then the wefts were removed, and the fabric was rewoven with unpatterned, monochrome permanent wefts. This method, developed in about 1905, allowed for the creation of varied curvilinear motifs.

24. *HEIYŌ-GASURI*: DOUBLE IKAT
Detail (20x) of cat. 63. Both warp and weft were stencil-dyed to create the designs for double-ikat *meisen*, usually using different stencils for each color on the wefts and the warps. The yarns had to be carefully aligned on the loom to create the complex patterns. Use of this method peaked in 1930–50, and it is the signature technique of the Isesaki *meisen* producers.

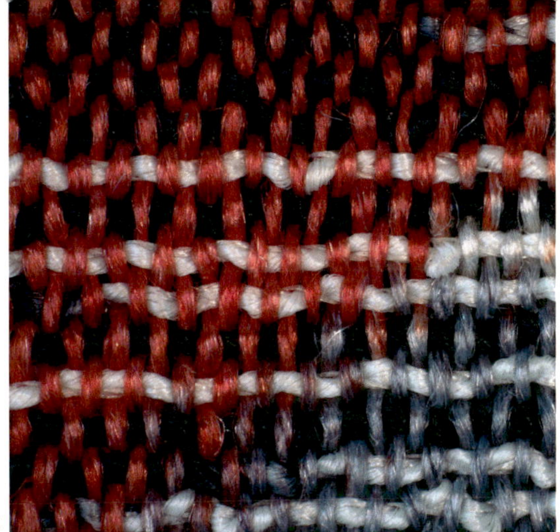
25

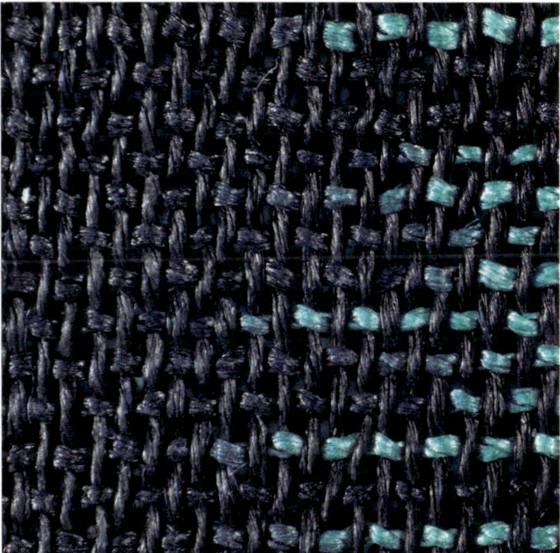
26

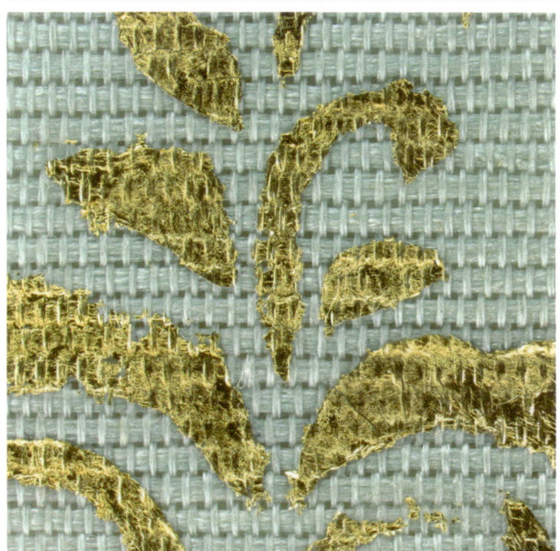
27

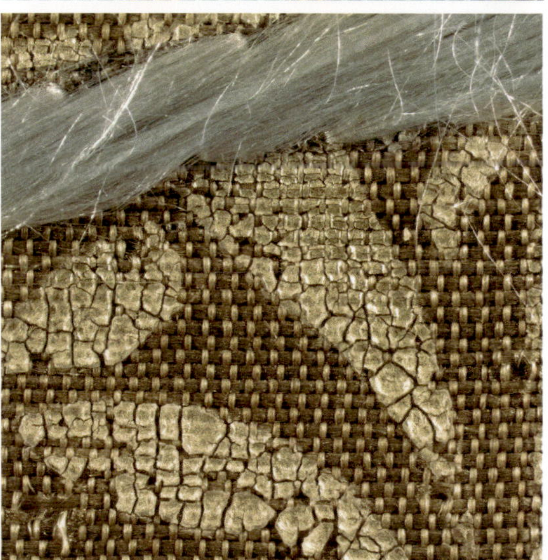
28

25. *HANHEIYŌ-GASURI*: PARTIAL DOUBLE IKAT
Detail (20x) of cat. 59. A simpler and less time-consuming technique for *meisen* than the complex *heiyō-gasuri*, it entailed weaving unraveled stencil-dyed (*hogushi*) warps with tied-resist-dyed (*kasuri*) wefts; the latter had only simple, large motifs in white or bright colors, creating accents in the design. Another advantage of *hanheiyō-gasuri* was that it could be woven on automated looms.

26. *YOKOSŌ-GASURI*: ALL-WEFT IKAT
Detail (20x) of cat. 60. A resist-dyed, all-weft *kasuri* technique used for *meisen*, it produced multicolored, free-form, continuous patterns in large repeats. The warps were monochrome. Many *meisen* were produced by this method in 1940–50.

SURFACE DECORATION

27. *SURIHAKU*: STENCIL-PASTED FOIL APPLICATION
Detail (10x) of cat. 4. In this metal-leafing technique, a patterned design of gold leaf (*kinpaku*) or silver leaf (*ginpaku*) is applied with a stencil. The method is like that for *kata-zome*: first a thin layer of rice paste is spread over the stencil, serving as an adhesive, and then the foil is laid on top and pressed into the fabric. These beautiful, shimmering metallic patterns were often used in early luxury *kosode* and in Noh theatrical costumes.

28. *NUIHAKU*: FOIL APPLICATION WITH EMBROIDERY
Detail (10x) of cat. 3. Like *surihaku*, this technique uses gold leaf and/or silver leaf to create a design or, in the case of *nuihaku*, to fill the fabric's ground. In *nuihaku*, silk embroidery (*nui*) is added to create patterns against the metallic ground. *Nuihaku* is often used to make a Noh costume that came to be known by the same term.

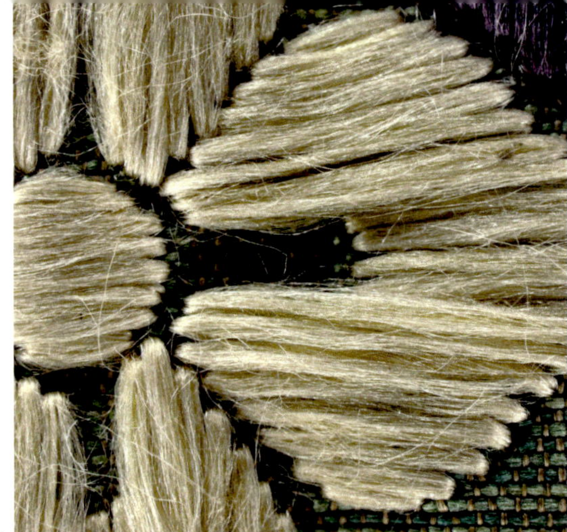

29

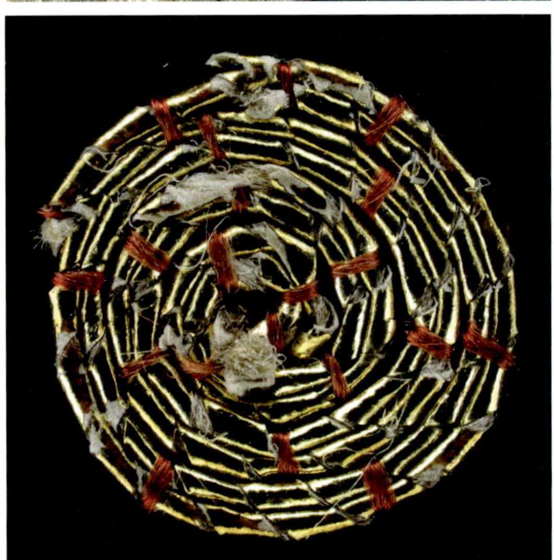

30

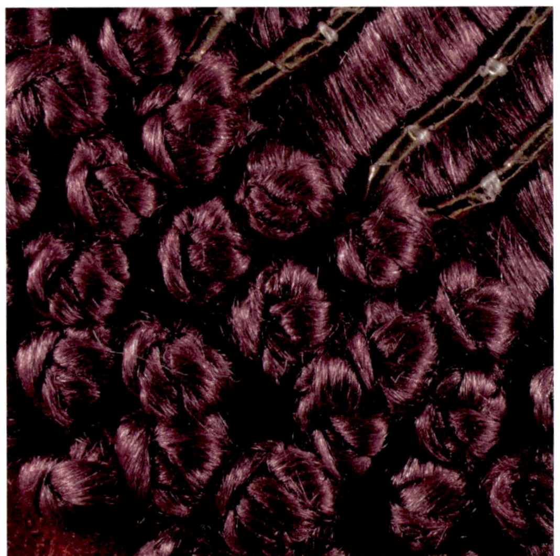

31

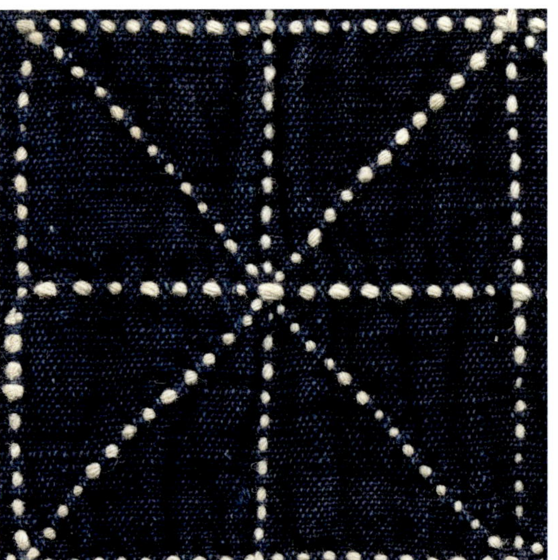

32

29. *HIRA-NUI*: SATIN STITCH
Detail (10x) of cat. 3. A single stitch that creates a long float and is laid alongside subsequent satin stitches to fill a pattern. The earliest type of satin stich uses minimal thread on the back; a second type carries the thread on both the front and the back, making the fabric appear reversible. Often silk floss without twist or ply is used to create a smooth, lustrous pattern.

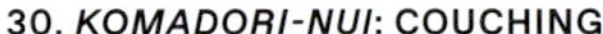

30. *KOMADORI-NUI*: COUCHING
Detail (10x) of cat. 47. An embroidery technique that lays threads on the surface of the fabric, usually creating a pattern, and secures them with perpendicular stitches. This technique is used primarily for metal thread and thick or textured threads that cannot easily be pulled through the fabric with a needle. Couching allows round metal threads (gold and silver strips wrapped around a silk core) to be fully visible and avoids wasting the precious metals on the back of the fabric. Variations of *komadori-nui* include single, paired, or grouped threads secured with variously spaced colored threads. In the early Edo period, white couching was usually used to secure gold threads, but red couching was commonly used later. White or gray couching secured silver threads, accentuating the metal's color.

31. *SAGARA-NUI*: KNOT
Detail (10x) of cat. 13. A round, flat knot made by passing the needle through and around a loop of thread twice, without overlapping, and then into the fabric a short distance from the first stitch. This technique creates uniform knots that add texture to an otherwise flat design. Multiple knots filling an area or motif, as in this example, are known as *sagara-zume*.

32. *SASHIKO*: JAPANESE DECORATIVE QUILTING
Detail of cat. 29. Thick, sometimes doubled, white cotton thread pierces several layers of fabric—mainly indigo-dyed cotton or bast-fiber folk textiles—in running stitches. This kind of simple stitching was probably first used to sew together layers of fabric to create thicker, warmer, and more durable clothes; it then became valued as a decorative technique. In the Edo and Meiji periods, the stitching was used to create geometric patterns that distinctly contrasted with the ground fabric and covered entire garments worn by farmers and fishermen.

NOTES

JAPANESE FASHION, FROM EDO TO THE MODERN ERA

1. Inoue Tsūjo, *Inoue Tsūjo zenshū* [Collected works of Inoue Tsūjo] (Marugame: Kagawa Kenritsu Marugame Kōtō Gakkō Dōsōkai, 1973), pp. 47–48. Quoted in Marcia Yonemoto, *The Problem of Women in Early Modern Japan* (Oakland: University of California Press, 2016), p. 1.
2. Penelope Francks, "Was Fashion a European Invention? The Kimono and Economic Development in Japan," *Fashion Theory: The Journal of Dress, Body & Culture* 19, no. 3 (2015), pp. 331–61.
3. Linda Welters and Abby Lillethun, *Fashion History: A Global View* (London: Bloomsbury Academic, 2018), pp. 1–7.
4. Jane Schneider, "Cloth and Clothing," in *Handbook of Material Culture*, eds. Christopher Tilley et al. (London: SAGE, 2006), pp. 203–20.
5. Jennifer Craik, *Fashion: The Key Concepts* (Oxford and New York: Berg, 2009), pp. 63–102, 105–30.
6. Eugenia Paulicelli, *Writing Fashion in Early Modern Italy: From* Sprezzatura *to Satire* (Farnham, Surrey, UK: Ashgate, 2014), pp. 3–4.
7. Risako Doi, "Beyond *The Greater Learning for Women*: Instructional Texts (*Joshiyō ōrai*) and Norms for Women in Early Modern Japan" (master's thesis, University of Colorado, 2011), pp. 1–12.
8. *Onna chōhōki* [Illustrated handbook on daily life for women, "The great treasure for women"] (Edo, 1692), quoted in Yonemoto, *The Problem of Women*, p. 76.
9. Tokyo National Museum, ed., *Kimono* [Kimono: Fashioning identities], exh. cat. (Tokyo: Asahi Shinbunsha, 2020), pp. 8–9.
10. Nagasaki Iwao, *Kimono Beauty: Shikku de modanna yosōi no bi — Edo kara Shōwa* [Kimono Beauty: The beauty of chic and modern clothing from Edo to Shōwa], exh. cat. (Tokyo: Tokyo Bijutsu, 2013), pp. 40–44.
11. Ihara Saikaku, *Nihon eitaigura* [*Japan's Eternal Storehouse*] (1688), in *Early Modern Japanese Literature: An Anthology, 1600–1900*, ed. Haruo Shirane (New York: Columbia University Press, 2002), p. 134.
12. Anna Jackson et al., eds., *Kimono: Kyoto to Catwalk*, exh. cat. (London: Victoria and Albert Museum; London: V&A Publishing, 2020), pp. 37–51.
13. Yabuta Yutaka, "Rediscovering Women in Tokugawa Japan" (lecture, Harvard University, Japan Forum, sponsored by the Edwin O. Reischauer Institute of Japanese Studies, February 11, 2000).
14. Kaibara Ekiken, *Women and Wisdom of Japan* (translation of *Onna daigaku*), eds. Launcelot Cranmer-Byng and Shaporji Aspaniarji Kapadia (London: John Murray, 1909), pp. 38–39.
15. Kaibara, *Women and Wisdom of Japan*, p. 44.
16. Quoted in Doi, "Beyond *The Greater Learning for Women*," p. 70.
17. Donald H. Shively, "Sumptuary Regulation and Status in Early Tokugawa Japan," *Harvard Journal of Asiatic Studies* 25 (1964–65), pp. 123–64.
18. William B. Hauser, "Textiles and Trade in Tokugawa Japan," in *Textiles in Trade: Proceedings of the Textile Society of America 2nd Biennial Symposium* (Washington, D.C.: Textile Society of America, 1990), pp. 117–20.
19. Nakaoka Tetsuro et al., "The Textile History of Nishijin (Kyoto): East Meets West," *Textile History* 19, no. 2 (November 1988), pp. 117–42.
20. William B. Hauser, "The Diffusion of Cotton Processing and Trade in the Kinai Region in Tokugawa Japan," *The Journal of Asian Studies* 33, no. 4 (August 1974), pp. 633–49.
21. High-quality *gofuku* were distinct from garments made of cotton and pongee, which were called *futomono*.
22. Jackson, *Kimono: Kyoto to Catwalk*, pp. 81–90.
23. Nagasaki Iwao, "Edo jidai ni okeru gofuku chūmon no gutaiteki purosesu ni kansuru kenkyū" [Study of the general order process of attire in the Edo period], *Kyoritsu Joshi Daigaku Katei Gakubu Kiyō* 63 (2017), pp. 37–72.
24. Yonemoto, *The Problem of Women*, p. 14.
25. Nagasaki, "Edo jidai ni okeru gofuku chūmon," pp. 45–52.
26. Yonemoto, *The Problem of Women*, p. 5.
27. Nagasaki Iwao, "Designs for a Thousand Ages: Printed Pattern Books and Kosode," in *When Art Became Fashion: Kosode in Edo-Period Japan*, eds. Dale Carolyn Gluckman and Sharon Sadako Takeda, exh. cat. (Los Angeles: Los Angeles County Museum of Art; New York: Weatherhill, 1992), pp. 95–104.
28. Tokyo National Museum, *Kimono*, p. 14.
29. Marcia Yonemoto, "The Perils of the 'Unpolished Jewel': Defining Women's Roles in Household Management in Early Modern Japan," *U.S.–Japan Women's Journal*, no. 39 (2010), pp. 38–62.
30. Okayama Art Museum, *Daimyō konrei chōdo: Kaikan nijusshūnen kinen tokubetsuten* [Daimyo wedding sets: Special exhibition to commemorate the museum's twentieth anniversary], exh. cat. (Okayama: Okayama Art Museum; Kyoto: Hatsubai Kyoto Shoin, 1984), pp. 122–41.
31. Museum of Kyoto, ed., *Konrei no iro to katachi: Kinsei kōgei no hana* [Colors and forms of wedding ceremonies: The splendor of early modern decorative arts], exh. cat. (Kyoto: Museum of Kyoto, 1997), pp. 6–12, 17–23.
32. Amy Stanley, "Fashioning the Family: A Temple, a Daughter, and a Wardrobe," in *What Is a Family?: Answers from Early Modern Japan*, eds. Mary Elizabeth Berry and Marcia Yonemoto (Oakland: University of California Press, 2019), pp. 174–94.
33. Shin-ichiro Yoshida and Dai Williams, *Riches from Rags: Saki-ori & Other Recycling Traditions in Japanese Rural Clothing*, exh. cat. (San Francisco: Museum of Craft and Folk Art, 1994), pp. 11–29.
34. Quoted in Audrey Yoshiko Seo, "Adoption, Adaptation, and Innovation: The Cultural and Aesthetic Transformations of Fashion in Modern Japan," in *Since Meiji: Perspectives on the Japanese Visual Arts, 1868–2000*, ed. J. Thomas Rimer, trans. Toshiko McCallum (Honolulu: University of Hawai'i Press, 2012), p. 475.
35. Yuko Fukatsu-Fukuoka, "The Evolution of *Yūzen*-Dyeing Techniques and Designs after the Meiji Restoration," in *Appropriation, Acculturation, Transformation: Proceedings of the Textile Society of America 9th Biennial Symposium* (Oakland, Ca.: Textile Society of America, 2004), pp. 406–9.
36. Anna Jackson, "Dress in the Meiji Period: Change and Continuity," in *Kimono: The Art and Evolution of Japanese*

Fashion: The Khalili Collections, ed. Anna Jackson (London: Thames and Hudson, 2015), pp. 112–50.

37. Anna Cesaratto et al., "A Timeline for the Introduction of Synthetic Dyestuffs in Japan during the Late Edo and Meiji Periods," *Heritage Science* 6 (2018), pp. 6–22.
38. Nagasaki, *Kimono Beauty*, pp. 124–52.
39. Julia Sapin, "Merchandising Art and Identity in Meiji Japan: Kyoto *Nihonga* Artists' Designs for Takashimaya Department Store, 1868–1912," *Journal of Design History* 17, no. 4 (2004), pp. 317–36.
40. Younjung Oh, "Shopping for Art: The New Middle Class' Art Consumption in Modern Japanese Department Stores," *Journal of Design History* 27, no. 4 (2014), pp. 351–69.
41. Hatsuda Tōru, *Hyakkaten no tanjō: Meiji, Taishō, Shōwa no toshi bunka wo enshutsushita hyakkaten to kankōba no kindaishi* [The birth of department stores: The modern history of department stores that created the urban culture of the Meiji, Taishō, and Shōwa periods] (Tokyo: Sanseidō, 1993), pp. 174–75.
42. Louise Young, "Marketing the Modern: Department Stores, Consumer Culture, and the New Middle Class in Interwar Japan," *International Labor and Working-Class History* 55 (April 1999), pp. 52–70.
43. Higuchi Atsuko, "Meiji-makki ni okeru kimono zuan no kindaisei: 'Genroku moyō' wo chūshin ni" [The modernity of kimono design in the late Meiji period: Focusing on Genroku patterns], *Bijutsushi* 68, no. 20 (March 2019), pp. 247–64.
44. Jinno Yuki, *Shumi no tanjō: Hyakkaten ga tsukutta teisuto* [The birth of taste: The taste created by department stores] (Tokyo: Keiso Shobo, 1994), pp. 139–97.
45. Usui Kazuo, "'Tomorrow I'll Go to Mitsukoshi': The Department Store, a Dream or a Threat of Modernity?," in *Marketing and Consumption in Modern Japan* (London: Routledge, 2014), pp. 75–102.
46. Yamanouchi Yuki, "1920 nendai no meisen ichiba no kakudai to ryūkō dentatsu no shikumi" [The expansion of the *meisen* market in the 1920s and the structure of the transmission of fashion information], *Keiei Shigaku* 44, no. 1 (2009), pp. 3–33.
47. Several articles connecting the style of Art Nouveau with that of Ogata Kōrin were published in the *Mitsukoshi Times* in 1908–9.
48. Kendall H. Brown, "Delirious Japan: Politics, Culture and Art in the Taishō and Early Shōwa Periods," in *Kimono: The Art and Evolution*, pp. 154–65.
49. Seo, "Adoption, Adaptation, and Innovation," p. 481.
50. Elise K. Tipton, "*Atarashii Onna*: The New Japanese Woman," in *Fashioning Kimono: Dress and Modernity in Early Twentieth-Century Japan*, ed. Annie Van Assche, exh. cat. (London: Victoria and Albert Museum; Milan: 5 Continents, 2005), pp. 38–44.
51. Nagasaki, *Kimono Beauty*, pp. 169–201.
52. Penelope Francks, "Kimono Fashion: The Consumer and the Growth of the Textile Industry in Pre-War Japan," in *The Historical Consumer: Consumption and Everyday Life in Japan, 1850–2000*, eds. Penelope Francks and Janet Hunter (London: Palgrave Macmillan, 2012), pp. 151–75.

THE TIGER'S LEAP: KIMONOS AND COUTURE

1. Fukai Akiko, "Fashion," in *Japanese Design: A Survey since 1950*, eds. Kathryn B. Hiesinger and Felice Fischer, exh. cat. (Philadelphia: Philadelphia Museum of Art, 1994), p. 37.
2. Edward W. Said, *Orientalism* (New York: Pantheon Books, 1978).
3. Fukai Akiko, "Japonism in Fashion," in *Japonism in Fashion: Kimono across the Sea*, exh. cat. (Kyoto: The Kyoto Costume Institute; Tokyo: Heibonsha, 1994), p. 2.
4. Ulrich Lehmann, *Tigersprung: Fashion in Modernity* (Cambridge, Mass.: MIT Press, 2000). Walter Benjamin, "Theses on the Philosophy of History," in *Illuminations* (London: Jonathan Cape, 1970), p. 263.
5. Shuji Takashina quoted in Fukai Akiko, "The Discovery of Abstraction in Twentieth-Century Fashion," in *Fashion Game Changers: Reinventing the 20th-Century Silhouette*, eds. Karen Van Godtsenhoven, Miren Arzalluz, and Kaat Debo, exh. cat. (Antwerp: Mode Museum; London: Bloomsbury, 2016), p. 165.
6. Josephine Rout, *Japanese Dress in Detail*, exh. cat. (London: Victoria and Albert Museum; London: Thames and Hudson, 2020), p. 7.
7. Younjung Oh, "Shopping for Art: The New Middle Class' Art Consumption in Modern Japanese Department Stores," *Journal of Design History* 27, no. 4 (2014), p. 353.
8. Mei Mei Rado, "The Hybrid Orient: Japonisme and Nationalism of the Takashimaya Mandarin Robes," *Fashion Theory: The Journal of Dress, Body & Culture* 19, no. 5 (2015), p. 596.
9. Rado, "The Hybrid Orient," p. 590.
10. Rado, "The Hybrid Orient," p. 606.
11. Rado, "The Hybrid Orient," p. 583.
12. Fukai, "The Discovery of Abstraction," p. 165.
13. Allie Yamaguchi, "Kimonos for Foreigners: Orientalism in Kimonos Made for the Western Market, 1900–1920," *The Journal of Dress History* 1, no. 2 (Autumn 2017), p. 103.
14. Fukai, "Japonism in Fashion," p. 7.
15. Harold Koda and Andrew Bolton, eds., *Poiret*, exh. cat. (New York: The Metropolitan Museum of Art, 2007), p. 52.
16. Fukai, "Japonism in Fashion," p. 8.
17. Fukai, "The Discovery of Abstraction," p. 163.
18. Fukai Akiko, "Visions of the Body: Body Images and Fashion in the 20th Century," in *Visions of the Body: Fashion or Invisible Corset*, ed. Fukai Akiko, exh. cat. (Kyoto: The Kyoto Costume Institute, 1999), p. 3.
19. Fukai, "The Discovery of Abstraction," p. 183.
20. Betty Kirke, *Madeleine Vionnet* (San Francisco: Chronicle Books, 1998), pp. 32–33.
21. Fukai, "The Discovery of Abstraction," p. 183.
22. Kirke, *Madeleine Vionnet*, p. 46.
23. Miren Arzalluz, "Iconoclastic Visions of the Silhouette: Cristóbal Balenciaga," in *Fashion Game Changers: Reinventing the 20th-Century Silhouette*, pp. 65–67.
24. Arzalluz, "Iconoclastic Visions," p. 67.
25. Fukai, "Japonism in Fashion," p. 9.
26. Bernadine Morris, "Loose Translators," *New York Times*, January 30, 1983, Fashion, sec. 6, p. 43.
27. Fukai, "Fashion," p. 37.
28. "An Acquired Taste—Like Oysters," *Women's Wear Daily*, June 1, 1966, p. 1.
29. Hanae Mori quoted in Ayaka Sano, "Overcoming the Oriental Past: Hanae Mori's American Dream, 1965–1976" (master's thesis, New York University, 2020), p. 19.
30. Fukai, "Japonism in Fashion," p. 10.
31. Issey Miyake quoted in June Weir, "The Japanese Designer Who Paved the Way," *New York Times*, January 30, 1983, Fashion, sec. 6, p. 42.

32. Geraldine Stutz, president of Henri Bendel, quoted in Morris, "Loose Translators," p. 43.
33. Rei Kawakubo quoted in Morris, "Loose Translators," p. 40.
34. Morris, "Loose Translators," pp. 40, 43.
35. Yohji Yamamoto quoted in John Duka, "Yohji Yamamoto Defines His Fashion Philosophy," *New York Times,* October 23, 1983, sec. 1, p. 63.
36. Yohji Yamamoto quoted by The Kyoto Costume Institute, webpage for "Jacket, Dress, Pants," collection of The Kyoto Costume Institute on Google Arts and Culture, https://artsandculture.google.com/asset/jacket-dress-pants-yohji-yamamoto/XAFNfgT9jA6-ow?hl=en.
37. Bernard Rudofsky, *The Kimono Mind: An Informal Guide to Japan and the Japanese* (Garden City, N.Y.: Doubleday, 1965).
38. Richard Martin, "Our Kimono Mind: Reflections on 'Japanese Design: A Survey since 1950,'" *Journal of Design History* 8, no. 3 (1995), p. 215.

MEISEN AND *OMESHI*: KIMONOS FOR THE MASSES

1. Arai Masanao, "Ito kara hajimaru monogatari" [A tale beginning with a thread], in *Meisen, Taishō-Shōwa no oshare kimono* [*Meisen*, the fashion kimono of the Taishō-Shōwa period], Bessatsu Taiyo (Tokyo: Heibonsha, 2004), pp. 124–34. Arai Masanao, "*Meisen*: Its Times and Techniques," in *Nyūyōkā ga miserareta bi no sekai: Jon shī Uebā korekushon* [A New Yorker's view of the world: The John C. Weber collection], ed. Miho Museum, exh. cat. (Kōka: Miho Museum, 2015), pp. 430–33. See also Nagasaki Iwao, ed., *Kimono modanizumu: Suzaka kurashikku bijutsukan meisen korekushon* [Kimono modernism: *Meisen* collection of the Suzaka Classic Museum], exh. cat. (Suzaka: Suzaka Classic Museum, 2015), pp. 8–16, 138–46.
2. According to an accounting ledger, the *Kamaire-chō*, in 1802 the Hoshino family commissioned neighboring farms in the Kiryū area to hand-reel silk cocoons. It appears that the yarns spun in January 1802 were composed of 54.9 percent raw silk and 45.1 percent *tama-ito*. Despite the advancements in sericulture technology, the percentage of waste cocoons was still surprisingly high.
3. *Kenpu chōhōki* [Precious records of silk clothing] (1789), in *Tsūzoku keizai bunko* [Library of ordinary economics] 2 (Tokyo: Nihon Keizai Sosho Kankōkai, 1916), p. 137.
4. Nihon Orimono Shinbunsha, ed., *Senshoku jiten* [Dictionary of textiles] (Osaka: Nihon Orimono Shinbunsha, 1931), p. 780.
5. Naoko Inoue, "Silk Waste, Spun Silk, and *Meisen* Kimono," in *Linking Cloth/Clothing Globally: The Transformations of Use and Value, ca. 1700–2000*, ed. Miki Sugiura, an Institute of Comparative Economic Studies Publication (Tokyo: Hosei University Publishing, 2019), pp. 232–57.
6. The author created a graph based on statistics from *Zenkoku meisen seisandaka tōkei* [National *meisen* production data], research conducted by Arai Kōichi for the National Meisen Federation in about 2000; see Isesaki Meisen Archives, http://iga.justhpbs.jp/comparison.html. The rapid decline in production from 1935 may be attributed to the shift in production from *meisen* to *omeshi*.
7. Mutō Kazuo, a researcher specializing in *meisen* and *tsumugi* (hand-spun pongee silk) textiles, estimates that approximately 400 million *meisen* kimonos were manufactured altogether, under the assumption that one bolt was used to make one kimono. This estimate includes approximately 200 million garments in 1912–37, plus 100 million from the Edo through the Meiji period, and an additional 100 million from 1938 through the 1940s. See Nihon Hōsō Shuppan Kyōkai, ed., "Meisen, yon-oku mai no yume: Fudangi kara baketa kindai no ryūkō kimono" [*Meisen* kimonos, 400 million dreams: The everyday wear that changed into modern fashion], *NHK Shiru wo tanoshimu: Rekishi ni kōkishin* [NHK–Enjoy knowing and have an interest in history] (Tokyo: Nihon Hōsō Shuppan Kyōkai, 2007), pp. 167–72.
8. Ōmori Tetsuya, Arai Masanao, and Sawabe Machiko, *Vivid meisen: Kirameki no kimonotachi, "Taishō roman" kara "Shōwa modan" e* [Vivid *meisen*: Kimono avant-garde in the early 20th century], exh. cat. (Kyoto: Seigensha, 2016), pp. 176–83.
9. Kobanawa Heiroku, "Isesaki meisen zuisō" [Isesaki *meisen* essays], *Isesaki Shiwa* 2, no. 4 (April 1959), pp. 20–21.
10. Isesaki Orimono Kyōdōkumiai, ed., *Isesaki orimonoshi* [Isesaki weaving history] (Isesaki: Isesaki Meisen Kaikan, 1966), p. 27.
11. Imperial Cabinet Statistical Bureau, ed., *Dai Nippon teikoku tōkei nenkan* [Imperial Japanese statistical yearbook] 59 (Tokyo: Imperial Cabinet Statistical Bureau, 1941), p. 5.
12. Kimura Rokusuke, *Saikin Ashikaga orimono hyōhon to kaisetsu* [Recent examples of Ashikaga textiles and their descriptions] (Tokyo: Hōbunkan, 1931), pp. 12, 18–20.
13. Japan, Ministry of Justice, Investigation Bureau (Chōsabu), ed., *Setai chōsa shiryō* [Research material on the state of the society] 39 (Tokyo: Japan, Ministry of Justice, Investigation Bureau, 1942), p. 64. Japan's output of 330,000 pounds surpassed the United States' 312,000 pounds, Great Britain's 119,700 pounds, Germany's 110,000 pounds, and Italy's 104,300 pounds.
14. Isesaki Orimono Kyōdōkumiai, ed., *Isesaki orimonoshi*, pp. 213–14.
15. Nihon Orimono Shinbunsha, ed., *Shiire hoten* [Special handbook for textile buyers] (Osaka: Nihon Orimono Shinbunsha, 1935), p. 58.
16. Shakaibu (a student club) of Ashikaga Girls' High School, ed., *Ashikaga meisen no kenkyū* [Research on Ashikaga *meisen*], series 5 (Ashikaga: Ashikaga Girls' High School, 1955), p. 20.

THEATRICAL COSTUMES

1. Monica Bethe, "Colour, Texture and Tailoring: The Role of Costumes in Nō and Kyōgen," in *Theatre of Dreams, Theatre of Play: Nō and Kyōgen in Japan*, ed. Khanh Trinh, exh. cat. (Sydney: Art Gallery of New South Wales, 2014), pp. 43–51.
2. Kawakami Shigeki, "The Development of the *Karaori* as a Noh Costume," in *Miracles & Mischief: Noh and Kyōgen Theater in Japan*, in collaboration with Sharon Sadako Takeda et al., exh. cat. (Los Angeles: Los Angeles County Museum of Art, 2002), pp. 100–122.
3. Nagasaki Iwao, "Patronage: Daimyo, Actors, and Noh Costumes," in *Miracles & Mischief*, pp. 124–44.
4. Kirihata Ken, *Nō shōzoku: Okayama Bijutsukan zō Ikeda-ke denrai* [Noh costumes in the Okayama Art Museum from the Ikeda family collection] (Kyoto: Kyoto Shoin, 1986), vol. 2, pp. 64–83.
5. Kirihata Ken, *Kyogen Costumes: Suo (Jackets) and Kataginu (Shoulder-Wings)* (London: Thames and Hudson, 1980), pp. 12–20.

6. Kirihata Ken, "Kyōgen Costumes: The Fascinating World of Dyed Textiles," in *Miracles & Mischief*, pp. 160–76.

WARRIORS AND FIREFIGHTERS

1. Ikeda Hiroshi, "Japanese Armor: An Overview," in *Art of the Samurai: Japanese Arms and Armor, 1156–1868*, ed. Morihiro Ogawa (New York: The Metropolitan Museum of Art, 2009), pp. 37–43.
2. Fukuoka Yuko, *Jinbaori no sozai to gihō ni kansuru kagakuteki bunseki to senshokushiteki kenkyū* [Research on the techniques and material analysis of *jinbaori*] (PhD diss., Kyoritsu Joshi Daigaku, 2008), pp. 8–25.
3. Kyoto National Museum, ed., *Miyako no mōdo: Kimono no jidai* [Kyoto style: Trends in 16th–19th-century kimono] (Kyoto: Shibunkaku Shuppan, 2001), pp. 15–18.
4. Ichinomiya City Museum, ed., *Jinbaori: Bushi no fasshion* [Fashion of the samurai: Fabrics from overseas], exh. cat. (Ichinomiya: Ichinomiya City Museum, 2011), pp. 33–38.
5. Tokyo National Museum, ed., *Kimono* [Kimono: Fashioning identities], exh. cat. (Tokyo: Asahi Shinbunsha, 2020), pp. 194–210.
6. Nobuko Shibayama, Report from The Metropolitan Museum of Art's Scientific Research Department (New York: The Metropolitan Museum of Art, 2013).
7. With thanks to Nagasaki Iwao, professor in the Department of Textile and Clothing at Kyoritsu Women's University, Tokyo, for his contribution to an earlier version of this entry.
8. With thanks to Nagasaki Iwao.
9. Nishiyama Matsunosuke, Shirai Kazuo, and Tani Minezo, *Edo san hikeshi zukan: Machibikeshi, jōbikeshi, daimyō-bikeshi no shirushi* [An illustrated book of Edo firefighters' insignia and costume: Townspeople, *hatamoto*, and daimyo] (Tokyo: Iwasaki Bijutsusha, 1988), pp. 188–97.
10. Kirihata Ken, *Shomin no senshoku* [Textile art of the commoners], vol. 9 of *Nihon no senshoku* [Japanese textile art], ed. Yamanobe Tomoyuki (Tokyo: Chūō Kōronsha, 1982–83), pp. 100–109.

EDO FASHIONS

1. Monica Bethe, "Color: Dyes and Pigments," in *Kosode: 16th–19th Century Textiles from the Nomura Collection*, eds. Naomi Noble Richard and Margot Paul, exh. cat. (New York: Japan Society and Kodansha International, 1984), pp. 58–77.
2. Anna Jackson, ed., *Kimono: Kyoto to Catwalk*, exh. cat. (London: Victoria and Albert Museum; London: V&A Publishing, 2020), p. 93.
3. Kawabarata Kōji, "Miyazaki Yūzensai to yūzen-zome" [Miyazaki Yūzensai and *yūzen*-dyeing], *Kyoto Sangyō Daigaku Nihon Bunka Kenkyūjo Kiyō* 22 (2017), pp. 220–54.
4. Endō Takako and Katanuki Toyoaki, "Kosode hinagata-bon ni miru Noh-kyoku ishō—Kakitsubata moyō wo chūshin ni" [Designs inspired by Noh plays featured in pattern books—focusing on the iris motif], *Toshokan Jōhō Media Kenkyū* [Library information media research] 11, no. 2 (2014), pp. 1–22.
5. Translated by John T. Carpenter, Mary Griggs Burke Curator of Japanese Art at The Metropolitan Museum of Art, New York.
6. The poem is in the "Early Spring" section of the eleventh-century anthology *Japanese and Chinese Poems to Sing (The* Wakan rōei shū*)*, trans. J. Thomas Rimer and Jonathan Chaves (New York: Columbia University Press, 1997).
7. Frank Feltens, "Sartorial Identity: Early Modern Japanese Textile Patterns and the Afterlife of Ogata Kōrin," *Ars Orientalis* 47 (2017), pp. 117–57.
8. Tomoko Sakomura, "Japanese Games of Memory, Matching, and Identification," in *Asian Games: The Art of Contest*, eds. Colin Mackenzie and Irving Finkel, exh. cat. (New York: Asia Society Museum, 2004), pp. 253–71.
9. Museum of Kyoto, ed., *Konrei no iro to katachi: Kinsei kōgei no hana* [Colors and forms of wedding ceremonies: The splendor of early modern decorative arts], exh. cat. (Kyoto: Museum of Kyoto, 1997), pp. 61–99.
10. Matsuzakaya Art Museum, ed., *Kosode: Edo no ōto kuchūru; Matsuzakaya Kyōto, Senshoku Sankōkan no meihin* [*Kosode*: Haute couture kimonos of the Edo period; Kyoto Matsuzakaya, masterpieces of the reference museum], exh. cat. (Tokyo: Nihon Keizai Shinbunsha, 2008), pp. 17–18.
11. Shibuya Kuritsu Shōto Bijutsukan, ed., *Ainu no yosooi to hare no hi no kimono* [Ainu attire kimono for halle day: For the opening of the National Ainu Museum], exh. cat. (Tokyo: Shibuya Kuritsu Shōto Bijutsukan, 2021), pp. 10–17, 62–78.

MODERN KIMONOS

1. Nihon Orimono Shinbunsha, ed., *Dai Nippon orimono nisen-ropphyakunen-shi* [Textiles of imperial Japan: 2,600 years of history], vol. 2 (Osaka: Nihon Orimono Shinbunsha, 1940), p. 601. Iida Tetsutarō and Nomura Satoru, eds., *Hyakusen-kai hyakai-shi* [The history of Hyakusen-kai at its centennial] (Tokyo: Takashimaya Co., Ltd., 1971), pp. 162–272.
2. Tamamushi Satoko, "Kōrinkan no hensen 1815–1915" [Changes in the perception of Kōrin 1815–1915], *Bijutsu Kenkyū* 371 (March 1999), pp. 1–70.
3. With thanks to Anna Jackson, Keeper of the Asian Department at the Victoria and Albert Museum, London, for her contribution to an earlier version of this entry.
4. With thanks to Anna Jackson.
5. Fujii Kenzō, "Taishō Shōwa no meisen kimono no ryūkō" [The fashion for *meisen* kimonos, 1900–1930], in *Meisen: Taishō Shōwa no oshare kimono* [*Meisen*: Fashionable clothing in the Taishō and Shōwa periods], eds. Fujii Kenzō and Fujimori Takeshi (Tokyo: Heibonsha, 2004), pp. 114–22.

SELECTED BIBLIOGRAPHY

Allen, Laura W., Julia Meech, Eric C. Rath, and Melinda Takeuchi. *Seduction: Japan's Floating World: The John C. Weber Collection*. Exh. cat. San Francisco: Asian Art Museum, 2015.

Arzalluz, Miren. *Cristóbal Balenciaga: The Making of a Master (1895–1936)*. London: V&A Publishing, 2011.

Atkins, Jacqueline M., ed. *Wearing Propaganda: Textiles on the Home Front in Japan, Britain, and the United States, 1931–1945*. Exh. cat. New York: The Bard Graduate Center for Studies in the Decorative Arts, Design, and Culture. New Haven: Yale University Press, 2005.

Brandon, Reiko Mochinaga. *Bright & Daring: Japanese Kimono in the Taishō Mode; From the Oka Nobutaka Collection of the Suzaka Classic Museum*. Exh. cat. Honolulu: Honolulu Academy of the Arts. Tokyo: Unsōdō Publishing, 1996.

Brown, Kendall H., ed. *Deco Japan: Shaping Art and Culture, 1920–1945*. Exh. cat. New York: Japan Society. Alexandria, Va.: Art Services International, 2012.

Brown, Kendall H., and Sharon A. Minichiello. *Taishō Chic: Japanese Modernity, Nostalgia, and Deco*. Exh. cat. Honolulu: Honolulu Academy of Arts, 2002.

Burnham, Dorothy K. *Warp & Weft: A Dictionary of Textile Terms*. New York: Scribner, 1981.

Dalby, Liza Crihfield. *Kimono: Fashioning Culture*. New Haven: Yale University Press, 1993.

Dees, Jan. *Taishō Kimono: Speaking of Past and Present*. Exh. cat. Rotterdam: Kunsthal Rotterdam. Milan: Skira, 2009.

Deslandres, Yvonne, with Dorothée Lalanne. *Poiret: Paul Poiret, 1879–1944*. Translated by Paula Clifford. New York: Rizzoli, 1987.

Earle, Joe, ed. *Serizawa: Master of Japanese Textile Design*. Exh. cat. New York: Japan Society. New Haven: Yale University Press, 2009.

Emery, Irene. *The Primary Structures of Fabrics: An Illustrated Classification*. Washington, D.C.: Textile Museum. New York: Watson-Guptill Publications/Whitney Library of Design, 1995.

Fujii Kenzō and Fujimori Takeshi, eds. *Meisen: Taishō Shōwa no oshare kimono* [*Meisen*: Fashionable clothing in the Taishō and Shōwa periods]. Tokyo: Heibonsha, 2004.

Fukai Akiko, ed. *Fashion: A History of the 18th to the 20th Century; The Collection of the Kyoto Costume Institute*. Cologne: Taschen, 2002.

Fukai Akiko. *Kimono to Japonisumu: Seiyō no me ga mita Nihon no biishiki* [The kimono and Japanism: The reception of Japanese aesthetics in the West]. Tokyo: Heibonsha, 2017.

Fukui Sadako. *Kaitei: Nihon no kasuri bunkashi* [Revision: The history of Japanese *kasuri* culture]. Kyoto: Kyoto Shoin, 1981.

Geczy, Adam. *Fashion and Orientalism: Dress, Textiles and Culture from the 17th to the 21st Century*. Oxford: Berg, 2013.

Gluckman, Dale Carolyn, and Sharon Sadako Takeda, eds. *When Art Became Fashion: Kosode in Edo-Period Japan*. Exh. cat. Los Angeles: Los Angeles County Museum of Art. New York: Weatherhill, 1992.

Godtsenhoven, Karen Van, Miren Arzalluz, and Kaat Debo, eds. *Fashion Game Changers: Reinventing the 20th-Century Silhouette*. Exh. cat. Antwerp: Mode Museum. London: Bloomsbury, 2016.

Gordon, Andrew. *Fabricating Consumers: The Sewing Machine in Modern Japan*. Berkeley: University of California Press, 2011.

Guth, Christine. *Art of Edo Japan: The Artist and the City, 1615–1868*. New York: Harry N. Abrams, 1996.

Hamada Nobuyoshi. *Taishō Kimono: Beauty of Japanese Modernity in 1910s & 1920s*. Tokyo: PIE Books, 2015.

Hay, Susan Anderson. *Patterns and Poetry: Nō Robes from the Lucy Truman Aldrich Collection at the Museum of Art, Rhode Island School of Design*. Providence: Museum of Art, Rhode Island School of Design, 1992.

Howell, David. *Geographies of Identity in Nineteenth-Century Japan*. Oakland: University of California Press, 2005.

Jackson, Anna. *Japanese Country Textiles*. New York: Weatherhill, 1997.

Jackson, Anna, ed. *Kimono: The Art and Evolution of Japanese Fashion: The Khalili Collections*. London: Thames and Hudson, 2015.

Jackson, Anna, ed. *Kimono: Kyoto to Catwalk*. Exh. cat. London: Victoria and Albert Museum. London: V&A Publishing, 2020.

Jō Kazuo and Watanabe Naoki. *Nihon no fasshon: Meiji, Taishō, Shōwa, Heisei* [Japanese fashion: Meiji, Taishō, Shōwa, Heisei periods]. Kyoto: Seigensha, 2007.

Kawamura Yuniya. *The Japanese Revolution in Paris Fashion*. Oxford: Berg Publishers, 2004.

Kennedy, Alan. *Japanese Costume: History and Tradition*. Paris: A. Biro, 1990.

Kirihata Ken, ed. *Kagayakeru kosode no bi: Tsujigahana kara yūzen-zome; Kyōto Tabata-ke korekushon zenyō hatsukōkai* [The splendor of *kosode* from Tsujigahana to *yūzen*-dyeing]. Exh. cat. Kyoto: Takashimaya; Osaka: Umeda Hankyu. Osaka: Asahi Shinbunsha, Cultural Projects Division, 1990.

Kirke, Betty. *Madeleine Vionnet*. San Francisco: Chronicle Books, 1998.

Koda, Harold, and Andrew Bolton. *Poiret*. Exh. cat. New York: The Metropolitan Museum of Art, 2007.

Koizumi Kazuko, ed. *Shōwa no kimono* [Shōwa-period kimono]. Tokyo: Kawade Shobō Shinsha, 2006.

Koriyama City Museum of Art, ed. *Taishō no kagayaki moga jidai no yosooi ōtokuchūru to kimono* [Radiance of the Taishō period's "modern girls" and their apparel, haute couture and kimono]. Exh. cat. Koriyama: Koriyama City Museum of Art, 2004.

Koyama Shizuko. *Ryōsai Kenbo: The Educational Ideal of "Good Wife, Wise Mother" in Modern Japan*. Translated by Stephen Filler. Leiden: Brill, 2013.

Kyoto Costume Institute, ed. *Mōdo no Japonisumu: Kimono kara umareta yutori no bi* [Japanism in fashion: Comfortable beauty born from kimonos]. Exh. cat. Kyoto: The Kyoto Costume Institute, 1994.

Kyoto National Museum, ed. *Miyako no mōdo: Kimono no jidai* [Kyoto style: Trends in 16th–19th-century kimono]. Exh. cat. Kyoto: Kyoto National Museum. Kyoto: Shibunkaku Shuppan, 2001.

Li, Vivian, ed. *The Kimono in Print: 300 Years of Japanese Design*. Exh. cat. Worcester, Mass.: Worcester Art Museum. Leiden: Hotei Publishing, 2020.

Li, Vivian, and Christine D. Starkman, eds. *Kimono Couture: The Beauty of Chiso*. Exh. cat. Worcester, Mass.: Worcester Art Museum. Lewes, U.K.: Giles, an imprint of D. Giles Limited, 2020.

Martin, Richard, and Harold Koda. *Orientalism: Visions of the East in Western Dress*. New York: The Metropolitan Museum of Art, 1994.

Maruyama Nobuhiko. *Edo mōdo no tanjō: Mon'yō no ryūkō to sutā eshi* [The birth of Edo fashion: Popular motifs and star designers]. Tokyo: Kadokawa Gakugei Shuppan, 2008.
Matsuzakaya Art Museum, ed. *Kosode: Edo no ōto kuchūru* [*Kosode*: Haute couture kimono of the Edo period]. Exh. cat. Nagoya: Nagoya City Museum of Fine Arts. Tokyo: Nihon Keizai Shinbunsha, 2008.
Matsuzakaya Art Museum, ed. *Utsukushiki wa no iro no sekai—KIMONO* [The world of beautiful Japanese colors—KIMONO]. Exh. cat. Nagoya: Matsuzakaya Art Museum, 2021.
McDermott, Hiroko, and Clare Pollard. *Threads of Silk and Gold: Ornamental Textiles from Meiji Japan*. Exh. cat. Oxford: Ashmolean Museum, 2012.
Miho Museum, ed. *Nyūyōkā ga miserareta bi no sekai: Jon shī Uebā korekushon* [A New Yorker's view of the world: The John C. Weber Collection]. Exh. cat. Kōka: Miho Museum, 2015.
Milhaupt, Terry Satsuki. *Kimono: A Modern History*. London: Reaktion Books, 2014.
Moes, Robert, Amanda Mayer Stinchecum, and William B. Hauser. *Mingei: Japanese Folk Art; From the Montgomery Collection*. Exh. cat. Pittsburgh: Frick Art Museum. Alexandria, Va.: Art Services International, 1995.
Morishima, Yuki, and Rie Nii, eds. *Kimono Refashioned: Japan's Impact on International Fashion*. Exh. cat. San Francisco: Asian Art Museum of San Francisco, 2018.
Morishita Misako. *Edo no hanayome: Muko erabi to buraidaru* [Brides in the Edo period: Finding a husband and wedding arrangements]. Tokyo: Chuokoron-sha Inc., 1992.
Mostow, Joshua S., Norman Bryson, and Marybeth Graybill, eds. *Gender and Power in the Japanese Visual Field*. Honolulu: University of Hawai'i Press, 2003.
Museum of Kyoto, ed. *Kyō no kosode: Dezain ni miru Nihon no eregansu* [Kyoto kimonos: Inspired grace and elegance from Momoyama to Edo]. Exh. cat. Kyoto: Museum of Kyoto. Osaka: Mainichi Shinbunsha, 2011.
Nagasaki Iwao. *Kimono Beauty: Shikku de modanna yosōi no bi—Edo kara Shōwa* [Kimono Beauty: The beauty of chic and modern clothing from Edo to Shōwa]. Exh. cat. Tokyo: Tokyo Bijutsu, 2013.
Nagasaki Iwao, ed. *Kimono modanizumu: Suzaka kurashikku bijutsukan meisen korekushon* [Kimono modernism: *Meisen* collection of the Suzaka Classic Museum]. Exh. cat. Suzaka: Suzaka Classic Museum, 2015.
Nagasaki Iwao and Yumioka Katsumi. *Meiji, Taishō, Shōwa ni miru kimono monyō zukan* [Illustrated guide of kimono patterns of the Meiji, Taishō, and Shōwa eras]. Tokyo: Heibonsha, 2005.
Nagoya City Museum, ed. *Moyō wo kiru* [Wearing patterns]. Exh. cat. Nagoya: Nagoya City Museum, 2020.
National Museum of Japanese History, ed. *Edo mōdo daizukan: Kosode mon'yō ni miru bi no keifu* [Edo à la mode: Aesthetic lineages seen in *kosode* kimono motifs]. Exh. cat. Sakura: National Museum of Japanese History, 1999.
Ōmori Tetsuya, Arai Masanao, and Sawabe Machiko. *Vivid Meisen: Kirameki no kimonotachi, "Taishō roman" kara "Shōwa modan" e* [Vivid *meisen*: Kimono avant-garde in the early 20th century]. Exh. cat. Rome: Japan Cultural Institute; Ashikaga: Ashikaga Museum of Art. Kyoto: Seigensha, 2016.
Oyama Yuzuruha. *Kosode: Edo dezain no iki* [Edo fashion: *Kosode* robes]. Tokyo: Tokyo National Museum, 2019.
Oyama Yuzuruha. *"Tsujigahana" no tanjō: "Kotoba" to "senshoku gihō" o meguru bunka shigengaku* [The birth of "Tsujigahana": Cultural resources and vocabulary related to dyeing and weaving techniques]. Tokyo: Tokyo Daigaku Shuppankai, 2012.
Peck, Amelia, ed. *Interwoven Globe: The Worldwide Textile Trade, 1500–1800*. Exh. cat. New York: The Metropolitan Museum of Art, 2013.
Proser, Adriana G., and Melinda Takeuchi. *The Art of Impermanence: Japanese Works from the John C. Weber Collection and Mr. and Mrs. John D. Rockefeller 3rd Collection*. Exh. cat. New York: Asia Society, 2020.
Rathbun, William Jay, ed. *Beyond the Tanabata Bridge: Traditional Japanese Textiles*. Exh. cat. New York: Thames and Hudson, in association with the Seattle Art Museum, 1993.
Sano Ayaka. "Overcoming the Oriental Past: Hanae Mori's American Dream, 1965–1976." Master's thesis, New York University, 2020.
Sato, Barbara. *The New Japanese Woman: Modernity, Media, and Women in Interwar Japan*. Durham, N.C.: Duke University Press, 2003.
Sittenfeld, Michael, ed. *Five Centuries of Japanese Kimono: On This Sleeve of Fondest Dreams*. Exh. cat. Chicago: The Art Institute of Chicago, 1992.
Stinchecum, Amanda Mayer. *Kosode: 16th–19th Century Textiles from the Nomura Collection*. Edited by Naomi Noble Richard and Margot Paul. Exh. cat. New York: Japan Society, 1984.
Sudjic, Deyan. *Rei Kawakubo and Comme des Garçons*. New York: Rizzoli, 1990.
Takahashi Haruko. *Nenpyō: Kindai nihon no minari bunka* [Chronology: The appearance culture of modern Japan]. Tokyo: Sangensha, 2007.
Takeda, Sharon Sadako, Monica Bethe, and Hollis Goodall-Cristante. *Miracles & Mischief: Noh and Kyōgen Theater in Japan*. Exh. cat. Los Angeles: Los Angeles County Museum of Art, 2002.
Takeda, Sharon Sadako, and Luke Shepherd Roberts. *Japanese Fishermen's Coats from Awaji Island*. Exh. cat. Los Angeles: UCLA Fowler Museum of Cultural History, 2001.
Tanabe, Willa J. *Painting with Threads: The Art of Japanese Embroidery*. Exh. cat. Honolulu: University of Hawai'i Art Gallery, 2006.
Thakar, Karun, and Anna Jackson. *Kimono Meisen: The Karun Thakar Collection*. Stuttgart: Arnoldsche, 2015.
Tipton, Elise K., and John Clark, eds. *Being Modern in Japan: Culture and Society from the 1910s to the 1930s*. Honolulu: University of Hawai'i Press, 2000.
Tokyo National Museum, ed. *Kimono* [Kimono: Fashioning identities]. Exh. cat. Tokyo: Ashai Shinbunsha, 2020.
Trede, Melanie, ed. *Arts of Japan: The John C. Weber Collection*. Exh. cat. Berlin: Museum of East Asian Art, 2006.
Van Assche, Annie, ed. *Fashioning Kimono: Dress and Modernity in Early Twentieth-Century Japan*. Exh. cat. London: Victoria and Albert Museum. Milan: 5 Continents, 2005.
Vollmer, John E., ed. *Re-envisioning Japan: Meiji Fine Art Textiles*. Milan: 5 Continents, 2016.
Wada, Yoshiko Iwamoto, and Arai Masanao. "Kimono Mode and Marketing: Popular Textiles for Women in Early Twentieth-Century Japan." *Research Journal of Textile and Apparel* 15, no. 1 (2011), pp. 108–23.
Yamanobe Tomoyuki and Fujii Kenzō. *Kyoto Modern Textiles: 1868–1940*. Kyoto: Kyoto Textile Wholesalers Association, 1996.
Yamauchi Yuki. "Why was *meisen*, Japan's traditional working clothes, accepted well in the market as everyday clothes and stylish garments between 1900 and 1930?" *Doshisha Shogaku* 65, no. 5 (2014), pp. 767–81.
Yokohama Museum of Art, ed. *Fasshon to ato uruwashiki tōzai kōryū* [The elegant other: Cross-cultural encounters in fashion and art]. Exh. cat. Yokohama: Yokohama Museum of Art. Tokyo: Rikuyosha, 2017.

INDEX

(Page references in *italics* refer to illustrations.)

This catalogue is published in conjunction with *Kimono Style: The John C. Weber Collection*, on view at The Metropolitan Museum of Art, New York, from June 7, 2022, through February 20, 2023.

The exhibition is made possible by the Mary Livingston Griggs and Mary Griggs Burke Foundation Fund, 2015.

This publication is made possible by the Florence and Herbert Irving Fund for Asian Art Publications. Additional support is provided by the Richard and Geneva Hofheimer Memorial Fund.

Published by
The Metropolitan Museum of Art, New York
Mark Polizzotti, Publisher and Editor in Chief
Peter Antony, Associate Publisher for Production
Michael Sittenfeld, Associate Publisher for Editorial

Edited by Nancy E. Cohen
Production by Lauren Knighton
Designed by Lucinda Hitchcock and Cara Buzzell
Bibliographic editing by Alicia Badea
Image acquisitions and permissions by Josephine Rodriguez
Translations from Japanese by Monika Bincsik and Ayaka Sano

Principal photography is by Paul H. Lachenauer, Imaging Department, The Metropolitan Museum of Art. Photomicrography is by Kristine M. Kamiya, associate conservator in the Department of Textile Conservation, The Metropolitan Museum of Art.

Additional photography credits: Collection of Akabori Museum of Local History, Isesaki City, photo by Ubukata Shiego: fig. 36; Collection of Cirotex Co. Ltd., Isesaki, Japan: figs. 40, 41, 42; Graph by Arai Masanao based on research by Arai Kōichi: fig. 38; Bibliothèque Nationale de France, Paris: fig. 24; International Center for Japanese Studies (Nichibunken): fig. 4; Isesaki Textile Manufacturers' Association: fig. 43; Photo by Ishii Katsu: fig. 35; Photo by Kobayashi Kichitaro, Kobayashi Yoshiki: fig. 44; Image © The Metropolitan Museum of Art: figs. 2, 3, 10, 14, 15, 22, 23, 25, 26, 27, 28, 30, 31, 32, 34; Image © The Metropolitan Museum of Art, photo by Paul H. Lachenauer: figs. 1, 7, 8, 13, 16, 17, 29, 33; Photograph © 2022 Museum of Fine Arts, Boston: figs. 5, 6, 12; New York Public Library: fig. 9; Toppan Inc. Printing Museum, Tokyo: fig. 19

Typeset in Canela, Favorit, and Noto Sans by Matt Mayerchak
Printed on 135 gsm GardaPat Bianka
Printing, binding, and color separations by Trifolio S.r.l., Verona, Italy
Cover illustrations: front, *meisen* kimono, ca. 1930–40 (detail of cat. 57); back, over robe (*uchikake*), first half of 19th century (detail of cat. 26)

Pages 4–5: Fireman's jacket (*hikeshi-banten*), mid-19th century. Detail of cat. 15
Page 6: Daimyo firefighter's jacket, first half of 19th century. Detail of cat. 12
Page 10: Summer robe (*hito-e*), early 19th century. Detail of cat. 18
Page 32: Iida & Co./Takashimaya. Tea gown, ca. 1900. Detail of fig. 23
Page 46: *Meisen* summer kimono, ca. 1940–45. Detail of cat. 60
Pages 56–57: Kyōgen suit (*suō*), mid-19th century. Detail of cat. 5
Pages 70–71: Daimyo firefighter's ensemble (*kaji shōzoku*) for samurai woman, first half of 19th century. Detail of cat. 13
Pages 86–87: Over robe (*uchikake*), first half of 19th century. Detail of cat. 26
Pages 114–15: *Meisen* jacket (*haori*), ca. 1935–45. Detail of cat. 59

First printing

The Metropolitan Museum of Art
1000 Fifth Avenue
New York, New York 10028
metmuseum.org

Distributed by
Yale University Press, New Haven and London
yalebooks.com/art
yalebooks.co.uk

Cataloguing-in-Publication Data is available from the Library of Congress.
ISBN 978-1-58839-752-2